£17.99

Doing Social Psychology Resea

To Professor Halla Beloff
who encourages diversity

Edited by

GLYNIS M. BREAKWELL

Doing Social PSYCHOLOGY

Research

BPS Blackwell

350 Main Street, Malden, MA 02148-5020, USA
108 Cowley Road, Oxford OX4 1JF, UK
550 Swanston Street, Carlton, Victoria 3053, Australia

First published 2004 by The British Psychological Society
and Blackwell Publishing Ltd

Library of Congress Cataloging-in-Publication Data

Doing social psychology research / edited by Glynis M. Breakwell. – 1st ed.
p. cm.
Includes bibliographical references and index.
ISBN 1-4051-0811-8 (alk. paper) – ISBN 1-4051-0812-6 (pbk : alk. paper)
1. Social psychology – Research – Methodology.
I. Breakwell, Glynis M. (Glynis Marie)

HM1019.D65 2004
302–dc22   2003015768

A catalogue record for this title is available from the British Library.

Set in 10/12pt Meridien
by Graphicraft Limited, Hong Kong
Printed and bound in the United Kingdom
by MPG Books, Bodmin, Cornwall

For further information on
Blackwell Publishing, visit our website:
http://www.blackwellpublishing.com

CONTENTS

CONTRIBUTORS

Julie Barnett is a Research Fellow in the Department of Psychology, University of Surrey, UK.

Peter Bibby is a Lecturer in Psychology in the School of Psychology at the University of Nottingham, UK.

Glynis M. Breakwell is Vice Chancellor of the University of Bath, UK.

Peter Bull is a Senior Lecturer in the Department of Psychology, University of York, UK.

Tom Farsides is a Lecturer in Social Psychology in the Department of Psychology at the University of Sussex, UK.

Eamonn Ferguson is a Reader in Health Psychology in the School of Psychology at the University of Nottingham, UK.

Chris Fife-Schaw is a Senior Lecturer in the Department of Psychology, University of Surrey, UK.

Richard H. Gramzow is Assistant Professor, Department of Psychology, Northeastern University, Boston, MA.

Geoffrey Haddock is a Senior Lecturer in the School of Psychology at the University of Cardiff, UK.

Lorne Hulbert is Psychology Lecturer in the Department of Psychology at The University of Kent at Canterbury, UK.

Susan Miles is a Research Associate in the School of Medicine, Health Policy and Practice, University of East Anglia, Norwich, UK.

Mike Osborn is a consultant Macmillan psychologist at the Royal United Hospital, Bath, UK.

Gene Rowe is a Senior Research Scientist in the Consumer Science group at the Institute of Food Research, Norwich, UK.

Adam Rutland is a Lecturer at the Centre for the Study of Group Processes, Department of Psychology, University of Kent, Canterbury, UK.

Jonathan A. Smith is Senior Lecturer in Psychology at Birkbeck College, University of London.

Mark Van Vugt is Senior Lecturer in Social Psychology, University of Southampton, UK.

Vivian L. Vignoles is Lecturer in Social Psychology, University of Sussex, UK.

Sue Wilkinson is Ruth Wynn Woodward Endowed Professor in the Department of Women's Studies, Simon Fraser University, Canada.

| CHAPTER ONE |

Introduction: Approaches to Data Collection and Data Analysis

Glynis M. Breakwell

The Purpose of the Book

Doing social psychology research is a fascinating adventure. It is a route to understanding in a systematic way the individuals and the social world around you. It encourages you to ask and start to answer difficult but fundamentally important questions. What threatens identity? Why do people rebel? How are risks communicated effectively? How do leaders command? How are sexual relationships developed? How do minorities gain influence? How do people react under intense pressure? How do the mass media represent societal crises? How does the public behave when faced with a terrorist attack? The list of interesting questions is probably endless and the ones chosen as the priorities for research vary according to the values of the social psychologist involved, the availability of funding for the work and the theoretical preoccupations of the time. It is, however, true to say that in the main social psychology research is focused on issues that matter.

The interesting questions are invariably complex, usually even more complex than they appear at first sight. The prime skill of a social psychology researcher lies in refining the question and crystallizing out something that is capable of being answered. The second vital skill of the social psychology researcher lies in choosing from the vast arsenal of research methods that are available the one that is best suited to address the question posed. To develop this second skill, it is necessary to gain a thorough understanding of all the tools that reside in the arsenal.

There are now many books to help students of psychology learn about the research methods they might use. This one is specifically aimed at undergraduates who want to learn about some of the data collection methods and data analysis approaches that are used in social psychology. It is not comprehensive in coverage of all the myriad methods used, but those selected for inclusion are very commonly used or they are methods that arouse much student interest. The selection is deliberately broad. The book is not designed to proselytize any particular epistemological orientation or set of methodological principles. It is designed to give the reader an opportunity to judge what a variety of methods can offer. Each is described in an honest and open way, and a real effort is made to explain its weaknesses as well as its strengths.

However, it is inevitable that any book on methods in social psychology will find itself drawn into the epistemological debates that have enlivened the discipline for at least 30 years. Questions emerge naturally about the feasibility of hypothesis testing, the value of experimentation, the limitations of measurement, the objectivity of data, the ethics of manipulation, the role of reactance to the process of research, the implications of sample structure, the pitfalls of prediction and so on. Here these issues are not extracted and dissected as formal philosophical problems. Instead, they are addressed as they need to be, embedded in the consideration of each of the methods.

This is not a book that is designed to explain the details of the various statistical techniques that can be employed. Where a statistical technique is the most obvious candidate for use, in combination with a specific research design and form of data collection, it is described here. However, the descriptions of statistical procedures are not meant to be stand-alone expositions. Some chapters are more elaborate and explicit about the statistics to be used than others. These tend to be the chapters where the technique of data collection employed is less important for the question posed than the way the data that are collected are subsequently treated. Essentially, in this book the reader is introduced to a statistical technique as an intrinsic element in the research method, rather than as an end in its own right. The chapters are designed to expose the logic that indicates which statistical test is best matched to the data collected. Understanding the assumptions that underlie statistical tests is often best achieved in the context of their repeated application. This book offers an opportunity to see the diversity of approach to the use of statistics that exists in social psychology.

The Organization of the Book

Each chapter describes a method and illustrates how it can be applied to a particular research question drawn from the substantive topics that are typically included in current social psychology courses. The topics covered include identity processes, attribution, stereotyping, attitude change, social influence, communication, and group dynamics. The chapters provide a succinct overview of the theoretical arguments that surround the topic. In the main, this means that each chapter can be used as a discrete and independent basis for gaining an understanding of both the method and the social psychological problem to which it is applied.

The chapters are written by researchers well known for using the specific techniques they describe. The strategy adopted in inviting contributors was to seek them from UK institutions that are very active in social psychology research. Authors were asked to present the method and outline the design for an exercise that would illustrate its use – in the way they might for their own undergraduate students. This means that there is diversity across chapters in the approaches taken. Some are more heavily concerned with the philosophical and logical rationale underlying the method they describe. Others are clearly more concerned with the practicalities of executing the method rigorously. It is useful for undergraduates to be exposed to these varieties in emphasis; there are many routes to achieving a good understanding of a research method.

Most chapters include three broad structural elements:

- Description of the method and its applications – a succinct outline of the generic features of the method (what it is, how to do it, what it can be used for, its strengths and weaknesses), its links to particular theoretical models and exemplars of classic studies that have used it to good effect.
- Specific exercise – a description of a training exercise that can be pursued by the individual students or as part of a methods course; identifying a research question and showing how the method can be used to address it. It identifies step by step what needs to be done in order to utilize the method. The forms of analysis that might be used with the information collected are explained (if the

analytical approach is not already obvious because it is intrinsic to the method).

- Notes for course leaders – a brief description for course tutors who might wish to use the exercise of the assumptions it makes about the level of experience of the student, the time it takes, the materials needed, the preparatory reading required and so on. While this element of the chapters is directed at course leaders, it may be valuable for students as well, allowing them to locate the method within a matrix of real constraints.

However, each chapter takes on a unique shape and style. There is no excessive standardization of format across chapters since this can be boring and sometimes undermines the very real differences in approach included.

Some chapters address fundamentally the same technique (e.g. interviewing) but they do so from quite different perspectives or with different emphases. This is a valuable element of a contributed book on methods. The subtle differences between contributors in their representation of a technique highlight the need for students critically to evaluate assertions that are made about the characteristics of any method.

Some chapters are targeted at students who have had little previous research methods training. Others are more appropriate for students who have already been introduced to the basic techniques. Chapters are clearly categorized as introductory or more advanced so that the reader or course leader using them can be selective. The book is intended to be a useful resource throughout undergraduate studies. It could be used as the basis for developing expertise in social psychology research methods in short bursts but in a cumulative fashion throughout the full period of an undergraduate course. Equally, it could be used as the framework for a single intensive injection of methods within a brief but cohesive programme focused on social psychology.

Data Collection Methods: Elicitation and Recording

Data collection is in reality about two intimately connected activities: data elicitation and data recording. Data elicitation is about accessing the information, opening it up for examination. Data recording is about codifying the discovered information in a way that allows the research question to be addressed.

What is a data elicitation method? It is a way of getting information. So you could gain information by observing what people do (*observation*). For example, you could stand on a busy road with a machine that measures the speed of the motor cars that pass in order to determine the number of speeding offences on that road. Alternatively, you could gain information by asking people questions about what they do, think or feel (*self-report*). To extend the earlier example, you could ask people who drive along the particular stretch of road whether they ever exceed the speed limit on it and how often. Those questions could be asked verbally through some form of an interview or they could be asked in written form through some form of a questionnaire. The answers people are allowed to give could be open-ended (without any constraint imposed by you) or they could be structured to varying degrees (limited in format by you in advance – e.g. through the use of rating scales). Some methods of data collection involve no direct contact with the object of the research. These rely essentially upon archives (i.e. records) or artefacts as sources of data (*archival*). So, for instance, you might find out what people who are long dead were doing in the nineteenth century by examining archives reflecting their behaviour. For example, in order to understand something about family structures, you might look at parish records to determine how old people were when they married in the nineteenth century. To continue with the earlier example in the context of the use of archives, you could use criminal records of automobile speeding fines on the target stretch of road to quantify the level of compliance with road use restrictions.

Observation, self-report and archival methods of data elicitation dominate in social psychology. Most others are merely variants of these three prime types. They are essentially different ways of structuring the observation, shaping self-report or accessing the archive. For instance, face-to-face interviews rely on self-report but so too do self-completion questionnaires. Equally, the use of focus groups as a method of discovery relies upon observation but the measurement of physiological variation is also a type of observation.

The data that observation, self-report and archival methods reveal can then be recorded in many different ways. All three can be used to generate either qualitative or quantitative data records (and sometimes both at the same time). The form of the data is not intrinsically dictated by the method of data elicitation used. When you use observation you can choose to give a qualitative account of what happens or you can decide to report a quantified breakdown of what happens. For instance, you could observe the meeting of two people in a railway station in terms of their demeanour, their movement to a table in a café, what they order to drink, whether they look happy when they part. Alternatively, you could decide to report how many times they touch each other and the interval of time between each such contact. The object in both cases may be to understand how people behave in public places and in both cases the data elicitation method is observation. However, one approach to recording the data is clearly qualitative and the other obviously quantitative. The dichotomy between qualitative and quantitative methods is not a division in the approach to data elicitation at the macro-level but a distinction in the way data are recorded and then subsequently analysed.

Crucially, the way data are recorded matters. This is not simply because the way they are recorded will radically influence the way they can be subsequently treated (i.e. analysed, and this does not simply involve statistical analysis). It is also because the way data are recorded reflects the underlying theoretical and epistemological beliefs of the researcher. Differences in data elicitation methods are less revealing of these distinctions in belief than differences in data recording. Both Popperian hypothesis testers and social constructionists may use observation within the context of an interview but they are exceedingly unlikely to do the same things with the data thus collected. In learning about a method, it is always important to examine how data elicitation and recording may be related. All data elicitation techniques allow for a variety of recording methods. Choosing the best recording method is as important for the question you are addressing as choosing the most appropriate data elicitation method.

Research Designs

When learning about research methods it is also worth remembering that the same data elicitation method can be used in many different types of research design. Essentially, the label 'research design' is simply shorthand for the overall structure of the study to be undertaken. It specifies the components that comprise the study. It should identify the logical relationships between those components. The researcher should be able to explain how each component in the research design is necessitated by the research question that is being addressed. The chapters in this book describe how research designs are built up from a research question. The various approaches to developing the research design that are included here illustrate that the key to a good study is a very systematic unpicking of each aspect of the research question. A thorough understanding of what it is you really want to ask or actually want to know is the vital basis for good research. Ambiguity or under-specification in the research question leads to poor research because it can result in the wrong data being elicited or data being recorded ineffectively or data analysis being misdirected. Getting the specification of the research question correct is the prime precursor of effective research.

It should already be evident that experimental and non-experimental research designs are not distinguishable on the basis of the data elicitation and recording methods they may employ. The logical distinctions between experimental, quasi-experimental and non-experimental research designs are explained in various chapters in this book. Suffice it to say here that the distinction hinges not upon the method of data elicitation or recording but upon the extent to which the researcher can and chooses to introduce structured manipulation of the participants in the study. Experimental designs involve systematic manipulation. Non-experimental designs involve no manipulation. Manipulation essentially comprises an intentional intervention on the part of the researcher that is designed to affect the participants in the study and lead to recordable outcomes. Manipulation is deemed to be intentional. It should not be confused with the unintended effects that the researcher might have upon study participants simply by attempting to elicit data. The chapters in this book illustrate a range of approaches to manipulation and their relationships to the research designs that can be used.

Figure 1.1 summarizes the various levels that coexist and can be described in piece of research. The figure can be used as an aide memoir when thinking about how to describe the methodological components of any study.

Each of the chapters in this book can be characterized in terms of the first three levels described in Figure 1.1. Table 1.1 provides that summary. Table 1.1 can be used in order for the reader to make a quick selection of a chapter that provides information relevant to particular forms of research activity. It can be used by a course leader to map out the sequence in which chapters might be included in a methods course. The table illustrates that chapters overlap in the research skills that they depict. It is consequently useful in planning comparisons between different approaches to one research tool (e.g. alternative ways of using self-report data from interviews or quasi-experimental designs).

Level 1: Research design		
Experimental	Quasi-experimental	Non-experimental
Level 2: Data elicitation		
Observation	Self-report	Archival

Each can be done through many media (e.g. written, audio, visual, artefactual). Each may involve varying degrees of interaction between the researcher and the subject of the research. Technological developments (e.g. closed circuit televisual recording, computer-assisted questionnaire administration or online web-based techniques) are dramatically modifying the nature of the interaction between researcher and researched.

Level 3: Data recording

Data recording can be structured prior to initiating data elicitation or can have structure imposed post hoc. Some structuring prior to analysis is inevitable if the research is to involve more than direct description.

The structure imposed can take many forms. It might be unitary (e.g. indicating presence or absence of the entity), or frequency-based, or intensity-based (e.g. rating or scaling approaches) or thematic (i.e. identifying patterns in the information collected).

Level 4: Data treatment and analysis

Data may be analysed using qualitative or quantitative techniques. The same data can often be analysed using both types of technique.

Figure 1.1   Methodological levels of a research study

Table 1.1 Chapter coverage

Chapter	Research design	Data elicitation			Data recording	
		Observation	Self-report	Archival	Pre-structured	Post-structured
Chapter 2	Experimental		X		X	
Chapter 3	Experimental		X		X	X
Chapter 4	Quasi-experimental	X	X		X	
Chapter 5	Quasi-experimental		X	X	X	X
Chapter 6	Quasi-experimental		X		X	
Chapter 7	Non-experimental		X		X	
Chapter 8	Non-experimental		X		X	X
Chapter 9	Quasi-experimental	X	X	X		X
Chapter 10	Non-experimental	X	X			X
Chapter 11	Non-experimental		X			X
Chapter 12	Non-experimental		X		X	
Chapter 13	Non-experimental		X		X	X
Chapter 14	Non-experimental	X				X

CHAPTER TWO

Experimental Research Designs

Lorne Hulbert

This chapter presents the basic logic of experimental research designs and includes a simple illustrative exercise. No previous knowledge of the approach is assumed.

Introduction

Certain archetypal personages like Dr Jekyll and Frankenstein help form our early understanding of experimentation. Similarly, history provides many examples of famous 'experiments'. For example, in 1752, the colonial American philosopher-politician-raconteur Benjamin Franklin conducted his 'kite experiment'. Franklin thought to demonstrate that lightning – or *'electric fire'* – was indeed electricity, and could be used for other purposes. In his autobiography, he provides what we might today call a 'Method section' for this experiment, with enough detail to allow for replication, should one be so inclined.[1]

Philadelphia, October 19

As frequent Mention is made in the News Papers from Europe, of the Success of the Philadelphia Experiment for drawing the Electric Fire from Clouds by Means of pointed Rods of Iron erected on high Buildings, &c. it may be agreeable to the Curious to be inform'd, that the same Experiment has succeeded in Philadelphia, tho' made in a different and more easy Manner, which any one may try, as follows.

Make a small Cross of two light Strips of Cedar, the Arms so long as to reach to the four Corners of a large thin Silk Handkerchief when extended; tie the Corners of the Handkerchief to the Extremities of the Cross, so you have the Body of a Kite; which being properly accommodated with a Tail, Loop and String, will rise in the Air, like those made of Paper; but this being of Silk is fitter to bear the Wet and Wind of a Thunder Gust without tearing. To the Top of the upright Stick of the Cross is to be fixed a very sharp pointed Wire, rising a Foot or more above the Wood. To the End of the Twine, next the Hand, is to be tied a silk Ribbon, and where the Twine and the silk join, a Key may be fastened. This Kite is to be raised when a Thunder Gust appears to be coming on, and the Person who holds the String must stand within a Door, or Window, or under some Cover, so that the Silk Ribbon may not be wet; and Care must be taken that the Twine does not touch the Frame of the Door or Window. As soon as any of the Thunder Clouds come over the Kite, the pointed Wire will draw the Electric Fire from them, and the Kite, with all the Twine, will be electrified, and the loose Filaments of the Twine will stand out every Way, and be attracted by an approaching Finger. And when the Rain has wet the Kite and Twine, so that it can conduct the Electric Fire freely, you will find it stream out plentifully from the Key on the Approach of your Knuckle. At this Key the Phial may be charg'd; and from Electric Fire thus obtain'd, Spirits may be kindled, and all the other Electric Experiments be perform'd, which are usually done by the Help of a rubbed Glass Globe or Tube; and thereby the Sameness of the Electric Matter with that of Lightning compleatly demonstrated.

Reports like Franklin's convey the popular idea of what an experiment is: given an idea about reality, the environment is manipulated to discover whether the result is consistent or not with the idea. Using knowledge of modern research methods, however, we would not call Franklin's experiment an experiment. Because of this we would – all other things equal – be doubtful about the conclusions Franklin draws from the results. Indeed if Franklin were to submit this research for publication in a psychological journal, it would probably be rejected on the grounds that his primary claim – lightning causes a key to carry an electrical charge – is not sufficiently supported by his research design! The procedure of the kite experiment lacks essential elements of modern experimental design that allow researchers to support conclusions like those made by Franklin.

Experimental design and procedure is at first glance complicated, and it is therefore discussed at length in this chapter. However, an important organizing principle for understanding experimental design is to remember throughout that what experimental procedures are designed to do is to allow the demonstration of a *causal relationship* between *constructs*. In the kite experiment, the important constructs are lightning and an electrified key, and the tested causal relationship is that the lightning *causes* the electricity in the key.[2]

Does the kite experiment allow us to conclude that the hypo-thesized causal relationship between lightning and the electrified key exists? Strictly speaking, the answer is no. At a fundamental level, how could Franklin conclude that it was the lightning, and not some other result of the kite being elevated in a storm, that caused the key to be charged? Importantly, when considering experiments the ques-tion, 'Are there potential alternative constructs that might have caused the effect?' must be asked. The experimental method has developed to address this question explicitly, and experimental procedures are the set of techniques that have been developed to help answer the question negatively. The potential to infer causation by eliminating alternative causes is the defining characteristic of experiments, relat-ive to other research methods.

There are many fine basic texts on the nature of research and experimentation (Cook & Campbell, 1979; Runkle & McGrath, 1972) some of which are discussed in this more limited chapter. Here, we attempt to condense this information, and discuss experimentation within the context of actual experiments in social psychology. First we consider (very briefly) a philosophy of causation in order to begin a discussion of the relationship between causation and experimenta-tion. Then we will consider the basis, design, procedure and results of a published social psychological experiment to give a framework for a more abstract discussion of experimentation *per se*. Finally, after brief discussion of tangential aspects of the experimental method, an exercise will be given to help practise designing good experiments.

The Philosophy of Causation

Humans spend much of their time trying to know the causes of things. Some thinkers propose that this factor distinguishes humans from other animals. Under the rubric *attribution theory*, social psycho-logy has attempted to understand how humans infer causal relation-ships between people's personality (including our own) and their behaviours. For instance, if our constructs are a 'person's sincere belief about the National Health Service' and 'a person's statement that the National Health Service should be abolished', when can we conclude that the sincere belief causes the statement? According to *correspondent inference theory* (Jones & Davis, 1965), we would be more likely to conclude that a person's sincere belief caused the statement if they have acted in a way that may lead to negative consequences; as for instance if a politician were to make this statement to a pensioner's group rather than to health insurance executives.

The point to make is that people have *implicit* characteristic rules for determining that constructs are in causal relationships. However, these human rules often diverge from *objective* criteria for demonstrating that one construct causes another. Given that human intuition can be biased, an honest thinker must conclude that the use of intuition to discover truths about reality – which is after all, what science is all about – must be helped along with alternative mechanisms. Research methods are the alternative mechanisms psychologists use for testing possible causal relationships. Different research methods, like human intuition, have different strengths and weaknesses. While a debate about the relative value of one research method over another can be attractive, it is probably more useful to understand the strengths and weaknesses of each.

Because abstract rules about causation exist, we can analyse logically the potential of any research method to show a causal relationship. When research methods are analysed according to these criteria, we find that a well done experiment is most likely to satisfy these *logical* demands. So what are these rules, then? Experimentation as a tool to assist causal inference has developed – and is developing – primarily to match the eighteenth-century philosopher David Hume's *three criteria for demonstrating causation*: temporal precedence of the cause over the effect; covariance between the cause and effect; the exclusion of all other possible causes. Hume held that if these three criteria were met in a given demonstration, then causation could be assumed.

The first of Hume's criteria was that there should be *temporal precedence* of the hypothesized cause over the effect. This is a fancy way of saying that the supposed cause should come before the effect in time. In the case of Franklin's experiment, and assuming that the key was not charged before the kite was flown in the storm, we can show that the lightning appeared before the key was electrified. Although most research methods meet this criterion, others, like survey research, may sacrifice it to optimize other criteria (in this case, being able to study an important construct that is out of the experimenter's control, like domestic violence or culture).

The second of Hume's criteria is more difficult to demonstrate than the first, but is usually fulfilled by most research methods. This is that there should be *covariance* between the hypothesized cause and the effect. That is to say, when the supposed cause occurs, then the effect also occurs. Similarly, when the supposed cause does not occur, then neither does the effect. Thus the cause and effect *covary*, or vary together. Unfortunately, the kite experiment does not really meet this criterion. We need more information, or more *conditions* under which the effect *might* occur. For instance, what happens if there is rain, but no lightning? Or, for that matter, what happens if the kite isn't attached to the key? In general, to demonstrate covariance, a comparison must be made. In the kite experiment, there is no comparison condition, and so we cannot conclude that lightning and electricity in the key covary.

The third and final of Hume's criteria is the most difficult to demonstrate, and the one most relevant to a comparative discussion of experiments. This criterion might be called the *exclusion principle*. According to Hume, in order to infer causation, in addition to demonstrating temporal precedence and covariance, we must also *exclude* all other possible alternative causes. Franklin has failed to use any procedure to meet the third of Hume's criteria. How do we know that something else did not just happen to cause the key to be electrified at the same time that lightning struck the kite? For instance, perhaps invisible angels electrified the key, or perhaps the lightning causes a psychokinetic illusion of electricity.

While all this is clearly unfair to Franklin, and these are absurd alternatives, the logical point remains: in the kite experiment, no attempt was made to ensure that other constructs were not causing the key to be electrified. In a properly conducted experiment, procedures are used – as much as possible – to *control* for alternative causes, thus meeting the third of Hume's criteria for demonstrating causation. Thus we speak of *experimental control*, which is a set of procedures that help us to eliminate alternative causes in experiments.

Examination of a Simple Experiment

To continue this discussion, we consider an experiment by Bouas and Komorita (1996) about social dilemmas.[3] *Social dilemma* is the term for a very large number of different situations in which a group of people, all acting independently, must choose between actions that tend to maximize their *personal welfare* and actions that tend to maximize the good of the entire group (*collective welfare*). A social dilemma is a dilemma because of the way the situations are set up. If everyone in the group attempts to maximize their personal welfare, they will all be worse off than if they had acted to maximize collective welfare. There are many social dilemmas in everyday life. For instance, each individual must choose each day whether to drive or to use public transport to commute to work. It is individually rational to drive, because it is more convenient and comfortable. However, if everyone drives their car to work, the collective will suffer from too much smog and noise, and – more directly – it will take ever longer for an individual to get to work.

In the laboratory, a social dilemma is an abstract situation for groups in which group members (research participants) independently and anonymously make simple choices that do or do not result in some reward (e.g. money, vouchers, or school supplies) for all the group members. The choices and rewards are structured so that the basic characteristics of the social dilemma are maintained: acting for the self always gives more reward than acting for the group; but if all act for themselves, they will all be worse off than if they had all acted for the group. Social psychologists use laboratory social dilemmas to study *cooperation* (for more information about this research see Dawes, 1980; Komorita & Parks, 1995; Liebrand, Messick & Wilke, 1992).

IDENTIFICATION OF IMPORTANT
CAUSAL RELATIONSHIPS

Like all experimenters, Bouas and Komorita were interested in testing causal relationships. They were concerned with the constructs 'group discussion', 'group identity', and 'cooperation in a social dilemma'. Research has shown that a pre-choice group discussion causes people to act more cooperatively in social dilemmas, and some psychologists (e.g. Dawes, McTavish & Shaklee, 1977) believe that this is because group discussion fosters a sense of group identity among members. Others (e.g. Kerr & Kaufman-Gilliland, 1994) believe that group discussion only allows members to reach a consensus about mutual cooperation, to which members adhere subsequently. To help resolve this issue, Bouas and Komorita tested the idea that group discussion creates group identity, which is responsible for the increased levels of collective behaviour. In the same experiment, they tested whether group discussion allows for the development of within-group agreement to cooperate, and that this causes increased cooperation in social dilemmas.

EXPERIMENTAL DESIGN: CONDITIONS

To test these relationships, Bouas and Komorita measured participants' cooperation in the social dilemma, group identity, and perceived within-group agreement to cooperate. But they also created different *conditions* in their experiment. That is, they created different experiences for different sub-samples of the participants in their study, and took measurements following these experiences. There were three conditions in the experiment, one *control condition* and two *treatment conditions*:

- Control condition: a condition in which there was no group discussion and thus no fostering of group identity. Participants in this condition merely made choices on the social dilemma. Following common labelling customs, they called this condition the *control condition*.
- First treatment: a condition in which there was group discussion and thus group identity. In this condition, groups *discussed the dilemma itself*, which would allow the development of an agreement to act cooperatively. This condition is called the *discuss-the-dilemma* condition.
- Second treatment: a condition in which there was discussion again, but in this condition groups *discussed a salient issue* (tuition fees) but not the social dilemma. Bouas and Komorita reasoned that these groups should develop group identity, but not an agreement to act cooperatively. This condition is called the *discuss-tuition-fees* condition.

HYPOTHESES OF THE EXPERIMENT

The experimental conditions and measures were specifically designed to test the causal relationships of interest. Statements that explain the relationships between conditions, measurements and conclusions, are called *hypotheses*. The hypotheses for this experiment were:

Hypothesis 1: group identity causes cooperation.
If group identity causes collectively rational choice in social dilemmas, then the proportion of people choosing cooperatively in the two discussion conditions should be equal, and greater than the proportion in the control condition. This hypothesis predicts that the amount of cooperation will be high where there is any kind of group discussion (when group identity is high) but not otherwise. Thus amounts of cooperation are compared between conditions.

Hypothesis 2: agreement to cooperate causes cooperation.
Alternatively, if it is reaching a consensus about cooperating, rather than group identity, that affects choice in the social dilemma, then

cooperation should be higher in the discuss-the-dilemma condition (when perceived within-group agreement is high), relative to the other two conditions, which will be equal to each other.[4]

PARTICIPANTS

To conduct the study, Bouas and Komorita arranged for 160 female undergraduate students to come to the laboratory in groups of four to participate in a social dilemma. These students were randomly selected from a large pool of students who participate in research for partial credit in an introductory psychology course. Note that Bouas and Komorita are careful to tell us how many participants there were (160), with information about the participants (female undergraduate students) and also how and from where they were selected for the experiment. This information should be found in every experimental report.

EXPERIMENTAL PROCEDURE

Before group members arrived at the laboratory, or immediately afterward, which of the three conditions a given group would be in during the experiment was determined randomly (e.g. by roll of dice or table of random numbers), with the constraint that there were equal numbers of groups in each of the conditions by the end of the experiment. As we shall see, this seemingly trivial procedure is the most important of this group of important practices. If researchers do not randomly assign participants to conditions, then we conclude immediately that the research is not an experiment.

Once group members arrived, they were welcomed, seated separately, and told something about the experiment. In this phase, they were told whether the experiment would be distressful or embarrassing, and asked if they were sure they would like to participate. This is called getting participants' *informed consent* to participate. In a social dilemma experiment, informed consent might sound something like this:

> Hello and welcome to the experiment. In this experiment, you will be asked to make simple anonymous choices as part of a group. The combination of your choice and the other group members' choices will determine the numbers of points you all receive at the end of the experiment. The number of points you earn will determine whether

you win some money later in the year. The experiment is not in any way harmful or embarrassing, but if you'd rather not participate today, please let me know now by raising your hand.

Clearly, different experiments would have variations of this statement, but the informed consent procedure is an important part of the *ethics* of doing psychology experiments. The (few, if any) participants who decide at this point to opt out are dismissed without question or comment.

After informed consent was granted, participants were given written instructions, and they were asked to read along silently with a tape recording of those instructions. The instructions informed the students that they were in a group playing a social dilemma. Most of the instructions would concern how the social dilemma works, and about the choice between individually rational and collectively rational options. They are tape recorded and written to try to ensure that all participants are treated almost identically, and have the same knowledge, in all conditions. Treating participants as equally as possible in all conditions (excepting the relevant changes, of course) is a 'golden rule' of experimental research.

Importantly, words like 'social', 'dilemma', 'rational' and 'cooperation' are not used when the situation is described to participants. Rather, words like 'situation', 'earn points' and 'choice' are used. This standard procedure in social dilemma experiments is to prevent any *response biases* the participants might exhibit due to the norms associated with such words.

Afterwards, in group discussion conditions, the participants had 10 minutes to discuss, and then returned to partitioned cubicles to make their choices. When participants did not have a group discussion, they were given 10 minutes to make their choices. This is important so as to ensure that participants in all conditions have the same amount of *time* (regardless of group discussion) between instructions and choices. This procedure too is reported by Bouas and Komorita so that we see that they attempted to ensure that participants did not respond to elements of the procedure that were irrelevant to the causal hypothesis.

After the participants made their choices for the dilemma, but before they discovered how everyone else had chosen, they completed a short questionnaire. On the questionnaire participants responded to a scale developed by Hinkle, Taylor, Fox-Cardamone and Crook (1989) to assess their feelings of identity with the group. In addition, they indicated how many of the three other group members would make the cooperative choice. These measurements are called *manipulation checks*. They are designed to check that the conditions had the effects the experimenters intended. Discussion of any sort was assumed to increase group identity, but discussion about the dilemma was the only kind of discussion that was assumed to increase within-group agreement. The manipulation checks can support the conclusions the experimenters make.

After the participants filled out the questionnaires, they were individually told about the choices of all the group members, and were *debriefed* (i.e. informed about the procedure and purposes of the study), thanked and dismissed. Debriefing is the second part of experimental procedure that is explicitly concerned with ethics. By adhering to an ethical code, experimenters agree to debrief participants at the end of the experiment.

RESULTS

The results of the study are presented in Figure 2.1. What is left is to compare the results to each of the hypotheses, and to see which ones are rejected as plausible descriptions of the results. As can be seen, high levels of cooperative choice in the discuss-the-dilemma condition were found, relative to the other conditions. Thus Hypothesis 1 is rejected by the results of the experiment and Hypothesis 2 is not rejected.

Figure 2.1 also shows the results of the two manipulation checks. As can be seen, group identity was equally high in both discussion conditions, relative to the control condition. Also, perceived within-group agreement to cooperate was low in the control and discuss-tuition-fees condition, relative to the discuss-the-dilemma condition. Thus, Bouas and Komorita concluded that their conditions had the effects they assumed they would, and provided greater support for their conclusions.

CONCLUSIONS

Because Hypothesis 1 cannot explain the results of the study, Bouas and Komorita concluded that enhanced group identity following group discussion is not a cause of greater cooperation in the social dilemma. Rather, another factor must be important. Here they have proposed the development of within-group agreements about cooperating. This hypothesis was not rejected and awaits further testing. It is important to keep in mind the relative strengths of the conclusions that are

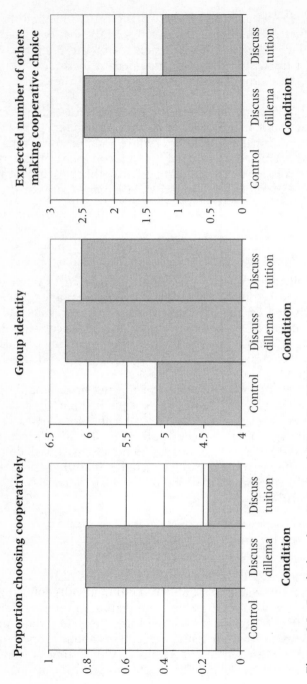

Figure 2.1 Results based on Bouas and Komorita (1996)

drawn in this case. Whereas the causal relationship between group identity and cooperation is *rejected*, the causal relationship between within-group agreement and cooperation was *not rejected*, implying, of course, that this relationship might be rejected in the future.

Demonstrating Covariance in Experiments

If we compare Bouas and Komorita's design to that of the kite experiment, we find many differences. First, Hume's *temporal precedence* criterion is satisfied, since the group discussion (or not) occurred before the participants made their choices. Second, Bouas and Komorita clearly demonstrated *covariance* between the supposed causes and effects by comparing the data from the different conditions of the experiment. For instance, in the discuss-the-dilemma condition, there was more cooperation, and when there was no group discussion about the dilemma, there was less cooperation. This demonstrates covariance for this relationship, and so the criterion is met. (Note again, however that rather than concluding that this relationship is true, we conclude that Hypothesis 2 has not been rejected.)

INDEPENDENT AND DEPENDENT VARIABLES

In experiments, we have special names for the constructs that are involved in the causal relationships. The supposed cause in an experiment is called an *independent variable* (often abbreviated as 'IV'). Using this terminology, we say that one condition is different from another when the conditions differ in amounts of the independent variable. To understand what an independent variable is, it is first important simply to understand that because it is a *variable*, it varies. For instance, in Bouas and Komorita, one independent variable was group identity, and it varied between some group identity (in the conditions where there was a group discussion) and less group identity (control condition). We call these the *levels of the independent variable*, meaning the 'amount' of the independent variable that is present in the different conditions. We say that the experimenter *controls the level of the independent variable* in the experiment by (in this example) controlling if and when a group discussion occurs.

In an experiment, the supposed *effect* in the causal relationship is called a *dependent variable* (usually abbreviated as 'DV'), or *dependent measure*. In Bouas and Komorita (1996) the three dependent variables were *choice in a social dilemma*, *group identity* and *perceived within-group agreement to cooperate*. Dependent variables are – like independent variables – variables, meaning that they vary. For instance, the group identity scale used by Bouas and Komorita is composed of nine questionnaire items, to which participants could give one of seven responses. Bouas and Komorita used the average of participants' responses to all nine questions, so this dependent variable varied between 1.0 and 7.0. Unlike independent variables, however, the *participants* 'control' the level of the dependent variables, by responding to the different stimuli presented to them.

There is more to be said about independent and dependent variables, in the context of the third of Hume's criteria. However, for now we can state that although experiments are sometimes very complex, a characteristic of all experimental research is that *covariance is demonstrated when a comparison is made between levels of the DV observed in at least two conditions that differ in levels of the IV*.

INTERACTIONS

Before we consider the relationship between experiments and the principle of exclusion, it is useful to discuss an important sort of comparison called an *interaction*. At one level an interaction is a comparison that is made for experiments in which there are more than two independent variables (n.b. not necessarily more than two *conditions*). Conceptually we say that an interaction *exists* when the effect (on the DV) of the two independent variables *together* is different from the effect of either one of them *alone*.

Good examples for explaining interactions are often pharmaceutical. For instance, we know that the effect of an antibiotic is to kill a harmful bacterium. Also we know that the effect of alcohol is to cause euphoria, relaxation and lack of coordination. What is the effect of the two drugs in combination? In one possibility, taking the two drugs results in all the effects of each drug occurring, but together. So the person taking both would feel quite euphoric and relaxed, and would as a bonus also lack harmful bacteria. We call this result *additive effects*. The other possibility (which is the reality) is that the two drugs in combination can cause severe illness or even death. Thus the two drugs *interact*, meaning that their joint effect is different from the effect of either alone.

Table 2.1 summarizes the differences between additive effects and interactions for this example. The two independent variables are *taking an antibiotic* and *taking alcohol*. Both independent variables have two levels: taking it or not taking it. When the two independent

Table 2.1 Interactions and additive effects

	No interaction between drugs (additive effects)	
	No alcohol	*Takes alcohol*
No antibiotic	No effects	Relaxation, euphoria, lack of coordination
Takes antibiotic	Kills harmful bacterium	Relaxation, euphoria, lack of coordination *plus* kills harmful bacterium
	Interaction between drugs	
	No alcohol	*Takes alcohol*
No antibiotic	No effects	Relaxation, euphoria, lack of coordination
Takes antibiotic	Kills harmful bacterium	Severe nausea, potential death

variables are *crossed* this creates four conditions: no antibiotic and no alcohol, no antibiotic and takes alcohol, takes antibiotic but no alcohol, takes antibiotic and takes alcohol. The cells of the top table shows what will happen under the additive effects hypothesis, and those of the bottom table show the results predicted by the interaction hypothesis.

An example of interaction from the research

As an example from social psychology, we consider the experiment of van den Bos, Bruins, Wilke and Dronkert (1999) concerning *procedural fairness*.[5] The idea of procedural fairness is that in competitive situations (e.g. criminal courts, negotiation and bargaining), some procedures are considered to be fairer than others (e.g. Tyler, 1994). For instance, in justice systems based on English Common Law, a trial by jury is thought to be fairer than a trial by magistrate, despite evidence that the two procedures lead to few or no substantive differences. The upshot is that a person's satisfaction with an outcome may depend upon the *procedure* used to achieve that outcome.

For example, suppose that in an important football match a penalty kick is given to your favourite side. If the striker scores the goal, this is a favourable outcome for you and you should be satisfied, and vice versa. To make your satisfaction into a dependent variable (i.e. to give numbers to satisfaction), we can suppose that if the striker scores the goal you gain one satisfaction 'point', but zero satisfaction points otherwise.

But when considering ideas of procedural fairness, we consider the fairness of the procedure used to determine that the defensive player fouled the opponent: it can be *fair* (the referee made a good call, e.g. as indicated by slow motion tape replay) or *unfair* (the referee made a bad call). How will the fairness of the procedure affect your satisfaction with the result of the kick? One hypothesis is that you do not care whether the penalty was given fairly or unfairly, and your satisfaction depends wholly upon whether the goal is scored. In this case, you would receive no satisfaction points if the penalty was or was not fairly given.

Another hypothesis is that your satisfaction would be affected by the fairness of the referee's call. To use the satisfaction DV again, you would score one satisfaction point if the penalty was fairly given, and zero otherwise. Thus you would be happiest when a fairly given penalty is scored (1 point from the score, and 1 point from the fairness for a total of 2 points), and as happy when an unfairly given penalty is scored as when an unfairly given penalty is missed (1 point from either the score *or* from the fairness). You would receive no satisfaction from a missed unfairly given penalty.

The top two tables in Table 2.2 show these two additive effects hypotheses. The top table shows the case when procedural fairness has no effect, and the middle table shows the case when procedural fairness has an effect. Note that the effects of both of the independent variables on the dependent variable 'add together' to complete the table.

Van den Bos et al. (1999) continued this argument for their experiment. They reasoned that a fan would always be more satisfied if the goal were scored, relative to not scoring. However, given that the goal was missed, the fan would be slightly mollified if the penalty was unfairly given – perhaps the fan might think something like, 'Oh well, it wasn't meant to happen anyway'. Van den Bos et al. called this the *reversal hypothesis*. The reversal hypothesis is an interaction hypothesis because it predicts that the effects of outcome favourability and procedural fairness together would be different from the effect of either alone.

To test the reversal hypothesis, van den Bos et al. asked 49 male and 35 female psychology students to participate in groups of five in a simulated organization. The experiment was conducted over a computer, and participants never truly interacted in any way. The students were informed that they would be randomly assigned to one of five

Table 2.2 Interactions and additive effects between outcome favourableness and procedural fairness

Additive effects, procedural fairness gives no satisfaction		
	Good call (0 satisfaction points)	*Bad call (0 satisfaction points)*
Scores goal (1 satisfaction point)	Satisfaction = 1	Satisfaction = 1
Misses goal (0 satisfaction points)	Satisfaction = 0	Satisfaction = 0

Additive effects, procedural fairness gives satisfaction		
	Good call (1 satisfaction point)	*Bad call (0 satisfaction points)*
Scores goal (1 satisfaction point)	Satisfaction = 2	Satisfaction = 1
Misses goal (0 satisfaction points)	Satisfaction = 1	Satisfaction = 0

Interaction found by van den Bos et al. (simplified)		
	Fair procedure	*Unfair procedure*
Higher position (1 satisfaction point)	Satisfaction = 2	Satisfaction = 2
Lower position (0 satisfaction points)	Satisfaction = 0	Satisfaction = 1

positions within the organization (the highest position rendering the greatest reward and the lowest rendering the least reward), but all were assigned to the middlemost of the five positions (the participants did not know this until the end of the study). Following an initial work period, participants took an examination that they were told would determine their placement in the hierarchy for the next phase.

However, rather than participants' actual score being used, a *randomly determined half* of the participants were told that their placements for the next phase were determined using only two of the 20 items on the exam and the other half were told that all 20 items were used. This procedure manipulated the first independent variable: *fairness of the procedure*. The first IV has two levels: *fair* and *unfair*. Then a randomly determined half of the participants in the unfair level of the fairness IV were told that they had been promoted to the next highest position. The remaining half were told they had been demoted. The same procedure was conducted for the people in the fair condition. This procedure manipulated the *favourableness of the outcome* independent variable. The second IV also has two levels: *favourable* and *unfavourable*.

By manipulating the two independent variables in the way described above, van den Bos et al. created four conditions of their experiment (fair/favourable, fair/unfavourable, unfair/favourable, unfair/unfavourable), each containing a randomly determined 21 of the participants. Each participant in the experiment experienced only one *condition*, but they experienced one level each of both IVs. This design matches that shown in Table 2.2, and once more participants did not know that they were placed in different conditions until the end of the experiment.

After participants were assigned a position for the second phase, they were asked how happy, content and agreeable they were about the outcome, and these were combined to form an overall measure of satisfaction (the DV). Before they left the laboratory, they were fully debriefed, including a description of the different things they were told that were in fact not true.

A simplified version of the result is shown in the last part of Table 2.2. As can be seen, the results differed from both possible additive effects results. Fairness of the procedure did not affect the high degree of satisfaction with the favourable outcome, but the unfavourable outcome following an unfair procedure was more satisfactory, relative to when an unfavourable outcome follows a fair procedure. Therefore, van den Bos et al. (1999) rejected the hypothesis that fairness and favourableness render additive effects. Furthermore, by examining the results more closely, they also concluded that the reversal hypothesis was not rejected, and thus this hypothesis awaits further testing.

As you read more about social psychology, you will soon discover the importance of interactions to the discipline. They can sometimes be difficult for beginners to understand, and making tables like those in Tables 2.1 and 2.2 will help you to extend and refine your understanding of them. Indeed, many social psychologists use tables like these to help them understand research they read about, as well as to plan and design their own research. Although part of the reason for their importance is their amenability to statistical analysis (ANOVA), being able to structure information like this turns out to be a powerful analytical tool. However, the final point to make about interactions is that, although they are more complex, and require quite a lot of initial understanding of an area of research before skill with them develops, they have as their basis the simple idea of making comparisons to show covariance.

(Striving to Satisfy) the Exclusion Principle

To summarize to this point, we have considered several common terms used by experimentalists like *causal relations, hypotheses, conditions, independent and dependent variables, levels of independent variables* and *interactions*, and we considered covariance between independent and dependent variables. In this section of the chapter, we will consider how experimental methods treat the problem of the exclusion principle, that is, of eliminating alternative potential causal constructs for a given effect.

The exclusion principle is satisfied in experiments by careful structuring of experimental design and experimental procedure. Although these labels overlap to some extent, it is relatively safe to define them independently. *Experimental design* is the specification of conditions, which at a more basic level is the specification of independent and dependent variables, and the order they are administered. *Experimental procedure* concerns the instantiation of experimental design, primarily, *what happens* in each condition, *who* is in each condition and *how* DVs are measured.

When considering the exclusion principle and experimental design and procedure, we think of a utopian methodological form in which all possible alternative causes in a causal relationship are eliminated. This ideal is achieved when the experimenter has complete *control* over the experimental design and procedure. We should take *experimental control* to mean *the degree of adherence to a set of guidelines and protocols that, if followed absolutely, lead to the ideal experiment.* In the traditional terminology of experimental method, these guidelines and protocols are problems of *manipulation* and *isolation*.

Manipulation in this sense means causing the level of the independent variable. An example from Bouas and Komorita (1996) is: *group identity can be manipulated by making groups have a discussion.* An example from van den Bos et al. (1999) is: *fairness can be manipulated by leading participants to believe that they were judged based on only two items of the exam.* So manipulation means 'cause', 'increase', 'decrease', 'make occur', 'cause to go away', 'change' or 'effect'.

Isolation is the most important element of being able to infer causation. By *isolation* we mean providing conditions that differ *only* in the level of the independent variable. An example is: *by comparing groups that discuss the social dilemma to groups that discuss tuition fees, an attempt was made to isolate the perception of within-group agreement to cooperate from group identity.* Bouas and Komorita's goal was to eliminate group identity as a rival to perceived agreement as the cause of cooperation. We can believe their conclusion that perceived agreement (rather than group identity) has not been rejected as the cause of cooperation *only to the extent we believe they isolated perceived agreement from group identity.* If covariance between perceived agreement and cooperation has been demonstrated, but they have not been isolated from each other, then we cannot choose between them as causal factors.

In the van den Bos et al. study, a more general isolation is attempted: *by comparing people who were judged based on only two items to those who were judged using 20 items, an attempt was made to isolate fairness of the judgement procedure from all other aspects of the judgement procedure.* Here, there is no specific potential alternative cause from which the IV is isolated, but rather the attempt is made to eliminate all other potential alternative causes. We can believe their conclusion that fairness of the judgement procedure (rather than some other aspect of the procedure) has not been rejected as the cause of satisfaction *only to the extent we believe they isolated perceived fairness of the procedure from all other aspects of the procedure.* If covariance between perceived fairness and satisfaction have been demonstrated, but perceived fairness has not been isolated from all other aspects of the procedure, then we cannot choose between fairness and some other aspect as causal factors.

In the next two sections, we consider techniques for isolating independent variables. Potential alternative causes are for convenience grouped under the labels of *artefacts* and *confounds*. The goal of the experimenter is to design and conduct experiments such that artefacts and confounds are *controlled*.

Designing Experiments to Control for Artefacts

Campbell and Stanley's volume (1963; see also its sequel, Cook & Campbell, 1979) is the foremost reference for understanding how ordering of the presentation of IVs and DVs helps ensure that an experiment will satisfy the principle of exclusion, and should be read for a fuller statement of what is discussed here. Certainly, the language used by Campbell and Stanley is so widely used that it is important to discuss it in any chapter concerning experimentation. They were concerned with the presence of *artefacts* in experiments. Artefacts are by-products of the practical necessities of doing psychological research that potentially cause the effect. Artefacts are not psychological factors *per se*, but they compromise our ability to test the causal relationship with respect to the IV.

In all, Campbell and Stanley identified 12 artefacts. Examples of these are *history* (things that occur – other than the independent variable – that change responses to a second measurement), *maturation* (changes in responses due simply to the passage of time) and *instrumentation* (changes due to differences between different measures of the same construct).

After identifying these artefacts, Campbell and Stanley considered a variety of different possible *experimental designs*, that is, orderings of IV manipulation and DV measurement. Simplifying, designs can be classified by asking three questions:

• Is the dependent variable measured before (pre-test) and after (post-test) the independent variable is manipulated, or is there only a post-test?
• Is there only one condition, or are there multiple conditions?
• Are participants randomly selected and assigned to conditions, or not?

The use of any one of these methods controls for one or more artefacts. The use of two or three of them controls for as many artefacts as possible. Research in social psychology will not be *described* as an 'experiment' if it does not answer 'yes' to the latter two questions, and often to all three. Rather than considering all the permutations of the responses to these questions, let us say that the simplest design that controls for as many artefacts as possible is the one in which there is no pre-test, there are multiple conditions and participants are randomly selected and assigned to conditions. Both Bouas and Komorita (1996) and van den Bos et al. (1999), have this sort of design: there were multiple conditions, no pre-test and random selection and assignment. Suppose that 'DV' means that there is a measure taken, and 'IV' means that the IV is manipulated, this design, called the 'post-test only, multiple conditions' design, is shown in Table 2.3. You can be sure of accounting for all possible artefacts if you use this design.

With respect to using a pre-test, there is a complication of which it is necessary to be aware. In a design in which there is a pre-test, multiple groups and random selection and assignment, the minimum

Table 2.3 Post-test only, multiple conditions design. 'IV' means the point when the independent variable is manipulated, and 'DV' means the point when the dependent variable is measured

	Time 1	Time 2
Condition 1:	IV	DV
Condition 2:		DV

Table 2.4 Pre-test, post-test, control group design

	Time 1	Time 2	Time 3
Condition 1:	DV	IV	DV
Condition 2:	DV		DV

number of groups necessary to account for all artefacts is four. Consider this case when there are only two groups: Campbell and Stanley call this the 'pre-test, post-test, control group' design. The pre-test, post-test, control group design is shown in Table 2.4.

Using this design, we might think that if in Condition 1, the DVs measured at Times 1 and 3 are different, while in Condition 2 the measures at both times do not change, then the IV must have caused the change. However, Campbell and Stanley have pointed out that this design has a potential artefact called *testing by IV interaction*. From our discussion of interaction, we know this means that the effect of the test (the measurement of the DV) and the IV together is different from the effect of either in isolation. Thus this artefact prevents us from concluding anything about the IV alone with confidence.

A simple example of this would be a poor social dilemma experiment: suppose that *after* participants played the social dilemma one time, the experimenters manipulated an IV intended to enhance the influence of group norms, and then a second test was made using the social dilemma. In this case, the pre-test is likely to change the effect of the IV, because if the group was cooperative before, then the group norm is clearly to be cooperative, and vice versa. Thus the effect of the pre-test and the IV interact to cause response in the post-test.

In sum, although it is often very useful to have an experiment with a pre-test, one must beware of the testing by IV interaction. A design that allows for the use of pre-tests, and controls for the testing by IV

Table 2.5 Solomon four-group design

	Time 1	*Time 2*	*Time 3*
Condition 1:	DV	IV	DV
Condition 2:	DV		DV
Condition 3:		IV	DV
Condition 4:			DV

interaction is called the 'Solomon four-group design'. This design is shown in Table 2.5. The Solomon design allows the experimenter to assess the possible effect of the treatment by IV artefact by comparing Condition 1 to Condition 3.

RIGOUR VERSUS PRACTICALITY

As an aside, we should note a non-substantive drawback to using the four-group design. Consider our faulty pre-test, post-test social dilemma experiment. Let's say that in our experiment we used groups of six people and, since we need multiple groups in both conditions, 10 groups in each condition are required. Thus, this experiment would require 10 (number of groups) × 6 (group size) × 2 (number of conditions) = 120 participants. If we wish to do the experiment and control for the treatment by IV artefact, then our requirement for participants would double to 240.

This example is interesting because it highlights an important conflict for social psychologists, and group process researchers in particular. We might call this the conflict between *rigour versus practicality*. Rigour here means the ideal experiment, with all the attendant procedural and design control necessary to meet the exclusion principle, and practicality is the experimenter's actual ability to conduct the ideal experiment. The use of the Solomon four-group design with a social dilemma is a good case. Here, because the supply of research participants is far more limited than our ability to violate principles of good research, the experimenter must either make compromises or avoid investigating cooperative behaviour.[6] Since the topic is important, most make the compromise. The difference between good and bad experimenters, however, is that the good one will understand this conflict, limit the conclusions made from this single experiment and resolve them in subsequent research.

We have not yet considered the third of the issues – random selection and assignment. All three of the designs above assume that participants are randomly selected and assigned. The importance of randomization, however, goes beyond the control of artefacts and is discussed later on in this chapter.

Conducting Experiments to Control for Confounding Variables

The reason that artefacts cause problems for experiments is because they represent alternative plausible causes of changes in the dependent variable. By controlling experimental design, we can account for most of them. Another kind of alternative cause is called a *confounding variable*, or *confound*. Unlike artefacts, confounds are usually taken to mean psychological meaningful variables (other than the IVs) that cause changes in the DV. For instance, in social dilemma experiments, there is some evidence that *gender* partially causes cooperation in the social dilemma (for discussion, see Sell & Griffith, 1993). If gender is not controlled in a social dilemma experiment, then it is available as an alternative cause when the results of the experiment are evaluated.

Confounds are a problem when they are *associated*, or *correlated*, with the independent variable. By *association* we mean that conditions varying in levels of the independent variable also vary in levels of the confounding variable. For instance in Bouas and Komorita's study, it would have been a basic design flaw if in one condition there were all women, and in another there were all men. In this case, how would we be able to determine whether changes in cooperation were caused by gender or by group identity? There are a variety of ways that potential confounds are dealt with in social psychological research. Note that this list is more *descriptive* than *prescriptive*, meaning that they are compromises for the sake of practicality.

CHECKING FOR THE CONFOUND'S EFFECT AFTER THE FACT OR DISCARDING DATA

One way to control for the effect of a potential confound is to assess the effect of the confound after the experiment is finished, and make conclusions accordingly if there is an effect, or combine the data as normal if not. For instance, if in a social dilemma experiment we included both men and women, and then *afterwards* discovered that there is the potential for a gender confound, we might check our results for men and then check the results for women. The ideal would be that there was no difference between men and women, and analysis would proceed as normal. Another possibility is simply to discard the data of some of the participants (e.g. men or women). This might happen in an experiment where the experimenter simply cannot control the potential confounding variable. Obviously in the ideal situation, the experimenter determines the criteria for determining who will be discarded before the experiment runs.

These practices are poor procedure, but they are found under certain circumstances. Sometimes we are simply unaware of a potential confound until too late (e.g. new research is published immediately after you conduct the experiment). Sometimes, as in the case of gender and cooperation, the effect is at best ephemeral, and the evaluation of the rigour versus practicality question might induce a willingness to risk the occurrence of the confound. Similarly, some confounds are completely 'off the wall' and unexpected, and it would be impractical to discard the data because of them. For instance, suppose in the middle of the week in which an experiment is run, the ventilation system begins rattling at random intervals. Cancelling the experiment would be a waste of time for you, your assistants and the people who have already participated. If such an unlucky event happens (and if you conduct enough experiments it probably will), then you should record in your data when the ventilation was rattling, and use this procedure.

Checking and discarding are often used when an experiment involves *deception*. Deception is sometimes used to make people believe something for the duration of the experiment which is not true. Deception was used by van den Bos et al. (1999) to manipulate the *fairness* IV (either 2 or 20 exam items were used to determine placement in the organization). If an experimenter decides to use deception (and this decision must be made with reason and sensitivity) then it is a good idea to check at the end of the experiment whether or not the participants were deceived. This kind of question is usually called a *suspicion check* (consistent with *manipulation* check). Afterwards, you can check for a suspicion confound using this procedure.

THE IMPORTANCE OF *A PRIORI* REASONING

The use of these strategies is less than perfect experimental procedure, and *planning* to use these procedures is definitely a poor way to proceed. The problem with planning to use them lies in the difference between *a priori* (before the fact) versus *a posteriori* (after the fact) reasoning. The assumption that experimental methods can test causal relationships validly depends upon matching data to hypotheses when those hypotheses have been specified *before* the data are collected. The reason for this is philosophical: it is likely we will be able to find *at least one* person, under *at least one* set of circumstances, for whom the hypothesized causal relationship is true. By extension, there is at least one person to support *every* causal relationship. If our goal in science is merely to succeed in identifying true causal relationships, one strategy is to ransack experimental data, checking potential confounds and discarding when necessary, to find this person. In the sense of pure experimentation this is counterproductive: In the extreme, the result of science would be an untenably large and confusing number of equally 'true' theories, many of which completely contradict others.[7] Thus the pure experimentalist would condemn these procedures.

HOLDING THE CONFOUND CONSTANT AND EXPERIMENTERS' BEHAVIOUR

Another way to control for a confound is simply to ensure that the level of the confound is *constant* (identical) in all conditions. Bouas and Komorita (1996) used this strategy in their experiment when they included only women participants. By asking only men or only women to participate in a social dilemma experiment, the gender variable will not influence the effect of the IV.

This procedure is by far the most commonly used. The attempt to hold confounds constant underlies much of the *behaviour of experimenters* when they collect data. A 'golden rule' about conducting experiments is that – apart from the manipulation of the IV, which obviously dictates differences – participants are treated exactly the same way in different conditions of the experiment. Experimenters might be very concerned about maintaining constant temperatures and lighting levels during experiments. They might ensure that sessions of the experiment are run at the same time of the day or that the experimenter wears the same clothes all the time.[8]

Much effort at control is focused on the behaviour of the experimenter. As social psychologists, we are well aware that people use many possible cues from other people to help them interpret and respond in all kinds of situations – particularly in unusual milieu like laboratories. Thus some effort is made to hold all these possibilities constant across conditions. At the extreme, experimenters may use a control procedure called *experimental blind*. When using an experimental blind, even the experimenter does not know which condition is operating when the data are being collected. Thus the experimenter cannot influence the results of the experiment by behaving in systematically different ways in different conditions. Despite sounding implausible, experimental blinds (or limited versions of it) are possible. For instance, van den Bos et al. (1999) used a computer to conduct their study: it would not be necessary for the experimenter to know what participants experienced during a particular session. The control provided by computerized data collection is a powerful reason for its use.

Similar kinds of controls used by Bouas and Komorita (1996) included using tape recorded instructions (so that understanding was constant across all conditions). An important example of control for small group research is when Bouas and Komorita gave participants who did not have group discussion 10 minutes to decide, simply to control for the extra time necessary to allow for discussion in other conditions (Campbell and Stanley's *maturation* artefact). Similarly, note that Bouas and Komorita are careful to state that there were only four participants per experimental session, controlling for the possibility that the *mere presence* (Zajonc, 1968) of other people would confound the results.

Note that some confounds, like mere presence effects, are known from previous social psychological research. Others, like consistency between instructions for different conditions, are more a matter of common sense. Usually, a researcher attempts to hold *everything* constant, but for the sake of brevity, reports in a journal article only those particular concerns of other researchers in the field. Sometimes, as when Bouas and Komorita say only that there were four people in every experimental session, the reason for this (mere presence) is not stated because other group process researchers understand this potential problem. Clearly, this kind of knowledge comes with experience. In the meantime, a novice experimenter should try to control everything, and read 'between the lines' of similar journal articles to discover what is important to report.

CONTROL VERSUS GENERALIZABILITY

The strongest objection to control by holding constant is that it limits the *generalizability* of the results of the experiment. The generalizability of the results of the experiment (sometimes called the experiment's *external validity*) signifies the proportion of all the humans (or in some cases, all the creatures) in the world for which the results are 'true'. The goal of psychology is, after all, to understand the behaviour of everyone, and these strategies compromise that goal. Even in the imaginary situation in which all humans participate in an experiment, the generalizability of the results may be limited to the specific procedures used by the researchers. For instance, van den Bos et al. (1999) manipulated fairness by manipulating the number of items used to judge participants. There are many possible procedures to manipulate fairness, and we cannot be sure that these other procedures will have the same effects. Similarly, the artificiality and paucity of the laboratory milieu plausibly can limit the generalizability of social psychological research to more natural settings.

Thus experimental control and generalizability are almost directly opposed. So in addition to considering *rigour versus practicality*, experimentalists are always concerned with issues of *control versus generalizability*. An experiment is inherently less generalizable than almost all other research methods. Its advantage over other methods is the use of control to (as much as possible) eliminate alternative causes. For this reason, it could be argued that the best strategy of all when doing experiments is to make the situation as artificial as possible in order to more easily isolate fundamentally interdependent social variables, thus capitalizing on the strengths of the experimental method. Certainly, such a consideration partially drives, for instance, the use of the abstract laboratory social dilemma to study cooperation.

BLOCKING

Blocking is a control procedure that ensures that a potential alternative causal construct occurs equally in all the levels of the independent variable. Figure 2.2 demonstrates this procedure for an experiment testing the effect of group identity on cooperation in the social dilemma using 24 participants. When manipulating group identity, the experimenter ensures that equal numbers of men and women are in both conditions. Thus if the experimenter finds differences in cooperation, it can be assumed that it was not gender that caused these differences, because the high cooperation of one particular sex would 'cancel out' the low cooperation of the other sex. However, if group identity causes cooperation, then its effect will still be seen since all the high group identity men and women are together in one condition, separate from the low group identity people in the other condition.

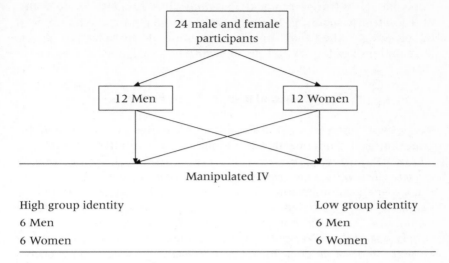

Figure 2.2 Blocking to control for a potential alternative cause

Blocking is commonly used to control for a special kind of confounding variable (or artefact) known as *order effects*. Order effects are relevant either when participants experience two or more treatments, or when participants are measured on more than two relevant dependent variables. In these cases, the experimenter may be concerned that the order in which the variables are manipulated (or measured) has an effect on the results of the study. When order effects are relevant, experimenters block the order of presentation to exclude order as a potential cause. This procedure is often flagged in reports of experiments by the phrase *'order was counterbalanced across conditions'*.

Blocking can be directly contrasted to holding constant as a control procedure. When holding constant, some levels of a confounding variable are prevented from occurring in the experiment, and when blocking, all levels are used, but divided equally across conditions. One disadvantage of blocking relative to holding constant is simply that of *identifying* all the confounds to be blocked. When discussing holding constant as a strategy, we saw that many possible confounds may be of concern (e.g. temperature, time of day). Moreover, should we be able to identify all relevant confounds, as the number of potential blocking variables increases, the number of required participants increases quickly. For instance, if gender does not cause cooperation, then the same experiment might be conducted with half the number of people. Thus the *rigour versus practicality* question plays a role in the decision to use blocking. In this case, we can increase generalizability by blocking rather than holding constant, at the expense of the impracticality of large numbers of required participants.

Randomization in Experiments

Recall that when discussing experimental design, we indicated the importance of randomization. Randomization is in effect the *sine qua non* of the pure experiment. There are two sorts of randomization: *random selection from the population*, and *random assignment to conditions*. If complete randomization is achieved, then all possible confounding variables are controlled for in the experiment. When there is randomization, an experiment meets the three criteria of causation as closely as possible. Without it, we can be fairly certain that a particular piece of research does not meet the strict definition of experiment.

RANDOM SELECTION OF PARTICIPANTS

If the participants in the sample are a true random selection from the population, we can be as sure as we possibly can (barring examining the entire population) that the experiment is generalizable to the population in question – consider how accurate pre-election surveys ordinarily are. Note that this is a slightly different issue from the one we have discussed. Even given complete random selection, the generalizability of the results – that is, *what can be generalised* – is still limited by the procedural controls in an experiment. Here we are discussing the degree to which this limited generalization can be made.

We are ordinarily interested in the population of all human social behaviour. You will find that most psychological research is conducted on undergraduate students. The degree to which this research is generalizable to the wider population is a matter of assumption, depending upon the particular variables under study. For instance, we would be hard pressed to justify the generalizability of research conducted using undergraduates about married couples' behaviour; whereas we would have an easier time when considering research about working in groups.[9]

Sears (1986) presents an excellent analysis of this problem, and this paper should be read for more information on it. You may sometimes find it difficult to see from a given research report *how* participants were selected from *what* subpopulation. Indeed, I provided you with more information than was available in the case of Bouas and Komorita (1996) because of my familiarity with the research of these psychologists. In general, if no further information is given, then you can expect that the selection procedure is much like my description of Bouas and Komorita's.

RANDOM ASSIGNMENT TO CONDITIONS

The easiest way to understand the importance of random assignment is to think again about blocking and holding constant. In blocking, potential confounding variables are equated across conditions. However, recall that we are unable to define all the potential confounding variables; if we could, we would be unable to conduct an experiment large enough to control all of them. By holding constant, we limit generalizability.

In addition to the problems with these strategies, we are always concerned about *Factor X*, in this case, the variable we did not and probably could never predict. To make the point philosophically, Factor X might be something absurd like the invisible angels or psychokinetic illusions we posited for the kite experiment, although it is more likely to be far more mundane. Factor X is always a potential confounding variable from which the IV is not isolated.

In experimental design, Factor X is controlled by determining randomly which participants are in which condition. This is done explicitly by using a table of random numbers, or by flipping a coin. By doing this, *on average*, equal amounts of all potential confounds will be in all the conditions of the experiment, and thus cancel each other out, similar to when we use blocking.

If complete randomization could ever be achieved in an experiment, then control procedures like blocking and holding constant would become unnecessary. Even a possible confound like mere presence effects could be *randomized out* of an experiment simply by including the total number of people present during the experiment as a variable to be randomized.

Thus, in conjunction with random selection, random assignment to conditions will allow us to isolate the IV in an experiment, thus satisfying the exclusion principle and allowing a valid test of a causal relationship. An experimenter will always indicate in a research report how participants were assigned to conditions.

The Not Demonstrably Perfect Experiment

The perfect experiment clearly specifies a causal relationship to be tested. Sufficient numbers of participants are *randomly selected* from the population, and *randomly assigned* to the *treatment and control conditions* of an experimental design which *eliminates all artefacts*. The experimenter has created the treatment and control conditions by *manipulating an independent variable in isolation* so as to prevent the influence of a confounding variable on the results. After participants experience the treatment (or not), the DV is measured. By comparing the level of the DV in the two conditions, all three of the criteria allowing the inference of causation have been met.

Randomization is critical to this endeavour, but when we examine the definition of the perfect experiment, we ask: *how many participants are required before all possible confounds are randomized out?* If the number of confounding variables is not known, the question cannot be answered. Moreover, randomization works *on the average*. In 10 throws of a coin, one may quite possibly attain 10 heads; similarly in an experiment, one might find that the confounding variable is *unequally* distributed between conditions. Additionally, if we *really* randomly assign our participants to conditions, there is nothing to guarantee that by the time we run out of participants, there will be no one in one of the conditions. Recall that in our discussion of the experiments of Bouas and Komorita and van den Bos et al. we said that participants were randomly assigned *subject to the constraint* that equal numbers of participants were in each condition. This eminently practical constraint already violates the assumption of random assignment.

In sum, the limitations imposed by practical constraints means we should not assume that random assignment to conditions guarantees isolation of the independent variable. Nevertheless, it is definitely the case that, *without* this procedure, a particular piece of research cannot *possibly be* an experiment. Thus random assignment to conditions is a *necessary but not sufficient* condition for satisfying the third of Hume's criteria for demonstrating causation. Given that experimenters do randomly assign participants to conditions, then the *not demonstrably perfect* experiment has been conducted. The not demonstrably perfect experiment has the procedures that are *necessary* to allow for a conclusion about cause to be made, but it may not in fact do so. Cook and Campbell (1979) call not demonstrably perfect experiments, *quasi-experiments* (discussed in several chapters of this volume), and we must assume that nearly all experiments in social psychology are quasi-experiments.

Rejection of Hypotheses and Programmatic Research

In sum, given experimental results, we must adjust the strength of our beliefs accordingly and abide by general protocols that follow directly. An important implication of inability to isolate independent variables from Factor X in fact underlies much of the confusion that arises in the study of statistics and research methods, namely, the idea that we only *reject* or *fail to reject* hypothesized causes. This idea was developed primarily by Karl Popper (1959), whose influence is such that what is presented in this chapter is sometimes given the general term of *Popperian science*. Because experimentalists never assume that they have been able to control for Factor X, they never conclude that the IV they have examined in an experiment is the definite cause of changes in the DV. Instead, they say that the potential cause has failed to be rejected, and awaits further testing.[10]

An important positive side effect of Popperian ideas (and indeed, of criticism of them) has been the emphasis in social psychology on the necessity to continue to test the same causal relationship. In experimental terms, we say that to retest a given effect is to *replicate the effect*. Replication has many positive benefits. In addition to being philosophically (and statistically) sound, it helps us to deal with experimental control issues. For instance, we depend on random assignment to distribute confounds equally over conditions, but we recognize the weakness of this strategy due to the potential for assignments that distribute the confound unequally. However, if we engage in the procedure two, three or more times, and the conclusions of these separate experiments support each other, our confidence in the result grows. Although no social psychologist would accept the results of one experiment as completely conclusive, probably all social psychologists gain great confidence in the validity of a conclusion based on several studies.

Thus as a general rule, social psychologists try to engage in *programmatic research*. In programmatic research, a single question is researched multiple times. Each experiment within a programme *replicates and extends* the results of previous experiments. For example, Bouas and Komorita (1996) replicated the finding that group discussion increases cooperation, and extended the finding to give evidence that within-group agreement to cooperate underlies this effect; van den Bos et al. (1999) replicated the effect of procedural fairness on outcome satisfaction, but extended the finding to situations involving negative outcomes.

Experimental Ethics in Brief

Research ethics have nothing to do with the abstract consideration of perfect experiments. Indeed, ethical procedures are potential confounds. Clearly, however, these procedures must be used. There is a hint of exploitation underlying experimental research. Participants (indeed, who until recently were called *subjects*) place themselves in the experimenter's care when they agree to do research. A cavalier attitude towards experimental participants must be avoided. Recent methodological treatises have emphasized the social exchange between researcher and participant, and have highlighted the desirability of making research a positive active experience for participants (e.g. Altman, 1988). More cynically, the enterprise of doing psychology ultimately will suffer from propagation of the stereotype of the scientist as contemptuous and devious.

Social psychology is particularly notorious for the use of *deception* in experiments. Some of our most famous (or infamous) research has used offensive or even potentially harmful deception to manipulate independent variables. All social psychologists develop their own ideas about what deception is acceptable and unacceptable in light of this questionable background. Although some believe that deception is never necessary, what is uniformly unacceptable is its indiscriminate use. Most social psychologists probably dislike the use of deception, but recognize its value and use it carefully. Despite the recognition that we vary in our feelings about deception, we all value a process of *formal ethical approval*. In your own work, get ethical advice from an objective (even authorized) source.

Professional bodies offer ethical guidelines for doing ethical research, to which you should adhere. In particular there are the American Psychological Association and British Psychological Society guidelines. When submitting reports of experiments to journals owned by these organizations, experimentalists must state explicitly that they have abided by these guidelines when they conducted their research. However, these guidelines can be complete only to the extent they become unmanageable. We all recognize that the researcher's judgement in combination with independent review is the best way to ensure doing ethical research.

However, there are at least two elements of doing ethical research that are normally a part of experimental procedure, these being *informed consent* and *debriefing*. We have already discussed these in the context of Bouas and Komorita (1996) and van den Bos et al. (1999). You need to engage in these two procedures when you do experiments.

Although this cannot substitute for a full consideration of the ethics of experiments, it is likely that if you plan these procedures rigorously and honestly, you will have designed an ethical experiment.

A Brief Note on Statistics in Experiments

Almost any kind of statistical analysis can be used for an experiment. Most of the statistics taught at undergraduate level have been developed to analyse data from experiments. The crucial aspect of the analysis is that it allows an assessment of the 'significance' of differences between two conditions. In general, however, if the dependent variable is discrete (e.g. yes/no, cooperate/do not cooperate) then χ^2 analysis is appropriate. If the data are continuous (e.g. a scale of outcome satisfaction) then the ANOVA should be used (or a t-test, if there are only two conditions). The ANOVA in particular is how interaction hypotheses can be tested easily.

Summary

This chapter has attempted to discuss not only about how experiments *should be done*, but also a little bit about the relationship between the perfect experiment and the typical 'experiment' in social psychology. It is hoped that you will use this chapter to help you to design your own experiments, to evaluate experiments you read about, to encourage you to read more about research methods, and to give you understanding of the ideal way to demonstrate causation to which you can compare the methods that generate the 'facts' you read about in your psychology courses.

In that vein, Table 2.6 shows the questions that can be asked about any research in psychology, and of experiments in particular. In the table the answers are given for the perfect experiment, and for the two experiments discussed in this chapter. These questions have been addressed in this chapter to one degree or another, and they are designed to help you to assess any particular experiment (including your own) against the perfect experiment.

What follows is a little exercise for you to attempt designing and conducting experiments about group performance. This exercise is yet another kind of group study. Relative to the social dilemma, however, the groups in this experiment will interact in a way that we recognize – they will *brainstorm*, or generate as many ideas as possible in a limited amount of time. Despite the differences between brainstorming

Table 2.6 Questions to be asked of research designs

Questions	Perfect experiment	Bouas and Komorita (1996)	van den Bos et al. (1999)
Development of causal hypothesis			
What is the causal hypothesis under question?	Any	Group identity causes cooperation in social dilemma	Procedural fairness mitigates dissatisfaction with negative outcome
What considerations have motivated the development of the causal hypothesis?	Any	Previous research, interest in cooperation	Previous research, interest in fairness-outcome relationship
What are the alternative causes of relevance to the experiment?	All	Within-group agreement to cooperate	Goodness of outcome
Is the experiment a replication, extension, both or neither?	Any	Replication, extension	Replication, extension
What are the hypotheses of the experiment?	Causal relationship indicated by covariance between conditions	(1) Group identity will not cause cooperation, (2) within-group agreement will	(1) Additive hypotheses, (2) Reversal hypothesis (interaction)
Experimental Design			
What is the dependent variable?	Measured effect construct	Cooperation in social dilemma	Outcome satisfaction
What is the independent variable?	Manipulated cause construct	Group discussion about dilemma or tuition fees or no discussion	(1) Fairness (2) favourability of outcome
Are manipulation checks included?	Not necessarily	Yes	Yes (not reported here)
Is the experimental design one that will eliminate most artefacts?	Yes (e.g. post-test only, two conditions)	Yes (post-test only, multiple conditions)	Yes (post-test only, multiple conditions)

Experimental procedure

Participants

What is the population of interest?	Social behaviour of all humans	Cooperation of all groups of all humans	Satisfaction of all humans
What is the population that is sampled?	Social behaviour of all humans	Cooperation of groups of four undergraduate females at large university (Illinois)	Satisfaction of undergraduates at medium-sized university (Essex)
What is the nature of the sample?	Any	160 female undergraduates	49 male and 35 female undergraduates
Is there random sampling?	Yes	Yes	Not reported

Procedure

What is a general description of the procedure used in the study?	Isolated IV is manipulated and DV is measured	See text	See text
Is there random assignment to conditions?	Yes	Yes, with constraint of equal numbers in conditions	Yes, with constraints of equal numbers in conditions
Are there any potential confounding variables blocked in the experiment?	No	No	No
Are there any potential confounding variables that are held constant in the experiment design?	No	Gender, time for choice in control condition, numbers of participants, etc.	Starting place in 'organization', instructions, etc.
What kinds of procedures are used to hold other variables constant?	Randomization	Scheduling of attendance, use of tape recorded instructions	Use of computer
(If there is deception) Is there a suspicion check?	Any	No deception	Deception but no check reported

Table 2.6 (cont'd)

Questions	Perfect experiment	Bouas and Komorita (1996)	van den Bos et al. (1999)
Results and conclusions			
What is the relationship between the data and the hypothesis?	Data consistent or inconsistent with hypothesis	Data inconsistent with Hypothesis 1, consistent with Hypothesis 2	Data inconsistent with Hypothesis 1, consistent with Hypothesis 2
Is the hypothesis rejected or not?	Depends on above	Hyp 1 rejected, Hyp 2 not rejected	Hyp 1 rejected, Hyp 2 not rejected
What kinds of experiments might be designed to replicate and extend this result?	Multiple	Multiple	Multiple
Ethics			
Has the experiment been deemed acceptable by an objective source?	Not necessarily	Not reported, but probably	Not reported, but probably
Is informed consent requested?	Not necessarily	Not reported but probably	Not reported, but probably
Is there deception?	Not necessarily	No	Yes
Is there a debriefing?	Not necessarily	Yes	Yes
Overall			
What kinds of sacrifices have been made in the interests of practicality?	None	Constraints on random sampling and assignment, ethical necessities	Constraints on random sampling and assignment, ethical necessities
How much has experimental control limited the generalizability of the results?	Generalizable to all people, but limited to specific procedures in study	Potentially considerable, e.g. only women in study. Representativeness undergraduates an important question.	Representativeness of undergraduates important
To what extent has the experiment really tested a causal relationship?	Perfectly	Not demonstrably perfectly	If available population sampled randomly, not demonstrably perfectly; otherwise, somewhat less rigourously conducted study

and social dilemmas, the controls used by Bouas and Komorita (1996) for their groups apply to this situation. So you can model your procedure on theirs. In addition, there are many references provided to allow you to investigate the other common designs and procedures for this particular context.

An Experiment to Test Group Superiority on Brainstorming Tasks

Intuitions about human interaction often lead to the conclusion that groups will be superior to individuals in a variety of tasks (Davis, 1992). For instance, our intuition may suggest to us that when solving abstract problems, groups would be superior to individual problem solvers simply because by exchanging information and checking others' mistakes, groups are more likely to solve a difficult problem than are individuals. Research has shown consistently that, whereas group *do* solve more problems than individuals, they do not solve as many problems as we would *expect* them to, relative to the fact that they possess members of high ability (e.g., Hill, 1982; Laughlin & Ellis, 1986; Lorge & Solomon, 1955; Davis & Restle, 1963).

An extremely plausible intuition underlies the idea that groups would be more *creative* than individuals, or would simply generate more ideas. In 1957, Osborn developed the group interaction procedure called *brainstorming*. Brainstorming is the term given to the idea that when trying to provide a solution for a difficult question or problem, the optimal procedure would be to give the problem to groups and ask them to generate as many solutions or ideas as possible – no matter how strange or impractical. Groups would be asked to engage in 'free-wheeling' discussion, to refrain from criticizing each others' ideas, and to build upon ideas of other members. The intuitions underlying the supposed effectiveness of brainstorming are powerful indeed. Shouldn't it be true that group members will be able to stimulate each other so as to develop more (and more good) ideas?

However, experiments examining brainstorming show that this is not the case. Although, to be sure, a group will produce more ideas than will a single individual, groups do not produce more ideas than they should be able to. For instance, suppose that several groups of four people are asked to generate ideas with respect to the question: how would the world be different if everyone after 1970 was born with two thumbs on each hand? Researchers would count the average number of *unique* ideas produced in these groups, and compare that number to the number of unique ideas that four individuals acting alone would produce. That is, the average number of ideas generated in a group of four people is compared to four times the average number of ideas an individual produces. When the number of individual ideas is multiplied in order to provide a comparison for interacting groups, we have created what is called a *nominal group*. Creating nominal groups is fundamental to the study of group performance: rather than comparing group to individual performance, group performance researchers compare group performance to what we would *expect* groups to produce.

When the comparison is made between nominal groups and real groups for brainstorming tasks, it turns out that over a large number of studies, with many different brainstorming problems (e.g. how can the education system be improved?), individuals outperform groups by almost two to one (Mullen, Johnson & Salas, 1991). Many reasons have been proposed for this difference, including *social loafing* (some group members do not perform because they know others will do the work; Diehl & Stroebe, 1987; Kerr & Bruun, 1983), *production blocking* (the necessity to wait for others to speak an idea before one can speak one's own ideas not only means more time is required, but also interferes with memory; Diehl & Stroebe, 1992) and *matching* (members who produce few ideas increase to match members who produce more ideas, and vice versa, leading to average performance overall; Brown & Paulus, 1996). Paulus and Dzindolet (1993) provide an integrative model wherein all these processes occur at different stages of group idea generation.

Another interesting aspect of group versus individual brainstorming is that when asked, people always say that groups will produce more ideas than individuals. This *includes* asking people who have been explained the idea of nominal groups (Paulus, Dzindolet, Poletes & Camacho, 1993; Stroebe, Diehl & Abakoumkin, 1992).

SPECIFYING NOMINAL GROUPS

As an exercise, you can try to replicate (and possibly extend) one or more of these results. The critical thing about doing group performance research is in specifying the nominal group. In general there are two possibilities with respect to brainstorming. One possibility (the most rigorous) is to specify conditions so that there are equal numbers of *individual participants* in both group and nominal group conditions. So for instance, if you were conducting this as an exercise in a large class, you could divide the class into halves randomly, and form groups and nominal groups (randomly of course) from those halves.

Another possibility (the more practical) is to specify conditions so that there is *one* individual for each group. Then, when the data are analysed, multiply the number of ideas produced by each individual by the group size. So for instance if the group size is equal to three and there are 72 people in the class, create 18 groups of three people each for a total of 54 individuals in the group condition. The remaining 18 people would serve as individuals. After the experiment, there would be data from 18 groups and 18 individuals. Before computing the average number of ideas produced by individuals, multiply each individual's data by three to create the nominal groups.

TREATMENT OF DATA

Some coding of data is required: numbers of unique items must be counted, particularly for nominal groups. For nominal groups of three (i.e. the first procedure above), if two individuals record the same idea, this is only counted once; for nominal groups formed from one person only, this is not important. It is not strictly necessary that group discussions are tape recorded. One member might be appointed as the group 'recorder'. This is however, is a procedural variant relative to most previous studies. These data can be analysed with an ANOVA or a t-test.

EXTENSIONS AND TIPS

The exercise can be made more complex (potentially to allow for extensions) by including more dependent variables (e.g. coding the *quality* as well as the number of ideas, or asking participants if groups or individuals would produce more ideas), or by devising manipulations of some of the factors referenced above (e.g. a manipulation of social loafing like the one used by Diehl & Stroebe, 1989), or by including different brainstorming topics. Like all group performance researchers however, you will soon run into some of the common practical constraints (notably, numbers of participants, numbers of experimenters, space and time).

It is possible to try out different experimental designs, and to attempt to assess the presence of artefacts in the data. Clearly innocuous deceptions might be attempted (e.g. at the level of participants' beliefs about other members' or their own past performance levels, or about the consequences of their group's performance, obviously under careful supervision). Consider blocking variables as an exercise (e.g. gender or age) only, since these variables have not been identified in the literature as being relevant to brainstorming performance. Be explicit about how all things other than the independent variable are held constant across conditions (e.g. instructions and experimenter's behaviour). The use of suspicion and manipulation checks, if necessary, are highly recommended. Be sure that alternative hypotheses are specified in terms of conditions and independent variables to make interpretation of the results easy. It is essential that random assignment to both conditions *and* to groups is undertaken formally. Use a table of random numbers, dice, playing cards or a computer programme to do this assignment.

Apart from analysing and interpreting the results of the experiment, answer the questions in Table 2.6 about the study that is done. Consider in particular issues of rigour versus practicality and control versus generalizability, which usually provide good understanding of the difficulty in planning experiments, likely problems with experimental results and ideas for further research.

NOTES

1   Excerpt from Franklin's *Autobiography, Letters and Other Writings*, from <www.bibliomania.com>.

2   In social psychology, typical kinds of constructs are *attitude, conformity, social influence* and *social identity*, and typical hypothesized causal relationships are 'Does social identity cause attitude?' or 'Do different amounts of social influence cause different amounts of conformity?'

3   A slight simplification of Bouas and Komorita's experiment is used here.

4   Experience in teaching research methods and statistics suggests the importance of cautioning students to always remember that hypotheses describe *potential* states of reality that will be tested.

5   Again, a simplified version of this experiment is used and some liberties are taken with some specifics. However, the gist of the experiment is preserved.

6   We should note that eight groups is probably the minimum requirement for a social dilemma experiment. For group problem-solving and decision-making experiments, as many as 20, and almost certainly more than 10, is required.

7   It needs to be noted that what is presented here is the strict experimentalist's viewpoint, and I am deliberately under-representing the alternative viewpoint. There is a valid and fascinating argument for using this particular strategy, sometimes called 'perspectivism' or 'contextualism' (e.g. McGuire, 1989). If you are interested in science, McGuire's challenging and engaging work is highly recommended, as is Kerr's (1998) refutation of these strategies based on psychological grounds.

8 Anecdotes about the effects of particularly attractive experimenters on participants abound among social psychologists. Although one might find a hint of self-acclamation to such claims, the possibility cannot be denied.

9 One of my professors claims that, when once asked about the population involved in his research, he replied that he wanted to understand the behaviour of university undergraduates! Although he was being flippant, he was trying to teach me the importance of understanding the limitations of my research. Given that every experiment will have logical weaknesses relative to the ideal experiment, this understanding is the most important thing for you to develop.

10 A nice introduction to the ideal Popperian science is given by Platt (1964). However, the Popperian method is not without detractors, both in philosophy and psychology (e.g. Gergen, 1985; McGuire, 1973). Nevertheless, the ideal of the Popperian method is still highly influential in psychology.

REFERENCES

RESEARCH METHODOLOGY

Altman, I. (1988). Process, transactional/contextual, and outcome research: An alternative to the traditional distinction between basic and applied research. *Social Behaviour, 3,* 259–80.

Campbell, D. T. & Stanley, J. C. (1963). *Experimental and quasi-experimental designs for research*. Chicago: Rand McNally.

Cook, T. D. & Campbell, D. T. (1979). *Quasi-experimentation: Design & analysis for field settings*. Boston: Houghton-Mifflin.

Gergen, K. J. (1985) The social constructionist movement in modern psychology. *American Psychologist, 40,* 266–75.

Kerr, N. L. (1998). HARKing: Hypothesizing after the results are known. *Personality and Social Psychology Review, 2,* 196–217.

McGuire, W. J. (1973). The yin and yang of progress in social psychology: Seven koan. *Journal of Personality and Social Psychology, 26,* 446–56.

McGuire, W. J. (1989). A perspectivist approach to the strategic planning of programmatic scientific research. In Gholson, B., Shadish, W. R., Houts, A., & Neimeyer, R. (eds.), *Psychology of science: Contributions to metascience* (pp. 214–45). Cambridge, UK: Cambridge University Press.

Platt, J. R. (1964). Strong inference. *Science, 146,* 347–53.

Popper, K. R. (1959). *The logic of scientific discovery*. New York: Basic Books.

Runkle, P. J. & McGrath, J. E. (1972). *Research on human behavior: A systematic guide to method*. New York: Holt, Rinehart and Winston.

Sears, D. O. (1986). College sophomores in the laboratory: Influences of a narrow data base on social psychology's view of human nature. *Journal of Personality and Social Psychology, 51,* 515–30.

SOCIAL PSYCHOLOGY

Bouas, K. S. & Komorita, S. S. (1996). Group discussion and cooperation in social dilemmas. *Personality and Social Psychology Bulletin, 22,* 1144–50.

Brown, V. & Paulus, P. B. (1996). A simple dynamic model of social factors in group brainstorming. *Small Group Research, 27,* 91–114.

Davis, J. H. (1992). Some compelling intuitions about group consensus decisions, theoretical and empirical research, and interpersonal aggregation phenomena: Selected examples, 1950–1990. *Organizational Behavior and Human Decision Processes, 52,* 3–38.

Davis, J. H. & Restle, F. (1963). The analysis of problems and prediction of group problem solving. *Journal of Abnormal and Social Psychology, 66,* 103–16.

Dawes, R. M. (1980). Social dilemmas. *Annual Review of Psychology, 31,* 169–93.

Dawes, R. M., McTavish, J. & Shaklee, H. (1977). Behavior, communication, and assumptions about other people's behavior in a commons dilemma situation. *Journal of Personality and Social Psychology, 35,* 1–11.

Diehl, M. & Stroebe, W. (1987). Productivity loss in brainstorming groups: Toward the solution of a riddle. *Journal of Personality and Social Psychology, 53,* 497–509.

Diehl, M. & Stroebe, W. (1992). Productivity loss in idea-generating groups: Tracking down the blocking effect. *Journal of Personality and Social Psychology, 61,* 392–403.

Hill, G. W. (1982) Group vs. individual performance: Are N+1 heads better than one? *Psychological Bulletin, 91,* 517–39.

Hinkle, S., Taylor, L., Fox-Cardamone, D. L. & Crook, K. (1989). Intragroup identification and intergroup differentiation: A multicomponent approach. *British Journal of Social Psychology, 28,* 305–17.

Jones, E. & Davis, E. E. (1965). From acts to dispositions: The attribution process in person perception. In Berkowitz, L. (ed.), *Advances in experiment social psychology, Vol 2* (pp. 219–66, New York: Academic Press.

Kerr, N. L. & Bruun, S. E. (1983). Dispensability of member effort and group motivation losses: Free-rider effects. *Journal of Personality and Social Psychology, 44,* 78–94.

Kerr, N. L. & Kaufman-Gilliland, C. M. (1994). Communication, commitment, and cooperation in social dilemmas. *Journal of Personality and Social Psychology, 66,* 513–29.

Komorita, S. S. & Parks, C. D. (1995). Interpersonal relations: Mixed-motive interaction. *Annual Review of Psychology, 46,* 183–207.

Laughlin, P. R. & Ellis, A. L. (1986). Demonstrability and social combination processes on mathematical intellective tasks. *Journal of Experimental Social Psychology, 22,* 177–89.

Liebrand, W. B. G., Messick, D. M. & Wilke, H. A. M. (1992). *Social dilemmas: Theoretical issues and research findings.* New York: Pergamon.

Lorge, I. & Solomon, H. (1955). Two models of group behavior in the solution of Eureka-type problems. *Psychometrika, 20,* 139–48.

Mullen, B., Johnson, C. & Salas, E. (1991). Productivity loss in brainstorming groups: A meta-analytic review. *Basic and Applied Social Psychology, 12*, 3–23.

Osborn, A. F. (1957). *Applied imagination.* New York: Scribner.

Paulus, P. B. & Dzindolet, M. T. (1993). Social influence processes in group brainstorming. *Journal of Personality and Social Psychology, 64*, 575–86.

Paulus, P. B., Dzindolet, M. T., Poletes, G. & Camacho, L. M. (1993). Perception of performance in group brainstorming: The illusion of productivity. *Personality and Social Psychology Bulletin, 19*, 78–99.

Sell, J. & Griffith, W. I. (1993). Are women more cooperative than men in social dilemmas? *Social Psychology Quarterly, 56*, 211–22.

Stroebe, W., Diehl, M. & Abakoumkin, G. (1992). The illusion of group effectivity. *Personality and Social Psychology Bulletin, 18*, 643–50.

Tyler, T. R. (1994) Psychological models of the justice motive: Antecedents of distributive and procedural justice. *Journal of Personality and Social Psychology, 67*, 850–63.

van den Bos, K., Bruins, J., Wilke, H. A. M. & Dronkert, E. (1999). Sometimes unfair procedures have nice aspects: On the psychology of the fair process effect. *Journal of Personality and Social Psychology, 77*, 324–36.

Zajonc, R. B. (1968). Attitudinal effects of mere exposure. *Journal of Personality and Social Psychology, 7*, 1–29.

CHAPTER THREE

Measuring Optimistic Bias

Chris Fife-Schaw & Julie Barnett

This chapter provides a detailed description of the ways in which optimistic bias may be measured. In illustrating how complex concepts such as optimistic bias require careful analysis of implications of different data-recording approaches, the chapter emphasizes the intimate links between the conceptualization of a theoretical construct and the way it is measured. The practical exercise included in the chapter entails an experimental research design. The authors provide instructions on the SPSS analysis to be used with the data generated. The exercise and statistical approach is most appropriate for advanced students.

The Research Area and Question

It has long been known that humans have a tendency to be optimistic about their chances in life. In many circumstances people will tend to believe that their own chances of success are better than they really are and that the chances of bad things happening to them are lower than they are, even for people in ostensibly the same situation. This tendency is known as 'optimistic bias' and sometimes, in the context of threats, as 'perceived invulnerability' (Klein & Helweg-Larsen, 2002).

Though this phenomenon was commented upon from time to time in the psychological literature, it was Neil Weinstein who first formally studied it among Rutgers University students. In an early study (Weinstein, 1980) he asked students to tell him how likely they were to experience 42 life events and how likely their classmates were to experience the same things. When considering positive events (e.g. getting a good job) the students saw themselves as more likely to succeed than their peers. When the event was negative (e.g. having an early heart attack) the students felt they were less at risk than their classmates were.

This phenomenon is not restricted to students. For example, Segerstrom, McCarthy, Caskey, Gross et al. (1993) showed that among 4,152 smokers, most thought their chances of becoming ill as a result of smoking was less than for other smokers. They also thought that their preferred brand of cigarette had a lower and less damaging tar content than it really did. Similarly, Middleton (1996) showed that bungee jumpers felt they were at less risk than fellow jumpers even though family and friends looking on saw no such difference in the risks being taken by their loved ones.

The phenomenon has been demonstrated in research into a whole range of behaviours and settings. The interesting research questions are now focused on defining the conditions under which optimistic bias occurs, because it does not occur in all people at all times, and on what effects this bias has on people's behaviour. An example of the former is research that shows that optimistic bias is less likely when the risk is thought not to be under the control of the individual and the individual has first hand experience of the hazardous outcome. Helweg-Larsen (1999) showed that people showed less evidence of an optimistic bias in respect of surviving earthquakes in the aftermath of the 1994 Northridge earthquake in California, even though they still displayed an optimistic bias with respect to other hazards. More recently Harris et al. (2000) were reasonably successful in eliminating the optimistic bias phenomenon by varying the in-group/out-group status of the 'other' that is judged.

An example of the research into the effects of optimistic bias on behaviour is the case of AIDS/HIV. Many young people believe themselves highly unlikely to catch the disease and consequently see little point in taking preventative measures to avoid infection like using condoms (e.g. Abrams, Abraham, Spears & Marks, 1990). Looking at beliefs about successes, those who expect success at exams may get over-confident and fail to prepare themselves for tests as well as their more anxious peers (Goodhart, 1986).

This is therefore an important topic of study for social psychologists and in this chapter we are going to look at ways of measuring optimistic bias. More specifically, we will look at how measurement method can influence the apparent extent of optimistic bias.

Description of the Methods and their Applications

Central to the assessment of unrealistic optimism is the comparison of oneself with others, and the methodologies used reflect this focus. Although some attention has been paid to unrealistic optimism in relation to absolute risk (Rothman, Klein & Weinstein, 1996), because of the difficulties involved in assessing absolute risks, the measurement of unrealistic optimism is essentially comparative.

There are two main ways in which unrealistic optimism has been measured (Weinstein & Klein, 1996; Otten & van-der-Pligt, 1996; Klein & Weinstein, 1997). The first involves a *direct comparison*. Here there is one rating scale and participants are asked whether their own risk is smaller, greater or the same as the risk of another. The main disadvantage of using this scale is that when changes in the level of unrealistic bias are observed in relation to some sort of manipulation or intervention, there is no way of telling whether it is the representation of 'self' or 'other' risk that has changed.

The second way involves an *indirect comparison*. Here there are two rating scales and people are asked to provide separate risk estimates for themselves and others. A variant on this indirect procedure is when it is used in a between-groups rather than within-groups design. Here different groups are asked to assess the probability for self and for other (Heine & Lehman, 1995; Harris, 1996). Either numerical or verbally labelled scales can be used with either measurement procedure. However, Otten and van der Pligt (1996) note that the two procedures tend to be associated with different verbal labels/numerical values of the response scale and also in the number of categories that the response scale provides.

Given that there are different approaches to measuring optimistic bias, a question that arises is whether the degree of unrealistic optimism obtained is attributable to the type of measurement used rather than the bias itself. This can be explored in two ways: first whether there are differences between the indirect and direct methods of assessment, and secondly whether there are order effects in relation to self/other ratings.

In relation to the first point, as might be expected most studies use either one technique or the other. However, there is some suggestion that the two techniques do vary in the extent to which unrealistic optimism is expressed (Heine & Lehman, 1995; Otten & van-der-Pligt, 1996). The latter authors address this question directly saying that, 'relative to the indirect procedure, the direct procedure provides a much stronger comparative frame' (pp. 83–4).

Schwarzer (1994) also notes evidence that the two techniques are distinct to some extent, suggesting that the direct procedure tends to elicit social comparisons with 'abstract stereotypes of victims' rather than with an existing reference person or group. However, Klein and Weinstein (1997) note that as few studies employ more than one approach it is impossible to evaluate the two techniques.

In relation to the second issue, Otten and Van der Pligt suggest that most studies that use indirect assessments do not report the effects of the order in which the assessments are made (i.e. whether risk to the self is assessed before or after the risk to others). Of those that do, some report finding no order effects (Perloff & Fetzer, 1986; Whalen, Henker, O'Neil & Hollingshead, 1994; Klein, 1996) and others suggest that there are (Dolinski, Gromski, & Zawisza, 1987; Hoorens & Buunk, 1993).

Otten and van der Pligt (1996) address the issue of presentation order in some detail and relate it to theoretical work on self/other comparisons. The crux of their argument is that 'the measurement procedure determines the comparison standard when judging self–other probabilities and that the others-as-standard perspective enhances optimism relative to the self-as-standard perspective' (p. 81; see also Wanke, Schwarz & Noelle-Neumann, 1995). They draw upon the work in relation to an asymmetry effect in self–other similarity ratings where judgements of self relative to others constitutes an 'others-as-standard' perspective and where judgements of others relative to self constitutes a 'self-as-standard' perspective. Self is judged as being less similar to others in relation to the former frame of reference. When applied to probability judgements about self and other, with the question form systematically varied, a similar pattern is found, that is, a larger discrepancy between self and other (greater unrealistic optimism) when there is an 'other-as-standard' perspective.

Several explanations for such an asymmetry have been suggested. Hoorens and Buunck (1993) found this effect in relation to unrealistic optimism estimates rather than estimates of similarity, and offer a motivational explanation in terms of identity-protecting processes. They say, 'individuals may not like the idea of seeing their own future as similar to that of others. Indeed the best way to be different is being better' (p. 299). This explanation is linked with that of Codol (1987) who suggested that the potential threat of being similar to another varies in relation to whether the reference point for comparison is self or other. He suggests that the threat is greater when the reference point is the 'other' and this leads to a heightened tendency to differentiate self from other. Similar results in relation to perceptions of interpersonal distance are also interpreted in terms of 'personal identity affirmation and defence' (Codol, Jarymowicz, Kaminska-Feldman & Szuster-Zbrojewicz, 1989).

A second explanation is offered by Otten and van der Pligt (1996) in response to their finding that in the direct measurement condition there is significantly more unrealistic optimism in the 'other-as-standard' frame of reference than in the 'self-as-standard'. They suggest that the latter formulation may emphasize that claiming invulnerability is at the expense of others (i.e. that higher risk is attributed to others) and that this claim may be seen as inappropriate. They suggest that this may lead to better scrutiny of the arguments and thus lead to less difference being placed between self and other. The nature of this explanation is similar to that suggested by Blanz, Mummendey and Otten (1997) in relation to the positive–negative asymmetry evidenced in social discrimination (Blanz, Mummendey & Otten, 1995). The nature of this asymmetry is that in-group favouritism found in respect of positive resources is absent in relation to negative resources and they locate their explanation for this 'valence asymmetry' in relation to justice and normative evaluations of positive and negative outcomes: 'The normative account suggests a generally differential perception of the appropriateness of ingroup-favouring decisions depending on the valence of stimuli . . . Subjects hold normative ideas about appropriate allocation behaviour, and these ideas are apparently sensitive to contextual inputs such as stimulus valence' (Blanz et al., 1997, p. 167).

They found that overall, in-group favouritism and social discrimination within the negative domain was perceived as less justified than within the positive area and in conclusion suggest that 'People refer to certain normative orientations when they evaluate the appropriateness of a particular distribution of stimuli between different recipients. Dependent on these normative orientations, a distribution might be judged as more or less appropriate or just' (Blanz et al., 1997, p. 175).

A Specific Exercise

DEMONSTRATING HOW METHOD OF MEASUREMENT AFFECTS AMOUNT OF BIAS

This example exercise is intended to demonstrate the optimistic bias effect and assess the degree to which different methods of measuring optimistic bias influence the amount of bias displayed. The study is a between-subjects design with two factors being manipulated. The first factor has two conditions that reflect the two different ways of measuring optimistic bias described above, namely the direct and indirect methods. The second factor deals with the frame of reference that the respondent is being encouraged to use, namely self-as-reference and other-as-reference. As there are two factors each with two conditions there is a total of four conditions in the study.

The dependent variable is the extent of optimistic bias being shown by the respondents. In this example we will be asking people about the likelihood of a range of life events and aggregating these responses. We could look at a single life event but this would make for a very short study and is in any case rarely seen in the research literature.

The study has the following hypotheses:

1 Both measurement procedures yield evidence of optimistic bias.
2 The direct method will yield a stronger optimistic bias effect than the indirect method.
3 The level of optimistic bias will be greater for the other-as-reference condition.

These hypotheses are based on the literature and the study design is a simplified, though typical, example of the kind of study common in this literature.

ASSUMPTIONS OF THE STUDY

1 It assumes that it would be unlikely for most people in a group to have a lower probability for an event if the probabilities of the event occurring are normally distributed. At a group level (i.e. people in one cell of the experimental design) we would expect the mean likelihood of an event occurring to be the same for the self and others if there is no bias operating.
2 The explicit comparative wording used in the direct procedure is assumed to make comparison more obvious than the indirect method.
3 The order of presentation for the indirect procedure is assumed to determine whether a self-as-standard or other-as-standard context is primed.
4 The particular events we are asking people about are not individually of interest. We will aggregate across events for the present purposes though it is not necessary to do this.

PROCEDURE

You will need to draw a sample of people who will be prepared to spend 5 to 10 minutes answering a single questionnaire for you.

		Factor I Comparison method	
		Direct	Indirect
Factor II Reference perspective	Other-as-reference	Direct Other-as-reference (A)	Indirect Other-as-reference (C)
	Self-as-reference	Direct Self-as-reference (B)	Indirect Self-as-reference (D)

Figure 3.1   The four cells of the study design

This sample could be of any kind of person you like but in order to give your study the necessary statistical power to correctly reject a false null hypothesis you will need to find at least 84 respondents (see Notes for Course Leader). If you are working in a lab class you can detail your classmates to collect a proportion of the sample each.

There will be four versions of the questionnaire, reflecting the four cells of the study design as shown in Figure 3.1. As this is an experiment we must have control over which respondent is exposed to which conditions of the two experimental factors. Ideally respondents should be randomly allocated to receive one of the four questionnaire types (as numbered in the figure). This could be done simply by placing the forms in order in a pile running A,B,C,D,A,B,C,D,A, and so on, and distributing them from the top of the pile as you encounter people. More elaborate random allocation systems are possible but this should work well enough for the present purposes.

Respondents should be encouraged to fill in the questionnaire individually and reasonably quickly. You can either collect then at the time of distribution (preferable) or have them returned to a convenient location.

Materials

The materials of this study consist simply of the four questionnaires and some clear instructions for respondents to follow. If conducting this study with the public you might like to have some cheap pens available too.

INSTRUCTIONS TO RESPONDENTS

A clear set of instructions should be provided for respondents. These can be spoken but are perhaps better written down. The instructions should indicate the broad purpose of the study, though you should not explain the research hypotheses explicitly at this stage. As the optimistic bias phenomenon is unlikely to be demonstrated if the study respondents are previously made aware of it, it would be best to present this topic as being generally concerned with risk perceptions. The instructions should identify who you are and explain that participation is voluntary and anonymous – there is no need for them to be identified in any way on the forms.

The instructions should note that there are no 'correct' answers and that you would like their initial opinion – you do not want them to agonize over each response nor rush off to a library to conduct extensive research on each risk/hazard. The four questionnaire types have slightly differing formats but you will be asking them to circle one response per risk event (see below). Finally you should thank the respondent and tell them how and where they can receive feedback on the research. This could be simply that you explain the study on the spot if gathering respondents on a face-to-face basis or you may take their names and agree to send them a brief summary of the work at a later date.

BACKGROUND INFORMATION

You should include questions on the respondent's age and sex on all versions of the questionnaire so that you can describe your sample when reporting the study. It is probably sensible to request age information in age bands, say 18–21 yrs, 22–25 yrs, and so on.

TARGET LIFE EVENTS

We are interested in factors influencing the extent of optimistic bias displayed by differing methods so the target life events of the survey are potentially of less interest in and of themselves. To make the questionnaire seem realistic to respondents it would not make much sense to ask about a single life event, so you should aim to have 10 to 20 events on the questionnaire. This is a starting list of suggestions and you should feel free to add yours to the list or abandon this one in favour of your own. Currently it contains a 50/50 split of positive and negative life events so that you might choose to investigate whether the bias is equally likely for positive and negative events.

Catching an STD in the next year,
Not completing your degree on time,
Getting sunburn,
Getting skin cancer,
Having to stay in bed with flu,
Increasing your average course mark by 10 per cent,
Getting a good job,
Remaining healthy for X years,
Being happily married to one person for the rest of your life,
Winning a car in a magazine competition.

QUESTIONNAIRE FORMATS

Two of the four questionnaires will use the direct format and two the indirect approach. These will be crossed with the reference frame to give the following four formats:

Version A – Direct condition/other-as-reference

Thinking of an average person [student] of your age and sex, compare the probability that each of the following events will happen to you personally with the probability that each event will happen to this average person. *(Please circle one response per line.)*

	Very much *lower* than the average [student's] probability	Both probabilities are equal	Very much *higher* than the average [student's] probability

The probability for myself of. . . .

(Q1) Catching an STD
In the next year is: −5 −4 −3 −2 −1 0 1 2 3 4 5

(Q2) Not completing my
degree on time is: −5 −4 −3 −2 −1 0 1 2 3 4 5

etc . . .

Version B – Direct condition/self-as-reference

Thinking of an average person [student] of your age and sex. Compare the probability that each of the following events will happen to this average person [student] with the probability that these events will happen to you yourself. *(Please circle one response per line.)*

	Very much *lower* than my own probability	Both probabilities are equal	Very much *higher* than my own probability

The probability for this average person [student] of . . .

(Q1) Catching an STD
In the next year is: −5 −4 −3 −2 −1 0 1 2 3 4 5

(Q2) Not completing a
degree on time is: −5 −4 −3 −2 −1 0 1 2 3 4 5

etc . . .

Versions C and D – Indirect conditions

In the two indirect condition questionnaires respondents are asked both about their own risks and those of others, only the order of presentation is varied. One questionnaire version (C) asks about the 'other' first and the second (D) asks about the 'self' first. Of necessity the indirect questionnaires are longer and require twice as many responses from people as the direct method. The two wording formats appear below:

How probable do you think it is that each of the following events will happen to you?

	The event certainly will not happen	The event certainly will happen

(Q1) Catching an STD
in the next year   0 1 2 3 4 5 6 7 8 9 10

(Q2) Not completing a
degree on time   0 1 2 3 4 5 6 7 8 9 10

etc . . .

Thinking of an average person [student] of your age and sex, how probable do you think it is that each of the following events will happen to the average person [student] in the future?

	The event certainly will not happen										The event certainly will happen

(Q1) Catching an STD
in the next year   0   1   2   3   4   5   6   7   8   9   10

(Q2) Not completing a
degree on time   0   1   2   3   4   5   6   7   8   9   10

etc

Note that in the indirect conditions the question numbering must be sequential. If say, you have 10 events and the other-as-reference items are presented first (as in version C of the questionnaire) then the first self-as-reference question will be Q11, not Q1.

In all four questionnaires the events must appear in the same order otherwise it will be difficult to sort out later when we come to do the data analysis.

Analyses: Data Preparation

For the purposes of this study we will aggregate responses across the events rather than consider them individually. Assuming you are using SPSS for Windows to analyse your data, you should create a single data file with the following variables:

Variable name	What it is
CASENO	A number that you should write on each returned form so that you can identify it later if the computer picks up a problem with that case – this is good practice for all questionnaire-based data sets.
QTYPE	This should be a number that indicates which questionnaire the respondent completed. Code A = 1, B = 2, C = 3 and D = 4.

FAC1	Indicates the level of Factor I associated with the questionnaire type. Code Direct = 1 and Indirect = 2.
FAC2	Indicates the level of Factor II. Code 'Other-as-reference' = 1 and 'Self-as-reference' = 2. Although this variable and FAC1 might appear to duplicate information in the QTYPE variable it will be helpful to identify the factors in the ANOVA we will conduct later.
AGE	The respondent's age. If you requested this in categories as noted above you allocate a single number to each category, e.g. 18–21 yrs = 1, 22–25 yrs = 2 etc.
SEX	The respondent's sex. Code female = 1, male = 2.
qn1	The response to Q1. The 'N' is being used to indicate that the event is a negative one; if it had been a positive event the variable would have been called 'QP1'.
qn2 or qp2	The response to Q2.
qp3 or qp3	The response to Q3.

And so on. Remember that the indirect format questionnaires will generate more data than the direct format. SPSS will generate some 'system missing' values for the respondents who did the direct format questionnaires – this is highly desirable and not a problem. *Make sure you save the data frequently!*

A certain number of what might appear tricky data transformations are required before you can conduct the statistical analysis but in essence these are quite straightforward and should cause you few problems. To do this we need to take the following steps for each of the four questionnaire types:

VERSION A – DIRECT/OTHER-AS-REFERENCE

1 Multiply all individual responses by 2 – this will make the scores fall on a scale from −10 to +10 and thus comparable with the scores from the indirect questionnaires as described below.

2 For the *positive life events only*, reverse the signs of the scores so that, say, −8 becomes +8, +6 becomes −6.
3 Add up the resulting scores for each event and divide this number by the number of events on your questionnaire.

This gives the respondent's bias score. Scores below zero indicate the presence of optimistic bias, scores around zero indicate no bias and scores above zero would suggest an unlikely pessimistic bias.

VERSION B – DIRECT/SELF-AS-REFERENCE

1 Multiply all individual responses by 2 – this will make the scores fall on a scale from −10 to +10 and thus comparable with the scores from the indirect questionnaires as described below.
2 For the *negative life events only*, reverse the signs of the scores so that, say, −8 becomes +8, +6 becomes −6.
3 Add up the resulting scores for each event and divide this number by the number of events on your questionnaire.

This gives the respondent's bias score similar to the above.

VERSIONS C AND D – INDIRECT METHOD
(BOTH QUESTIONNAIRE TYPES)

1 For the *negative events*, subtract the 'other' score from the 'self' score.
2 For the *positive events*, subtract the 'self' score from the 'other' score.
3 Add up the resulting scores for each event and divide this number by the number of events on your questionnaire.

Although all of this looks complicated the basic idea here is simple.

The SPSS for Windows syntax for making these calculations is included below. To create a syntax file go to the 'FILE' menu and select 'New' and then 'Syntax'. Type in the commands below (you may omit the comments if you wish) and save the syntax file. To run the analyses simply highlight all the syntax and press the small black triangular 'Run' button.

```
* This syntax file will do all the necessary preparations for the
data analysis.
* This example assumes you have 10 events on the questionnaire.
* It assumes the first five events were negative and the second
five were positive.
value labels FAC1 1 'Direct' 2 'Indirect'. /* labels the levels of
the 2 factors to.
value labels FAC2 1 'Other-as-ref' 2 'Self-as-ref'. /* make the
output easier to read.
do if (qtype = 1).            /* selects only data for question-
                                 naire A.
compute qn1r = qn1*2.         /* creates new variables that are
                                 twice the old ones.
compute qn2r = qn2*2.
compute qn3r = qn3*2.
compute qn4r = qn4*2.
compute qn5r = qn5*2.
compute qp6r = qp6*2.
compute qp7r = qp7*2.
compute qp8r = qp8*2.
compute qp9r = qp9*2.
compute qp10r = qp10*2.
recode qp6r qp7r qp8r qp9r qp10r
(-10 = 10) (-8 = 8) (-6 = 6) (-4 = 4) (-2 = 2) (0 = 0) (2 = -2)
(4 = -4) (6 = -6) (8 = -8) (10 = -10).
                              /* reverses the scores for the posit-
                                 ive items only.
compute bias = (qn1r + qn2r + qn3r + qn4r + qn5r + qp6r +
qp7r + qp8r + qp9r + qp10r)/10.
                              /* computes an average bias score
                                 for later analysis.
end if.
do if (qtype = 2).            /* selects only data for question-
                                 naire B.
compute qn1r = qn1*2.         /* creates new variables that are
                                 twice the old ones.
compute qn2r = qn2*2.
compute qn3r = qn3*2.
compute qn4r = qn4*2.
compute qn5r = qn5*2.
compute qp6r = qp6*2.
compute qp7r = qp7*2.
```

```
compute qp8r = qp8*2.
compute qp9r = qp9*2.
compute qp10r = qp10*2.
recode qn1r qn2r qn3r qn4r qn5r
(−10 = 10) (−8 = 8) (−6 = 6) (−4 = 4) (−2 = 2) (0 = 0) (2 = −2)
(4 = −4) (6 = −6) (8 = −8) (10 = −10).
                              /* reverses the scores for the neg-
                              ative items only.
compute bias = (qn1r + qn2r + qn3r + qn4r + qn5r + qp6r +
qp7r + qp8r + qp9r + qp10r)/10.
                              /* computes an average bias score
                              for later analysis.
end if.
do if (qtype = 3).            /* selects the data for questionnaire
                              C.
compute d1 = qn1 − qn11.      /* subtract the 'other' from the
                              'self' for negative.
compute d2 = qn2 − qn12.      /* events.
compute d3 = qn3 − qn13.
compute d4 = qn4 − qn14.
compute d5 = qn5 − qn15.
compute d6 = qp16 − qp6.      /* subtract the 'self' from the
                              'other' for positive.
compute d7 = qp17 − qp7.      /* events.
compute d8 = qp18 − qp8.
compute d9 = qp19 − qp9.
compute d10 = qp20 − qp10.
compute bias = (d1 + d2 + d3 + d4 + d5 + d6 + d7 + d8 + d9
+ d10)/10.
                              /* computes an average bias score
                              for later analysis.

end if.
do if (qtype = 4).            /* selects the data for questionnaire
                              D.
compute d1 = qn11 − qn1.      /* subtract the 'other' from the
                              'self' for negative.
compute d2 = qn12 − qn2.      /* events.
compute d3 = qn13 − qn3.
compute d4 = qn14 − qn4.
compute d5 = qn15 − qn5.
compute d6 = qp6 − qp16.      /* subtract the 'self' from the
                              'other' for positive.
compute d7 = qp7 − qp17.      /* events.
```

```
compute d8 = qp8 - qp18.
compute d9 = qp9 - qp19.
compute d10 = qp10 - qp20.
compute bias = (d1 + d2 + d3 + d4 + d5 + d6 + d7 + d8 + d9
+ d10)/10.
                            /* computes an average bias score
                            for later analysis.
end if.
execute.
```

There are several things to note about this. First, you must keep an eye on which questions were about negative events (the 'qn' variables) and which were the positive ones (the 'qp' variables). We have kept this example simple by having 10 events, the first five of which are negative – your questionnaires and data set may be different.

Second, syntax files like this are very useful since they can be saved and rerun at any time in the future, unlike a series of mouse 'clicks', which may be difficult to recall. Complex data manipulations are nearly always more easily achieved by using this command language and they make it possible for you to seek out errors and correct them if/when you make a mistake. There are more fancy commands that could have been used to achieve the same thing with fewer commands but they are less easy to understand and follow than the ones used here.

Third, you should note that the commands never recode the original variables into themselves, which would have the effect of changing your data file. Variables are always recoded into new variables (e.g. qn1r) so that your data file is not corrupted.

The variable 'bias' is now the indicator of how much optimistic bias was shown by each respondent. Values of 'bias' below zero indicate the presence of optimistic bias.

Analysis: Statistical Procedures

A simple initial analysis to address the first hypothesis is to calculate the mean bias score across all conditions and use a one-sample t-test to see if this mean is significantly different from zero. If the overall mean is negative *and* significantly different from zero then this would suggest that the optimistic bias is quite pervasive.

To run this analysis in SPSS (assuming the data is loaded up and the syntax has been run) click on: *Analyze/Compare Means . . . /One Sample T Test*.

Your 'test variable' is the variable 'bias' and the 'test value' is zero (0). You can either click on 'OK' to do the test now or click on 'Paste' to paste the necessary commands into your syntax file for use again later.

The key test of hypotheses 2 and 3 can be achieved by using a two-factor between-subjects analysis of variance (ANOVA). The hypotheses were that the direct method will yield a stronger optimistic bias effect than the indirect method and that the level of optimistic bias will be greater for the other-as-reference condition. This is to suggest we would expect main effects for Factor I, comparison method (FAC1) and Factor II, reference perspective (FAC2). To obtain this analysis click on: *General Linear Model/Univariate*.

The dependent variable is 'bias' and the Fixed Factor(s) are FAC1 and FAC2. There are no Random Factor(s), Covariate(s) or WLS Weight – these boxes can be ignored.

Click on *Options* . . . and highlight all the items in the top left-hand box and place them in the 'Display Means for:' box by clicking on the black triangle button, then click on 'Continue'. Click on the 'Plots' button and put 'FAC1' in the 'Horizontal Axis:' box and 'FAC2' in the 'Separate Lines:' box then press 'Continue'. Running this will produce the mean scores for the two factors as well as the means of each cell of the design and a simple graph to display these means. Again you can either click on 'OK' to do the test now or click on 'Paste' to paste the necessary commands into your syntax file for use again later.

Looking at the output, look at the table called 'Tests of Between-Subjects Effects'. A statistically significant effect (i.e. a 'Sig' value of less than 0.05) for Factor I would suggest that the indirect and direct methods of eliciting comparative risk judgements differed in the level of optimistic bias they revealed. You will need to look at the table of means for FAC1 to find out which method produced the most apparent bias (remember a score less than zero indicates optimistic bias).

Similarly if the effect for Factor II (FAC2), the reference frame used, is significant, then it will suggest that the amount of bias displayed will depend on whether the 'self' or 'other' is used as the frame of reference. The table of means for FAC2 should be investigated to work out which way around this is.

Finally, you should look to see whether the FAC1*FAC2 interaction is significant. If it is then this would suggest that the amount of bias recorded may depend on both the reference frame and the method of bias elicitation. One possibility is that the most bias is shown when the direct method is used *and* the frame of reference is the other. You will need to examine the table of means for the FAC1*FAC2 interaction to work this out. Here the graphical plot may help you to see what is going on.

Notes for Course Leader

The key lesson to be learned from this exercise is that question context matters. What might seem like a relatively straightforward thing to ask about nonetheless produces a situation that is fundamentally ambiguous. It is difficult to tell which is the 'right' way to ask a question, so it is important when making comparisons to ensure that the data-collecting context is as similar as possible (see Fife-Schaw & Rowe, 2000).

The second message to convey is how the study design and the mode of statistical analysis are intimately linked. We have a two-factor study that is analysed using a two-factor ANOVA. All the basics of experimental design in social psychology are present here to some degree or other. Indeed, the design and analysis allow us to test the effects of both factors separately and in interaction with one another – something that was not formally hypothesised. If appropriate the task could be simplified by simply looking at one level of the direct/indirect factor and conducting simple t-tests on the other factor.

The figure of 84 people was selected for the sample size based on an *a priori* power calculation. In Otten and van der Pligt's (1996) studies they revealed effect sizes between self-as-reference and other-as-reference in the order of 0.8 to 1 standard deviations. Assuming an alpha criterion of 0.05 one-tailed, an effect size of 0.8 and a desired power of 0.8 the minimum sample size required for a t-test to test the equality of the means of any two cells in the design is 42. As there are four cells the desired sample size was 84.

A range of variations on the basic paradigm is possible. It is possible to use any odd number of response categories and there is evidence to suggest that optimistic bias is more pronounced the fewer the number of response options available (Otten and van der Pligt, 1996). Some researchers use 101-point scales, some only 7-point scales – the number of points used could easily be incorporated into the class exercise as an additional factor to study. Here we have employed 11-point scales to increase the likelihood of demonstrating some bias without going to the extreme of a 7-point scale which can lead to respondents complaining that they have too few options available to them.

We have used an example where the questionnaire contains both positive and negative life events. It would be perfectly possible to expand the study design to add the negativity of the events as a within-subjects factor and thereby permit a more thorough investigation of the phenomenon.

To make the exercise feasible in the context of student lab classes we have not been able to insert a delay between asking respondents to make self and other indirect judgements. In many studies using the indirect method there is a filler task, or indeed in some cases a time gap of several weeks, between asking the 'self' and 'other' judgements. The present design is likely to accentuate the self vs. other comparison and thereby reduce the differences in the degree of bias yielded by the direct and indirect methods. Keen students might be encouraged to see what the effect of differing lengths of inter-judgement period has on the degree of bias obtained.

Extending the study further it would be interesting to assess the relationship between optimistic bias and actual risk taking. One possibility is to collect the data from students as above including the event 'Getting skin cancer from sunbathing'. In a second phase, without looking at the data, students would rate the respondent's degree of suntan. Obviously this would have to distinguish between intentional tanning and those people whose skin was naturally dark – this should not be difficult if the study is restricted to classmates. The hypothesis would be that those who have got a tan would display greater optimistic bias for that event than those without tans whilst there should be no systematic difference in bias displayed for other life events.

REFERENCES

Abrams, D., Abraham, C., Spears, R. & Marks, D. (1990). AIDS invulnerability, relationships, sexual behaviour and attitudes among 16–19 year olds. In P. Aggleton, P. Davies and G. Hart (eds.), *AIDS: Individual, cultural and policy dimensions*. Lewes, UK: Falmer Press.

Blanz, M., Mummendey, A. & Otten, S. (1995). Positive–negative asymmetry in social discrimination: The impact of stimulus valence and size and status differentials on intergroup evaluations. *British Journal of Social Psychology, 34*, 409–19.

Blanz, M., Mummendey, A. & Otten, S. (1997). Normative evaluations and frequency expectations regarding positive versus negative outcome allocations between groups. *European Journal of Social Psychology, 27*, 165–76.

Codol, J. P. (1987). Comparability and incomparability between oneself and others: Means of differentiation and comparison reference points. *European Bulletin of Cognitive Psychology, 7*, 87–105.

Codol, J. P., Jarymowicz, M., Kaminska-Feldman, M. & Szuster-Zbrojewicz, A. (1989). Asymmetry in the estimation of interpersonal distance and identity affirmation. *European Journal of Social Psychology, 19,* 11–22.

Dolinski, D., Gromski, W. & Zawisza, E. (1987). Unrealistic pessimism. *Journal of Social Psychology, 127,* 511–16.

Fife-Schaw, C. R. & Rowe, G. (2000). Extending the application of the psychometric approach for assessing public perceptions of food risk: Some methodological considerations. *Journal of Risk Research, 3*(2), 167–79.

Goodhart, D. E. (1986). The effects of positive and negative thinking on performance in an achievement situation. *Journal of Personality and Social Psychology, 51,* 117–24.

Harris, P. (1996). Sufficient grounds for optimism?: The relationship between perceived controllability and optimistic bias. *Journal of Social and Clinical Psychology, 15*(1), 9–52.

Harris, P., Middleton, W. & Joiner, R. (2000) The typical student as an in-group member: eliminating optimistic bias by reducing social distance. *European Journal of Social Psychology, 30,* 235–53.

Heine, S. J. & Lehman, D. R. (1995). Cultural variation in unrealistic optimism: Does the West feel more vulnerable than the East? *Journal of Personality and Social Psychology, 68,* 595–607.

Helweg-Larsen, M. (1999). (The lack of) optimistic biases in response to the 1994 Northridge earthquake: The role of personal experience. *Basic and Applied Psychology, 21*(2), 118–29.

Hoorens, V. & Buunk, B. P. (1993). Social comparison of health risks: Locus of control, the person-positivity bias, and unrealistic optimism. *Journal of Applied Social Psychology, 23,* 291–302.

Klein, C. & Helweg-Larsen, M. (2002) Perceived control and the optimistic bias: A meta-analytic review. *Psychology-and-Health, 17*(4), 437–46.

Klein, W. M. (1996). Maintaining self-serving social comparisons: Attenuating the perceived significance of risk-increasing behaviors. *Journal of Social and Clinical Psychology, 15,* 120–42.

Klein, W. M. & Weinstein, N. D. (1997). Social comparison and unrealistic optimism about personal risk. In B. P. Buunk & F. X. Gibbons (eds.), *Health, coping, and social comparison* (pp. 63–94). Hillsdale, NJ: Lawrence Erlbaum.

Middleton, W. (1996). Give 'em enough rope: Perception of health and safety risks in bungee jumpers. *Journal of Social and Clinical Psychology, 15*(1), 68–79.

Otten, W. & van-der-Pligt, J. (1996). Context effects in the measurement of comparative optimism in probability judgments. *Journal of Social and Clinical Psychology, 15,* 80–101.

Perloff, L. S. & Fetzer, B. K. (1986). Self–other judgments and perceived vulnerability to victimization. *Journal of Personality and Social Psychology, 50,* 502–10.

Rothman, A. J., Klein, W. M. & Weinstein, N. D. (1996). Absolute and relative biases in estimations of personal risk. *Journal of Applied Social Psychology, 26,* 1213–36.

Schwarzer, R. (1994). Optimism, vulnerability, and self-beliefs as health-related cognitions: A systematic overview. *Psychology and Health*, *9*, 161–80.

Segerstrom, S. C., McCarthy, W. J., Caskey, N. H., Gross, T. M. et al. (1993). Optimistic bias among cigarette smokers. *Journal of Applied Social Psychology*, *23*(19), 1606–18.

Wanke, M., Schwarz, N. & Noelle-Neumann, E. (1995). Asking comparative questions: The impact of the direction of comparison. *Public Opinion Quarterly*, *59*, 347–72.

Weinstein, N. D. (1980). Unrealistic optimism about future life events. *Journal of Personality and*

Weinstein, N. D. & Klein, W. M. (1996). Unrealistic optimism: Present and future. *Journal of Social and Clinical Psychology*, *15*, 1–8.

Whalen, C. K., Henker, B., O'Neil, R. & Hollingshead, J. (1994). Optimism in children's judgments of health and environmental risks. *Health Psychology*, *13*, 319–25.

CHAPTER FOUR

A Quasi-experimental Study of Stereotyping

Adam Rutland

This chapter introduces a simple quasi-experimental research design in order to examine whether stereotype content is dependent upon the group context in which it is elicited. Aspects of the theory of self-categorization are used to formulate the research hypotheses. A questionnaire checklist approach to data elicitation is described. Factor analysis is used as a technique for scale construction. The chapter is suitable for introductory level students who have limited prior experience of quasi-experimental studies using questionnaires.

Research Topic: Stereotypes

The experimental study of stereotypes has been prevalent within social psychology ever since Walter Lippman introduced the term in 1922. He, as a journalist, appropriated the term from the world of printing where a stereotype is the metal cast that is used to produce repeated and matched images of a character. When Lippman applied the phrase 'stereotype' to human perception he was referring to how people tend to employ the same character to their impression of a group and its members. For example, when a white British male views all blacks as 'lazy', or all women as 'emotional', or all Germans as 'aggressive', he is using the same cast or character to describe all members of the specific group. Therefore, stereotypes can be thought of as beliefs about the characteristics of groups of individuals (e.g. Ashmore & del Boca, 1981; Stangor, 2000).

It is useful conceptually to distinguish between social and individual stereotypes, though in an important sense all stereotypes are social since they relate to social categories and are essentially social in origin. Many of the cognitive representations of groups, or stereotypes held by individuals, are shared with other individuals in our culture (Stangor & Schaller, 1996). Indeed some researchers have argued that social stereotypes realize their power, and thus become a topic of interest, because they are widely shared by a large number of individuals (Haslam, Turner, Oakes, McGarty & Reynolds, 1998; Haslam, Oakes, Reynolds & Tuner, 1999). Therefore these social psychologists have concentrated on the study of social or shared stereotypes, while others have stated that 'stereotypes are belief systems that reside in the minds of individuals' (Hamilton, Stroessner & Driscoll, 1994, p. 289) and favoured the study of stereotypes held by individuals where consensuality is an irrelevance.

Differences between these two approaches to the experimental study of stereotypes, one favouring the study of individual stereotypes and the other the study of social stereotypes, are reflected at a methodological level. Individual stereotypes are normally assessed using the methodologies of cognitive psychology. A stereotype, within this approach, is taken to be a *prototype* or *schema*, namely a cognitive representation stored in memory that contains linkage between a social category and associated traits (Dovidio, Evans & Tyler, 1986). Specific individuals from a social category (i.e. *exemplars*) also form part of our stereotypes in memory (Bodenhausen, Schwartz, Bless & Wanke, 1995). Other contemporary models of individual stereotypes have regarded them as examples of cognitive neural networks in the mind (Kunda & Thagard, 1996).

Experimental research on individual stereotypes focuses on what produces stereotype activation within an individual and the cognitive consequences of such activation. Indirect measures of stereotyping are favoured. These normally involve the recording of response latencies to stimuli once a social category has been introduced within an experiment. Such indirect measures are based explicitly on the idea that, because associative links are formed in memory between category labels and stereotypes, the related stereotypes should be automatically activated when exposed to the category label (Bargh, 1999). The automatic activation of associated stereotypes, once the category has been made salient, is used as a subtle cognitive measure of whether a stereotype has been utilized (Banaji & Hardin, 1996; Dovidio et al., 1986). A stereotype has been *primed* once it has been activated and is currently accessible in memory. Thus indirect measures of stereotyping within experimental studies aim to present a social category, and then to measure the extent to which associated stereotypes are primed. Indirect measures of stereotyping have the advantage of reducing the potential for self-presentation. This is when research participants may attempt to present themselves in a positive light by seemingly avoiding stereotyping. When directly measuring a stereotype, participants may not be willing to admit to socially undesirable negative beliefs, and therefore inhibit their stereotype expression. However, indirect measures avoid this problem, since once the category label is presented, the associated traits should automatically become accessible, and the participants should be unable to avoid the activation of related stereotypes.

Indirect measures have their advantages, especially when assessing individual stereotypes. However, they tell us little about the content of social stereotypes and the extent to which a stereotype is consensually shared within a group. It is also important to understand the content and consensuality surrounding social stereotypes (Haslam et al., 1998; Haslam et al., 1999; Stangor & Lange, 1994), since when members of the same group agree about the content of a stigmatized out-group stereotype they tend to treat members of that group in *similar* ways. Other measures of stereotypes, therefore, are needed to investigate experimentally the issues of stereotype content and consensuality. Traditionally this has been achieved using one form or another of an adjective checklist. This involves simply giving people a list of social categories and a list of traits that might be perceived as stereotypical of each. The participants are required to indicate, by checking them off, which traits they think are true of which group. The percentage approach is another form of checklist technique, in which participants are given a list of social categories and traits and asked to note down what percentage of the group has each of the traits. Open-ended approaches have also been used to measure the content of stereotypes. These are favoured by some researchers who argue against providing individuals with pre-selected traits that might be viewed as stereotypical, because it limits stereotyping to the traits chosen by the researcher and the participant may have other very different stereotype traits in mind (Reicher, Hopkins & Condor, 1997). Typically, in the open-ended approach to stereotype research, participants are given only the social category and asked either to describe it in their own words or list the traits they see as typical of the group (e.g. Ford & Stangor, 1992; Rutland, 1999). The researcher then studies the descriptions or traits produced to see what stereotypes are favoured.

This chapter will focus upon the use of the adjective checklist method in experimental studies that measure the changing content of stereotypes. Until the 1960s this checklist technique was common in experimental studies that were very much concerned with monitoring and describing the sharedness of stereotype content within particular groups. Katz & Braly (1933) pioneered this method of assessing stereotype content when they asked undergraduates from Princeton University to assign five traits from a list of 84 to a range of different nationalities and ethnic groups. For example, 84 per cent of Princeton students described Negroes as superstitious and 75 per cent as lazy, 78 per cent assigned the trait scientifically minded to the Germans and 48 per cent saw Americans as industrious. The adjective checklist method allows the content of a stereotype to be examined, in addition to the degree of consensus about the stereotype content. Indeed, Katz & Braly (1933) found high between-subject uniformity in content within their Princeton Study. In fact only 10.1 per cent of the traits on the checklist were required to explain half of all the subjects' trait selections (the figure should have been 50% if the selection had been maximally idiosyncratic). In the six decades or so since the original study by Katz and Braly (1933), several quasi-experimental studies have used their technique to document the changing content and degree of consensus of the stereotypes of certain groups in the United States. Several studies showed, for example, that different generations of participants selected different traits to describe groups (e.g. Karlins, Coffman & Walter, 1969). In addition, over the short term, content also changed as a function of both international upheavals (e.g. Seago, 1947) and changes in inter-group relations (e.g. Diab, 1963).

The fact that sharedness was a necessarily coexistent feature of stereotype content allowed researchers to examine other questions that proved of interest. Importantly, issues regarding changes or rigidity in stereotypes were examined through the measurement of sharedness (the percentage of subjects who assigned a particular trait at a particular time or in a particular context). For example, Diab (1963) utilized the Katz and Braly technique to investigate experimentally how the content and consensus surrounding national stereotypes varied in line with manipulation of the context in which particular groups were judged. This study found significant differences in the nature of stereotypes attributed by Arab-Moslem students in Beirut to five national groups in two experimental conditions. This study used a simple between-subjects experimental design. In 'Condition A' participants were asked to select from a list of 99 adjectives those that seemed necessary to best characterize 13 groups: Turks, Russians, Negroes, Chinese, Italians, French, Germans, Americans,

English, Japanese, Jews, Lebanese and Irish. 'Condition B' was similar to 'Condition A' in all respects except one, namely, the *number and kind* of groups presented. Participants were asked to characterize five of the groups from the other condition (Russians, Americans, French, Germans and English) and two additional groups (Algerians and Egyptians). It was found that the Arab-Moslem participants described the French more unfavourably in the second condition, because of the implicit contrast with the Algerians. In addition, the stereotype of the English became more negative under the second condition, possibly due to a contrast effect with the Egyptians. While the design of this study does not allow for firm conclusions about how contrasts with particular countries affect the stereotypes of other countries, it nevertheless shows that the number and kind of groups present in the context can affect stereotype content.

Stereotype Content is Context-dependent

The specific exercise described in this chapter will address the issue of variability in the content of stereotypes experimentally, using the Katz and Braly checklist technique. Context effects on the content of stereotypes may be explained as evidence of erroneous and distorted information processing about groups. Indeed, the 'cognitive miser' approach (Hilton & von Hippel, 1996; Fiske & Taylor, 1991) views stereotyping itself as a default option for social judgement that is used when we do not have sufficient cognitive resources (time, ability and motivation) to perceive people in individual terms.

However, this exercise will be based upon an alternative explanation that draws upon previous experimental research in the tradition of self-categorization theory (Oakes, Haslam & Turner, 1994; Spears, Oakes, Ellemers & Haslam, 1997; Turner, Hogg, Oakes, Reicher & Wetherall, 1987). Self-categorization theory (SCT) argues that social categorization is inherently comparative and that it does not reflect the fixed absolute properties of self and other but has comparative relational properties (Oakes et al., 1994). Therefore, SCT would predict that the stereotypes associated with social categories will vary with changes in the comparative context (Oakes et al., 1994; Turner et al., 1987; Turner, Oakes, Haslam & McGarty, 1994). Stereotyping or group-level perception is not represented by SCT as a product of faulty information processing due to cognitive capacity constraints, but as a result of a concern to discover social meaning with the aim of enriching social perception. Stereotypes are not seen by SCT as static knowledge structures stored in the head ready to be activated, but rather a product of the on-going multiplicative relationship between perceiver readiness (or accessibility) of the category and its perceived fit to the current social reality (Oakes, 1987; Oakes et al., 1994). SCT contends that accentuation effects and the desire to maximize, on the relevant dimensions of comparison, the metacontrast ratio (Oakes, 1987; Turner, 1987) can explain the context dependence of stereotypes. Therefore, people are motivated to maximize differences between groups and similarities within groups, so producing the best differentiation between stimuli in the social context.

Several SCT studies have shown the relationship between manipulations of context and stereotype content, in either a *post hoc* (e.g. Haslam, Turner, Oakes, & McGarty, 1992; Cinnirella, 1998) or *a priori* manner (e.g. Hopkins, Regan & Abell, 1997; Rutland & Cinnirella, 2000). For example, Haslam et al. (1992) found that the social stereotyping of Americans by Australian students varied with experimental manipulations of the context related to the hostilities in the Persian Gulf conflict 1990–91 between Iraq and the Western allies (e.g. America, Britain and Australia). They examined social stereotyping of Americans by Australian university students at the start and at the end of the conflict. The focus was on how the assignment of standard stereotypical traits to Americans were affected by large-scale social change resulting from the Gulf conflict, and by variation in the frame of reference provided by relevant comparison groups. Haslam and colleagues used a mixed design in their experiment, with three experimental conditions as the between-subject factor and repeated measures (before and after the conflict) as the within-subject factor. Participants were asked to characterize people from the United States both at the start and at the end of the conflict. The United States appeared as one of a list of countries which participants might have been asked to characterize. Manipulation of the frame of reference was achieved by expanding this list across three conditions. In a *restricted range* (RR) condition the other countries were Australia and Britain; in a *medium range* (MR) condition the other countries were Australia, Britain and the Soviet Union; while in an *extended range* (ER) condition the other countries were Australia, Britain, the Soviet Union and Iraq. The findings showed that the stereotypes of the Americans were significantly more negative at the end of the conflict than at the beginning in the RR condition and also at the start of the conflict in the ER condition, with Iraq in the frame of reference. Haslam and colleagues concluded that the content of the American stereotype held by Australian students was dependent on the number and type of nations in the comparative context. This experiment shows that stereotype content is inherently variable, comparative and context-dependent.

SCT states that the 'cognitive miser' approach is not supported by the fact that stereotype variability is not random but closely related to changes in the comparative context. For example, Hopkins et al. (1997) showed that Scottish self-stereotypes systematically varied depending on the frame of reference created by experimental manipulations. Hopkins and colleagues successfully predicted that a comparative context that included Greeks would result in Scottish self-stereotypes varying along the salient dimensions of hard-working and warmth. Their predictions were based upon the findings from research on perceived differences between northern and southern countries (e.g. Linssen & Hagendoorn, 1994) and perceived differences between Scots and the English (e.g. Hopkins & Reicher, 1996). They also successfully predicted that a comparative context involving the English would produce variability in Scottish self-stereotypes only along the relevant warmth or sociability dimension.

Self-categorization theorists have successfully utilized the Katz & Braly checklist technique in their experimental studies of stereotype content variability. Nevertheless, this method has been roundly maligned by a host of influential reviewers. For example, some researchers (Augoustinos & Walker, 1995; Brigham, 1971; McCauley, Stitt & Segal, 1980) have contended that the checklist methodology is weak because it may artificially force stereotyping and offers no possibility of identifying idiosyncratic personal stereotypes. In addition, it has been argued that the method obstructs the analysis of psychological processes (Brigham, 1971) and ignores the possibility that traits may mean very different things to each participant (Condor, 1990). Self-categorization theorists have responded to these criticisms of their adopted methods by claiming that stereotypes are worth investigation *only* because groups hold them. Moreover, they claim that the group origins and effects of stereotypes can only be imagined without a group-based measure that quantifies their shared nature (Haslam et al., 1998; Oakes et al., 1994; Stangor & Lange, 1994). The Katz and Braly checklist is the only available method that provides such a measure. SCT acknowledges that this technique does elicit a group-based response, though this is exactly the response of most relevance to, and predictive of, attitudes and behaviour when social identity is salient. Thus a group response is of most interest. The critique that the meaning of individual traits is not fixed would also apply to *any* quantitative measure of the sort regularly gathered by stereotype researchers (e.g. based upon rating scales or memory recall). This criticism becomes less significant if the stereotype research focuses less on offering a definitive account of stereotype content and more on understanding the social psychological processes behind stereotyping.

For instance, it might identify how stereotype content is shaped by the comparative context and by inter-group relations (Haslam et al., 1992; Hopkins et al., 1997; Oakes et al., 1994; Rutland & Cinnirella, 2000).

A Specific Exercise

THE RESEARCH QUESTION

In the remaining pages of this chapter a specific exercise is outlined that uses a quasi-experimental research design to examine context effects on stereotype content. The research question under investigation will be: do national in-group stereotypes vary in relation to experimental manipulations of the national out-groups in the context? To answer this question the exercise will involve manipulating the comparative context in different experimental conditions, and determining whether this affects the content of the national in-group stereotype. The Katz & Braly checklist technique will be used to assess the content of the national in-group stereotype within this experiment. The exercise will be modelled on the experiment described by Hopkins et al. (1997). This experiment examined context effects on the Scottish national in-group stereotype. Hopkins and colleagues were able to predict *a priori* how manipulating the comparative context will affect each dimension of the Scottish in-group stereotype. This was possible because previous research had identified the salient features of the Scottish stereotype, especially in relation to significant national out-groups (e.g. the English).

Before starting this exercise it is important to consider carefully what national in-group will be the focus of the study. For example, amongst a Scottish sample one could use either British or Scottish national identity as the topic under investigation. Rightly Hopkins et al. (1997) chose Scottish identity since evidence suggests that Scottish people have a stronger sense of identification with Scotland than with Britain (Huici, Ros, Cano, Hopkins, Emler & Carmona, 1997; Rutland & Cinnirella, 2000). So think about the choice of in-group. Furthermore, thought must also be given to exact national out-groups to be used within the experiment. It would be wise to select groups where there has been previous research into how the in-group perceives these out-groups. This research should help you identify how the out-group may contrast stereotypically with the in-group. Pilot work should be conducted before the main experiment that will help you confirm your choice of in-group and out-groups (see below). Depending upon your choice of the in-group and the out-groups you might be able to make *a priori* predictions concerning the effect of manipulating the comparative context on the content of the national in-group stereotype. The more background literature there is available concerning how the national in-group perceives the out-groups the easier it should be to predict how the experimental manipulation will affect the in-group stereotype. Hopefully, this should result in some experimental hypotheses stating whether and how the in-group stereotype will vary with each condition. If it is not possible to make specific predictions, then the experiment should just aim to disprove the null hypothesis.

THE EXPERIMENTAL DESIGN

This exercise will utilize an experimental between-subjects design. The research question will be most effectively tested using three conditions (though more conditions may be added depending upon the number of out-groups felt appropriate). One should be an intra-group condition, when only the participants consider the national in-group. The other two should be inter-group conditions, with the national in-group being implicitly contrasted with a national out-group. Participants in all conditions should be asked to stereotype their national in-group on a questionnaire rating scale, where they are required to state how typical a checklist of various stereotypical traits are of their national in-group. In the first, or intra-group, condition participants should only complete the questionnaire rating scale to measure their national in-group stereotype. This condition is effectively a 'control' since it does not encourage any inter-group comparison, whereas the remaining two inter-group conditions will invite such comparisons, since the participants in these two inter-group conditions will first complete a stereotype rating scale for a national out-group and then immediately for the national in-group. The questionnaire rating scale used for the in-group and out-group should be exactly the same, so to facilitate inter-group comparison on the same stereotype traits.

THE EXPERIMENTAL MATERIALS

The only material required will be a questionnaire for use in each experimental condition. Importantly the traits along which the national in-group stereotype will be measured must be determined. Initially this will involve selecting traits from pre-existing research on national stereotyping (e.g. Cinnirella, 1998; Hewstone, 1986; Hopkins et al., 1997; Linssen & Hagendoorn, 1994; Peabody, 1985; Pennebaker, Rime & Blankenship, 1996; Poppe & Linessen, 1999; Rutland & Cinnirella, 2000).

Once you have selected a collection of traits from the available literature (though you may add in additional traits which you feel are very appropriate for the national in-group) these should be tested in a pilot study. In conducting a pilot study I suggest you use approximately 30 traits. Ask members from the national in-group within your class to rate the percentage of the in-group and the two out-groups which possess these 30 traits (a third of the class could rate the in-group, a third one of the out-groups and the other third the remaining out-group). Some of the traits will not differentiate between the in-group and the two out-groups. Others will differentiate between the in-group and the others, but the direction of the differentiation will be the same for each out-group (e.g. the British will be seen as more hard-working than both the Greeks and the Portuguese). You need to choose traits for the main experiment which differentiate between the in-group and the out-groups, but ideally the out-groups would also be different in terms of valence on these traits. I would aim to choose about 20 to 24 traits. Remember the number of traits you select will determine the number of participants you will need in the experiment, because you will be performing factor analysis on these traits. It is statistically appropriate to have approximately four or five participants for each item or trait in a factor analysis. Therefore, if you choose 20 to 24 traits you will need somewhere between 80 and 125 participants.

Once you have decided upon the traits to be used in the questionnaire, you should construct the questionnaires that will be used in each experimental condition. I suggest you use one sheet of paper for each group (therefore, you will need two sheets in the inter-group conditions and only one in the intra-group condition). List your chosen traits on the sheet in no particular order. Ask the participants at the top of each sheet to say how much each trait applies to the group in question by circling a number from 1 ('not at all') through to 7 ('very much'). In the intra-group condition the participants will only complete one sheet, rating their national in-group on the chosen traits, and no mention will be made of any other specific out-groups. In the other two inter-group conditions they will first rate the out-group on the same chosen traits as in the intra-group condition. Once they have completed this sheet they should turn the page and rate the national in-group on the same traits. No explicit instructions should be given in the inter-group conditions to judge the groups in relation to each other, and the participants should not know that they will have to rate the in-group until they have finished rating the out-group and turned the page. The questionnaires will need to be reproduced using a photocopier.

THE PARTICIPANTS

The participants would be best recruited through convenience sampling of volunteer students from your university or college campus. This will be aided by the fact that the questionnaire should be quick to complete. The students must subjectively categorize themselves as members of the national in-group (and hold a passport if that is appropriate). The allocation of students to each condition should be random and there should be approximately equal numbers of students in each experimental condition. The researcher should briefly introduce the study to each participant as an investigation into his or her perceptions of certain social groups, and once the questionnaire is complete the participant should be fully debriefed. Amongst themselves, the class should equally distribute the responsibility of collecting completed questionnaires for each condition.

THE STATISTICAL ANALYSIS

Next the data from the completed questionnaires should be entered into a computer-based statistical package (e.g. SPSS). It would make sense if each member of the class were responsible for entering the data from the questionnaires they collected into the computer-based software. Remember that data should always be entered in its rawest form. In addition, ensure that all members of the class are entering the data using the same number of variables and with the variables in the same order. This is because once all the data from the questionnaires have been entered the individual data files can be merged into a complete data set for the whole class. The variable 'condition' will be your independent variable and this will be defined depending upon whether the participant was in the intra-group condition or one of the inter-group conditions. The dependent variables will be the ratings of the national in-group on the chosen traits. However, in the two inter-group conditions you should also enter the ratings on the traits for the two out-groups. The merged data set should be shared amongst all members of the class.

Before you start the statistical analysis to test your experimental hypotheses you should engage in scale construction. At the moment your number of dependent variables is equal to the total number of traits chosen for the experiment. It is not statistically advisable to have this many dependent variables. Therefore, the ratings of the national in-group on the chosen traits should be reduced through factor analysis (varimax rotation).

Various books explain how to perform factor analysis using the computer-based statistical package SPSS (e.g. Kinnear & Gray, 1999; Green, Salkind & Akey, 1997). If you need more detail concerning the procedure to follow within SPSS when undertaking factor analysis I suggest you read these texts. The book by Tabachnick & Fidell (1996) also provides a good introduction to the rationale and principles behind the use of factor analysis. Factor analysis will reduce the data to a small number of factors or stereotype dimensions. You should only consider factors with eigenvalues over 1 and ones that explain a reasonably high level of variance in your data. Each factor should also have constituent trait or item loadings. In general, a trait can be considered as loading on a factor if the factor loading is above 0.5. The factor loadings will determine whether a particular trait should be linked with a specific factor. Having decided the number of factors to work with, compute composite scales by summing across each constituent trait and dividing by the number of traits contributing to the scale (this can be performed using SPSS). Thus for each participant the appropriate number of scales (each having a minimum of 1 and a maximum of 7) should be created to correspond to the number of factors you have decided upon. The same factor structure identified by the factor analysis should also be used to compute composite scales for the stereotype factors or dimensions of the two national out-groups. Therefore, for example, if you had a four-factor solution (the stereotype factors being warm, work, organization and dominant) you should have computed four composite scales to measure 'warmth', 'work', 'organization' and 'dominance' amongst the national in-group and the two national out-groups.

Now you have constructed all the necessary scales, which will be your dependent variables, you can conduct the main statistical analysis. First, the in-group's perceptions of the two out-groups deserve consideration. In particular, it would be interesting to know the perceptions of the in-group in relation to the out-groups. Paired sample t-tests should be used to determine differences between the in-group and the two out-groups on the composite scales, which measure the stereotype dimensions. These paired sample t-tests should adopt the Bonferroni-adjusted criterion of $p = .001$, given the likelihood of a small n value. Next you need to examine the between-condition differences on the national in-group stereotype (as constituted by the composite scales). MANOVA should be used to identify a multivariate effect for condition across the stereotype dimensions or composite scales. This analysis will treat the composite scales as the dependent variables and the condition as the independent variable. In addition to determining any multivariate effect of condition a MANOVA should also conduct one-way ANOVAs on each of the composite scales, with condition again as the independent variable. These ANOVAs should help you pinpoint whether any effect of condition is specific to a particular scale or stereotype dimension. This will be necessary if you made specific predictions regarding how manipulating the comparative context will affect the particular stereotype dimensions of the national in-group stereotype. The use of the above statistical techniques should allow you to accept or reject the hypotheses you choose before you conducted the experiment.

Notes for the Course Leader

The exercise outlined above assumes that the students have an intermediate level understanding of social psychology. While a basic knowledge of experimental research into stereotyping would be useful it is not absolutely essential. However, a core understanding of the principles behind self-categorization theory would help the students understand the rationale for the experiment. The books by Oakes et al. (1994) and Spears et al. (1997) provide good introductions to the self-categorization theory approach to stereotyping. The class size should be approximately 20 to 40 students, since a large sample of participants will need to complete a short questionnaire and a significant number of students should be available to distribute the questionnaires. This means that a relatively large pool of participants should be available to the class, so they can be recruited via convenience sampling (most probably near your college or university). It might be advisable to try to recruit participants through large-scale lecture classes, given the questionnaire will be very short, though I would advise collecting the data for each experimental condition in separate lecture classes, since students are likely to talk to their colleagues sitting next to them and this would be problematic if they were in different experimental conditions.

It is anticipated that the practical exercise should take a minimum of two hours, though this will depend upon the amount of pilot work required and the time needed to recruit the appropriate number of participants. If possible it might be wise to split the exercise over two time slots, so the students have enough time to recruit participants on a on-to-one basis using convenience sampling. There are some additional features you could add to the exercise if time permits. Previous research (e.g. Cinnirella, 1998; Rutland & Cinnirella, 2000) has examined the effect of manipulating the comparative context on self-categorization (or social identification) and attitudes. Self-categorization theory (SCT) not only contends that stereotyping is tied to the inter-group context; it also argues that *self-categorization* itself and related cognitions (e.g. attitudes and beliefs) are inherently comparative and should vary with experimental manipulations of the frame of reference (Oakes et al., 1994; Turner et al., 1987; Turner et al., 1994). Cinnirella (1998) used a three-condition between-subjects design in his experiment on English university students. In one condition the participants stereotyped the British only, while in another they stereotyped the Italians only and in the third condition both the British and Italians were stereotyped together. So this final condition encouraged inter-group comparison and the others were intra-group conditions. In addition to assessing the student's national stereotypes Cinnirella also measured the student's degree of social identification with Britain and Europe immediately after they had completed the stereotyping tasks. The student's attitude to the European Community and European integration was also assessed within this experiment, using questionnaire rating scales. It was found that in the inter-group condition compared to the intra-group conditions the student's identification with Europe decreased and their attitudes became more negative.

Research by Rutland & Cinnirella (2000) also investigated context effects on national and European identification. This research used Scottish students and investigated how manipulation of the comparative context affects Scottish, British and European self-categorization. The first experimental study described by Rutland and Cinnirella (2000) adopted a similar procedure to Hopkins et al. (1997), though in this four-condition experiment the English, Germans and Australians were the national out-groups and measures were taken of three social identities (Scottish, British and European) after the stereotyping task. Social identification was measured using a seven-item scale adopted before by Cinnirella (1997) and broadly compatible with measures typically used in quantitative studies of social identity using social identity theory (see Brown, Condor, Mathews, Wade & Williams, 1986; Hogg & Abrams, 1988). The findings showed that the Scottish student's identification with Europe decreased with the inclusion of the Germans and English in the frame of reference. However, the student's Scottish and British identity was not affected by the context manipulation and their European identity was not affected by the addition of the Australians to the comparative context. Rutland &

Cinnirella explained these findings with reference to the importance of category accessibility, fragility and relations and conducted a second questionnaire-based study to support their argument.

The exercise might prove more interesting if additional measures of social identity (e.g. national and European) and attitudes (e.g. towards the European Union and European integration) were included at the end of the questionnaires after the stereotype trait-rating task, especially given the findings of the studies by Cinnirella (1998) and Rutland & Cinnirella (2000). However, as Rutland and Cinnirella (2000) note, context effects on self-categorization are not straightforward and it may be necessary to conduct additional preliminary research if you wish to predict *a priori* how the inclusion of national out-groups in the comparative context will affect self-categorization at different levels of abstraction. It might be necessary to initially conduct a study similar to the second study described by Rutland & Cinnirella (2000) if you intend to make specific predictions regarding context effects on self-categorization. Taken together, you may feel these additions to the exercise will make it too long and cumbersome.

One person could run the exercise, though this person must be knowledgeable enough to introduce the topic and explain the rationale behind the experimental procedure. However, if the class size is large then one teaching assistant might be advisable, especially when the students are designing their questionnaires and entering their data into a computer-based statistical package. During the exercise the students will need access to computers for designing the questionnaire and conducting the statistical analysis, and they will need access to photocopiers to reproduce the questionnaire. The students should have had some prior methodological and statistical training. They need to be statistically competent handling multivariate tests and factor analysis. They should also be familiar with the use of between-subjects designs within experimental psychology.

REFERENCES

Ashmore, R. D. & Del Boca, F. K. (1981). Conceptual approaches to stereotypes and stereotyping. In D. L. Hamilton (ed.), *Cognitive processes in stereotyping and intergroup behavior* (pp. 1–35). Hillsdale, NJ: Erlbaum.

Augoustinos, M. & Walker, I. (1995). *Social cognition: An integrated introduction.* London: Sage.

Banaji, M. R. & Hardin, C. D. (1996). Automatic stereotyping. *Psychological Science, 7,* 136–41.

Bargh, J. (1999). *The cognitive monster: The case against the controllability of automatic stereotype effects.* New York: Guilford.

Bodenhausen, G. V., Schwarz, N., Bless, H. & Wanke, M. (1995). Effects of atypical exemplars on racial beliefs: Enlightened racism or generalized appraisals? *Journal of Experimental Social Psychology, 31*, 48–63.

Brigham, J. C. (1971). Ethnic stereotypes. *Psychological Bulletin, 76*, 15–38.

Brown, R. J., Condor, S., Mathews, A., Wade, G. & Williams, J. A. (1986). Explaining intergroup differentiation in an organization. *Journal of Occupational Psychology, 59*, 273–86.

Cinnirella, M. (1997). Towards a European identity? Interactions between the national and European social identities manifested by university students in Britain and Italy. *British Journal of Social Psychology, 35*, 19–31.

Cinnirella, M. (1998). Manipulating stereotype rating tasks: Understanding questionnaire context effects on measures of attitudes, social identity and stereotypes. *Journal of Community and Applied Social Psychology, 8* (5), 345–62.

Condor, S. (1990). Social stereotypes and social identity. In D. Abrams & M. Hogg (eds.), *Social identity theory: Constructive and critical advances* (pp. 230–49). Hemel Hempstead, UK: Harvester Wheatsheaf.

Diab, L. (1963). Factors affecting studies of national stereotypes. *Journal of Social Psychology, 59*, 29–40.

Dovidio, J., Evan, N. & Tyler, R. (1986). Racial stereotypes: The contents of their cognitive representations. *Journal of Experimental Social Psychology, 22*, 22–37.

Fiske, S. & Taylor, S. (1991). *Social cognition* (2nd edn.). New York: McGraw-Hill.

Ford, T. E. & Stangor, C. (1992). The role of diagnosticity in stereotype formation: Perceiving group means and variances. *Journal of Personality and Social Psychology, 63*, 356–67.

Green, S. B., Salkind, N. J. & Akey, T. M. (1997). *Using SPSS for Windows: Analyzing and understanding data*. Upper Saddle River, NJ: Prentice Hall.

Hamilton, D. L., Stroessner, S. J. & Driscoll, D. M. (1994). Social cognition and the study of stereotyping. In P. G. Devine, D. L. Hamilton & T. M. Ostrom (eds.), *Social cognition: Contributions to classic issues in social psychology* (pp. 291–321). New York: Springer-Verlag.

Haslam, S. A., Oakes, P. J., Reynolds, K. J. & Turner, J. C. (1999). Social identity salience and the emergence of stereotype consensus. *Personality and Social Psychology Bulletin, 25*, 809–18.

Haslam, S. A., Turner, J. C., Oakes, P. J. & McGarty, C. (1992). Context-dependent variation in social stereotyping 1: The effects of intergroup relations as mediated by social change and frame of reference. *European Journal of Social Psychology, 22*(1), 3–20.

Haslam, S. A., Turner, J. C., Oakes, P. J., McGarty, C. & Reynolds, K. J. (1998). The group as a basis for emergent stereotype consensus. In W. Stroebe & M. Hewstone (eds.), *European Review of Social Psychology*, vol. 8 (pp. 203–39). Chicester, UK: John Wiley & Sons.

Hewstone, M. (1986). *Understanding attitudes to the European Community: A social-psychological study in four member states*. Cambridge, UK: Cambridge University Press.

Hilton, J. L. & von Hippel, W. (1996). Stereotypes. *Annual Review of Psychology*, 47, 237–71.

Hogg, M. A. & Abrams, D. (1988). *Social identifications: A social psychology of intergroup relations and group processes*. London: Routledge.

Hopkins, N. & Reicher, S. D. (1996). The construction of social categories and the processes of social change: Arguing about national identities. In G. M. Breakwell & E. Lyons (eds.), *Changing European identities: Social psychological analyses of social change* (pp. 69–93). Oxford: Butterworth-Heinemann.

Hopkins, N., Regan, M. & Abell, J. (1997). On the context dependence of national stereotypes: Some Scottish data. *British Journal of Social Psychology*, 36, 553–63.

Huici, C., Ros, M., Cano, I., Hopkins, N., Emler, N. & Carmona, M. (1997). Comparative identity and evaluation of socio-political change: Perceptions of the European Community as a function of the salience of regional identities. *European Journal of Social Psychology*, 27, 97–113.

Karlins, M., Coffman, T. L. & Walters, G. (1969). On the fading social stereotypes: Studies in three generations of college students. *Journal of Personality and Social Psychology*, 13, 1–16.

Katz, D. & Braly, K. (1933). Racial stereotypes of one hundred college students. *Journal of Abnormal and Social Psychology*, 28, 280–90.

Kinnear, P. R. & Gray, C. D. (1999). *SPSS for Windows made simple* (3rd edn.). Hove, UK: Psychology Press.

Kunda, Z. & Thagard, P. (1996). Forming impressions from stereotypes, traits and behaviors: A parallel constraint satisfaction theory. *Psychological Review*, 103, 284–308.

Linssen, H. & Hagendoorn, L. (1994). Social and geographical factors in the explanation of the content of European national stereotypes. *British Journal of Social Psychology*, 33, 165–82.

McCauley, C., Stitt, C. L. & Segal, M. (1980). Stereotyping: From prejudice to prediction. *Psychological Bulletin*, 87, 195–208.

Oakes, P. J. (1987). The salience of social categories. In J. C. Turner, M. A. Hogg, P. J. Oakes, S. D. Reicher & M. S. Wetherell (eds.), *Rediscovering the social group: A self-categorization theory* (pp. 117–41). Oxford: Blackwell.

Oakes, P. J., Haslam, S. A. & Turner, J. C. (1994). *Stereotyping and social reality*. Oxford: Blackwell.

Peabody, D. (1985). *National characteristics*. Cambridge, UK: Cambridge University Press.

Pennebaker, J. W., Rime, B. & Blankenship, V. E. (1996). Stereotypes of emotional expressiveness of Northerners and Southerners: A cross-cultural test of Montesquieu's hypothesis. *Journal of Personality and Social Psychology*, 70(2), 372–80.

Poppe, E. & Linssen, H. (1999). In-group favouritism and the reflection of realistic dimensions of difference between national states in Central and Eastern European nationality stereotypes. *British Journal of Social Psychology*, 38, 85–102.

Reicher, S., Hopkins, N. & Condor, S. (1997). Stereotype construction as a strategy of influence. In R. Spears, P. Oakes, N. Ellemers & S. A. Haslam (eds.),

The social psychology of stereotyping and group life (pp. 94–118). Blackwell: Oxford.

Rutland, A. (1999). The development of national prejudice, in-group favouritism and self-stereotypes in British children. *British Journal of Social Psychology, 38*, 55–70.

Rutland, A. & Cinnirella, M. (2000). Context effects on Scottish national and European self-categorization: The importance of category accessibility, fragility and relations. *British Journal of Social Psychology, 39*, 495–519.

Seago, D. W. (1947). Stereotypes: Before Pearl Harbour and after. *Journal of Social Psychology, 23*, 55–63.

Spears, R., Oakes, P., Ellemers, N. & Haslam S. A. (1997) (eds.), *The social psychology of stereotyping and group life.* Blackwell: Oxford.

Stangor, C. (2000) (ed.), *Stereotypes and prejudice: Essential readings.* Hove, UK: Psychology Press.

Stangor, C. & Lange, J. (1994). Mental representations of social groups: Advances in conceptualizing stereotypes and stereotyping. *Advances in Experimental Social Psychology, 26*, 357–416.

Stangor, C. & Schaller, M. (1996). Stereotypes as individual and collective representations. In C. N. Macrae, C. Stangor & M. Hewstone (eds.), *Stereotypes and stereotyping* (pp. 3–40). New York: Guilford.

Tabachnick, B. G. & Fidell, L. S. (1996). *Using multivariate statistics* (3rd edn.). New York: Harper Collins Publishers.

Turner, J. C. (1987). A self-categorization theory. In J. C. Turner, M. A. Hogg, P. J. Oakes, S. D. Reicher & M. S. Wetherell (eds.), *Rediscovering the social group: A self-categorization theory* (pp. 42–67). Oxford: Blackwell.

Turner, J. C., Hogg, M. A., Oakes, P. J., Reicher, S. D. & Wetherell, M. S. (1987) (eds.), *Rediscovering the social group. A self-categorization theory.* Oxford: Blackwell.

Turner, J. C., Oakes, P. J., Haslam, S. A. & McGarty, C. (1994). Self and collective: Cognition and social context. *Personality and Social Psychology Bulletin, 20*, 454–63.

CHAPTER FIVE

The Design and Analysis of Quasi-experimental Field Research

Eamonn Ferguson & Peter Bibby

This chapter explores some of the issues relating to quasi-experimental research in field settings. Research in the field setting is research conducted outside the constraints of the laboratory and where random allocation to groups is not generally feasible. The chapter discusses a number of issues relating to (1) random allocation, (2) causation, (3) types of quasi-experimental designs and their reliability and validity and (4) types of analytic strategy that can be used with data elicited. The chapter is designed for the student with some experience of using basic social psychology research methods. Nevertheless, it treats the issues involved in field research thoroughly from the most elementary to the more sophisticated. The chapter reviews some issues introduced in chapter 2 with a different gloss and development. It also introduces the student to some more recent advances in statistical techniques (e.g. SEM).

Approaches, Randomization and Causation

There are a number of investigative strategies that the researcher can adopt when conducting research (see Dane, 1990). First, descriptive studies tell us what is happening, where and when, to whom, or by whom. Second, it is possible to ask questions about covariation. That is, as one variable changes (gets bigger or smaller) does a second variable change in some proportional manner (also get bigger or smaller)? Finally, it is possible to ask questions about causality.

Experiments are designed in an attempt both to show causality (X causes Y) and provide an explanation of the results. The philosopher David Hume is credited with one of the more detailed early expositions of causality. Based on a set of general principles Hume's basic ideas are that X (the cause) temporally precedes Y (the effect), and that X and Y must meet at some point in time and space. An X leads to a particular Y; however, if a number of Xs lead to a single Y then these Xs have something in common.

Within psychology the analysis of variance (ANOVA) style experiment is the classic technique for demonstrating causality experimentally. Here levels of one or two independent variables are varied and their independent (main effects) and conjoint (interactive) effects observed with respect to some outcome measure (dependent variable or DV). This approach is derived from John Stuart Mill's *joint method*: 'If X then Y' and 'If not-X then not-Y'. However, the method is an example of *concomitant variation* [Y = F(X): that is, Y varies as a function of X]. That is, in many experimental studies there is no temporal sequence of events, rather the researcher is making statements pertaining to concomitant variation. Therefore, the experimental method shows that the presence of a variable is an important sufficient but not necessary cause of variation in a DV.

While simple causal prediction is important, real advances come when causal prediction is supplemented with explanation. Manicas and Secord (1983) argue that the causal properties of variables under exploration are important for aiding explanation. They use the example of salt (NaCl) dissolving in water (H_2O). Understanding the chemical structure of both salt and water provides an explanation of the causal relation. This means that one must have a precise theory about the causal properties of the objects under consideration.

An important distinction in this context is between *open* and *closed* systems. The salt and water system is reasonably closed, allowing prediction. Field research generally operates in *open* systems. Therefore, we cannot talk about cause *per se*, rather we must work within a *probabilistic* framework. Experiments allow a degree of closure to be placed on the system that is to be investigated. Manicas and Secord (1983) argue that under conditions of *closure* explanation and prediction (causation) can be equivalent. That is, in an open system (field studies) we may be in a position to explain (if the causal properties are known) but not in a position to predict accurately (as other explanations cannot be ruled out: see subsection on 'Internal reliability' below; cf. Lipsey & Cordray, 2000).

One implication is that theory and data from a number of levels of analysis (e.g. physiological, ontological, psychological, anthropological, sociological, neurological) are needed if explanation is desired. Thus to make predictions and explain how a stress management programme works it is necessary to understand and assess behavioural change from physiological (neuro-immunology), cognitive (stress appraisals), behavioural (coping), social (inter-actions and support), economic (company resources), organizational (company support) and political (government initiatives) points of view. Within each of these 'levels' the important causal properties need to be identified and their interacting mechanism studied. However, this does not mean disciplines like psychology can be reduced to biology or physics as the subject matter is different, in the same way that biology cannot be reduced primarily to chemistry (see Manicas & Secord, 1983).

One main problem with field work then is getting a degree of closure and ruling out as many alternative explanations as possible. One major way that this is achieved in experimental work is through the use of *random allocation to groups*. That is, each potential participant has an equal chance of being placed in any condition. Randomization may be achieved in a number of ways (see Roberts & Torgerson, 1998). First, there is *simple randomization*, where participants are allocated on the toss of a coin or using random number tables. This can lead to groups that are unequal in sample size. Second, *block randomization* may be used, and this has the advantage of producing more equal sample sizes. Here two conditions (A & B) may be expressed in blocks of four (e.g. AABB, ABAB). This produces six blocks of four. One block of six is selected at random and four participants, selected at random, are assigned to that sequence. Then another block of four is selected at random and so on. A third approach is termed *stratified randomization*. Here a set of individual characteristics that are believed to have an important influence on the outcomes (e.g. personality, health status) are identified and separate randomization lists drawn up using block randomization. When considering public health campaigns or training interventions randomization usually occurs at the group rather than the individual level (see Roberts & Sibbald, 1998). The main issue here is that clusters of individuals within groups may systematically vary as a function of the groups (group level randomization cannot control for individual level variability). In such cases special analytic strategies known as multi-level modelling are required (see below).

It is random allocation that is the main demarcation between experiments and quasi-experiments. The important fact is that due to lack of random allocation there is no guarantee that groups are equivalent:

they are *non-equivalent* with respect to their membership. This presents a number of important issues for the reliability and validity of both measures and experimental design. These are discussed in the next section.

Reliability and Validity

Whenever research is conducted the onus on the researcher is to make sure that the research is both reliable and valid. Reliability is concerned with the extent to which the measures taken can be reproduced. Issues of validity focus on the extent to which a given finding can be said to show what it is claimed to show. Neither of these issues are simple and both have important ramifications for the design of studies.

Reliability is the cornerstone of validity. Without being able to establish that the measures we take of people's behaviour are reliable it is impossible to argue that these measures show what it is that they purport to show. The notion of validity is based on the idea that a measure really does measure what we say it measures each time it is used.

TEST–RETEST RELIABILITY

Whenever a participant in the research study is given a psychological test or a questionnaire it is important to understand the reliability of that measure. A simple example of a reliable measuring instrument is a set of kitchen scales. When an ingredient for a recipe is weighed we expect that the scales will be accurate and we will obtain the quantity we require. We also expect that the next time we follow the recipe the scales will give us the same amount of that ingredient when we weigh it. This is an example of test–retest reliability. We will only trust the scales if we believe that every time we use them to measure a particular quantity they give us the same quantity. The scales can be said to have test–retest reliability if over time measurement of quantity is stable.

Psychological tests and questionnaires rarely have the level of accuracy that we have come to expect of kitchen scales. There is nearly always some fluctuation in the scores we obtain from participants when we measure them several times. The simplest way to establish a measure's test–retest reliability is to administer the measure to a group of participants and administer it again later. The correlation between the two sets of scores obtained provides an accurate representation of the test–retest reliability. A large positive correlation usually indicates a high level of test–retest reliability. A smaller correlation coefficient often suggests a lower level of test–retest reliability.

Unfortunately, a high correlation over time does not always indicate good test–retest reliability and a low correlation does not guarantee low test–retest reliability. Participants who complete questionnaires twice may well be able to remember what they did the first time they completed the questionnaire and try to use their memory to guide their responses on the second time. If the interval between the two times a measure is administered is too short the correlation that measures the test–retest reliability may be artificially inflated by the effect of memory. Thus a high correlation may not indicate high test–retest reliability. A low correlation has a similar, but different, temporal problem. For at least some measures we would expect participants' responses to change over time. For example, measures of state anxiety are likely to vary from time to time. This reflects not only a temporal component but also a situational effect, that is, different situations are likely to lead to different responses to a measure of anxiety. To estimate the test–retest reliability of a state measure such as anxiety, participants should be tested in identical situations at time one and time two. The American Psychological Association insists that for psychological tests the user's manuals should specify the most favourable time period between measurements to maintain high test–retest reliability. Further, it is recommended that the users should be informed about what kinds of actual changes in participants' lives can be expected to impact on the test–retest reliability.

INTER-RATER RELIABILITY

A second kind of reliability is inter-rater reliability. For some kinds of research administering psychological tests or questionnaires is not appropriate. Instead two or more judges may be asked to rate a behaviour. For example, judges may be shown a number of video clips of children playing and asked to rate the extent to which they thought the children were cooperating in their play or playing independently. The amount of agreement between the judges is an indication of the inter-rater reliability.

Regrettably, percentage agreement as a measure of inter-rater reliability can lead to problems of interpretation. Percentage agreement as a measure of inter-rater reliability can in some situations confound accuracy and variability (Cohen, 1960). For example, Table 5.1 shows the results of two judges rating children for independent and

Table 5.1   Two cases of 90% agreement

Set 1		

Judge A		
Judge B	Independent	Cooperative
Independent	18	1
Cooperative	1	0
90% agreement between judges A & B		

Set 2		

Judge C		
Judge D	Independent	Cooperative
Independent	9	1
Cooperative	1	9
90% agreement between judges C & D		

cooperative play in one set (Set 1) of video clips and a second pair rating children for a second set (Set 2) of video clips.

For both Set 1 and Set 2 there is 90 per cent agreement between the judges, which would seem to indicate a high degree of inter-rater reliability. However, in Set 1 there is very little variability judged in the video clips. It could be the case that judges A & B would not have achieved such a high percentage agreement if there had been more variability in the video clips. A second issue that arises with percentage agreement is that it does not take account of chance factors. Cohen (1960) developed a statistic, κ, kappa, that takes into accounts variations due to chance.

At the same time as percentage agreement leads to problems if not examined carefully, simply correlating the scores of the judges can also lead to misinterpretations. A correlation coefficient has a different kind of problem when compared to percentage agreement. Two judges may correlate highly but one set of scores could be substantially lower in value than the other set of scores. In this case the judges do not agree except in terms of ranks.

INTERNAL CONSISTENCY RELIABILITY

The final kind of reliability considered here is internal consistency reliability (also known as reliability of components, Rosenthal &

Rosnow, 1991). When there are several items on a questionnaire or a scale within a questionnaire it is important to establish that those items are consistent with respect to each other. A number of approaches have been taken to establishing that test items have internal consistency. The Spearman–Brown procedure uses the inter-correlations among the items on test based on Pearson's *r*. An alternative is the Kuder–Richardson formula 20 (KR-20) which is used when the items are scored dichotomously. Perhaps the most popular assessment of internal consistency reliability is Cronbach's alpha statistic. This statistic is based on splitting the data in half and calculating the correlation between the two halves for all possible divisions of the data. Kline (1986) points out that if we wish to claim that a scale has internal consistency reliability then we should never accept an alpha coefficient less than 0.7. However, it must be noted that a high alpha does not imply that a scale is unidimensional (see John & Benet-Martinez, 2000 for a fuller analysis of psychometric measurement issues). Application of factor analytic techniques (see Ferguson & Cox, 1993), may still be applied to explore a scale's dimensionality.

INTERNAL VALIDITY

According to Cook and Shadish (1994), Campbell's (1957) exposition of internal validity has been regularly misunderstood. Campbell used the term *internal validity* to refer to the extent to which the relationship between two variables was causal in the specific situation(s) that had been tested to date.

To claim that there really is a causal relationship between two variables it is necessary to be convinced that those variables have been adequately operationalized. In a study that looks at the impact of stress reduction on absenteeism in the workplace we can define what stress reduction is, but that is only the first step. It is essential to further specify the complete procedure that will achieve the goal of reducing stress. It is this complete procedure that serves as the operational definition of stress reduction. At the same time, absenteeism is not a straightforward concept. People can be away from work for a wide variety of reasons that may have nothing to do with stress, such as going on a training course or having to take time off to look after a sick child. Again the definition of absenteeism has to be operationalized in such a way as to reflect the expected impact of reducing stress; for example, absenteeism due to training course or family commitments need to be excluded from the measure.

Once variables have been operationalized it is possible to consider in detail whether there is sufficient reason to believe that any observed relationship between variables is indeed causal. Campbell (1957) did not intend that theoretically based statements about causality should be included in this process of identification. Rather the intention was simply to assess whether in the particular research circumstances it is possible to state that the observed relationship between two variables reflects cause and effect irrespective of any specific theoretical claims made about those cause and effect relationships. The aim of maintaining internal validity is to rule out any extraneous variables that may account for the findings.

THREATS TO INTERNAL VALIDITY

Cook and Campbell (1979), in their book on quasi-experimental designs, have detailed a number of problems that can reduce the internal validity of a research study. The following provides a short introduction to some of the issues they discuss. For a more extended discussion it is worth taking the time to read Cook and Campbell's book. Of the threats to validity listed below all are handled by appropriate randomization procedures, with the exception of diffusion of treatment effects. While randomization is powerful it is not a panacea and does not always protect the research from alternative explanations.

Attrition

Often in a field study participants can be lost for a variety of different reasons. For example, someone may be present at pre-test but on holiday at the post-test; others may decide to drop out through lack of interest; some participants may become ill or, in some cases, die. Usually it would be expected that this participant attrition would be evenly distributed across treatment groups. In this case there is no problem. However, it could be the case that one treatment group shows an abnormally high attrition rate in comparison to other groups. In designing a study we have to be careful not to accidentally create situations or use methods that lead to differential attrition.

Diffusion of treatment

When participants in a study work or live in close proximity it is likely that they will talk to each other. Part of their conversation may well be to discuss the research that is being conducted. This may impact on how a treatment works. For example, participants in the experimental group may talk to a control group about the experimental procedure. If the experimental procedure involves giving one group information and not giving the control group this information then this kind of interaction between participants could reduce the expected differences between the treatment and control groups. Therefore, even randomization does not control for this threat to internal validity. One way suggested to help to guard against diffusion effects, even for randomized designs, to is try to have units in the design that are temporally or geographically isolated (see West, Biesanz & Pitts, 2000).

History

During the course of a study (e.g. an intervention or longitudinal study) events can occur that the experimenter did not anticipate, and these could have an affect on the outcome of the research. A company could introduce a new workplace policy or the government could issue edicts about how teaching should take place in the classroom. Both may well change the way people respond during a study. In a pre-test/post-test design intruding environmental changes are most likely to occur when there is a longer delay between pre-test and post-test.

Instrumentation

Studies based on using observers to measure participants' behaviour are particularly prone to instrumentation effects. If exactly the same test is used at pre-test and at post-test we would know that the measuring instrument has not changed. However, if an observer is asked to judge some behaviour at pre-test and post-test it is quite possible that their experience of judging behaviour at pre-test changes the way that they conduct their observations at post-test.

Maturation

In research with children maturation is a particular problem. As children grow older they may become bigger, stronger, more sophisticated, more skilled, more co-ordinated and so on. Any of these *natural* changes could impact on the research findings. However, maturation does not simply refer to growing up; it also covers any predictable systemic effects that can change over the course of a study. For example, diseases such as multiple sclerosis show progressive changes that need to be taken into account when designing the study.

Regression to the mean

Regression to the mean occurs when we sample at both ends of a continuum. For example, we might look at people who have scored high on some measure of state anxiety and compare them against a group of participants who give very low scores. In a study where these participants are measured twice it is likely that high scores will fall and low scores will rise. They have nowhere else to go. Regression to the mean occurs whenever participants are selected because their scores are extreme, and reflects the tendency for those scores to be less extreme when participants are retested. During the course of a study extreme scores tend to move closer to the overall mean.

Sequencing

In any within-subjects design there is always the risk that as participants perform different tasks the order in which those different tasks are presented could have an impact on the outcome of the research. It could be that a particular sequence of tasks artefactually inflates or deflates subjects' performance. In general, sequencing effects can be controlled for by having more than one order of presentation of tasks or procedures.

Testing

An issue that is not dissimilar to sequencing is testing. In general repeated presentation of the same measuring instrument may lead to an increase in performance due to the participant learning about the instrument. This is particularly important when skill or knowledge are being assessed. This kind of practice effect can be overcome by designing two or more measuring instruments that reliably measure the same level of performance.

STATISTICAL CONCLUSION VALIDITY

Cook and Campbell (1979) pointed out that implicit in the notion of internal validity is that there is a causal relationship between two variables. Generally, for a relationship to be said to be causal it is necessary to demonstrate the presence of the relationship first.

Commonly, statistical procedures are used to assess whether a relationship exists between two variables. Statistical conclusion validity refers to the extent that the statistical methods used to assess the relationship are appropriate to the task given the variables being considered. One threat to statistical conclusion validity is the extent to which the collected data matches the assumptions of the statistical procedure to be employed. A second threat to statistical validity includes the reliability of the measures of the variables. A third threat to statistical conclusion validity reflects data 'fishing' (i.e. searching for statistically significant results in an atheoretical manner). Whenever there are a large number of possible statistical procedures available for analysing data the researcher should choose the most appropriate method and stick to it.

EXTERNAL VALIDITY

Campbell (1957) defines external validity as the extent to which a causal relationship can be generalized across different populations of participants, different times or eras, different ways of operationalizing the variables and different research or environmental settings.

It is completely reasonable to assume that a causal relationship between two variables only shows itself in a specific population, at a particular time, and in a precise environment. Such a study would lack external validity. However, Mook (1983, see also Mook, 2001) argues that we should be careful that the conclusions we might want to draw from a study are 'externally invalid'. He states:

> Many psychological investigations are accused of 'failure to generalize to the real world' because of sample bias or artificiality of settings. . . . Rather than making predictions about the real world from the laboratory, we may test predictions that specify what ought to happen in the lab. We may even regard 'artificial' findings as interesting because they show what can occur, even if it rarely does. . . . A misplaced preoccupation with external validity can lead us to dismiss good research for which generalization to real life is not intended or meaningful. (Mook, 1983, p. 379)

Generally, we should be careful in considering what kinds of generalizations we might wish to make. As Mook argues, external validity is really a question, not a criterion. It may be that a specific cause–effect relationship does not generalize to many circumstances, but that does not make it uninteresting.

While being careful about not being overly conservative about external validity that does not mean we should throw the baby out with the bath water. It may be interesting to know that stress reduction reduces workplace absenteeism in nurses for example, but if it does not apply to any other population then it is reasonable to question the external validity of that finding. It also means that any general statements we wish to make about real world implications of the finding are necessarily restricted.

CONSTRUCT VALIDITY

Construct validity involves establishing the extent to which the operationalized variables generalize to the theoretical cause and effect constructs that they are meant to represent. In other words, are the measures taken really measures of the theoretical concepts that they are supposed to measure? Campbell and Fiske (1959) attempted to statistically formalize this idea by separating construct validity into two components, convergence and divergence. Convergent validity is the extent to which a measure is highly correlated with other measures that purport to measure the particular theoretical construct. For example, if someone was developing a new questionnaire to measure extroversion it would have convergent validity if this new measure was highly correlated with a different, well-established measure of extroversion. Divergent (or discriminant) validity is based on the extent to which a measure is not correlated to other established measures that are known not to correlate with the theoretical construct being studied.

The following section describes some of the main experimental and quasi-experimental designs that can be used to try to establish well-founded statements about the relationship between causes and effects, given the issues of reliability and validity described above.

Research Design

Random allocation to groups allows the researcher to discount certain threats to the internal validity of experiments. These include (1) history effects, (2) statistical regression to the mean, and (3) attrition. It does not control for diffusion of treatment effects. When conducting field research the researcher is still interested in making causal statements and trying to explain the phenomena under study. Therefore, the ingenuity of the researcher in designing the appropriate controls to rule out alternative explanations is important (see Cook & Shadish, 1994). While a variety of statistical procedures, such as analysis of covariance (ANCOVA), can be used to deal with non-equivalences, solutions based on good design should always override statistical corrections. Two main classes of quasi-experiment are described: (1) interrupted times series designs (ITSDs) and (2) regression discontinuity designs.

INTERRUPTED TIMES SERIES DESIGNS (ITSDs)

For an ITSD the outcome variable (denoted with O) is observed at numerous occasions over time and the effect of an intervention (denoted with X) is observed on the pattern within the data. The simple example adapted from Rosenthal and Rosnow (1991, p. 95) below should serve to illustrate this point.

Example 1: Simple ITSD

									Nature of the results
O	O	O	O	X	O	O	O	O	
3	3	3	3		3	3	3	3	No change
3	3	3	3		4	5	6	7	Upward drift
3	3	3	3		4	4	4	4	Upward constant
3	3	3	3		4	5	5	6	Gradually upwards
3	3	3	3		3	6	3	3	Pulse function

In the above example there are four measurement points prior to an intervention (X) and four after it. The first possibility shows no change in the pattern. The second possibility shows that, after the intervention, scores on the time series goes up at each measurement point and continue to rise steadily. In the third case there is an increase post-intervention and this remains constant. In the fourth possibility there is a gradual increase (less steep than possibility 2). Finally there is a pulse function, where no initial change is followed by a dramatic change and then a return to base level. The important point to take away from this is that ITSDs allow the researcher to explore the full nature of how X influences O. If multiple time points were not considered, and just one point in the post-intervention period, then the 'no change' and 'pulse functions' would be indistinguishable as would 'upward drift', 'gradual upward' and 'upward constant'. At two post-intervention points 'gradual upwards' and 'upwards drift' are indistinguishable. This highlights the importance of ITSDs to help tease out immediate, delay and constant effects of interventions. It may also be the case, although not illustrated above, that the intervention is detrimental, moving scores down to 2 or 1 after an initial improvement. Again multiple assessments help to tease these effects out. Similarly, it is important to have many pre-intervention assessments to identify trends.

History effects may be problematic with this simple pre–post design. To try to rule these out additional time series should be considered (see example 2).

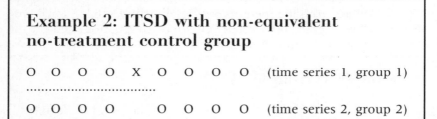

Example 2: ITSD with non-equivalent no-treatment control group

O O O O X O O O O (time series 1, group 1)

O O O O O O O O (time series 2, group 2)

In this case an additional time series is considered, but no intervention is introduced. The dotted line (.....) indicates that the two time series are from different non-equivalent groups. For example, the intervention introduced into the first group might be educational resources in one school, whereas another school has no intervention. Alternatively it might be a stress management programme introduced into one organization but not another. In terms of an educational intervention it might be expected that, in the post intervention period, an upward drift is seen in group 1 and no change in group 2.

An additional design is shown in example 3.

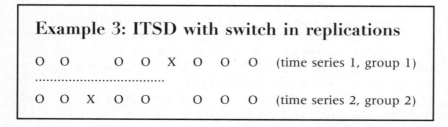

Example 3: ITSD with switch in replications

O O O O X O O O (time series 1, group 1)

O O X O O O O O (time series 2, group 2)

In this case the intervention introduced in group 2 is, at a later stage introduced to group 1. It would be predicted that the changes seen in group 2 are replicated when the intervention is introduced to group 1. This then helps to indicate that the intervention has some causal role in relation to the outcome and it is not just a function of some group non-equivalence.

REGRESSION DISCONTINUITY

In regression discontinuity designs, participants are assigned to treatments on the basis of a quantitative assignment variable (see West, Biesanz & Pitts, 2000). For example, scores on a measure of occupational stress may be used to divide a sample into those with high or low stress levels (this is a quantitative assignment variable). Following this those who report high levels of current stress are placed on the stress management programme and those that do not are not (see Figure 5.1). The question then is 'Does the stress management programme in some way influence the level of reported future stress?' The analytic strategy is to plot the regression slope between the current level of stress and the level of stress recorded at some future time point for those in the no training group and those in the training group.

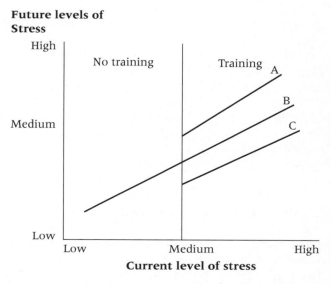

Figure 5.1 A graphical representation of the different possible outcomes of a regression discontinuity design

If the regression line in the training group is a continuation of the line plotted for the no training group (line B) then there is no additional discernible effect of training over what would be expected from a simple regression. However if the slope shows a discontinuity, as in lines A and C, then a discernible effect for training is shown, that is, there is a deviation in the slope from that which would be expected if no intervention occurred. Line A shows that the training programme was actually detrimental, maybe by raising unnecessary fears. Line C shows that the training programme had some beneficial effects, in that the level, but not the magnitude, of the slope is shifted downwards (see Campbell, 1979 for more examples). Similar sorts of regression analyses can be applied when groups are split on a quantitative assignment variable, but when no intervention is introduced (see e.g. Ferguson & Bibby, 2002). West et al. (2000) provide more detail on the application of regression analyses to this type of design.

SEMI-EXPERIMENTS

Vaught (1977) introduced the concept of the semi-experiment. A semi-experiment is a halfway house between true experiments and quasi-experiments. The basic idea behind the design of semi-experiments is *randomization after assignment*. Suppose we wanted to compare (1) drug therapy, (2) psychoanalysis and (3) cognitive behavioural therapy for depression. The principle steps for conducting a semi-experiment are as follows. We have three groups G1 (Drug therapy), G2 (Psychoanalysis) & G3 (Cognitive behavioural therapy). It may not be possible to randomly allocate people to the three groups. For example subjects assigned to G1 may adversely react with the drugs and so they could be re-assigned to G2 and G3. For others their GP may not want to refer them for psychotherapy and so on. Once all groups have been assigned they are then randomly allocated into a control and experimental (i.e. randomization after assignment) groups.

RANDOMIZED FIELD STUDIES

While some of the issues pertaining to randomization have been discussed above, it is worth considering the possibilities of doing randomized field studies. Within the medical sciences randomized control trials (RCTs) are widely used. Cook and Shadish (1994) suggest that randomized field studies are possible when supply exceeds demand. One way they suggest of achieving this is to advertise the study. However, such advertising will have the drawback of creating diffusion of treatment effects. Furthermore, random allocation should be conducted by an independent research service. If professionals, particularly if they have a vested interest, conduct the randomization, they may include people in the treatment group who they think will 'benefit'. Also those in treatment or placebo conditions may seek other treatments. The quality of a social intervention (e.g. is the training programme always delivered to the same standard?) may also affect results. Lipsey and Cordray (2000) refer to these quality issues and others as within-programme variations that can influence the nature of the outcome of an intervention. Other within-programme issues they discuss include people attaining services externally to the intervention and how well individuals engage with a service. They argue that these effects apply equally to control groups and measures of within-programme variation should be assessed as a way of helping to interpret any outcome results. All of these issues (some of which apply equally to ITSDs such as quality control, seeking alternative treatments), as well as ethical issues surrounding RCTs, make truly random field studies difficult but not impossible.

The following section discusses some of the statistical procedures that can be used to analyse the above designs.

Multivariate Statistical Techniques for Analysing Field Studies

For most field studies it is rare to consider single independent variables (IVs) and single dependent variables (DVs). More often than not there will be multiple variables either of one kind or the other or both. This section will consider the three most commonly used techniques for analysing data when there are either multiple IVs or multiple DVs.

Questions commonly asked by researchers in the field concern the degree of relationship between variables, the differences between groups of participants or the prediction of group membership. Table 5.2 shows four commonly used techniques that can help researchers explore these kinds of issues.

For the purposes of this chapter we will not be considering ANOVA since it is such a commonly used technique covered in numerous introductory methods texts. Instead we will be focusing on the multivariate techniques of multiple linear regression, multivariate analysis of variance and discriminant functions analysis. Detailed introductions

Table 5.2   Common research questions and their associated statistical techniques with respect to the number of DVs, IVs and covariates (extraneous variables)

Question	DVs	IVs	Covariates	Technique
Is there are relationship between measured variables?	One	More than one	None	Simultaneous linear regression
	One	More than one	Some	Hierarchical regression
Are there differences between groups of participants	One	One or more	None	ANOVA
			Some	ANCOVA
	More than one	One or more	None	MANOVA
			Some	MANCOVA
Can group membership be predicted?	One	One or more		Discriminant functions analysis

to each of these techniques can be found in Tabachnick and Fidell (1996), alongside a number of other multivariate techniques.

MULTIPLE LINEAR REGRESSION

Multiple linear regression (MLR) is not a single statistical technique but rather a set of techniques that assist researchers when asking questions about the nature and degree of relationship between a single DV and multiple IVs. For example, a researcher may want to know what factors are related to performance on tests of academic ability. Motivation, effort and anxiety may all be related to how well somebody does on a particular test. MLR works by assuming that there is a straightforward relationship between the IVs and the DV:

$$Y' = B_0 + B_1X_1 + B_2X_2 + B_3X_3 + \ldots B_nX_n \qquad [5.1]$$

Y' is the predicted value of the DV, B_0 is the intercept (the value of the DV when all the IVs are zero) and the Bs are the coefficients associated with the IVs. These coefficients specify the best fitting linear relationship between the DV and the IVs.

For the example of test performance this equation becomes:

$$\text{Predicted test performance} = B_0 + B_1(\text{Motivation}) + B_2(\text{Effort}) + B_3(\text{Anxiety}) \quad [5.2]$$

It is possible using MLR to ask a number of general and specific questions about the relationship between the IVs and the DV. First, we can ask: how good is the regression equation overall? Does it provide a good fit to the data that has been observed? Second, having identified whether a fit is better than chance, what is the degree of fit? What proportion of variability in the DV scores can be accounted for by the regression equation? Third, having obtained an overall picture of the relationship between the regression equation and the DV we can ask which of the IVs are most important. Are all the IVs significantly contributing to the overall relationship? What are the individual relationships between the IVs and the DV? How strong are these relationships?

The overall test of the regression equation examines the statistical significance of the multiple R. The multiple R is the correlation between the predicted and observed values of the DV. When this correlation is significant there is a non-zero fit to the data. A second important statistic is the multiple R^2. This is the proportion of variability in the DV that is explained by the regression equation. It is quite common for the multiple R to be statistically significant while the proportion of variability accounted for is quite small, for example $R = .3$, $R^2 = 0.09$ (9% of the variance).

The next step is to examine the IVs one at a time. Each IV can have a zero or non-zero relationship with the DV. For example, test performance might be predicted by Equation 5.2; however, the B coefficient associated with anxiety could be not greater than zero, whereas the other two are. In this case, it may be possible to argue that while motivation and effort are important predictors of test performance, anxiety is not. A second feature of the B coefficient is that it tells us the nature of the relationship between an IV and the DV. If the B coefficient has a positive value then there is a positive relationship between the IV and the DV. Similarly if B is negative there is a negative relationship.

A distinction is made when using MLR between three different types of regression procedure: simultaneous (or standard), hierarchical (or sequential) and stepwise (or statistical). In simultaneous MLR all the independent variables are entered into the regression equation at the same time. This allows the researcher to ask questions about the relative contributions of the different IVs to the DV when the pattern of correlations between the IVs have been taken into account.

Sometimes a specific IV may have an apparently small relationship with the DV when entered into the regression equation but a large correlation with the DV when examined in isolation from the other IVs. In this circumstance the researcher has to be careful to interpret correctly the unique and shared variability that is accounted for by this IV.

Hierarchical regression allows the researcher to enter IVs into the regression equation in a pre-specified order. Each IV is then assessed in relation to the contribution it makes to the regression equation at the point at which it is entered. This method requires the researcher to identify an appropriate order of entry into the regression equation. Such an order is usually generated on the basis of logical or theoretical factors. In particular, IVs that are considered to be causally prior are entered into the equation early as are IVs assigned superior theoretical value. Essentially, causally prior or theoretically important IVs act as covariates for less important IVs. This suggests an alternative approach to entering variables into the regression equation. When a potentially confounding or extraneous variable has been identified and measured this can be entered into the regression equation early so that the impact of the theoretically important variables can be assessed appropriately.

Stepwise regression uses statistical criteria to determine the order of entry into the regression equation. This technique is at best controversial and at worst it is used to fish around in the data to try to find effects. It should be avoided whenever possible to reduce the likelihood of threats to statistical construct validity.

MULTIVARIATE ANALYSIS OF VARIANCE (MANOVA)

The next statistical method to be considered examines whether there are differences between groups of participants when more than one DV has been measured. For example, a researcher may be interested in the impact of a particular training schedule on people's working practices. After random allocation of participants to a training group and suitable control groups, and the implementation of the training schedule, participants' recollection of the course, their knowledge of new facts and their ability to follow new procedures could all be measured. Rather than considering each of these DVs separately MANOVA allows the researcher to ask whether the IV has an impact on the DVs in combination.

MANOVA works by constructing a new DV which is a linear combination of the original DVs that maximizes the separation between the different groups of participants. It then examines this new DV to identify differences between the groups. Different linear combinations of the original DVs are constructed for each IV or interaction between IVs in the analysis.

This procedure leads to a number of distinct advantages over the traditional method of ANOVA. First, it avoids the inflation of Type I errors associated with conducting multiple univariate ANOVAs on many DVs. Second, it increases the likelihood of identifying the points at which the IV has an impact, simply because more measures of the IV's potential impact have been taken. Third, it can occasionally identify differences that could not be found by conducting separate ANOVAs.

When 'nuisance' variables have been identified and measured it is relatively straightforward to conduct a MANCOVA (multivariate analysis of covariance) to control statistically for the influence of the covariate on the DV. The addition of the covariate to the analysis can effectively remove noise from the analysis, and adjusts the means of the treatment groups to take account of the relationship between the covariate and the DV. With a known confounding variable this technique can increase the power of the statistical analysis.

DISCRIMINANT FUNCTIONS ANALYSIS

The third question that can be asked by researchers is whether it is possible to predict membership of groups. Discriminant functions analysis (DFA) is a commonly used technique for predicting group membership. It works by assuming that if there are reliable differences in mean scores of different groups on a variety of measures then it will be possible to predict in which group a participant belongs. In effect, it is a reverse of the MANOVA technique but the emphasis is different. It is more like regression analysis than traditional ANOVA methods. One of the major advantages of DFA is that once participants have been classified as belonging to particular groups it is possible to assess the adequacy of that classification.

A researcher may be interested in trying to identify those people who are successful at job interviews and those who are less successful. The researcher may have reason to believe that personality variables are important determinants in who is likely to be offered a job after interview. The researcher could measure these variables and then use them to predict who was offered a job and who was not. DFA is an excellent tool for performing these kinds of analyses.

DFA works by constructing classification functions that are linear combinations of the IVs. The number of classification functions generated depends on the number of groups of participants to be classified and the number of predictor variables. The first classification function maximizes the separation between the groups. A second classification function, if available, then tries to separate the groups still further by taking advantage of associations not captured by the first classification function. This process of constructing more classification functions continues until no more functions are available. Each of the classification functions is tested to establish whether the groups are reliably different along that dimension. It is quite possible that none, some or all of the classification functions are reliable indicators of group membership.

Once the classification functions have been assessed for predictive value, the individual IVs can be examined. The easiest way to identify which IVs are important for each of the discriminant functions is by examining the correlations between the IVs and the discriminant functions. These correlations not only indicate which IVs make a statistically significant contribution to the discriminant functions but also the nature of the relationship.

Having assessed how many discriminant functions are necessary to predict group membership and what IVs are important for making those predictions the next step is to assess the quality of the prediction. There are two basic indicators of quality or prediction: the overall success at predicting group membership and the successful prediction of individuals within a particular group. Table 5.3 shows

Table 5.3   Two examples of 75% success using DFA

	Situation 1	
	Predicted	
Actual	Group A	Group B
Group A	75%	25%
Group B	25%	75%
75% overall success		

	Situation 2	
	Predicted	
Actual	Group A	Group B
Group A	100%	0
Group B	50%	50%
75% overall success		

two example classification outputs for a DFA. In both cases the predictions are equally successful; 75 per cent of the cases are correctly allocated on the basis of the predictions made by the discriminant functions, and this is true for both groups. However, the second case shows that the discriminant function was 100 per cent successful for Group A but only 50 per cent successful for Group B. It is useful to examine these kinds of outputs carefully so that such phenomena are not missed.

Like MLR, DFA can be conducted in one of three ways: simultaneous, hierarchical and stepwise entry of the predictor variables (IVs). The reasons for adopting one method in preference to another are the same as those for MLR.

Recent Developments in Statistical Analysis

In this section three techniques for dealing with ITSDs will be discussed: (1) auto-regressive integrated moving average (ARIMA) models, (2) structural equation modelling (SEM) and (3) multi-level models (MLM).

AUTO-REGRESSIVE INTEGRATED MOVING AVERAGES (ARIMAs)

ITSDs by their nature involve multiple assessments over time. As such, statistical models designed specifically for this type of data are particularly useful for analysing ITSDs. A time series for a simple ITSD (Y_t) may be analysed by comparing the pre-time series (TS pre) with the post-time series (TS post).

$$Y_t = TS\ pre + TS\ post + error \qquad [5.3]$$

Simple regression analysis cannot deal with this type of data as successive errors in the time series will be correlated and ordinary least squares (OLS) regression assumes errors are independent. Therefore, errors and t-values are inflated and there is a major problem for statistical construct validity.

It is often better to think of a time series as being composed of a noise effect (N) and the intervention effect (I). There are three types of noise: (1) *trend*, which is general drift up or down in a series; (2) *seasonality* – a time series may spike every year or six months; and (3) *random error*. Even when effects of trend and seasonality have been modelled there may still be random variation about the mean.

ARIMA models are designed to assess the effect of these sources of noise and the effect of I. That is, they model the stochastic processes that generate the time series. A times series may be described as a series of random variations (or shocks). ARIMA tries to predict these shocks.

An important assumption underlying time series analysis is that of *stationarity*. That is, the means, variances and auto-correlations are invariant under time translations (i.e., auto-correlations depend only on the time lag between observations). This means that if the data is not stationary then it needs to be de-trended (e.g. remove seasonal variations). Once the analyst has chosen the most appropriate ARIMA model (see McDowall, McCleary, Meidinger & Hay, 1987 for the specific details of how this is achieved) the adequacy of that model must be tested. To do this, the residuals (what is left over once the ARIMA model has predicted the sequence) are examined. These should be statistically indistinguishable from white noise (randomness). That is, all that is left after the model has been specified is randomness.

Once an adequate ARIMA model has been identified the analyst can then see what effect an intervention has on that model. Does the ARIMA model change? Do the estimated model parameters change? McDowall et al. (1987) argue that in order to model the effect of an intervention the analyst must have a good theoretical idea of how the intervention will alter the shape of the series. Will it be an upward drift or an upward constant? Knowing which is expected, the effect of the intervention can be realized. West and Hepworth (1991) provide an excellent introduction to time series analysis for psychologists.

STRUCTURAL EQUATION MODELLING (SEM)

Given a pattern of covariance between a set of variables (e.g. self-blame attributions, life stress, neuroticism and depression) structural equation modelling (SEM) allows the researcher to examine a variety of theoretical models that can account for this covariation (see Figure 5.2). A number of points are worth noting from Figure 5.2. First, a correlation matrix with four variables has six pair-wise associations; the theoretical models may specify that fewer associations (three in the first case, four in the second and five in the third, association are depicted by arrows) can account for all the variability within those six associations. For example, Model 2 states that neurotic people are more likely to experience life stress and that both increased levels of

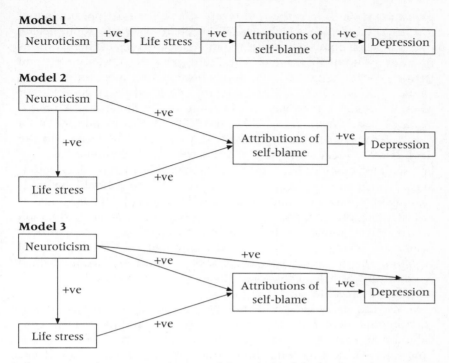

Figure 5.2   Three potential SEMs of the relationships between four variables

life stress and neuroticism produce more attributions of self-blame (e.g. 'it was my fault') and these attributions, but not stress or neuroticism, produce increased level of depression. The second important fact is that the arrows (called paths, partial regression coefficients) do not indicate causality (especially in cross-sectional data). Only with the appropriate design (intervention study, random allocation, appropriate control, longitudinal data etc.) can potential causal statements be entertained (e.g. Ferguson, James, O'Hehir & Sanders, 2003).

To aid the analyst a number of *fit indices* are available which the researcher can use to decide between competing theoretical models. There are a number of fit indices that vary between 0 and 1 with values approaching unity indicating good fit. Some of these are stand-alone indices and others assess the proportion of improved fit between a target model and a baseline model. Some of these coefficients indicate good fit with values close to 1 (e.g. the Tucker–Lewis Index, TLI) and others estimate error with lower values close to zero indicating good fit (e.g. the root mean square error of approximation, RMSEA) (see Bollen and Long, 1993). There has been some debate over the years about which values and combinations of these various fit indices should be taken to indicate good fit. Recently Hu and Bentler (1999) suggested a two-index presentation with, for example, values of the TLI of .95 and the RMSEA of .06 indicating good fit. For example Model 1 may have a TLI value of .86 and RMSEA of .12, Model 2 may have a TLI of .90 and a RMSEA of .08 and Model 3 a TLI of .97 and a RMSEA of .04. Here Model 3 is the best fit to the data. If two models have similar fits a chi-square difference test can be used to distinguish between these models. For each model a stand-alone chi-square statistic can be computed. This should be non-significant, indicating that covariation explained by your model is not significantly different statistically from the original correlation matrix. For example, Model 2 may have a chi-square of 9.3 with 10 degrees of freedom and Model 3 a chi-square of 2.7 with 9 degrees of freedom. The difference here is 6.6 with 1 degree of freedom (which is significant at .01). Therefore, Model 3 is significantly better fit to the data than Model 2.

SEMs can be used in a number of ways to analyse quasi-experimental data. First, they can be used to model the relative contribution of extraneous variables (see Loehlin, 1987). For instance, how effective is a training intervention when previous experience, demographics and so on are included in a model? Second, SEMs can be used to see how the direction or strength of paths change as a function of an intervention (see Ferguson, Dodds, Craig, Flannigan & Yates, 1994). Third, SEMs can be used to model the temporal relations in a data set. Finally, SEMs can be used to compare groups who receive different interventions to see if the pattern within the data is the same and if not where the differences lie. These four possibilities are not mutually exclusive.

MULTILEVEL MODELLING (MLM)

Data to be analysed in field studies is very often hierarchical in nature (see Figure 5.3). For example, a two-level data hierarchy may have daily records of stress and coping (level 1) nested within person (level 2). A three-level hierarchy may have daily records of stress and coping (level 1) nested within person (level 2) which in turn are nested within organizations (level 3).

The kinds of regression techniques we have already discussed cannot cope statistically with such data structures. Therefore, a statistical

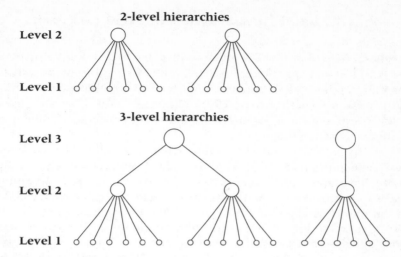

Figure 5.3   Hierarchical data structures

approach known as MLM has been developed specifically to deal with such data structures (see Raudenbush & Bryk, 2002; Snijders & Bosker, 1999). Within MLM the outcome at one level of analysis (slopes and intercepts) become the variables to be predicted by variables at the next level. For example, the researcher may wish to explore how daily coping relates to daily negative mood (i.e. the regression slope between these level 1 variables). Furthermore, the researcher wants to know how these slope are affected by personality (a level 2 variable). Thus scores on personality are used to predict the regression slopes from level 1. Level 1 effects may be seen as fixed (constant across persons) or random (varying from person to person). Level 2 variables may include other person factors (e.g. did or did not receive training, age, gender). Level 3 variables, in this case, may be public or private sector organizations, profit made each year, and so on. MLM may also be used to conducted meta-analyses with effects sizes coefficients at level 1 and moderators at level 2 (Ferguson, James, Maddeley, 2002). MLM is a very important development for the analysis of field studies. For more detailed discussions of MLM and its applications see Affleck, Zautra, Tennen and Armeli (1999), Ferguson (in press), Reis and Gable (2000) and Nezlek (2001).

Having examined a variety of design and analytic strategies we now turn to a number of ethical and practical issues facing those conducting field research.

Practical and Ethical Issues of Field Research

In general there a number of ethical issues that apply to any research. The British Psychological Society (BPS) published a document discussing ethical principles for conducting research with human participants (British Psychological Society, 1995). The main issues that are raised include competence, consent, withholding information, debriefing, withdrawal and confidentiality.

With respect to competence, researchers should reflect on their own competence and not attempt to conduct research for which they do not have appropriate preparation. Informed consent is a central aspect of ethical research. Wherever possible the researcher should inform participants about the objects of the research programme. In particular, investigators should pay attention to informing participants about all those aspects of the research that may influence participation in the research. Sometimes informing participants about the goals of the research may influence the outcome of the research. In those circumstances it may be reasonable to withhold information about the research. It is important in such situations to consult widely – for example, put research plans forward to ethics committees – about the appropriateness of such a procedure prior to conducting the research, and participants should be fully debriefed after the research has been conducted. Debriefing is an essential part of conducting research with human participants. Each participant should be fully informed about the research and have any questions they ask fully answered. Participants are entitled to withdraw from a programme of research at any time during the research. Finally, any information obtained about a participant during a study is confidential unless the participant has given prior consent. It is important, however, to remember that the participant can withdraw that consent at any time during or after the study. (For further details see Lindsay & Colley, 1995; British Psychological Society, 1995).

There are specific ethical issues associated with some of the field research we have discussed. For example, it is unethical to randomly allocate people to high versus low chronic life stress (e.g. carers vs not carers of long-term ill) or to particular job roles. In this case the quasi-experiment is optimal. However, the other major ethical concern pertains to the random allocation to people or groups to interventions. This is particularly the case for randomized control trials (RCT), where one group receives an intervention that might be helpful and the other no intervention (see Sibbland & Roland, 1998). However, the no-intervention group will usually receive the intervention once the RCT has finished.

A major ethical issue in any intervention, be it quasi-experimental or an RCT, is how long the intervention should last (cf. Abrams, 1998). That is, how long is required to identify a benefit and how long after this should the trial continue to ensure that effect is sustainable and genuine? Given all the issues, briefly discussed, it has been argued by some that where major adverse effects are unlikely and that a 'rescue' intervention can be provided if difficulties arise then it is in fact unethical not to do RCT (see Trauma, Reynolds, Moore & McQuay, 1998).

There are also a number of practical issues associated with quasi-experiments and RCTs. Often in organizational research (e.g. evaluation of a training programme) it is hard to convince an organization to pay money for nothing to happen (the control group or groups in a Solomon's 4 groups design) so such controlled trials/intervention are rare. Another practical issue is one of participant preference (see Torgerson & Sibbald, 1998). That is, if participants are aware of an intervention (as may be required with informed consent) they may have a strong preference to be included in the active intervention or control group. Torgerson and Sibbald (1998) describe what they term 'patient preference trials' where given two conditions A and B there are four groups, those randomized to A and B who did not express preference and those in A and B who expressed a preference for either A or B.

We now want to put these issues into practice.

Intervention Research: Some Practice Scenarios

The following section contains three scenarios and a number of questions designed to get you to think more clearly about the issues described above. These scenarios and the ensuing questions can be used to form the basis of a tutorial.

Scenario 1: An intervention to reduce driver error
Consider the following scenario:
Driver error has been implicated in a number of recent 'near miss' incidents (e.g. trains missing warning signals) on a major rail system. You are asked to develop and evaluate a preliminary training programme to alleviate this problem.

Scenario 2: A stress management programme
Consider the following scenario:
An organization has noticed problems with its staff in terms of lateness, absenteeism and general low morale. They believe that stress is the cause and ask you to devise and evaluate a stress management programme.

Scenario 3: A study of teacher satisfaction
Consider the following scenario:
A government agency has asked you to examine current and past levels of teacher satisfaction in the light of changes to government policy over the last 10 years. They believe that changes in policy have differentially impacted teachers of lower and higher rank within the teaching profession. You have been asked to establish the correctness of this hypothesis.

CHECKLIST

For each of the above scenarios use the following checklist to help you to consider what may be the most appropriate design and analytic strategies as well as ethical concerns.

Question	Possible Answers	Reason
What research design is most appropriate?	Randomized field trial Quasi-experiment Semi-experiment Experiment	
What are the most likely threats to internal validity?	Attrition Diffusion of treatment History Instrumentation Maturation Regression to the mean Sequencing Testing	
What other validity concerns are important?	External validity Statistical conclusion validity Construct validity	
What statistical techniques are most appropriate	Multiple linear regression MANOVA Discriminant functions analysis ARIMA Structural equation modelling Hierarchical linear modelling	

Question	Possible Answers	Reason
What ethical considerations are important?	Competence Consent Withholding of information Debriefing Withdrawal Confidentiality	

Notes to the Course Leader

This chapter and the above tutorial activities are designed for second and third year undergraduate students. The authors have not assumed that students have used any of the statistical procedures that we have discussed. Rather, we have provided a brief glimpse of some of the statistical techniques that are available for analysing the kinds of multivariate data often collected in field settings.

We envisage that the materials will be used as the foundation for a tutorial with between six and 15 students. The scenarios and checklist should be used to stimulate discussion about the issues that we have raised in this chapter. It's worth remembering that there is no one right answer for each of the scenarios and that it is possible to consider several different research designs to approach each of the problems.

The basic preparation we would recommend is reading this chapter. For more information on quasi-experimental designs see Campbell (1969) or Cook & Campbell (1979). In our experience there are no gentle introductions to multivariate statistics but Tabachnik and Fidell (1996) provides extensive discussions of the common multivariate methods we have discussed. The ARIMA, HLM and SEM techniques are discussed in a variety of different specialist texts and journal articles. For ARIMA and time series approaches McDowell et al. (1987) and West and Hepworth (1991) are excellent texts; for MLM, Affleck et al. (1999) and Arnold (1992) provide a good introduction for psychologists, as Tabachnick & Fidell (1996) do for SEM.

The following is the above checklist with major considerations for scenario 1 detailed in column 3.

What research design is most appropriate? What other designs might also work?	Randomized field trial Quasi-experiment Semi-experiment Experiment	Pre–post test design with suitable control groups (RCT). The most appropriate design is called a Solomon's 4 groups design (see below)
What are the most likely threats to internal validity? How will these threats impact on the research?	Attrition Diffusion of treatment History Instrumentation Maturation Regression to the mean Sequencing Testing	Attrition, diffusion of treatment, and regression to the mean are the most important threats to internal validity for this scenario. This does not preclude the possibility that the other threats to validity will also have an impact.
What other validity concerns are important? How might you deal with these concerns?	External validity Statistical conclusion validity Construct validity	Correct sampling is required to generalize to the company as a whole. Therefore external validity of the research is an important consideration.
What statistical techniques are most appropriate? What other techniques might be used?	Multiple linear regression MANOVA Discriminant functions analysis ARIMA Structural equation modelling Hierarchical linear modelling	The answer to this question depends on the research design. With the Solomon's 4 groups design ANOVA is the most appropriate statistical analysis. However, a MANOVA may be appropriate if there are multiple DVs.
What ethical considerations are important? Are there any others that might be specific to this scenario?	Competence Consent Withholding of information Debriefing Withdrawal Confidentiality	All the ethical issues listed are important. However, a specific ethical issue for this scenario pertains primarily to safety. Observing behaviour can often change it and the driver may not work as safely as usual. Removing people to go on a training course may mean that trains are not always staffed by the best people.

Table 5.4 The Solomon's 4 group design (adapted from Rosenthal and Rosnow, 1991)

Pre-training measures	Intervention	Post-training assessments
Yes	Yes	Yes
Yes	No	Yes
No	Yes	Yes
No	No	Yes

A Solomon's 4 groups design allows the researcher to explore the effect of assessments made prior to the intervention on the assessments taken after (they have to be the same in both cases).

REFERENCES

Abrams, K. (1998). Monitoring randomised controlled trials. *British Medical Journal, 316*, 1183–4.

Affleck, G., Zautra, A., Tennen, H. & Armeli, S. (1999). Multilevel daily process designs for consulting and clinical psychology: A preface for the perplexed. *Journal of Consulting and Clinical Psychology, 67*, 46–754.

Arnold, C. (1992). An introduction to hierarchical linear models. *Measurement and Evaluation in Counselling and Development, 25*, 58–90.

Bollen, K. A. & Scitt Long, J. (1993). *Testing structural equation models*. London: Sage.

British Psychological Society (1995). Code of conduct. *The Psychologist, 8*, 4452–3.

Campbell, D. (1957). Factors relevant to the validity of experiments in social settings. *Psychological Bulletin, 54*, 297–312.

Campbell, D. (1969). Reforms as experiments. *American Psychologist, 24*, 409–29.

Campbell, D. T. (1979). Reforms as experiments. In J. Bynner and K. M. Stribley (eds.), *Social research: Principles and procedures* (pp. 79–112). Harlow, UK: Longman/Open University Press.

Campbell, D. & Fiske, D. (1959). Convergent and divergent validation by the multitrait-multimethod matrix. *Psychological Bulletin, 56*, 81–105.

Cohen, J. (1960). A coefficient of agreement for nominal scales. *Educational and Psychological Measurement, 20*, 37–46.

Cook, T. & Campbell, D. (1979). *Quasi-experimentation: Design and analysis issues for field settings*. Chicago: Rand-McNally.

Cook, T. & Shadish, W. (1994). Social experiments: Some developments over the past fifteen years. *Annual Review of Psychology, 45*, 545–80.

Dane, F. (1990). *Research methods*. Pacific Grove, CA: Brooks/Cole.

Ferguson, E. (in press). The use of diary methods in clinical and health psychology. In J. Miles and P. Gilbert (eds.), *A handbook of research methods in clinical and health psychology*. Oxford: Oxford University Press.

Ferguson, E. & Bibby, P. A. (2002). Predicting future blood donor returns: Past behavior, intentions and observer effects. *Health Psychology, 21*, 513–18.

Ferguson, E. & Cox, T. (1993). Exploratory factor analysis: A users guide. *International Journal of Selection and Assessment, 1*, 84–94.

Ferguson, E., Dodds, A., Craig, D., Flannigan, H. & Yates, L. (1994). The changing face of adjustment to sight loss: A longitudinal evaluation of rehabilitation. *Journal of Social Behavior and Personality, 9*, 287–306.

Ferguson, E., James, D. & Maddeley, L. (2002). Factors associated with success in medical school: Systematic review of the literature. *British Medical Journal, 324*, 952–7.

Ferguson, E., James, D., O'Hehir, F. & Sanders, A. (2003). A pilot study of the roles of personality, references and personal statements in relation to performance over the 5 years of a medical degree. *British Medical Journal, 326*, 429–31.

Hu, L. & Bentler P. M. (1999). Cutoff criteria for fit indexes in covariance structure analysis: Conventional criteria versus new alternatives. *Structural Equation Modeling, 6*, 1–55.

John O. P. & Benet-Martinez, V. (2000). Measurement: Reliability, construct validation and scale construction. In H. T. Reis and C. M. Judd (eds.), *Handbook of research methods in social and personality psychology* (pp. 339–69). Cambridge, UK: Cambridge University Press.

Kline. P. (1986). *A handbook of test construction: Introduction to psychometric design*. London, Methuen.

Lindsay, G. & Colley, A. (1995). Ethical dilemmas of members of the society. *The Psychologist, 8*, 448–51.

Lipsey, M. W. & Cordray, D. S. (2000). Evaluation methods for social intervention. *Annual Review of Psychology, 51*, 345–75.

Loehlin, J. (1987). *Latent variables models*. Hillside, NJ: Erlbaum.

Manicas, P. & Secord, P. (1983). Implications for psychology of the new philosophy of science. *American Psychologist, 38*, 399–413.

McDowall, D., McCleary, R., Meidinger, E. & Hay, R. (1987). *Interrupted times series analysis*. London: Sage.

Mook, D. (1983). In defense of external invalidity. *American Psychologist, 38*, 379–87.

Mook, D. G. (2001). *Psychological research: The ideas behind the methods*. New York: W. W. Norton.

Nezlek, J. B. (2001). Multilevel random coefficients analyses of event- and interval-contingent data in social and personality psychology research. *Personality and Social Psychology Bulletin, 27*, 771–85.

Raudenbush, S. & Bryk, A. (2002). *Hierarchical linear models: Applications and data analysis methods* (2nd edn.). Newbury Park, CA: Sage.

Reis, H. T. & Gable, S. L. (2000). Event-sampling and other methods of studying everyday experiences. In H. T. Reis and C. M. Judd (eds.), *Handbook* of research methods in social and personality psychology (pp. 190–222). Cambridge. UK: Cambridge University Press.

Roberts, C. & Sibbald, B. (1998). Randomising groups of patients. *British Medical Journal, 316*, 1898.

Roberts, C. & Torgerson, D. (1998). Randomisation methods in controlled trials. *British Medical Journal, 317*, 1301.

Rosenthal, R. & Rosnow, R. (1991). *Essentials of behavioral research: Method and data analysis* (2nd edn.). New York: McGraw-Hill.

Sibbland, B. & Roland, M. (1998). Why are randomised controlled trials important? *British Medical Journal, 316*, 1210.

Snijders, T. & Bosker, R. (1999). *Multilevel analysis: An introduction to basic and advanced multilevel modelling*. London: Sage.

Tabachnick, B. & Fidell, L. (1996). *Using multivariate statistics* (3nd edn). New York: Harper Collins.

Torgerson, D. & Sibbald, B. (1998). What is a patient preference trial? *British Medical Journal, 316*, 360.

Trauma M., Reynolds, D., Moore, A. & McQuay, H. (1998). When placebo controlled trials are essential and equivalence trials are inadequate. *British Medical Journal, 317*, 875–80.

Vaught, R. (1977). What if subjects can't be randomly assigned? *Human Factors, 19*, 227–34.

West, S. G. & Hepworth, J. T. (1991). Statistical issues in the study of temporal data: Daily experiences. *Journal of Personality, 59*, 609–61.

West, S. G., Biesanz, J. C. & Pitts, S. C. (2000). Causal inference and generalization in field settings: Experimental and quasi-experimental designs. In H. T. Reis and C. M. Judd (eds.), *Handbook of research methods in social and personality psychology* (pp. 40–84). Cambridge, UK: Cambridge University Press.

CHAPTER SIX

The Impact of Social Value Orientation on Decision Making in Social Dilemmas: A Survey Exercise

Mark Van Vugt & Richard H. Gramzow[1]

This chapter introduces the basic principles of designing a self-report questionnaire to be used in a survey. It provides guidance on survey sampling issues and employs in the course exercise a quasi-experimental design in a field setting. The aim of the exercise is to examine the impact of social value orientation on decision making in a real-life social dilemma. The specific hypothesis tested is whether cooperators behave more cooperatively (and less competitively) in a social dilemma than do individualists and competitors. To this end, students develop a survey to examine reactions to a naturally occurring dilemma that they choose. They then administer the survey, along with an existing measure of social value orientation, to test this hypothesis. The exercise is appropriate for introductory level students.

Social Dilemmas

Social dilemmas are situations in which there is a conflict between a person's immediate self-interest and the broader interest of the group to which that person belongs (Van Vugt, 1998). Many small-scale inter-personal conflicts, as well as large-scale societal conflicts, share the features of a social dilemma. For managing these conflicts, it is important to understand how individuals approach these problems and how they respond to them. An important predictor of decision making in social dilemmas is an individual's social value orientation (Van Lange, Otten, De Bruin & Joireman, 1997). Social value orientation (SVO) is an individual difference variable that reflects a stable personal preference for how outcomes are distributed to oneself and others (McClintock, 1972). The three most common orientations are cooperation, individualism and competition.

Many of the smaller and larger problems that we face in our lives have the properties of a social dilemma. Let's look at some examples.

1 Melanie and Craig have just started dating each other. On Sundays, when both of them are free from work, Mel likes to take long walks in the country. Mel would prefer Craig to come along. Craig, however, plays football early Sunday morning, and he is usually too tired to go out for a walk afterwards. How do Mel and Craig solve this conflict of interests? If they want to spend some time together on Sundays, one of them will have to make a sacrifice.

2 Anna, a university student, does not have a computer at home. Instead she uses the student computer network room in her department to do her course work. Because there are only a limited number of network computers available, she frequently needs to wait until there is one free. According to departmental rules, each student is only allowed to work one hour per day on a network computer. But Anna has noticed that there are many students who do not obey this rule. Anna is tempted to do the same, but she realizes that that would be quite selfish. What does she do?

3 Nick is deeply concerned about the impact of human activity on the natural environment. He has read some distressing stories in the newspaper about the effects of car use on the environment. He is willing to give up driving his car to work. However, to take a more environmentally desirable option like public transport, he would have to get up 15 minutes earlier each morning. Furthermore, he would have to give up the flexibility and comfort of using his car.

These three stories are all examples of social dilemmas, because they contain a conflict between a person's self-interest (play football on Sundays, infinite use of shared computer, commute by car) and the interests of others or society (go out for a walk, restrict use of shared computers, commute by public transport). Formally, a social dilemma can be defined by the following two properties (Dawes, 1980):

- Each person is individually better off making a competitive or 'selfish' choice than making a cooperative choice;
- If all (or most) individuals choose to be competitive, then everyone is worse off than if they all choose to cooperate.

In Example 1 Craig would be better off if he could play football on Sundays, yet if both he and Melanie insist on their own preferences, they will both be worse off because they are not able to go out together. Similarly, in Example 2 Anna is personally better off not to limit herself in using the shared network computers, but if none of her fellow students cooperate, each of them is worse off. Finally, although Nick in Example 3 is tempted to continue commuting by car, he knows that it could have devastating implications for the environment if everyone acted this way.

The term *social dilemma* is a generic term for a broad class of problems that create strong pressures on individuals and groups. An individual faced with a social dilemma is caught between two competing forces: to act competitively by serving his or her own interests, or to act cooperatively by serving the needs of the group or society. Such dilemmas are also regarded as conflicts between two different definitions of rationality: the rationality of the individual versus the rationality of the collective.

The notion of a social dilemma was first described by Garrett Hardin (1968) in his famous parable of the Tragedy of the Commons in which a number of herdsmen destroy a common pasturage because each of them decides to add an extra animal to their flock. Traditionally, a distinction is made between two classes of social dilemmas: the commons or resource dilemma and the collective action or public goods dilemma (Van Vugt, 1998). The resource dilemma refers to a set of problems that require cooperation to preserve a valuable resource, such as a communal pasturage, rain forest, or a common computer network room. Public good dilemmas are situations which require cooperation in the form of people contributing to creating a valuable good, such as a collective team effort, a community leisure centre, or a national education system.

Another way of classifying social dilemmas is by whether competitive decision making will have an immediate or delayed negative effect on the common interest (Messick & Brewer, 1983). The negative effects of some behaviours, notably the environmentally destructive behaviours (car use, energy use), are dispersed in time. In contrast, the behavioural consequence of not wanting to pay for a taxi after a night out with friends will have an immediate effect on the well-being of the people involved. Hence, it is useful to make a distinction between social dilemmas, on the basis of whether they involve taking (resource) or giving (public good) and whether the effects of these actions are either immediately visible or delayed in time. It is easy to see why the delayed problems are hardest to solve, because people experience the positive effects (taking the car) immediately, whereas the positive effects of cooperation will only be visible in the distant future (the preservation of a rain forest).

Motives Behind Cooperation in Social Dilemmas

In view of the above, it is hard to believe that people would find satisfactory solutions to these social dilemmas. As it stands, there is no incentive to change from a selfish strategy to a cooperative strategy, unless one can be certain that the others involved will cooperate as well. The quest for solutions to social dilemmas has influenced much research in social psychology. Researchers have suggested numerous ways in which cooperation between individuals can be promoted, and many of them have been investigated in laboratory research (for reviews, see Komorita & Parks, 1994; Liebrand, Messick & Wilke, 1992; Van Vugt, Snyder, Tyler & Biel, 2000).

Structurally, cooperation can be promoted by giving incentives for cooperation. In Example 3, Nick might be more tempted to use public transport to get to work if his employer would be willing to refund his travel costs. Or it could be made impossible to act competitively (e.g. no car parking spaces at work).

Cooperation can be promoted by social-psychological factors as well. Allowing communication between individuals dramatically increases their cooperation (Dawes, McTavish & Shaklee, 1977), and so does the creation of a shared group identity (De Cremer & Van Vugt, 1999). Making people accountable for their decisions also helps (Jorgenson & Papciak, 1981), as does making people believe that their individual contributions are critical (Van de Kragt, Orbell, & Dawes, 1983). In Example 3, Nick can be persuaded by a campaign stressing that all contributions to a better environment are relevant.

But there is also evidence to suggest that cooperation in social dilemmas emerges even without such facilitating factors. For example, even in an anonymous laboratory situation (where people interacted with strangers via computers), around 30 per cent of participants donated their money to the group during a social dilemma game, rather than keeping the money for themselves (Dawes et al., 1977). When these people were asked why they cooperated, they often mentioned reasons related to morality (e.g. 'cooperation is clearly more ethical'), fairness (e.g. 'I considered it fair to the group to contribute) and trust (e.g. 'I expected others to do the same').

How can this cooperative behaviour be explained? Looking at these findings, the assumption that all individuals in social dilemmas pursue their immediate self-interest must be relaxed somewhat. Perhaps not all people respond in the same way when they are faced with a social dilemma. Some persons may assign as much weight to the interests of other people as they do to their own interests (or even more). Thus, a characteristically 'selfish' Anna may not be persuaded by the departmental computer distribution rule. However, a characteristically 'cooperative' Anna might accept it because of the benefits that this will have for other students. Hence, there may be stable personality variables that could partially explain why persons differ in the degree of cooperative and competitive behaviour that they exhibit in social dilemmas.

Social Value Orientation

One of the more promising personality variables that could explain differences in behavioural decision making in social dilemmas is social value orientation. Social value orientations refer to stable patterns of preferences for particular outcome distributions between oneself and inter-dependent others (McClintock, 1972; Messick & McClintock, 1976). Theoretically, there are many different value orientations possible, but the accumulating research points to three fundamental orientations: cooperation – maximizing outcomes for oneself and others, while minimizing outcome differences (i.e. equality); individualism – maximizing outcomes for oneself, regardless of those of others; and competition – maximizing outcomes for oneself relative to those of others (Van Lange et al., 1997).

There are several instruments available for measuring social value orientation (Komorita & Parks, 1994). However, the decomposed games measure is probably the simplest, and can be administered easily in a survey study. The decomposed games method has excellent psychometric qualities, such as high internal consistency and high test–retest reliability. Moreover, it does not appear to be affected by social desirability bias. The evidence for the predictive utility of this instrument largely stems from experimental social dilemma research. There is, as yet, limited research into the ecological validity of the decomposed games measure. This exercise is designed to address this gap in the literature.

The decomposed games method consists of nine items (see Appendix 6.1). Each item contains three alternative outcome distributions, with points – representing valuable outcomes – for both oneself and another person who remains anonymous. To limit the influence of accountability or social desirability, it is emphasized to participants that they will not see or meet this person. Each of the three outcome distributions associated with each item represents a particular orientation. Here is an example item:

	Option A	Option B	Option C
Points for self	500	560	500
Points for other	500	300	100

Option A represents the cooperative orientation, because it involves the highest possible joint outcome (500 + 500 = 1,000), compared to Option B (560 + 300 = 860) and Option C (500 + 100 = 600). Option B represents the individualist option, because it contains the highest individual outcome (560), relative to Options A and C (both 500). Finally, Option C reflects a competitive orientation, because it involves the greatest difference between outcomes for self and other (500 − 100 = 400), relative to Option A (500 − 500 = 0) and Option B (560 − 300 = 260).

In a typical study using the decomposed games procedure, each participant is classified into one of three groups (cooperators, individualists or competitors) if at least six out of nine of his or her responses are consistent with that orientation. Usually, this method yields a distribution of orientations similar to the following: cooperators (60%), individualists (25%), competitors (10%) and unclassifiable (5%). The individualist and competitor orientations are frequently combined into a single 'pro-self' orientation. This is because predictions often do not differ for these two orientations, and combining them increases statistical power. The pro-self group is then contrasted with the 'pro-social' group, which consists only of people with a cooperative orientation (De Cremer & Van Vugt, 1999).

Origins of Social Value Orientation

Where do these systematic differences in social value orientation come from? To answer this, we need to take a developmental perspective on these orientations. A recent set of studies conducted in the Netherlands (Van Lange et al., 1997) suggests that social value orientations may be shaped by social interactions in early childhood. When examining relations between social value orientation and attachment style (Bowlby, 1969), it was found that cooperators exhibited greater levels of secure attachment than individualists and competitors. In addition, cooperators exhibited relatively lower levels of avoidant attachment. These researchers argued that the family situation during childhood could partly explain these patterns. On average, cooperators grew up in larger families than individualists and competitors. But the gender of participants' siblings appeared to be more influential than the absolute number of siblings. Cooperators had more sisters, on average, than did individualists and competitors.

The fact that social value orientation is associated with attachment style and family structure does not mean necessarily that these orientations remain stable over a lifetime. For example, in a set of studies that followed American children from nursery school to second grade (McClintock & Moscovitz, 1969), it was found that individualism was the dominant orientation when children were three to four years old. However, by the time these children were six and seven, there was an increase both in cooperative and in competitive orientations. Moreover, this developmental pattern was found across various societies (America, Mexico, Belgium, & Greece), suggesting that this is a universal phenomenon. One explanation for this pattern is that competition and cooperation are more complex orientations than individualism, because they require a higher level of mental ability. For example, in the decomposed game measure, the individualistic option requires people to look simply at their own outcomes, whereas the cooperative and competitive options require people to make a more complex transformation (either by adding or subtracting scores for self and other).

During the transition from early to later adulthood, there is a further shift in orientations. The percentage of cooperators in the population increases over time, whereas the proportion of individualists and competitors decreases. This could indicate that people become more pro-social over time, perhaps because they perceive more of the benefits of cooperation, or because they depend more on others for their help and service.

Finally, you might expect there to be sex differences in the prevalence of different social value orientations. Findings from the available research on this topic are inconsistent. Some research supports the stereotypical view that men are more competitive than women (Van Lange et al., 1997). However, the opposite has been found as well. Some researchers have argued that differences in social value orientation between men and women are culturally specific (Knight & Kagan, 1981). The argument is that, in most cultures, there is more pressure on women to conform to the dominant cultural value. Thus, in individualistic cultures (e.g. the USA), women tend to be more individualistic. However, in collectivistic cultures (e.g. Korea), women tend to be more cooperative than men.

Evidence for Impact of Social Value Orientations

The original research on social value orientations was conducted in the laboratory in an effort to predict choices in the classic Prisoner's Dilemma game. This was followed by research that examined the impact of these orientations within social dilemmas with a greater ecological validity, such as the resource dilemma and the public good dilemma. For example, in a study by Kramer, McClintock & Messick (1986), it was found that participants classified as pro-socials (cooperators) took less from a common resource pool that was depleting than did people classified as pro-selfs (individualists and competitors). These latter participants did not adjust their harvests to a shrinking resource situation, which led the resources to become exhausted.

The role of social value orientation has also been established in the domain of public goods. For example, a set of studies by De Cremer & Van Vugt (1999) showed that pro-social participants were willing to contribute more of their money to provide a common good for their group – an extra financial reward – than were pro-self participants.

A possible explanation for these results is that cooperators, relative to individualists and competitors, assign greater weight to the outcomes for the group. However, it is also possible that individualists and competitors simply have less trust in the cooperative tendencies of others. Because they do not want to run the risk of being exploited by other group members, they choose what appears to be the safest option, which is not to cooperate. This explanation is supported by research that suggests that pro-socials and pro-selfs have very different beliefs about the world. Pro-selfs think that everyone else is competitive and, therefore, cannot be trusted to cooperate. Pro-socials are much more variable in their beliefs about others' orientations. It is easy to see how distrust may become a self-fulfilling prophecy that prevents group members from reaching cooperative solutions to problems.

Although there is considerable support for the impact of social value orientation in social dilemmas generated in the laboratory, much less is known about their role in understanding social dilemmas in the real world. If social value orientation is an important personality factor, we must demonstrate its influence on behaviour during social dilemmas outside the laboratory.

As we noted previously, there is as yet little research on this topic. There is some evidence that social value orientation predicts strategies during negotiation situations. Pro-social negotiators tend to be more considerate and fairer towards their negotiation partner (De Dreu & Van Lange 1995). Also, social value orientation has been found to predict behaviour in helping situations. Pro-social students donate more of their time as volunteer participants in experiments (McClintock & Allison, 1989).

Finally, there is some evidence for the role of social value orientation in environmental decision making. The first author and several colleagues examined whether car drivers could be persuaded to switch to a more environmentally friendly public transport option (Van Vugt, Van Lange, & Meertens, 1996). We argued that this decision posed a social dilemma because, from a collective environmental viewpoint, it would be better if many people used public transport. At the same time, however, each person would be better off by taking his or her car, because this was personally the more convenient option. A survey with several travel scenarios was administered to about 200 car commuters in the Netherlands. For each scenario the commuters indicated whether they would prefer to take their car or public transport. Before they completed the survey, they also filled in the decomposed games instrument (see Appendix 6.1). Based on their responses to the decomposed games measure, commuters were categorized into either the pro-social group or pro-self group. Across all scenarios, pro-social commuters were more willing to give up driving their cars than were pro-self commuters. Secondary analyses revealed that pro-social commuters were much more concerned about environmental pollution, and much less concerned about their travel flexibility than pro-self commuters.

Specific Hypothesis under Investigation in the Exercise

We can now formulate the central hypothesis of the research that should be carried out following this chapter: in the context of a naturally occurring social dilemma, there should be a difference in decision making between cooperators, individualists and competitors. Based on the review above, it is predicted that pro-social people (cooperators) will be more willing to cooperate in such situations than pro-self people (individualists and competitors). Likewise, pro-self people will be more likely to compete than pro-social people.

Survey Exercise

STEP 1: CHOOSE THE DILEMMA AND RELEVANT CONCEPTS

The first step is to identify a naturally occurring social dilemma. In small groups, generate a working definition of 'social dilemma' based on the preceding discussion. Next, generate a list of current events that fit this definition. For example, as we were writing this chapter, much of Britain came to a standstill. Protesters who were angry over the high cost of petrol blockaded oil refineries throughout England, Scotland and Wales. Most petrol stations closed within a day or two, and the few that did remain open were forced to restrict sales to the emergency services. In addition, many food staples (such as bread and milk) were swept off the shelves within 24 hours. Alarmingly, these shortages were not due to a reduction in the total amount of petrol, milk and bread available to consumers. Instead, the shortages resulted from 'panic buying'. That is, individuals bought more than they really needed, largely out of fear that supplies would run out in the near future. Many people realized that this was why supplies were being depleted, but that awareness only contributed to the impulse to stock up before everything was gone. Had consumers stuck to their normal buying patterns, the effects of the blockades would have been far less immediate, and perhaps less severe.

The example above represents a short-term dilemma, having an immediate effect on the common interest. Other social dilemmas may represent patterns of behaviour over longer periods of time that have delayed effects on the common interest (such as patterns of public transportation, recycling or water use). In addition, the 'panic buying' situation represents a dilemma over shared resources (i.e. a 'commons dilemma'). Other social dilemmas may represent a need for collective action (i.e. a 'public good dilemma'). Finally, some social dilemmas may be worldwide problems like the environment, whereas others may be more localized, affecting relatively small groups like university departments or close relationships.

Theoretical variables you wish to measure

After you have identified a real-life social dilemma, you need to construct a questionnaire that will assess behaviours relevant to this dilemma. This questionnaire will serve as the dependent measure in your study. Before developing the specific items for the questionnaire, however, you should first identify the theoretical variables you wish to measure. We are interested in predicting the degree to which people behave cooperatively or competitively with respect to this specific social dilemma. Based on the introductory discussion above, how would you define cooperative and competitive behaviours? At this point, we are referring to conceptual definitions of these behaviours, not to specific examples of cooperative or competitive behaviour.

Operationalize these variables

Now that you have provided conceptual definitions for the variables, you need to operationalize them. An operational definition specifies the operations, or procedures, that you will use to measure the variable. In this case, you will be constructing a questionnaire to measure cooperative and competitive behaviours relevant to the social dilemma that you have selected. The specific items that you include in the questionnaire, and the techniques you use to administer it, will constitute your operational definitions.

Survey research

Survey research is a complex scientific enterprise. Many universities have entire departments dedicated to the creation and administration of sophisticated surveys. It would be unrealistic for us to meet the standards required of formal survey research. Instead, we will describe how things should be done *ideally*, and it will be your job to decide what is actually possible, or practical, for you to do. This will also allow you to identify some of the strengths and limitations of your study.

STEP 2: DEVELOP THE QUESTIONNAIRE

How should you start developing the questionnaire? It may be helpful to approach this task in several stages. The first stage is to generate behaviours, the second is to choose a response scale, the third is to carefully word each item, and the fourth is to select the items you wish to retain for the final version of the questionnaire.

Generate behaviours

List as many specific examples of cooperative and competitive behaviours as possible. Depending on the scope of the dilemma, you may be able to produce several dozen or only a handful. For some dilemmas (e.g. conflicts in close relationships or groups), you can probably think of many examples; for other dilemmas (e.g. water or energy conservation), examples may be less forthcoming. It may help to interview people (such as friends, parents and flatmates) informally about the topic. Don't worry too much about the wording of the behaviours at this point. Just get down as many as possible on paper. Your goal is to increase the *content validity* of the final questionnaire. Content validity is the degree to which your measure taps the range of behaviours relevant to the dependent variable you wish to assess.

Response scales

Now that you have a pool of behaviours, you need to decide how to format the items on your questionnaire. The first decision is whether to use open-ended or closed-ended questions. Open-ended questions give respondents considerable flexibility in their responses (e.g. 'What actions do you take to conserve water?' or 'How much are you willing to sacrifice in your relationship?'). This format provides a wide range of responses, which may help you discover answers that you did not anticipate. However, the data from open-ended questions are difficult to score. They require a great deal of interpretation on the part of the researcher, which will limit the reliability and validity of the questionnaire. They also lead respondents to give answers that may not be directly comparable to one another (e.g. 'a lot' vs. '5 gallons per week'), making the data difficult to analyse meaningfully. You may want to use open-ended questions when interviewing people during the item generation phase, but you will probably want to use closed-ended questions during the actual survey.

There are several issues you will need to consider as you construct closed-ended questions. First, what *scale of measurement* will you use for each item: nominal, ordinal, interval or ratio? A nominal scale makes use of discrete categories. For example, yes/no questions are on a nominal scale – as are questions about biological sex (males or females) and political party affiliation (Labour, Conservative, Liberal Democrat, Green, etc.). With nominal scales, there are no quantitative differences among the response alternatives. That is, the alternatives are not numerically different, and the order of the alternatives is largely arbitrary.

An ordinal scale provides response alternatives that are in rank order. For example, results from an Olympic race can be presented using an ordinal scale (i.e. first place, second place, third place, etc.). Likewise, you would be using an ordinal scale if you asked, 'How often do you recycle?' and provided as possible responses 'never', 'daily', 'weekly', 'monthly', and 'yearly'. Psychological variables that use the Likert response format (see below) are often on ordinal scales, including such diverse measures as test anxiety, self-esteem and marital satisfaction. With ordinal scales, you begin to be able to quantify the variable to some degree, but you cannot determine absolute differences among the responses (e.g. 'daily' and 'monthly' are not equally different from 'weekly').

Interval scales provide a more precise way to quantify variables, because the response alternatives are real numbers that represent relative differences in the magnitude of each response. Temperature is typically measured on an interval scale. Interval scales that have an absolute zero point are referred to as ratio scales. For example, results from an Olympic race can be presented using an interval scale by providing the precise time at which each participant finishes. An advantage of ratio scales is that differences in magnitude remain constant over the range of responses. Thus an Olympic finishing time of 45 seconds is twice as fast as a finishing time of 90 seconds. However, 70 degrees Fahrenheit (an interval scale) is not twice as warm as 35 degrees. For the statistical analyses that you will be doing, it is probably best to use interval or ratio scales (or, at the very least, ordinal scales).

The format of the *response scale* that you provide for each item will need to be coordinated with the scale of measurement. You could select a multiple-choice format for nominal scales. The options can be mutually exclusive, for example:

Which political party did you vote for in the last election? (Select only one)

    a. I didn't vote   d. Conservative Party
    b. Green Party   e. Liberal Democrat Party
    c. Labour Party   f. Other

Or, they can be nonexclusive, for example:

> Which of the following materials do you regularly recycle?
> (Check all that apply)
>
> ___ Glass bottles   ___ Glass jars
> ___ Tins   ___ Aluminium cans
> ___ Plastic milk jugs   ___ Newspaper

For ordinal scales, you would provide response alternatives that fall along a continuum. For example, the Likert-type format below is quite common.

> I think recycling is important.
>
> Strongly agree   Strongly disagree
> 1   2   3   4   5   6   7
>
> How likely are you to participate in a new curbside recycling program?
>
> Very unlikely   Very likely
> 1   2   3   4   5   6   7

Note that the number of values in the Likert scale (seven in the example above) is completely arbitrary. You could just as easily use a five-point scale, a 10-point scale, or a three-point scale. Likewise, the numbers themselves (1 to 7) do not represent actual values. In fact, we could use letters instead of numbers (A to G). Or, we could use negative values (−3 to +3).

For interval and ratio scales, you need to be specific about the numerical scale you want participants to use. For example:

> How many days per week do you shower/bathe? (Please use a value between 0–7).
> During a normal week, how many round trips do you take by bus? (Please use a value between 0–50).
> How much do you weigh (in stones)?

Question wording

In constructing the items for your questionnaire, be sure to avoid double-barrelled questions. This is when a single item actually contains two or more questions. For example, you would not want to include items such as: 'More people should travel to work by bus or train'. A respondent may agree that bus travel should be increased, but not train travel, or vice versa. It is best to separate such items into two separate questions.

In addition, the way an item is phrased can sometimes lead respondents to answer in one direction. An example of a leading question would be: 'People should feel free to throw their aluminium cans on the ground to pollute the Earth for all eternity'. It is better to use neutral phrasing, which will reduce the influence of social desirability bias.

Some statements are so vague that they apply to almost everyone. For example, 'Do you think the environment is important?' or 'Have you ever thrown away any recyclable goods?' Be as specific as possible, so that you are likely to get a wide variety of responses. For example, 'Counting today, how many glass bottles or jars have you thrown in the bin in the last seven days?' Likewise, avoid terms that are poorly defined. For example, words such as 'frequently' and 'seldom' could be defined differently by different respondents. It is better to be specific (e.g. '5 or more times per week' or '2 or 3 times per month').

Finally, you will want to reduce the possibility that response sets will influence your data. A response set is when a participant consistently provides the same response, regardless of the content of the item. For example, some participants will tend to agree with most statements (response acquiescence), whereas others will tend to disagree with most statements (response deviation). It is good practice, therefore, to alternate the direction in which items are phrased. In the present exercise, this can be accomplished by providing statements that refer to both cooperative behaviours and to competitive behaviours. In addition, you should alternate the response scales, such that higher values sometimes indicate agreement with a statement and sometimes indicate disagreement with a statement. To avoid errors, however, be sure that it is clear to participants that you have switched the response scale.

Item selection

Now that you have a set of carefully worded items, you need to select which of these items you will include in the final questionnaire. You should try to have an even balance of cooperative and competitive behaviours, and you should try to avoid duplicate items. In addition, you should check how actual respondents are likely to react to the items. The best way to do this is through pilot testing. You should interview several people, taking them through the questionnaire item by item. The purpose is to ensure that they interpret the items in the way you intend, that the scales capture the true variety of response, that the response scales match the wording of the items and that the items are phrased in a neutral fashion that limits social desirability biases. In the end, you should aim to have at least five cooperative behaviours and five competitive behaviours in your questionnaire.

STEP 3: SELECT THE SAMPLE

After determining the content and structure of the questionnaire, you will need to identify the population you wish to study. The population is the total set of potential participants in your study, and is determined by your research objectives. Usually, the relevant population for a study is extremely large. For example, if you want to know how many people in Wales have diabetes, then your population is all the people in Wales. If you want to know whether a new advertising campaign in Manchester is effective in reducing pre-teen smoking, then your target population is all pre-teens in Manchester. If you want to know whether caffeine increases reaction time, then your population is, effectively, everyone on planet Earth. Basically, the population represents all those about whom you want to draw conclusions from your data.

If you collect data on every member of the population, then you have conducted a *census*. For most research objectives, a true census is not possible because the population is too large. This is why most researchers conduct a *survey*, in which they select a sample from the larger population. How this sample is selected can have important implications.

In formal survey research, researchers often use probability sampling. One form of probability sampling is random sampling, whereby each member of the population has an equal chance of being selected for the sample. So, if your population consists of all pre-teens in Manchester, then ideally you would select a random sample from this population. That way, you would be confident that the results you obtain from your sample will be representative of the population as a whole.

In reality, true random sampling is often extremely difficult, and sometimes impossible. Because of practical concerns, researchers often chose non-probability sampling. The most common forms are convenience sampling and quota sampling. Convenience sampling is what it sounds like – basing the sample on volunteers who are readily available. Quota sampling involves determining sub-groups from the population that are of interest (e.g. males and females, liberals and conservatives, working-class and middle-class). The researcher then ensures that these sub-groups are reflected in the same proportion within the sample as they are in the population (e.g. 50% males and 50% females). Much of the psychological literature is based on non-probability samples (e.g. undergraduate students who participate for course credit). This is not necessarily a major flaw, but it does mean that the results may not be representative of the true population of interest.

A standard sample size for formal survey research is 1,200 participants. This allows the researcher to estimate true population values and effects with considerable accuracy (provided the sampling methods were sound). It is unlikely that you will be able to obtain a sample this large. Therefore, it is a good idea to estimate the effect size that you expect, and to determine the sample size that would be necessary for an effect size of that magnitude to be statistically significant. There are formal procedures to do this, known as power analysis. However, we can also suggest some simple rules of thumb. If you expect very small effect sizes (e.g. a point-biserial $r < .20$ or a Cohen's $d < .40$), then you typically will need a sample size above 250. For moderate effect sizes (e.g. $r = .30$ or $d = .60$), a sample size of 100 is usually sufficient. If your sample size falls below 50, you will only be able to detect quite large effects (e.g. $r > .40$ or $d > .80$). These guidelines come from the definitive work on the subject (Cohen, 1988), but most good introductory statistics texts demonstrate procedures for estimating power and effect size.

STEP 4: COLLECT THE DATA

Now that you have the questionnaire, and have identified the size of your sample, you need to decide how you will administer the question. First, carefully select the title of the questionnaire. It is best to keep the title neutral and brief. You don't want to put potential participants on the defensive with a title such as 'Sexual Perversion Test'. Second, don't forget the basics: ethical approval for the study, informed consent and debriefing. Third, decide where and when respondents will complete the questionnaire. Generally, it is best if participants have a quiet place to complete the questionnaire, away from other people. Fourth, if you have two or more questionnaires, decide upon which order they should be completed by participants. Ideally the order of questionnaires should be varied. For reasons of simplicity, administer the social value orientation measure before the questionnaire about the specific social dilemma.

STEP 5: PREPARE THE DATA

After collecting the data and entering them into the computer you will need to do some preliminary analyses to inspect the data.

Item frequencies

After you have entered the data, the first step in the analysis will be to check the frequencies for all items in the questionnaire and SVO measure. Produce a frequency table for each item, and check to make sure that the values for each item are in the correct range for that item's response scale. For example, if the frequency table shows a value of 23 for an item measured with a seven-point scale, then you know that there is an error in the raw data. You will need to track down and fix such errors. Also, be sure that any missing values are being treated as such.

Scale construction

Now that the data have been screened at the item level, you need to consider how you will combine the items into larger scales. Let's assume that your questionnaire has seven cooperative behaviours and seven competitive behaviours. How are you going to combine the 14 responses? One possibility is to use each participant's mean (average) response for the seven cooperative behaviours as an index of cooperation and his or her mean response for the seven competitive behaviours as an index of competitiveness. This would result in two dependent measures. A second possibility is to combine the cooperative and competitive behaviours together into a single scale. In order to do this, you would first need to recode the competitive behaviours such that higher values indicate less competitiveness rather than more competitiveness. You can then take the average across all 14 items as an index of cooperation. For the remainder of this section, we will assume that you wish to construct separate cooperative and competitive scales.

Internal consistency

Before you actually construct the scales, you first need to determine whether you are justified in combining the items. Typically, you would only create an overall scale if all of the component items assessed the same construct. If the items do measure the same construct (e.g. cooperativeness), then they should be inter-correlated with one another. This is a type of scale reliability, referred to as internal consistency. For example, a self-esteem scale might contain 10 items, each designed to measure some aspect of self-esteem (e.g. 'I take a positive attitude toward myself' and 'I feel that I have a number of good qualities'). You would expect these 10 items to correlate with one another, such that participants who indicate high self-esteem on one item will also indicate high self-esteem on the other nine items. Likewise, you would expect that participants who indicate low self-esteem on one item will also indicate low self-esteem on the other nine items. To check the degree of inter-correlation, you could produce a table containing the correlations among the 10 items, but this would be difficult to interpret because there would be a total of 45 correlations in the table. Luckily, there is a single index that can be used to assess the degree of inter-correlation among a set of items. For items measured on continuous scales (i.e. Likert, interval, and ratio scales), researchers typically use Cronbach's alpha. This is a standard analysis contained in most statistical software packages. Cronbach's alpha can range from 0 to 1.0, with higher values indicating greater inter-correlation among the items. Generally, an alpha above .70 indicates a satisfactory degree of internal consistency.

What happens if your alpha is below .70? A low alpha indicates that at least some of the items in your scale are not correlated with one another. Most software packages allow you to obtain diagnostic information for the individual items. This generally comes in the form of the correlation between the individual item and the total scale. If this is low, then the item does not reflect the overall scale very well. In addition, you can usually obtain a value that represents the alpha with that item deleted. If the alpha with the item deleted is higher than the alpha with the item in the scale, then you would consider dropping the item. It is best to drop just one item at a time, as the overall scale will change as each item is deleted. As a cautionary note, it is necessary to recode items such that high values on all items represent high values on the construct you wish to measure. If you don't do this, then your alpha estimates will not be valid. Negative item-total correlations are often a sign that certain items have not been recoded properly.

Constructing sub-scales

Assuming that your reliability analyses support the formation of one or more sub-scales, you need to decide how to combine items into larger scales. To do this, you need to construct a new variable for each scale. Most likely, this will either be the sum of all of the items that comprise the scale, or it will be the average of all the items that comprise the scale. It doesn't usually matter which way you combine the items. However, we prefer to use the average of the items because this retains the original scale. For example, if your scale is composed of five items assessed on seven-point scales, then each respondent's average on the five items would also fall along the seven-point scale. By contrast, a respondent's sum across the five items would fall between 5 and 35.

If the items you wish to combine into an overall subscale were not measured using the same response scale, then you must first standardize each variable. You can then sum or average the new standardized variables to produce the sub-scale.

Forming groups

Appendix 6.1 describes how to construct three groups based on responses to the SVO. You will need to create a new variable, and to assign a value for each participant based on his or her responses to the SVO (1 = cooperative, 2 = individualistic, 3 = competitive). Depending on how many people are in your survey, you may want to create a second variable that combines the two pro-self groups (individualist and competitive) into one group for comparison with the pro-social group (i.e. 1 = pro-social, 2 = pro-self).

STEP 6: ANALYSE THE DATA

Descriptive statistics

Examine the descriptive statistics for the key variables in your study. First, look at the distribution of groups based on the SVO measure. As this is a nominal variable, does it make sense to report the mean and standard deviation for this variable? Basically, you want to describe the percentage of respondents who were classified into each of the three groups. Next, look at the distribution for your continuous dependent measures (i.e. the sub-scales you created). What are the mean levels of cooperative and competitive behaviour? Is there a great deal of variability in responses? Are these variables normally distributed?

Correlation between dependent measures

Check whether the measures of cooperative and competitive behaviour are correlated with one another. If they are, does it make sense to combine them into a single scale?

Hypothesis testing

The primary hypothesis provided in the introduction was that pro-social people will be more willing to cooperate in a real life social dilemma than pro-self people (individualists and competitors). Likewise, it was predicted that pro-self people will be more likely to compete than pro-social people. How would you test these hypotheses statistically? (If your group has chosen different hypotheses, then your analysis will have to be tailored to those hypotheses.)

The two hypotheses are specified as differences between one group (cooperators) and two other groups (individualists and competitors). First, examine the mean levels of cooperation and competition for each of the three groups. Are the patterns of means consistent with this hypothesis?

Next, test for statistical significance. To test for differences between more than two independent groups, researchers typically use a one-way analysis of variance (ANOVA). Because you have two dependent measures (cooperation and competition), you will need to perform two separate ANOVAs. For each ANOVA, if the *F*-statistic is significant ($p < .05$), then this indicates that the probability that the means are equal is extremely low. Unfortunately, this *F*-statistic is an omnibus test that is not sufficient to address your hypothesis. This is because you don't know which of the three groups differ from one another.

To test your specific hypothesis, you will have to follow up the omnibus test with more specific comparisons. One option is to use a contrast statement (e.g. the pro-social group compared to the average of the individualistic and competitive groups). This has the advantage of allowing you to match the statistical test directly to your hypothesis. A second option is to test for differences between specific pairs of means (i.e., cooperators vs individualists, cooperators vs competitors, and individualists vs competitors). This allows you to determine which specific groups differ from one another. Thus you might expect cooperators to differ significantly from individualists and competitors, but for there to be no significant difference between the latter two groups.

The one drawback to testing pairwise comparisons is that you will have to adjust for multiple comparisons. This is because you are testing three 1df comparisons, whereas the omnibus *F*-statistic is based on

2 df. The problem is that you need to keep the alpha level (usually .05) that you used to determine the significance of the omnibus test the same when you perform the follow-up tests. There are a number of procedures to adjust for multiple comparisons (e.g. Bonferroni, Scheffe, Tukey's HSD, or Dunnet), which are standard in most computer software packages.

Alternative strategy

If you have decided to combine the individualist and competitor groups into a single pro-self group, then you will probably want to do t-tests for independent means rather than univariate ANOVAs. This is because readers usually expect to see t-tests when comparing differences between two groups. You will need to do a separate t-test for each of your dependent measures (cooperative behaviours and competitive behaviours). One advantage of the t-test procedure is that it allows you to address your predictions efficiently. You will not have to perform follow-up tests, because there are only two means being compared. The disadvantage is that you may be combining two groups (individualists and competitors) whose means are not descriptively similar.

Advanced statistics

Advanced students should consider using a multivariate analysis. Researchers often use multivariate analyses when they have two or more dependent measures that are correlated with one another. Multivariate tests generally are more powerful than univariate tests. Thus if the cooperative and competitive scales are inversely correlated with one another, you may want to precede the two univariate ANOVA analyses with a single multivariate analysis of variance (MANOVA). If the multivariate test is significant, then you can examine the univariate F-statistics to determine whether there are significant differences for each of your dependent measures. Similarly, if you are conducting t-tests rather than ANOVAs, you may want to precede these with a MANOVA. If the MANOVA is significant, then you can examine the separate univariate t-tests for cooperative and competitive behaviours.

STEP 7: WRITE UP RESEARCH

Once you have analysed the data with regard to the main hypothesis of your research, the time has come to write up the results. Obviously it would be nice to find that your results confirm the hypothesis. But do not worry if this is not the case. Quite often it is more interesting to read why a particular hypothesis did not receive support. Researchers can then take this into account in conducting subsequent research.

It goes beyond the purpose of the chapter to give you guidelines about how to write up your research. For specific technical instructions about how to write up the results of your survey research, we'd like to refer you to the *APA Publication Manual* (4th edn.). For more general information about the rules for scientific writing in psychology, there are other books available like Sternberg's *The Psychologist's Companion* (1988).

Appendix 6.1: Decomposed Games Instrument to Measure Social Value Orientation (from Van Lange et al., 1997, printed with permission from APA)

INSTRUCTIONS

In this task we ask you to imagine that you have been randomly paired with another person whom we will refer to simply as 'Other.' This other person is someone you do not know and that you will not knowingly meet in the future. Both you and the other person will be making choices by circling either letter A, B or C. Your own choices will produce points for both yourself and 'Other'. Likewise, Other's choice will produce points for him/her and for you. Every point has value: the more points you receive the better for you and the more points 'Other' receives, the better for him/her.

Here is an example of how this task works:

	A	B	C
You get	500	500	550
Other gets	100	500	300

In this example, if you chose A you would receive 500 points and Other would receive 100 points. If you chose B you would receive 500 points and Other 500, and if you chose C you would receive 550 and the other 300. So you see that your choice influences both the number of points you receive and the number of points Other receives.

Before you begin making choices, please keep in mind that there are no right or wrong answers – choose the option that you, for whatever reason, prefer most. Also remember that the points have value: the more of them you accumulate the better for you. Likewise, from Other's point of view, the more points s/he accumulates the better for him/her.

TASK

For each of the nine choice situations, circle A, B or C depending on which column you prefer most:

		A	B	C
1	You get	480	540	480
	Other gets	80	280	480
		A	B	C
2	You get	560	500	500
	Other gets	300	500	100
		A	B	C
3	You get	520	520	580
	Other gets	520	120	320
		A	B	C
4	You get	500	560	490
	Other gets	100	300	490
		A	B	C
5	You get	560	500	490
	Other gets	300	500	90
		A	B	C
6	You get	500	500	570
	Other gets	500	100	300
		A	B	C
7	You get	510	560	510
	Other gets	510	300	110

		A	B	C
8	You get	550	500	500
	Other gets	300	100	500

		A	B	C
9	You get	480	490	540
	Other gets	100	490	300

NOTE FOR INSTRUCTORS

Participants are classified when they make six or more consistent choices. Cooperative choices are 1c, 2b, 3a, 4c, 5b, 6a, 7a, 8c, 9b; individualistic choices are 1b, 2a, 3c, 4b, 5a, 6c, 7b, 8a, 9c; and competitive choices are 1a, 2c, 3b, 4a, 5c, 6b, 7c, 8b, 9a.

NOTE

1   Although preparation of this chapter was a truly cooperative effort, the first author is primarily responsible for the theoretical component and the second author for the exercise component of the chapter. Portions of this chapter were written while the first author was on sabbatical leave at the Free University of Amsterdam.

REFERENCES

Bowlby, J. (1969). *Attachment and loss, Vol. 1: Attachment*. London: Hogarth.

Cohen, J. (1988). *Statistical power analysis for the behavioral sciences* (2nd edn.). Hillsdale, NJ: Erlbaum.

Dawes, R. M. (1980). Social dilemmas. *Annual Review of Psychology, 31*, 169–93.

Dawes, R. M., McTavish, J. & Shaklee, H. (1977). Behavior, communication and assumptions about other people's behavior in a commons dilemma situation. *Journal of Personality and Social Psychology, 35*, 1–11.

De Cremer, D., & Van Vugt, M. (1999). Social identification effects in social dilemmas: A transformation of motives. *European Journal of Social Psychology, 29*, 871–93.

De Dreu, C. K. W. & Van Lange, P. A. M. (1995). Impact of social value orientations on negotiator cognition and behavior. *Personality and Social Psychology Bulletin, 21*, 1178–88.

Hardin, G. (1968). The tragedy of the commons. *Science, 162*, 1243–8.

Jorgenson, D. O. & Papciak, A. S. (1981). The effects of communication, resource feedback, and identifiability on behavior in a simulated commons. *Journal of Experimental Social Psychology, 17,* 373–85.

Knight, G. P. & Kagan, S. (1981). Apparent sex differences in cooperation–competition: A function of individualism. *Developmental Psychology, 17,* 783–90.

Komorita, S. S. & Parks, C. D. (1994). *Social dilemmas.* Dubuque, IA: Brown & Benchmark.

Kramer, R., McClintock, C. G. & Messick, D. M. (1986). Social values and cooperative response to a simulated resource conservation crisis. *Journal of Personality, 54,* 101–17.

Liebrand, W. B. G., Messick, D. M. & Wilke, H. A. M. (1992). *Social dilemmas: Theoretical issues and research findings.* Oxford: Pergamon Press.

McClintock, C. G. (1972). Social motivation – a set of propositions. *Behavioral Science, 17,* 438–54.

McClintock, C. G. & Allison, S. T. (1989). Social value orientation and helping behavior. *Journal of Applied Social Psychology, 19,* 353–62.

McClintock, C. G. & Moscovitz, J. M. (1976). Children's preference for individualistic, competitive, and cooperative outcomes. *Journal of Personality and Social Psychology, 34,* 543–55.

Messick, D. M. & Brewer, M. B. (1983). Solving social dilemmas: A review. In L. Wheeler & P. Shaver (eds.), *Review of personality and social psychology* (vol 4, pp. 11–44). Beverly Hills, CA: Sage.

Messick, D. M. & McClintock, C. G. (1968). Motivational basis of choice in experimental games. *Journal of Experimental Social Psychology, 4,* 1–25.

Sternberg, R. J. (1988). *The psychologists' companion.* New York: Cambridge University Press.

Van de Kragt, A. J. C., Orbell, J. M. & Dawes, R. M. (1983). The minimal contributing set as a solution to public goods problems. *American Political Science Review, 77,* 112–22.

Van Lange, P. A. M., Otten, W., De Bruin, E. M. & Joireman, J. A. (1997). Development of prosocial, individualistic, and competitive orientations: Theory and preliminary evidence. *Journal of Personality and Social Psychology, 73,* 733–46.

Van Vugt, M. (1998). The conflicts of modern society. *The Psychologist,* June, 289–92.

Van Vugt, M., Snyder, M., Tyler, T. & Biel, A. (2000). *Cooperation in modern society: Promoting the welfare of communities, states, and organizations.* London: Routledge.

Van Vugt, M., Van Lange, P. A. M. & Meertens, R. M. (1996). A social dilemma analysis of travel mode judgements. *European Journal of Social Psychology, 26,* 373–95.

CHAPTER SEVEN

On Using Questionnaires to Measure Attitudes

Geoffrey Haddock

This chapter describes strategies for measuring attitudes. Essentially, it introduces a number of explicit (i.e. direct) and implicit (i.e. indirect) techniques designed to produce quantitative records of a complex construct. The exercise presented relies upon an experimental research design. The chapter is suitable for introductory level courses.

Defining Attitude and Measuring Attitudes

People like some things and dislike others. For instance, I like the music of Bruce Springsteen and feel negatively about the use of capital punishment. A social psychologist would say that I possess a positive attitude towards the music of Bruce Springsteen and a negative attitude towards the death penalty. Understanding differences in attitudes across people and uncovering the reasons why people come to like and dislike different things has interested social psychologists since the field's inception. Indeed, almost 70 years ago, Gordon Allport (1935, p. 198) asserted that the attitude concept is probably 'the most distinctive and indispensable concept in . . . contemporary social psychology'. That statement remains equally valid today; the study of attitudes remains at the forefront of social psychological research and theory.

In this chapter, I introduce the attitude concept and discuss how attitudes can be measured. First, I will define the term 'attitude'. We will see that although different theorists provide somewhat different conceptualizations of the term, there is consensus that expressing an attitude involves making an evaluative judgement about an attitude object. Second, I will turn my attention to how attitudes have traditionally been measured within social psychology, concentrating on direct and indirect strategies that psychologists have developed to measure attitudes. Third, I will introduce a research exercise that the reader can carry out.

What is an Attitude?

Like most concepts within psychology, there is no universally agreed upon definition of attitude (Olson & Zanna, 1993). Listed in Table 7.1 is a set of definitions that have been offered by some of the field's most influential thinkers. Let's look at some of these definitions in greater detail. In their influential text *The psychology of attitudes*, Eagly & Chaiken (1993) define an attitude as 'a psychological tendency that is expressed by evaluating a particular entity with some degree of favor or disfavor' (p. 1). Fazio (1995) defines an attitude as 'an association in memory between a given object and a given summary evaluation of the object' (p. 247). Petty & Cacioppo (1981) define an attitude as 'a general and enduring positive or negative feeling about some person, object, or issue' (p. 7). Finally, Zanna & Rempel (1988) define an attitude as 'the categorization of a stimulus object along an evaluative dimension' (p. 319). Despite the differences inherent in

Table 7.1 Some recent definitions of attitude

Researchers	Definition
Eagly & Chaiken (1993)	A psychological tendency that is expressed by evaluating a particular object with some degree of favor or disfavor
Fazio (1995)	An association in memory between a given object and a given summary evaluation of the object
Greenwald (1989)	The affect associated with an attitude object
Kruglanski (1989)	A special type of knowledge, notably knowledge of content is evaluative or affective
Petty & Cacioppo (1981)	A general and enduring positive or negative feeling about some person, object, or issue
Zanna & Rempel (1988)	The categorization of a stimulus object along an evaluative dimension

these definitions, they all emphasize the notion that reporting an attitude involves the expression of an *evaluative judgement* about a stimulus object. Indeed, most attitude theorists would argue that evaluation is the predominant aspect of the attitude concept (Olson & Zanna, 1993). Once attitudes have been formed, they predispose an evaluation in response to the attitude object. In other words, reporting an attitude involves making a decision of liking versus disliking, approving versus disapproving, or favouring versus disfavouring a particular issue, object or person.

An attitude, when conceptualized as an evaluative judgement, can vary in two important ways (see Eagly & Chaiken, 1993). First, attitudes can differ in *valence*, or direction. Some attitudes that I possess are positive (like my attitude towards Bruce Springsteen), others are negative (like my attitude towards capital punishment), and yet others are neutral (like my attitude towards tomato juice). Second, attitudes can differ in *strength*. For example, while one person might feel extremely positively about the European single currency, a second person might feel only somewhat positively about the same issue.

So far, I have used a number of examples when describing my own attitudes. This leads to the following question – can *anything* be an attitude object? Basically, any stimulus that can be evaluated along a dimension of favourability can be conceptualized as an attitude object. As noted by Eagly & Chaiken (1993), some attitude objects are abstract (e.g. 'liberalism'), others are concrete (e.g. my computer). Furthermore, one's own self (e.g. self-esteem) and other individuals (e.g. a particular politician) can also serve as attitude objects, as can social policy issues (e.g. capital punishment) and social groups (e.g. people from Canada).

Attitudes are an important area of study as, not surprisingly, they predict behaviour. For example, a study by Fazio & Williams (1986) found a high correlation (approximately .70) between attitudes toward a political candidate and subsequent voting behaviour (as measured five months after the assessment of attitude). A meta-analysis that reviewed the results of over 100 studies on the attitude–behaviour relation discovered that on average, the correlation between opinions and actions was .38 (Kraus, 1995).

The Measurement of Attitudes

Attitudes, like most psychological constructs, are not directly observable. Rather, they can only be inferred from individuals' responses (Fazio & Olson, 2003; Himmelfarb, 1993). As a result, social psychologists have needed to develop various methodologies in order to effectively assess individuals' attitudes. In this section of the chapter, I describe some of the most commonly used techniques that have been developed over the past 75 years. This review is not exhaustive, and readers who are interested in other forms of attitude measurement (e.g. psychophysical measures, behavioural measures) are invited to read Fazio & Olson (2003) & Himmelfarb (1993).

In introducing different measures of attitude, I have elected to distinguish them on the basis of whether they are explicit (that is, direct) or implicit (that is, indirect). The distinction between explicit and implicit processes has a long history within psychology. Psychologists usually think of explicit processes as those that require conscious attention. In contrast, implicit processes are those that do not require conscious attention. Within the realm of attitude measurement, these terms are used to distinguish between attitude measures in which the respondent is aware or unaware that an attitude is being assessed. Put simply, explicit attitude measures directly ask respondents to indicate their attitude, whereas implicit attitude measures assess attitudes without needing to directly ask the respondent for a verbal report (Fazio & Olson, 2003).

DIRECT (EXPLICIT) MEASURES OF ATTITUDES

The vast majority of attitude measures can be conceptualized as direct indicators. Usually, these measures have been self-report questionnaires in which participants respond to direct questions about their opinions (e.g. 'What is your opinion about abortion?'). Initial research into attitude measurement via direct questionnaire measures is generally associated with the work of Thurstone (1928). In a seminal paper, Thurstone demonstrated how methods of psychophysical scaling could be adapted to the measurement of attitudes. Although a detailed description of the complete essence of Thurstone's work is beyond the scope of the present chapter (see Dawes, 1972; Eiser, 1990; Himmelfarb, 1993; Ostrom, 1989 for excellent reviews), a brief overview of his equal appearing intervals method (Thurstone & Chave, 1929) is warranted.

The equal appearing intervals (EAI) approach involves multiple stages (Himmelfarb, 1993). First, the researcher constructs a set of belief statements that are relevant to the attitude being measured. Assume for a minute that a researcher was interested in creating an EAI measure of attitudes towards capital punishment. The researcher would begin by deriving a pool of statements that are relevant to the issue (e.g. 'Capital punishment would decrease the homicide rate' and 'The death penalty should never be used'). Second, after the pool of belief statements has been developed, a group of judges is asked to locate each statement along intervals of an evaluative dimension. A score is assigned for each item that is equal to the value of the interval. For example, if judge A placed an item in the seventh interval, that item would have a score of 7 for that judge. The scale value for a particular item is derived by using the median of the scores assigned to that item across all judges. Thus, after the second stage, each item has been allocated a scale value score. In the third stage, the belief statements are given to the individuals whose attitudes are to be expressed. Respondents are asked to indicate the items with which they agree. A respondent's score is the mean (or median) of the scale value of the items to which they agreed. For example, if on a Thurstone EAI scale of attitudes towards capital punishment a respondent agreed with four items that had scale values of 5, 6, 6 and 7, this individual would have a score of 6.

Because he believed Thurstone's methodology to be too time-consuming, Likert (1932) developed a technique of summated ratings. In this approach, belief statements are written such that responses indicate either a favourable or unfavourable attitude. An example of a Likert scale to assess attitudes towards capital punishment is presented in the questionnaire below. For each item, respondents are asked to indicate their degree of agreement or disagreement. As you read the items presented in the questionnaire, you will notice that items can be written such that a strong positive attitude towards the death penalty will produce either a 'strongly agree' response (e.g. to item 2) or a 'strongly disagree' response (e.g. to item 3). Researchers create items that are worded in opposite directions in order to help avoid response sets. How are Likert scales scored? In a questionnaire like the example below, each response alternative is allocated a score (in this case from 1 to 5). Traditionally, a low score is taken to indicate a strong negative attitude and a high score is taken to indicate a strong positive attitude. Thus, for item 2 of our questionnaire, an individual who strongly disagrees with the statement will be allocated a score of 1, while a person who strongly agrees will be given a score of 5. For item 3 (a reverse keyed item), an individual who strongly disagrees with the statement is expressing a positive attitude (and hence is allocated a score of 5 for that item), whereas an individual who strongly agrees with that item is expressing a negative attitude (and thus is allocated a score of 1). To achieve a single score, a person's response on each item can be averaged to obtain a single score. For example, a respondent who answered E, D, A, E, and A to the items listed in the questionnaire would have a total score of 4.8 (after items 3 and 5 have been reverse coded).

An example of a Likert scale to assess attitudes towards capital punishment

The following statements are part of a survey on public attitudes. There are no right or wrong answers, only opinions. For each statement, indicate the number that best represents your personal opinion by using the following scale:

If you strongly disagree with the statement, indicate A
If you disagree with the statement, indicate B
If you neither disagree nor agree with the statement, indicate C
If you agree with the statement, indicate D
If you strongly agree with the statement, indicate E

1 Capital punishment should be instituted for
   people found guilty of murder.   _____
2 I would support a referendum for the institution
   of the death penalty.   _____
3 Capital punishment should never be used.   _____
4 Capital punishment is more appropriate than
   life imprisonment.   _____
5 I am against the use of the death penalty
   in all circumstances.   _____

Much of the early research on attitudes was designed to assess the degree to which group differences existed across a variety of attitude objects. This research was less interested in demonstrating how a particular individual might hold different attitudes towards different attitude objects. In order to address such questions, it was necessary to develop a methodology that would enable researchers to measure attitudes towards a variety of attitude objects along a common scale or metric. Among the efforts to develop such a technique, the method that has been the most influential is the *semantic differential* approach (Osgood, Suci, & Tannenbaum, 1957). An example of a semantic differential scale is shown below. In this technique, participants are given a set of bipolar adjective scales, each of which is separated into seven (or possibly five or nine) categories. Participants are asked to evaluate the attitude object by indicating the response that best represents their opinion. The bipolar adjectives typically include general evaluative terms such as favourable–unfavourable, good–bad and like–dislike. On a seven-point scale, a negative response can be coded as –3 and a positive response can be coded as +3. To the extent that the bipolar adjectives assess the same construct (i.e. a respondent's attitude), correlations among responses to each bipolar adjective item should be high. If they are sufficiently high (as normally indexed by a Cronbach α value above .70), scores on the individual items are averaged to form a single attitude score.

A semantic differential scale to measure attitudes towards capital punishment

Please respond to each scale by placing an 'x' in the box that best represents your opinion.

Capital Punishment

Bad	☐	☐	☐	☐	☐	☐	☐	Good
Negative	☐	☐	☐	☐	☐	☐	☐	Positive
Unfavourable	☐	☐	☐	☐	☐	☐	☐	Favourable

Issues relevant to the direct measurement of attitudes

Historically, direct measures of attitudes have dominated the empirical literature on the psychology of attitudes. However, despite their wide appeal, a number of issues relevant to these measures have been the source of concern. For example, sometimes individuals might not be aware of their underlying attitude toward an object (Fazio, Jackson, Dunton, & Williams, 1995; Greenwald & Banaji, 1995; Nisbett & Wilson, 1977). Further, research has determined that subtle differences in the way in which items are presented can influence responses to direct measures of attitude (see Haddock & Carrick, 1999a, 1999b; Schwarz, 1999; Schwarz, Strack, & Mai, 1991).

Probably the most important criticism about direct measures of attitude is that of impression management (e.g. socially desirable responding). Impression management refers to deliberate attempts to misrepresent (or fake) one's responses in a manner that allows the respondent to present themselves in a favourable way (Paulhus & John, 1998). To the extent that the researcher is interested in studying attitudes toward sensitive issues and/or issues relevant to norms of political or social appropriateness, individuals' responses might not necessarily reflect their own opinion, but instead may reflect a desire to present themselves in a positive manner. For example, in some cultures it may not be considered socially appropriate to express a prejudicial attitude toward a particular social group. In such contexts, the use of explicit direct measures of attitude may not provide an accurate portrayal of a respondent's attitude, as they may be reluctant to be perceived as prejudiced.

INDIRECT (IMPLICIT) MEASURES OF ATTITUDES

In an attempt to circumvent problems associated with direct measures of attitude, social psychologists have recently developed a number of indirect or implicit response strategies. While it is beyond the scope of the present chapter to review all of these approaches (see Fazio & Olson, 2003 for an excellent review), I would like to discuss two measures, the evaluative priming technique (see Fazio et al., 1995) and the Implicit Association Test (IAT; Greenwald, McGhee, & Schwartz, 1998).

Evaluative priming

Recall that Fazio (1995) defines an attitude as 'an association in memory between a given object and a given summary evaluation of the object' (p. 247). According to Fazio and colleagues, these associations can vary in strength, and the strength of the association determines the accessibility of an attitude. Let me describe this perspective more concretely by using an example. I really hate Marmite. Even thinking about Marmite sets off an immediate and strong negative reaction within me. I also dislike rice cakes, but my reaction is not as aversive.[1] Fazio's model would postulate that my (negative) attitude toward Marmite is more accessible than my attitude toward rice cakes.

How would one measure the accessibility of an attitude? Fazio and colleagues have measured this construct by determining how quickly an individual responds to an evaluative word following the brief presentation of the attitude object. In a typical accessibility study (see Fazio, 1995 for a description), a participant is seated in front of a computer. The attitude object is then briefly presented on the computer screen (e.g. the word Marmite). Shortly after the stimulus prime is presented, it is replaced by an evaluative adjective (e.g. disgusting). The participant's task is to indicate the connotation of the adjective as rapidly as possible. Of interest to the researcher is the latency (i.e. speed) with which the participant makes the evaluative judgement. In my case, the presentation of 'Marmite' should facilitate my response to a negative adjective and inhibit my response to a positive adjective. Furthermore, this effect should be more pronounced when I am presented with 'Marmite' rather than 'rice cakes'. Thus the strength of an association between an object and an evaluation determines the accessibility of an attitude (i.e. how quickly we report an evaluation).

Fazio and colleagues have used this approach in numerous studies, including domains in which explicit measures might be subject to social desirability concerns. For example, Fazio et al. (1995) adapted the evaluative priming paradigm to study prejudicial attitudes. In this study, participants were instructed that their task was to indicate the connotation of positive and negative adjectives. However, prior to the presentation of the target adjective, participants were briefly shown a photo of a black or a white person. Fazio et al. (1995) found that among white participants, the presentation of a black face produced faster responding to negative adjectives and slower responses to positive adjectives (relative to what was found in response to the presentation of white faces). Thus, in this study, a negative attitude towards black people would be represented by latency differences in the time required to categorize positive and negative adjectives after the presentation of a black face.

The Implicit Association Test

The second indirect procedure I would like to describe is the Implicit Association Test (IAT; Greenwald et al., 1998). I will present an example of procedures that would use the IAT to assess implicit gender attitudes. In a typical IAT study, participants are seated at a computer and asked to classify attitude objects (i.e. targets) and words. (See below for a description of an IAT that does not require the use of a computer.) Participants are instructed to make their responses as quickly as possible; the computer will record the time it takes them to respond. A computer-based IAT study involves five separate blocks. In block 1 of a gender IAT, participants are presented with a variety of male and female names. They would be instructed to make one response (e.g. press the 's' key on a keyboard) when they see a male name and make a different response (e.g. press the 'k' key) when they see a female name. They are asked to perform this task (and all others in the test) as quickly as possible (individual blocks will contain multiple trials). In block 2, participants are presented with a variety of positive and negative words. Again, they would be asked to make one response (press the 's' key) when a positive word appears on the screen and a different response (press the 'k' key) when a negative word appear on the screen. In block 3, participants are instructed that they will see names or words, and that they are to press the 's' key when they see a male name or positive word, and press the 'k' key when they see a female name or negative word. Block 4 is similar to block 2, but this time the responses are reversed, such that a participant now presses the 's' key when a negative word appears and the 'k' key when a positive word appears. Block 5 is similar to block 3, but this time participants are to press the 's' key when a male name or negative word appears, and the 'k' key when a female name or positive word appears. The key blocks are 3 and 5 – they measure the strength of association between an attitude object (in this case gender categories) and evaluations.

How does the IAT use these blocks to compute an attitude score? Imagine an individual who is more negative about women compared to men. For this individual, the task in block 3 should be quite simple. If they favour men against women, trials in which men are associated with positive words and women are associated with negative words should lead to fast responses, because the links between these categories and evaluations are congruent. Let's imagine that our participant's mean response time to trials in this block is 800ms. In contrast, responses in block 5 should take longer for this participant. Given their inherent preference for men over women, trials that associate women with positivity and men with negativity should take more time to elicit a response. Returning to our participant, let's imagine that their mean response time for this block is 1100ms. Thus our participant's mean response time for block 3 is shorter than that for block 5 by 300ms. This difference is referred to as the IAT effect (see Greenwald et al., 1998 for additional details about computing IAT effects).

The IAT, and other implicit measures (see Fazio & Olson, 2003) have become increasingly popular among attitude researchers. These types of measures have gained popularity because they assess attitudes without the necessity of asking the participant for a verbal report. As noted earlier, part of their appeal is due to the belief that responses on these measures are less likely to be affected by social desirability concerns (see Fazio & Olson, 2003). Interestingly, scores on implicit attitude measures tend to be only moderately correlated with explicit measures of the same construct. For interested readers who would like to learn more about the IAT (and even complete an on-line version of the measure), Greenwald, Banaji, and colleagues have developed very interesting and educational links on the World Wide Web (see e.g. <https://implicit.harvard.edu/implicit; http://www.briannosek.com/iat/>).

You might have noticed that the two implicit strategies I have discussed involve using computers to obtain response latencies. It is possible, however, to assess implicit attitudes without the benefit of a computer. Paper-and-pencil IAT tasks have recently been developed (see e.g. Lowery, Hardin, & Sinclair, 2001). Examples of a paper-and-pencil IAT are presented below. In this technique, stimuli (e.g. male and female names, positive and negative words) are presented as series of items running down the centre of a page. At the top of the page there are two categories on each side. Participants are asked to categorize both names and faces as quickly and accurately as possible, and are given a specific amount of time to perform this task (e.g. 20 seconds). In one block, male/positive and female/negative appear together (see Paper-and-pencil IAT#1). In another block, male/negative and female/positive appear together (see Paper-and-pencil IAT#2). As in the computerized version of the task, a participant who favours men against women should find it easier to complete the task in which male/positive and female/negative are categorized together. An IAT score is derived by computing the difference between the number of correct categorizations across the two blocks.

Paper-and-pencil IAT#1 (as used by Lowery et al., 2001)

Listed below is a list of names and words. Your task is to categorize each stimulus by placing an X on either the left- or right-hand side of the page. In this task, place an X to the left of the stimulus if the word is a male name or positive word; place an X to the right of the stimulus if the word is a female name or negative word.

Male Name OR   Female Name OR
Positive Word   Negative Word

Janet
Bomb
Andrea
Gentle
Robert
Integrity
Sharon
Honor
David
Affection

Martin
Sunrise
Steven
Crash
Frank
Failure
Claire
Brutal
Kevin
Honest
Judy
Noble
Alisha
Disease
Jeffrey
Health
Gordon
Ridicule
Margaret
Success
Betty
Abuse
Daniel
Rotten
Alan
Filth

Paper-and-pencil IAT#2 (as used by Lowery et al., 2001)

Listed below is a list of names and words. Your task is to categorize each stimulus by placing an X on either the left- or right-hand side of the page. In this task, place an X to the left of the stimulus if the word is a female name or positive word; place an X to the right of the stimulus if the word is a male name or negative word.

Female Name OR   Male Name OR
Positive Word   Negative Word

Janet
Bomb
Andrea
Gentle
Robert

Integrity
Sharon
Honor
David
Affection
Martin
Sunrise
Steven
Crash
Frank
Failure
Claire
Brutal
Kevin
Honest
Judy
Noble
Alisha
Disease
Jeffrey
Health
Gordon
Ridicule
Margaret
Success
Betty
Abuse
Daniel
Rotten
Alan
Filth

Issues Relevant to the Measurement of Attitudes

A sound measure of any psychological construct must be both reliable and valid. In its broadest sense, *reliability* refers to 'the degree to which test scores are free from errors in measurement' (American Psychological Association, 1985, p. 19). When we assess a psychological construct, we want the measure to be a true indication of the individual's status with respect to the construct being assessed. A measure that is not reliable (i.e. consistent) is of limited value. In the context of attitude measurement, reliability has two meanings. First, internal consistency refers to whether the individual items are assessing the same psychological construct. As noted earlier, items that assess the same construct should be positively correlated. Second, test–retest reliability refers to consistency in scores across time. A sound attitude measure should produce similar scores across repeated testing (in the absence of any true attitude change).

A number of studies have investigated the reliability of explicit and implicit measures of attitude. Explicit measures have been shown to exhibit high reliability. For example, semantic differential scales using the evaluative dimensions of good–bad, positive–negative, and favourable–unfavourable exhibit high internal consistency (Huskinson & Haddock, in press). Furthermore, a single item semantic differ-ential measure (the evaluation thermometer) has been shown to possess high test–retest reliability (Haddock et al., 1993). Given their recent introduction, less research has been conducted assessing the reliability of implicit measures of attitude. However, a recent paper by Cunningham, Preacher, & Banaji (2001) found that implicit measures, when considered as latent variables, possessed reasonably high internal consistency and test–retest correlations.

The *validity* of a scale refers to the extent that it assesses the con-struct it is designed to measure. Developing a valid measure of a psychological construct is not as simple and straightforward as one might expect. For example, testing the validity of a new measure of attitudes towards capital punishment would require demonstrating that the new measure is: (1) related to other measures of death penalty (e.g. convergent validity), (2) unrelated to measures of other constructs irrelevant to capital punishment (e.g. discriminant validity) and (3) predictive of future behavior (e.g. predictive validity).

A number of studies have investigated the validity of explicit and implicit measures of attitude. Explicit measures of attitude have been shown to be valid. For example, Haddock et al. (1993) demonstrated that a semantic differential measure of attitudes towards gay men was highly predictive of a subsequent measure of anti-gay discrimination (see Eagly & Chaiken, 1993, for more examples). Regarding implicit measures, Cunningham et al. (2001) and Fazio & Olson (2003) have found that implicit measures possess convergent and predictive validity. In one particularly compelling study using fMRI technology, Phelps, O'Connor, Cunningham, Funayama, Gatenby & Banaji (2000) found that an IAT measure of racial prejudice was highly predictive of amygdala activation when presented with pictures of black indi-viduals (the amygdala is an area of the brain associated with fearful evaluations).

Research Exercise: Implicit Gender Attitudes

In some of the examples I have provided to describe attitude measures, I have used the domain of gender attitudes. As you might expect, research has addressed whether, overall, there are differences in people's attitudes towards the categories 'women' and 'men'. Historically, research tended to demonstrate that men are evaluated more favourably than women, leading Del Boca, Ashmore, & McManus (1986, p. 121) to conclude that 'the social category female is not positively evaluated, at least not relative [to the social category] male'. However, recent research has documented a shift in gender attitudes (e.g. Eagly & Mladinic, 1989; Eagly, Mladinic, & Otto, 1991; Haddock & Zanna, 1994). For example, Eagly and Mladinic (1989), using semantic differential measures of attitudes toward women and men, found that attitudes towards women were more positive than attitudes toward men. Haddock & Zanna (1994) also found that the category 'women' was evaluated more favourably than 'men', and that this was true for both female and male respondents.

One question that is worthy of investigation concerns the degree to which there may be differences in gender attitudes using implicit measures. While females are preferred over males at an explicit level, does this pattern also occur for implicit measures? Do male and female respondents differ in their implicit gender attitudes? Another question might consider whether the favourability of an individual's implicit gender attitudes is related to their perceptions of female and male gender norms. These types of questions can be addressed within the proposed research exercise.

BACKGROUND READING AND FORMULATION OF RESEARCH QUESTION

The steps involved in the research exercise are as follows. First, it is recommended that you begin by reviewing some relevant literature. The papers of Eagly and colleagues (e.g. Eagly & Mladinic, 1989; Eagly et al., 1991) and Haddock & Zanna (1994) provide a good foundation regarding past research on the favourability of gender attitudes. Papers by Greenwald et al. (1998) and Lowery et al. (2001), as well as the websites mentioned earlier in this chapter, provide useful background regarding the IAT. Full references for these papers are listed at end of this chapter. These papers, which are written in an accessible format, will provide you with the necessary background information. Second, think about the precise research question that you wish to address in your study. While I have provided some questions, you could also quite easily develop your own research question. While considering the research question, you will also need to formulate a hypothesis (or hypotheses). Finally, you will need to consider the experimental design of your study. If, for example, you were interested in examining differences between male and female respondents on a gender-based IAT, your independent variable is the participant's gender, while the dependent variable is the IAT score.

DESIGNING THE EXPERIMENTAL MATERIALS

Once the research question(s) and design have been formulated, you will need to create the materials for your study. For the first research question I described (are there differences across males and females in the favourability of implicit gender attitudes?), you will need to develop an IAT. For the sake of simplicity, I would advocate using a paper-and-pencil version of the task, as in the examples above. These questionnaires are modelled after those developed by Lowery et al. (2001), who developed a paper-and-pencil IAT for assessing implicit racial attitudes. The first example provides instructions for a block in which male/positive and female/negative are paired, whereas in the second male/negative and female/positive are paired. In selecting the names and words, I have tried to use stimuli that appear with relatively equal levels of frequency. Remember that you will need to randomize the order in which different participants are presented with the two blocks. You might also wish to include practice blocks in which participants classify a list of names and a list of words.

Of course, should you decide to develop your own research question, you will need to make sure that the materials you develop in your questionnaire serve to answer the research questions being addressed in the study. You will also need to be certain that your data can be analysed using the appropriate test. Your course instructor will be able to assist in you at this phase of the research exercise.

CONDUCTING THE EXPERIMENT

Once the materials have been designed, it is now time to conduct the experiment. This phase of the research should be relatively short. You should aim to have between 60 and 80 participants in the study, with an approximately equal number of males and females.

DATA ENTRY AND ANALYSIS

Once the data have been collected they will need to be entered into a computerized statistics program (e.g. SPSS). While entering the data, you will need to maintain separate columns for each variable of interest. You will need to include columns for variables such as gender, age and the number of categorizations made within each block. You can compute the difference between these scores to compute an IAT score for each respondent (see Lowery et al., 2001 for additional details).

Finally, to assess whether there is a significant difference across your male and female respondents in the favourability of their implicit gender attitudes, you will need to conduct a t-test that compares the mean IAT scores for the two groups.

THINKING ABOUT THE RESULTS AND WRITING A RESEARCH PAPER

Once the data have been analysed, you will need to see how the outcome of the analyses relate to the question(s) that you hoped to address in the study. Was your hypothesis supported? If yes, your discussion section should include a statement of your conclusion plus a discussion of the implications of your study. If your hypothesis was not supported and the data were interpretable, are there other explanations for the results? In considering potential future studies that can be conducted in light of your results, remember that they should be linked with other relevant research findings. For additional advice on how to write a psychology research paper, see Sternberg (1993).

Notes for the Instructor

The research exercise is relatively straightforward and is aimed at undergraduate students at all levels of study. The studies that are most relevant to the exercise are written in a style that is accessible to undergraduate students. These studies should be read as a first step in the research process. Of course, students should also be encouraged to generate their own research questions.

The design of the study I have proposed is a between-subjects design with one manipulated variable. The materials are easy to develop and distribute. This study would require anywhere from 60 to 80 participants, suitable for a small group project. Given the brevity of the experimental materials, data can be collected over the course of an afternoon. The analyses required to carry out the project emphasize the use of a t-test.

PUTTING IT ALL TOGETHER

The study of attitudes is central to the field of social psychology. Over the years, researchers have developed a number of techniques to assess the favourability of individuals' opinions. The purpose of this chapter has been to introduce you to some of the different types of measures that have been developed, and to provide you with 'hands-on' experience with some of these assessment strategies.

NOTE

1   I would like to 'thank' my wife for introducing me to these products.

REFERENCES

Allport, G. W. (1935). Attitudes. In C. Murchison (ed.), *Handbook of social psychology* (pp. 798–844). Worcester, MA: Clark University Press.

American Psychological Association (1985). *Standards for educational and psychological testing*. Washington, DC: American Psychological Association.

Cunningham, W. A., Preacher, K. J. & Banaji, M. R. (2001). Implicit attitude measures: Consistency, stability, and convergent validity. *Psychological Science, 12,* 163–70.

Dawes, R. M. (1972). *Fundamentals of attitude measurement.* New York: Wiley.

Eagly, A. H. & Chaiken, S. (1993). *The psychology of attitudes.* Fort Worth, TX: Harcourt Brace Jovanovich.

Eagly, A. H. & Mladinic, A. (1989). Gender stereotypes and attitudes toward women and men. *Personality and Social Psychology Bulletin, 15,* 543–58.

Eagly, A. H., Mladinic, A. & Otto, S. (1991). Are women evaluated more favorably than men? An analysis of attitudes, beliefs, and emotions. *Psychology of Women Quarterly, 15,* 203–16.

Eiser, J. R. (1990). *Social judgment.* Pacific Grove, CA: Brooks/Cole.

Fazio, R. H. (1990). A practical guide to the use of response latency in social psychological research. In C. Hendrick & M. S. Clark (eds.), *Review of personality and social psychology* (vol. 11, pp. 74–97). Newbury Park, CA: Sage.

Fazio, R. H. (1995). Attitudes as object-evaluation associations: Determinants, consequences, and correlates of attitude accessibility. In R. E. Petty & J. A. Krosnick (eds.), *Attitude strength: Antecedents and consequences* (pp. 247–82). Hillsdale, NJ: Erlbaum.

Fazio, R. H., Jackson, J. R., Dunton, B. C. & Williams, C. J. (1995). Variability in automatic activation as an unobtrusive measure of racial attitudes: A bona fide pipeline? *Journal of Personality and Social Psychology, 69*, 1013–27.

Fazio, R. H. & Olson, M. A. (2003). Implicit measures in social cognition research: Their meaning and use. *Annual Review of Psychology, 54*, 297–327.

Fazio, R. H. & Williams, C. J. (1986). Attitude accessibility as a moderator of the attitude-perception and attitude-behavior relations: An investigation of the 1984 presidential election. *Journal of Personality and Social Psychology, 51*, 505–14.

Greenwald, A. G. (1989). Why attitudes are important: Defining attitude and attitude theory 20 years later. In A. R. Pratkanis, S. J. Breckler & A. G. Greenwald (eds.), Attitude structure and function (pp. 429–40). Hillsdale, NJ: Erlbaum.

Greenwald, A. G. & Banaji, M. R. (1995). Implicit social cognition: Attitudes, self-esteem, and stereotypes. *Psychological Review, 102*, 4–27.

Greenwald, A. G., McGhee, D. & Schwartz, J. (1998). Measuring individual differences in implicit cognition: The implicit association test. *Journal of Personality and Social Psychology, 74*, 1464–80.

Haddock, G. & Carrick, R. (1999a). How to make a politician more likeable and effective: Framing political judgments through the numeric values of a rating scale. *Social Cognition, 17*, 298–311.

Haddock, G. & Carrick, R. (1999b). The Queen Mother and I: Assimilation, contrast, and attitudes toward social groups. *European Journal of Social Psychology, 29*, 123–9.

Haddock, G. & Zanna, M. P. (1994). Preferring 'housewives' to 'feminists': Categorization and the favorability of attitudes toward women. *Psychology of Women Quarterly, 18*, 25–52.

Haddock, G., Zanna, M. P. & Esses, V. M. (1993). Assessing the structure of prejudicial attitudes: The case of attitudes toward homosexuals. *Journal of Personality and Social Psychology, 65*, 1105–18.

Himmelfarb, S. (1993). The measurement of attitudes. In A. H. Eagly & S. Chaiken (eds.), *The psychology of attitudes* (pp. 28–37). Fort Worth, TX: Harcourt Brace Jovanovich.

Huskinson, T. L. & Haddock, G. (in press). Individual differences in attitude structure: Variance in the chronic reliance on affective and cognitive information. *Journal of Experimental Social Psychology*.

Kraus, S. J. (1995). Attitudes and the prediction of behavior: A meta-analysis of the empirical literature. *Personality and Social Psychology Bulletin, 21*, 58–75.

Kruglanski, A. W. (1989). *Lay epistemics and human knowledge: Cognitive and motivational bases*. New York: Plenum.

Likert, R. (1932). A technique for the measurement of attitudes. *Archives of Psychology, 140*, 5–53.

Lowery, B. S., Hardin, C. D. & Sinclair, S. (2001). Social influence effects on automatic racial prejudice. *Journal of Personality and Social Psychology, 81*, 842–55.

Nisbett, R. E. & Wilson, T. D. (1977). Telling more than we know: Verbal reports on mental processes. *Psychological Review, 84*, 231–59.

Olson, J. M. & Zanna, M. P. (1993). Attitudes and attitude change. *Annual Review of Psychology*, 44, 117–54.

Osgood, C. E., Suci, G. J. & Tannenbaum, P. H. (1957). *The measurement of meaning*. Urbana: University of Illinois Press.

Ostrom, T. M. (1989). Interdependence of attitude theory and measurement. In A. R. Pratkanis, S. J. Breckler & A. G. Greenwald (eds.), *Attitude structure and function* (pp. 11–36). Hillsdale, NJ: Erlbaum.

Paulhus, D. L. & John, O. P. (1998). Egoistic and moralistic biases in self-perception: The interplay of self-deceptive styles with basic traits and motives. *Journal of Personality*, 66, 1025–60.

Petty, R. E. & Cacioppo, J. T. (1981). *Attitudes and persuasion: Classic and contemporary approaches*. Dubuque, IA: Brown.

Phelps, E. A. O'Connor, K. J., Cunningham, W. A., Funayama, E. S., Gatenby, J. C. & Banaji, M. R. (2000). Performance on indirect measures of race evaluation predicts amygdala activation. *Journal of Cognitive Neuroscience*, 12, 729–38.

Schwarz, N. (1999). Self-reports: How the questions shape the answers. *American Psychologist*, 54, 93–105.

Schwarz, N., Strack, F. & Mai, H. P. (1991). Assimilation and contrast effects in part-whole question sequences: A conversational logic analysis. *Public Opinion Quarterly*, 55, 3–23.

Schwarz, N., Knauper, B., Hippler, H., Noelle-Neumann, E. & Clark, F. (1991). Rating scales: Numeric values may change the meaning of scale labels. *Public Opinion Quarterly*, 55, 570–82.

Schwarz, N. & Sudman, S. (eds.) (1992). *Context effects in social and psychological research*. New York: Springer-Verlag.

Sternberg, R. J. (1993). *The psychologist's companion* (3rd edn). Cambridge, UK: Cambridge University Press.

Thurstone, L. L. (1928). Attitudes can be measured. *American Journal of Sociology*, ~, 529–54.

Thurstone, L. L. & Chave, E. J. (1929). *The measurement of attitude*. Chicago: University of Chicago Press.

Zanna, M. P. & Rempel, J. K. (1988). Attitudes: A new look at an old concept. In D. BarTal & A. W. Kruglanski (eds.), *The social psychology of knowledge* (pp. 315–34). Cambridge, UK: Cambridge University Press.

CHAPTER EIGHT

Modelling Identity Motives Using Multilevel Regression

Vivian L. Vignoles

This chapter illustrates how self-report data elicited using a single open-ended question ('Who am I?') tied to six simple rating scales in the context of a questionnaire completed during an interview can be analysed to test the relative viability of several theories of identity dynamics. The exercise described shows how a relatively simple data set can be manipulated statistically to test complex hypotheses. It emphasizes the importance in research of postulating and then examining alternative explanations for the patterns that are discovered in data sets. The exercise is suitable for intermediate and advanced level courses.

Self-esteem and Other Identity Motives

One of the least contested claims in social psychology is that most people are generally motivated to protect and enhance their *self-esteem*. A huge array of evidence supports this assertion. Research has shown that we typically pay more attention to, and show more confidence in, information which supports a positive self-evaluation, that we often engage in a variety of self- and group-enhancing strategies when making interpersonal and intergroup social comparisons, and that we generally see ourselves and members of our groups as 'better than average' on a wide range of evaluative dimensions. When our self-esteem is threatened, we tend to become sad or depressed, or we may engage in active attempts to minimize the damage to our identities: sometimes by adjusting our cognitions or behaviour, and sometimes by responding with hostility towards the source of the threat. (For reviews, see Baumeister, 1998; Gecas, 1982; Rosenberg, 1986; Taylor & Brown, 1988.)

However, in recent years, a number of researchers have suggested that other motives beyond self-esteem may be just as strongly implicated in identity processes and related behaviour (Abrams & Hogg, 1988; Breakwell, 1987; Deaux, 2000; Sedikides & Strube, 1995). Current theory and research into self-evaluation often focuses on three or four motivational processes, *self-enhancement, self-consistency, self-assessment* and – optionally – *self-improvement* (Sedikides, 1993; Taylor, Neter & Wayment, 1995), although there remains some ambiguity as to whether each process represents a distinct motive or whether these four processes should be viewed purely as alternative strategies for maintaining and enhancing self-esteem (Sedikides & Strube, 1997). Within the social identity tradition, optimal distinctiveness theory (Brewer, 1991) suggests that we are motivated to identify with social groups as a result of competing needs for *distinctiveness* – or differentiation from others – and *belonging* – or assimilation into social groups – while uncertainty reduction theory (Hogg, 2000) suggests that group identification is motivated by an overarching need for *meaning*. Synthesizing theories of individual and group identity, identity process theory (Breakwell, 1987, 2001) suggests that identity processes are directed towards preserving and enhancing *self-esteem, continuity, distinctiveness* and *efficacy*.

Evidence for the operation of identity motives falls mostly into two categories. On the one hand, researchers have documented a variety of 'cognitive biases', from the self-serving bias to the better-than-average effect (Alicke, Klotz, Breitenbecher, Yurak & Vredenburg, 1995; Zuckerman, 1979). The self has even been likened to a totalitarian political regime, fabricating and revising personal history (Greenwald, 1980). Sometimes it has been argued that these effects are 'purely cognitive' and can be explained without recourse to motivational constructs (Miller & Ross, 1975); however, recent theorists question the artificial separation of motivation and cognition in such arguments (Kruglanski, 1996). Supporting a motivational interpretation, a recent meta-analysis of the self-serving bias showed that effect sizes were significantly greater under conditions of self-threat (Campbell & Sedikides, 1999).

Another large body of research has examined the effects on cognitive, affective and behavioural outcomes of threatening or affirming aspects of the self-concept. Threats to individual and group identities have been shown to result in a variety of coping strategies, including changes in attributions, group identification, self-stereotyping, social attitudes, prejudice and even violence (Baumeister, Smart & Boden, 1996; Breakwell, 1988; Ethier & Deaux, 1994; Fein & Spencer, 1997; Pickett, Bonner & Coleman, 2002). However, many of these outcomes are avoidable if people are given the opportunity to cope with the threat by affirming or enhancing other relevant or irrelevant aspects of the self (Steele, 1988; Tesser, 2000). These studies show the dynamic nature of the self-concept: a huge variety of processes may come into operation to restore equilibrium when core motives are threatened.

An issue under-represented in all of these studies is what Deaux (1992) has called the 'multiplicity of identity'. Identity is composed of *multiple elements* and these elements can be inter-related in many different ways (see also Brewer, 1999). Yet most existing research has focused on single elements of identity, or at best multiple elements within a single domain. Content domains tend to be pre-selected by researchers, often for their theoretical or practical convenience, rather than examining which parts of identity may be relevant or salient to participants themselves. Arguably, this has quite serious implications for the generality of findings to other – perhaps more consequential – domains of identity content.

Moreover, most studies have looked at single motives in isolation, rather than considering the interplay of *multiple motives* in shaping identity. Where several motives have been studied together, research has focused almost exclusively on specific and usually artificial situations in which one motive is pitted against another (e.g. Brewer, 1991; Sedikides, 1993; Swann, Griffin, Predmore & Gaines, 1987). This leads to equally serious concerns about the possibility of generalizing to other – perhaps more ecologically valid – contexts. For example, it is frequently assumed that there is a 'fundamental opposition' between satisfying needs for differentiation and inclusion: the more an element of identity satisfies differentiation needs, the less it satisfies inclusion needs, and vice versa (Brewer & Gardner, 1996; Snyder & Fromkin, 1980): studies have often been formulated so as to reflect this 'fundamental opposition' without subjecting the assumed relationship between differentiation and inclusion to empirical scrutiny; yet it is actually not at all clear that the assumed opposition between differentiation and inclusion occurs in all or even most situations (Green & Werner, 1996; Vignoles, Chryssochoou & Breakwell, 2000).

The research exercise presented here addresses these concerns. I describe a method for evaluating the impact of multiple identity motives on the perceived centrality of multiple elements of identity without pre-specifying identity content or resorting to experimental manipulation. Participants will be allowed to specify their own identity elements. Predictions will be tested treating identity as a whole – rather than focusing on a limited selection of identity elements with a particular *a priori* relationship between them – and taking account of the empirical relationships between identity motives rather than assuming or constraining the nature of these relationships.

Rationale for the Method Described Here

Although this method involves the use of advanced statistical techniques, the central idea underlying it is actually quite simple. If the processes shaping identity are guided by a particular set of motives, then it should follow that elements of identity better satisfying these motives will be privileged by the processes, and will therefore be perceived as more central. Consider, for example, the motive for self-esteem: if I am motivated to increase my self-esteem, then it is likely that elements of my identity associated with feelings of high self-esteem (e.g. successful psychologist, engaged to be married) will become more central to me, whereas elements of my identity which do not enhance my self-esteem (e.g. bassist in a terrible rock band) will become less central. By extension, if I were to make a series of self-descriptive statements and then rate each statement for its association with feelings of self-esteem and for its centrality within my self-definition, you would expect to see a strong correlation between the two sets of ratings I have made – if I were not motivated to achieve higher self-esteem, it is hard to imagine why such a correlation would occur.

However, if the need for self-esteem is not my only motive, things get more complicated. Imagine, for example, that I also have a need for belonging: in this case, elements of my identity associated with stronger feelings of belonging (e.g. engaged to be married, bassist in a terrible rock band) should be more central, whereas elements of my identity which provide a weaker sense of belonging (e.g. successful psychologist) should be less central. Note that there is not a perfect match between which elements of my identity provide a greater sense of self-esteem and which provide a greater sense of belonging. Thus the centrality of each element to my self-definition may depend on a compromise between the demands of these two motives. In this scenario, if you wanted to predict which elements of my identity would be most central to me, you would need to run a multiple regression analysis of my responses with both self-esteem and belonging ratings as predictors.

Now consider that you have a list of partially overlapping theories, each of which proposes which motives may be most important in shaping my identity. This is actually the case: the SCENT model (Sedikides & Strube, 1997) suggests that *self-esteem* concerns will be the main determinant of which parts of my identity are most central. Optimal distinctiveness theory (Brewer, 1991) suggests that competing needs for *belonging* and *distinctiveness* will guide identity processes, although self-esteem will also be important. Uncertainty reduction theory (Hogg, 2000) suggests that the need for *meaning* will be my primary motivation, at least where group identities are concerned. Identity process theory (Breakwell, 2001) suggests that the perceived centrality of parts of my identity will be affected by pressures to maintain and enhance *self-esteem, continuity, distinctiveness* and *efficacy*. In order to evaluate these theories, you might try to establish which of the hypothesized motives are necessary to predict which parts of my identity are most central to me. If I were to make my series of self-descriptive statements and then rate each statement for its centrality within my self-definition and for its association with self-esteem, meaningfulness, belonging, distinctiveness, continuity and efficacy, you could compare models of identity motivation using a series of multiple regression models: which motives do you need in order to predict the perceived centrality of my identity elements?

Of course, it is more likely that you will want to test the applicability of different theories of identity motivation to a particular population, rather than running separate analyses within the responses of each single individual. Note that if you collect data from a sample of individuals, each of whom provides ratings of a series of identity elements, you will have a *nested* data structure, with two distinct levels of analysis: values in your data will vary between identity elements (level 1) and between individuals (level 2). A traditional multiple regression approach would ignore the clustering of identity elements within individuals, which might lead to an underestimation of error variance and hence an increased probability of Type I errors. This exercise introduces *multilevel regression modelling*, which models variance on two or more levels of analysis simultaneously and thus provides more accurate and reliable statistical inferences from nested data structures (Hox, 1995).

It should be acknowledged from the start that we cannot show identity processes in action using a correlational design. In particular, we cannot be sure to what extent the observed relationships are caused by processes shaping the perceived centrality of identity elements or the meanings of the elements themselves. Processes acting in both directions may be guided by identity motives (Ethier & Deaux, 1994), but their effects cannot easily be separated in this study. In this respect, the method outlined here in no way replaces existing experimental and longitudinal techniques for examining the processes shaping both structure and content of identity. However, this method also has particular strengths, notably in its holistic and comparatively non-reactive treatment of multiple elements of identity and multiple motives, which would be hard to reproduce using more controlled or artificial designs.

A Recent Study

Vignoles, Chryssochoou and Breakwell (2002a) used this method to study identity motivation among the population of UK Anglican parish priests. We were interested to compare the applicability to this population of three competing theoretical models: a *self-esteem model*, according to which the processes shaping identity are guided by a need to maintain self-esteem; *identity process theory*, according to which these processes are guided by multiple principles of maintaining self-esteem, distinctiveness, continuity and efficacy; and a *customized model*, including further principles of maintaining a sense of purpose and feelings of closeness to others, which we had previously found to be phenomenologically important among members of the Anglican clergy (Vignoles, 2000).

There were 149 participants, who each generated up to 12 identity elements and then rated each element on eight separate dimensions. Two questions measured the *perceived centrality* of each element within the participants' subjective identity structures. Six questions followed measuring associations of each element with feelings of *self-esteem, distinctiveness, continuity, efficacy, a sense of purpose,* and *closeness to others.* Following the rationale above, we expected that the priests' ratings of their identity elements for perceived centrality would be predicted by the degree to which each element was perceived as a source of self-esteem, distinctiveness, continuity, efficacy, purpose and closeness. We evaluated theoretical models of identity motivation by comparing multilevel regression models predicting perceived centrality with different combinations of these ratings.

Following the *self-esteem model*, we predicted that identity elements associated more strongly with self-esteem would be perceived as more central within participants' subjective identity structures. Supporting our prediction, the association of identity elements with self-esteem was a significant positive predictor of their perceived centrality ($p < .001$). The self-esteem model predicted an estimated 32.5 per cent of variance within participants in the perceived centrality of identity elements.

To test *identity process theory*, we hypothesized that including distinctiveness, continuity and efficacy ratings would substantially improve predictions of perceived centrality compared to a model with only the self-esteem rating as predictor. Supporting our prediction, including distinctiveness, continuity and efficacy ratings substantially improved predictions of perceived centrality compared to the self-esteem model ($p < .001$). Identity process theory predicted an estimated 49.7 per cent of variance within participants in the perceived centrality of identity elements, a substantial improvement in predictive value over the preceding model. We also computed four models, each assessing the effect of individually eliminating one of the predictors. All four predictors made significant individual improvements to the model fit (all $p < .001$). Thus, none of the four motives was superfluous within this model. These results were interpreted as strongly supporting the claim of identity process theory that principles of distinctiveness, continuity and efficacy should be given equal theoretical consideration to self-esteem as motives guiding identity processes.

Finally, to test the *customized model*, we hypothesized that purpose and closeness would behave similarly to the existing principles in predictions of perceived centrality, and that including these two constructs would significantly improve predictions compared to identity process theory. Both purpose and closeness were positive predictors of perceived centrality within this model, and including them in the model improved predictions of perceived centrality compared to identity process theory ($p < .001$). The customized model predicted an estimated 54.6 per cent of variance within participants in the perceived centrality of identity elements, a modest improvement in predictive value over identity process theory. As before, we also computed six additional models, each assessing the effect of individually eliminating one of the predictors. Five out of six predictors made significant individual improvements to the model fit (all $p < .001$). However the unique contribution of self-esteem was no longer significant within this model, indicating that the five other predictors had entirely accounted for the contribution of self-esteem ratings to the perceived centrality of identity elements observed in our previous models. Overall, the findings provided clear support for our argument that 'self-esteem is not the whole story', at least among Anglican parish priests in the United Kingdom.

Research Exercise

AIMS AND HYPOTHESES

The aim of this research exercise is to compare the predictive value of two models of identity motivation: the *self-esteem model* and *identity process theory*. Note that the exercise might be adapted to compare any number of theoretical models – however, these two models will suffice for current purposes. An additional aim is to explore whether there are significant *gender differences* in the relative strengths of each motive within identity process theory. Note that the same method might be used to compare identity motives between any two or more groups of participants.

The exercise is designed to test the following hypotheses: following the *self-esteem model*, it is predicted (H1) that those identity elements associated more strongly with self-esteem will be perceived as more central within participants' subjective identity structures. *Identity process theory* predicts that ratings of identity elements for associations with self-esteem, distinctiveness, continuity and efficacy will all be positive predictors of perceived centrality. However, an important issue here is to establish the *added value* derived from examining all four principles, rather than just a self-esteem principle. It is predicted (H2) that including distinctiveness, continuity and efficacy ratings will significantly improve predictions of perceived centrality, in comparison with a model incorporating only the self-esteem rating as predictor. As a more rigorous test of the importance of each motive within identity process theory, it is predicted (H3) that *each of these ratings individually* will be a significant positive predictor of perceived centrality after controlling for effects of the other three. Finally, in order to test for *gender differences*, it is predicted (H4) that there will be significant differences between male and female participants in the weights of one or more of these ratings as predictors of perceived centrality.

DATA COLLECTION

Participants and procedure

You should aim to collect data from about 50 male and 50 female participants from a population of your choice (or 50 in each group, if you are comparing a different set of groups). In an ideal world, participants would be randomly sampled from the population you have chosen: however, for this exercise, it will be acceptable to recruit participants opportunistically, as long as this is acknowledged when you report your findings. If you are working in a group, you may choose to collect a smaller amount of data each and then combine the data for your analyses, as long as you ensure that your participants are drawn from the same overall population.

Participants will be asked to fill in a questionnaire taking about 20 minutes. They should respond without discussing the questions with anyone else and should be encouraged to take reasonable care but not to agonize over each answer.

As in all social scientific research, you should give participants the right to withdraw from the study at any time, guarantee their anonymity, and – even if the study does not involve deception – you should provide some explanation afterwards of the study's aims. Ideally you will arrange a way of providing a summary of results for those who would like to know more about the study and its findings.

Questionnaire measures

The questionnaire will be the same for all respondents, and should include the following measures (see below for the questionnaire lay-out, which is important):

Generation of identity elements: first, participants will be asked to generate freely a series of identity elements. This can be done using a slightly reduced version of the Twenty Statements Test (Kuhn & McPartland, 1954), in which participants are asked to give 12 answers to the question 'Who am I?', fairly quickly, without worrying about the logic or importance of their answers. You may want to vary the number of answers requested, although too many may result in fatigue on the subsequent rating task while too few may provide insufficient variance in perceived centrality within the responses of each individual to test the main hypotheses.

Rating of identity elements: next, participants will be asked to rate the identity elements they have just specified on a series of dimensions, which measure the perceived centrality of each element within identity, as well as associations of each element with subjective feelings of self-esteem, continuity, distinctiveness and efficacy. Each dimension should be presented as a question at the top of a new page, with block of 12 seven-point scales positioned underneath to line up with the identity elements. Two questions can be used to measure perceived centrality:

> *How much do you see each of the answers you have written as central or marginal to your identity?*
> (rating scale: 1 = extremely marginal, 4 = intermediate, 7 = extremely central)
>
> *How important is each of these answers in defining who you are?*
> (rating scale: 1 = not at all important, 4 = intermediate, 7 = extremely important)

Associations of the identity elements with self-esteem, distinctiveness, continuity and efficacy can be measured using the following single-item measures:

> *How much does each of your answers give you a sense of self-esteem?*
> (rating scale: 1 = not at all, 4 = moderately, 7 = extremely)
>
> *How much do you feel that each of your answers distinguishes you from other people?*
> (rating scale: 1 = not at all, 4 = moderately, 7 = extremely)
>
> *How much does each of your answers give you a sense of continuity –between past, present and future – in your life?*
> (rating scale: 1 = not at all, 4 = moderately, 7 = extremely)
>
> *How much does each of your answers make you feel competent or effective in doing the things you do?*
> (rating scale: 1 = not at all, 4 = moderately, 7 = extremely)

Although – in an ideal world – it would be preferable to include several questions for each motive, single-item measures are used here to minimize the load on participants. Note that a similar approach has been used successfully to measure global self-esteem (Robins, Hendin & Trzesniewski, 2001), and the use of single-item measures has been established in other studies where participants are asked to make many repeated ratings on the same dimension (Reis, Sheldon, Gable, Roscoe & Ryan, 2000).

Demographic details: finally, you should collect sufficient demographic data to describe your sample. As a minimum, you should ask participants their sex (necessary to test H4) and their age. Depending on your chosen population, you may also include questions about occupation, marital status, ethnicity and/or nationality.

QUESTIONNAIRE LAYOUT

Note that the physical layout of your questionnaire is extremely important, as participants can easily get confused or lose their place while completing their ratings. It is essential that you present the first section of the questionnaire in such a way that participants can easily line up their identity elements with the rating scales. This not only minimizes your participants' effort in helping you with the study, it also ensures that you will have more accurate data, with fewer mistakes and fewer missing values.

Ideally, you should print the first section on a page which folds out from the main questionnaire, ensuring that the subsequent rating scales are always positioned at the same height on each page to match up with the identity elements. If this is not practical, you may altern-atively print the first section on a separate sheet from the main questionnaire, clearly numbering the 12 identity elements and the 12 rating scales for each question, and again making sure that the rating scales are always presented at the same height on the page as are the identity elements. In either case, a very useful trick is to use the 'shading' feature in Microsoft Word to shade lightly one row in three among the identity elements and the rating scales, which provides a visual cue to help participants reliably match up the two sections (see Figure 8.1; section A folds out from the back page of the answer booklet. The first page of section B, shown here, is the *second* page of the answer booklet, hidden by a cover sheet while participants com-plete section A.).

DATA ENTRY AND PRELIMINARY ANALYSES

These instructions assume that you will use SPSS for Windows to enter and prepare your data, and MIXREG to compute the multilevel regression models.

Data entry

You should create an SPSS data file, including the nine variables summarized in Table 8.1. Note that each row of your data file *does not* represent one participant, as is usually the case: each row of the data

Table 8.1 Variables for inclusion in your main SPSS data file

	Variable	Definition
1	part_no	You should give a unique number to each participant in your study and write this number on their questionnaire, so that you can check their responses in the event that you subsequently identify a possible mistake in your data entry
2	id_no	Similarly, you should number each identity element from 1 to 12 within the data of each participant
3	central1	Responses to the first centrality rating scale
4	central2	Responses to the second centrality rating scale
5	esteem	Responses to the self-esteem rating scale
6	distin	Responses to the distinctiveness rating scale
7	contin	Responses to the continuity rating scale
8	effica	Responses to the efficacy rating scale
9	sex	The participant's sex: code male = −1, female = 1

set is for one identity element, each column is for one variable. Thus, each participant will have 12 rows of data (unless they generated fewer than 12 identity elements in the first section): the first variable, part_no, will be used to identify which ratings came from whom.

When entering the data, you may find that some participants have missed one or two ratings. Do not worry about this, just leave those cells blank in the data file. However, be very careful when entering the data: it is easy to mistype values when you are trying to be fast! When you have finished entering the data from all participants, it is also good practice to check for any obviously mistyped values: use SPSS frequencies to look at all of your variables and make sure there are no impossible values (e.g. values less than 1 or greater than 7 in the rating scales, values other than −1 or 1 for sex). If anything arouses suspicion, you should find the relevant cells in the data file and look back at your questionnaires to correct them. Now save your data file. At this point, you should also *save a copy* with a different name, as you are about to make some changes, not all of which are reversible.

You should also create a second data file for the demographic information you requested from participants. Here, you will use this data file solely for descriptive statistics in order to characterize your sample when you report your findings.

Section A

Who am I?

There are 12 numbered blanks on the page below. Please write 12 answers to the simple question 'Who am I?'. Answer as if you were giving the answers to yourself, not ot somebody else. Write the answers in the order that they occur to you. Don't worry about the logic or 'importance' of your answers. Try to answer quickly.

1.
2.
3.
4.
5.
6.
7.
8.
9.
10.
11.
12.

Figure 8.1   Suggested questionnaire layout (adapted from Vignoles et al., 2002a)

Preparing your data

Before you run your multilevel regression analyses, you need to pre-pare the data file, so that MIXREG has the input it needs to calculate your results. You may follow the instructions below or run the SPSS syntax commands in Table 8.2.

Perceived centrality measure: first, you need to create your dependent variable from the first two rating scales in the questionnaire. Check

Section B

Now please look again at the 12 answers you gave to the question 'Who am I?' in section A. The next three questions refer to these 12 answrs you have given. Please answer each question 12 times, referring to each of your 12 previous answers.

How much do you see each of the answers you have written as central or marginal to your identity?

Extremely marginal...		...intermediate...			...extremely central	
1	2	3	4	5	6	7
1	2	3	4	5	6	7
1	2	3	4	5	6	7
1	2	3	4	5	6	7
1	2	3	4	5	6	7
1	2	3	4	5	6	7
1	2	3	4	5	6	7
1	2	3	4	5	6	7
1	2	3	4	5	6	7
1	2	3	4	5	6	7
1	2	3	4	5	6	7
1	2	3	4	5	6	7

Figure 8.1   *(cont'd)*

the correlation between central1 and central2: it should be quite high ($r > .5$), supporting the interpretation that these ratings are measuring the same underlying construct. Use 'SPSS compute' to calculate the mean of these ratings. Call this variable 'central'.

Deleting cases with missing data: for the analyses which follow, you will use only those identity elements for which there are no *missing data*. Therefore, you need to delete from your data file all identity elements for which there are missing values (make sure that you saved a copy of

Table 8.2 SPSS syntax for data preparation

Function	Syntax commands

Perceived centrality measure[a]	CORRELATIONS
	  /VARIABLES=central1, central2
	  /PRINT=TWOTAIL SIG
	  /MISSING=PAIRWISE.
	
	COMPUTE central = MEAN (central1, central2) .
	EXECUTE .

Deleting cases with missing data	COMPUTE missing = NMISS(central, esteem, distin, contin, effica, sex) . EXECUTE . FILTER OFF USE ALL . SELECT IF(missing = 0) . EXECUTE .
Intercept variable	COMPUTE intercpt = 1 . EXECUTE .

Participant-mean centring[b]	GLM
	Esteem distin contin effica BY part_no
	  /METHOD = SSTYPE(3)
	  /INTERCEPT = INCLUDE
	  /SAVE = RESID
	  /CRITERIA = ALPHA(.05)
	  /DESIGN = part_no .
	
	RENAME VARIABLES (res_1 = c_esteem)
	(res_2 = c_distin) (res_3 = c_contin)
	(res_4 = c_effica)

Cross-product terms	COMPUTE s_esteem = sex * c_esteem . COMPUTE s_distin = sex * c_distin . COMPUTE s_contin = sex * c_contin . COMPUTE s_effica = sex * c_effica . EXECUTE

Saving the data[c]	SAVE OUTFILE = 'identity.sav'
	  /COMPRESSED .
	SAVE TRANSLATE OUTFILE = 'identity.dat'
	  /TYPE=TAB /MAP /REPLACE .

These commands will perform all operations in the section on 'preparing your data'. You can type these commands into a single SPSS syntax file, select all of the text and press the run button to perform all of the operations in one go.

[a] Check this correlation in your SPSS output.
[b] Ignore the SPSS output for the GLM analysis.
[c] Run SPSS file info to check that variables are consistent with Tables 8.1 and 8.3.

the original data, in case you need to go back to it). To identify which identity elements have missing data, use 'SPSS compute' to calculate a new variable, 'missing', which is the sum of missing values in all variables [NMISS (central, esteem, distin, contin, effica, sex)]. You can now use 'SPSS select cases' to remove all identity elements for which there are missing data present. Use the 'select if condition is satisfied' option, with the condition missing = 0. Tick the 'unselected cases are deleted' box and run the procedure. You should find that identity elements for which there were missing data have now been deleted.

Intercept variable: for the multilevel regression analyses, you will need a 'variable' which represents the intercept in a regression equation. Using 'SPSS compute', simply create a new variable, 'intercpt', which is equal to 1. You should find this new variable – simply a column of 1's – at the end of your data file.

Participant-mean centring: note that the hypotheses in this exercise are concerned with predicting variance *within participants* in perceived centrality – which identity elements are perceived as more or less central *within* the responses of each individual participant – and not variance *between participants* – which participants rate their responses overall as more or less central. Between-participant effects (predicting individual differences in 'perceived centrality' as a function of individual differences in self-esteem, distinctiveness, continuity and efficacy) would have no obvious interpretation here, and would not provide evidence for identity motives.

If you conduct your analyses using the raw ratings of identity elements for satisfaction of each motive, your results will reflect a mixture of within-participant and between-participant effects. This is clearly not satisfactory, as you will be unsure whether your hypothesis tests are biased by the presence of non-meaningful between-participant effects. To obtain unbiased estimates of the *within-participant* regression weights in each model, you need to remove *between-participant* variance from all predictors. You can do this by *centring* values of each predictor around their mean value within the data of each participant (cf. Hofmann & Gavin, 1998).

A slightly unorthodox but nevertheless effective way of doing this is to run a MANOVA (using SPSS GLM Multivariate) on all predictor variables (esteem, distin, contin, effica) with part_no as a fixed factor, and save the unstandardized residuals. Ignore the output for this analysis, which is meaningless. At the end of your data file, you will find a new set of variables, 'res_1' to 'res_4', which are your four predictors, centred around their mean values within the data of each participant. You should rename these variables 'c_esteem', 'c_distin', 'c_contin' and 'c_effica'.

Cross-product terms: in order to test for gender differences (or other group differences), you will need to calculate interaction effects of sex with each of the four main predictors: do the regression weights of c_esteem, c_distin, c_contin and c_effica as predictors of central differ systematically according to whether the participant is male or female? In multilevel regression, as in traditional multiple regression, you can estimate interaction effects by introducing additional variables, known as *cross-product terms*, into your regression models (see Agresti & Finlay, 1999, pp. 404–8). Create these variables using 'SPSS compute': simply multiply each of your centred predictors (c_esteem, c_distin, c_contin and c_effica) by sex, to create four new variables, s_esteem, s_distin, s_contin and s_effica.

Saving the data: you need to save your data in two separate formats. For preliminary analyses, you should save the main data file in SPSS format. For the multilevel analyses, you must additionally save your data in tab-delimited (*.dat) format using the 'save as' function in SPSS. You must deselect the 'write variable names to spreadsheet' option, as MIXREG can read only numbers and not variable names in the data file: in your instructions to MIXREG, you will identify which columns in the data file refer to which variables. Call the file 'identity.dat'.

Table 8.3 lists the additional variables which should now be included in your data file. Before moving on to the next section, run 'SPSS file info' and check that the variables you have in your file are the same – and, crucially, in the same order – as are listed in Tables 8.1 and 8.3. If there are any differences (which should not be the case unless you have modified the exercise in any way), you will need to adjust your instructions accordingly when you run the MIXREG analyses described below.

Zero order correlations: when conducting research using any form of multiple regression, it is good practice to examine and report the *zero order correlations* between all variables used in the analysis. Use SPSS to look at the Pearson correlations between central, sex, the four participant-mean centred predictors and the four cross-product terms.

Ignore the significance values as these may be misleading because of the multilevel data structure: you will test the significance of your hypotheses shortly. Nevertheless, you can use the correlations to get an initial feel for your predictions. Look especially at the correlations of each predictor with central, your dependent variable. If identity process theory is correct, you should expect to see moderate to large positive correlations between each of the participant-mean centred predictors and perceived centrality, showing that identity elements associated more strongly with self-esteem, distinctiveness, continuity and efficacy also tend to be perceived as more central within identity.

Table 8.3 Additional variables created in your main data file

	Variable	Definition
10	central	Measure of perceived centrality for use in multilevel regression analyses (mean of CENTRAL1, CENTRAL2)
11	missing	Number of missing values for each identity element: should be equal to 0 for all identity elements after running select cases. This variable can now be disregarded
12	intercpt	Intercept for use in multilevel regression analyses: should be equal to 1 for all identity elements
13	c_esteem	Participant-mean centred responses to the self-esteem rating scale for use in multilevel regression analyses
14	c_distin	Participant-mean centred responses to the distinctiveness rating scale for use in multilevel regression analyses
15	c_contin	Participant-mean centred responses to the continuity rating scale for use in multilevel regression analyses
16	c_effica	Participant-mean centred responses to the efficacy rating scale for use in multilevel regression analyses
17	s_esteem	Cross-product of SEX and C_ESTEEM for calculating interaction effects in multilevel regression analyses
18	s_distin	Cross-product of SEX and C_DISTIN for calculating interaction effects in multilevel regression analyses
19	s_contin	Cross-product of SEX and C_CONTIN for calculating interaction effects in multilevel regression analyses
20	s_effica	Cross-product of SEX and C_EFFICA for calculating interaction effects in multilevel regression analyses.

If there are gender differences in the strengths of different identity motives, you should expect to see at least small correlations between one or more of the cross-product terms and perceived centrality: for any given motive, a negative correlation implies that the motive is stronger among males whereas a positive correlation implies that the motive is stronger among females.

MULTILEVEL REGRESSION MODELLING

Multilevel regression, also known as *hierarchical linear modelling* (Bryk & Raudenbush, 1992), is the most commonly used form of *multilevel*

modelling (Hox, 1995; Kreft & de Leeuw, 1998). Multilevel models are used wherever researchers need to separate effects occurring at two or more levels of analysis. These models are often used in educational psychology, where researchers need to distinguish effects attributable to differences between individuals from those which are attributable to differences between schools (see Bryk & Raudenbush, 1992). In such studies, the data collected is structured on two separate levels of analysis: pupils (level 1) are clustered within schools (level 2). Single-level analyses – which involve either ignoring the clustering of pupils within schools (level 1 analysis) or aggregating individual data to school level (level 2 analysis) – can give at best incomplete and at worst incorrect results (see Kreft & de Leeuw, 1998). On the other hand, multilevel modelling can be used to separate statistically effects occurring at these two levels of analysis.

In this exercise we also have a two-level data structure: identity elements (level 1) are clustered within participants (level 2). You will use the results of five multilevel regression analyses (summarized in Table 8.4) to test the four hypotheses of the exercise. The analyses you run will be based on principles of *model comparison*, similar to a traditional multiple regression approach in which predictors are entered in successive blocks (sometimes known as 'hierarchical' or 'nested' multiple regression analysis). As with *change statistics* in multiple regression, you will compare models of varying levels of complexity:

Table 8.4 Predictors included in each multilevel regression model

Predictor	Field	Model number				
		0	1	2	3	4
Fixed effects						
c_esteem	13	–	X	X	X	X
c_distin	14	–	–	X	X	X
c_contin	15	–	–	X	X	X
c_effica	16	–	–	X	X	X
sex	9	–	–	–	X	X
s_esteem	17	–	–	–	–	X
s_distin	18	–	–	–	–	X
s_contin	19	–	–	–	–	X
s_effica	20	–	–	–	–	X
Random effect						
intercpt	12	X	X	X	X	X

Dependent variable is central (field 10)

does making a simpler model more complex (by adding more predictors) significantly improve your prediction of perceived centrality? As with R^2 in multiple regression, you will calculate the proportion of variance in your dependent variable accounted for by each model. As with *B weights* in multiple regression, you will look at the *parameter estimates* for each predictor in your models: does each predictor contribute significantly and uniquely to your model of perceived centrality after accounting for the other predictors in the model?

Null model (model 0)

The first multilevel analysis you will run is to compute a *null model*, which you will use as a baseline for subsequent comparisons. Follow the steps outlined below to create your first MIXREG definition file.

1 Open MIXREG and click the 'default' button towards the bottom right.
2 You will see a window labelled 'configuration' into which you can now type your instructions to the program. In the 'title 1' box, type your name. In the 'title 2' box, type in a name for this model, 'Baseline model (model 0)'.
3 For this and for each successive analysis you perform, there will be three computer files involved. The 'definition file' summarizes the instructions you are currently giving to MIXREG: call this 'model0.def'. The 'output file' will contain the results of the analysis you are about to run: call this 'model0.out'. The 'input file' is the data file you saved earlier in dat format: double-click in the input file box and locate the data file ('identity.dat') where you saved it.
4 Now enter the number of data fields: this is the number of variables in your data file, which will be 20 if you have followed the research exercise exactly. MIXREG uses this information to identify where each row of data begins.
5 Now type in the field for level-2 units, which is the column number for the variable 'part_no' (if this was your first column of data – as suggested in Table 8.1 – then this number will be 1). MIXREG uses this information to identify which level 1 units (identity elements) belong to which level 2 units (participants).
6 Next, type in the dependent variable field, which is the column number of the variable 'central' (10 if you have followed the instructions) and the dependent variable label: 'central'. You have now told MIXREG where to find your dependent variable in the data file and how to label it in the output file.

7 Leave the remaining fields in the 'configuration' window as they are, and click on the 'variables' tab towards the top-left of the window. The 'variables' window is where you will enter your predictors for each analysis.

8 For the *null model* you have just one predictor, the intercept, which you should include as a random effect (meaning that the intercept can vary randomly between individuals, an essential feature of multilevel regression which I discuss below). Set the 'number of random effects' to 1 and the 'number of fixed effects' to 0. Now enter the 'field' column (which should be 12) and the 'label' 'intercpt'.

9 Now run the analysis (this will also save your definition file).

After a few seconds, an 'output window' will appear. The first part of this window describes the number of level 2 observations (participants) and the number of level 1 observations (identity elements) included in the analysis, which should be the same for all models, as well as descriptive statistics for all variables. Scroll down to the 'final results' section. This contains a number of important pieces of information, which you will need to use later. You may well find it easier to print the output files in this exercise, rather than copying everything from the screen.

The 'log likelihood' should be a large negative number. This is a measure of how well your regression model fits the observed data: the closer the log likelihood gets to zero, the better the fit of the model. You will use this value as a baseline, comparing it with the log likelihood of subsequent models using *likelihood ratio tests* to test whether these models fit the data significantly better than the null model.

Below this are three 'parameter estimates', which define the regression equation for the null model. The first value is the 'fixed parameter estimate' for the 'intercept', which here is an estimate of the true mean value of perceived centrality. The second is the 'random-effect variance estimate' for the intercept, an estimate of the amount of level 2 variance around this mean – the extent of differences between participants (also known as *level 2 residual variance*). The 'residual variance' reflects the amount of variance in perceived centrality which remains after accounting for the above parameters – that is, the total unexplained variance *within participants* in perceived centrality (also known as *level 1 residual variance*). Remember that we are not trying to model individual differences in perceived centrality in this exercise: our hypotheses concern *within-participant* variance only. Hence the 'residual variance' in the null model represents the total variance we are trying to predict: if the predictions are confirmed, you will see a reduction in residual variance in subsequent models, and you can use this baseline figure from the null model to estimate R^2_w, the *proportion of within-participants variance modelled*, similar to R^2 in multiple regression.

Testing the self-esteem model (model 1)

You are now in a position to run the *self-esteem model*, and test H1:

1 Close the output window and click on the 'configuration' tab to return to the first window in MIXREG. In the 'title 2' box, type in a new name: 'Self-esteem model' (model 1). Rename the definition and output files, 'model1.def' and 'model1.out'.
2 Now click on the 'variables' tab and change the 'number of fixed effects' to 1. Enter the 'field' (13) and the 'variable label' for 'c_esteem' and run the analysis.

You can test whether the self-esteem model fits your data significantly better than the null model using a *likelihood ratio test*. Look at the value of 'log likelihood' for this model. If the model fit has improved, then this value will be closer to zero than the value you noted down from the null model. To test whether the improvement is significant, calculate the *likelihood ratio statistic* for this model comparison, which is twice the difference between the two log likelihood values, or $2(LL_{model\ 1} - LL_{model\ 0})$. This statistic follows a χ^2 distribution with degrees of freedom equal to the number of parameters you have added to the model. Here, you have added just one predictor to the null model – the fixed slope for 'c_esteem' – so you can check the significance of the model using χ^2 tables with 1 degree of freedom. If the likelihood ratio statistic is higher than the critical value of χ^2 with 1df, then the self-esteem model is significantly better than the null model, and you have evidence supporting the first hypothesis.

A few lines below, you will see the 'fixed parameter estimate' for 'c_esteem'. Similar to a *B* weight in simple regression, this is the predicted increase or decrease in perceived centrality with an increase of one scale point in the self-esteem ratings. According to H1, this value should be positive, indicating that the more an identity element is associated with feelings of self-esteem, the more central it is perceived to be within identity. This value also has a 'p-value' associated with it: this represents the significance of 'c_esteem' as a predictor of perceived centrality after accounting for all other parameters in the model. Since, in this case, 'c_esteem' is the only predictor you have added to the null model, the significance test is equivalent to the likelihood ratio test you have just performed. Note however that, without the null model, you could not calculate the proportion of modelled variance (below), nor would you be able to test the overall fit of subsequent models with more than one predictor.

You probably also want to know *how well* the self-esteem ratings predict the perceived centrality of identity elements: how much variance in perceived centrality have you accounted for in the self-esteem model? Look at the 'residual variance' for the self-esteem model: this is how much *within-participants* variance you *have not* modelled in this analysis. If you compare this to the residual variance from the null model – which is the *total* within-participants variance in perceived centrality – you can work out how much within-participants variance you *have* modelled. Simply calculate the difference between the two values of residual variance and divide this number by the residual variance from the null model. This is the value of R_w^2. Multiply by 100 to express this value as a percentage. What percentage of the variance within participants in perceived centrality have you modelled?

Finally, look at the 'random-effect variance' term for the intercept: remember this is the amount of *between-participants* variance in perceived centrality you *have not* modelled. This value should be more or less unchanged from the null model: since the predictor you added, 'c_esteem', was centred within participants, it contains no between-participant variance and therefore could not have predicted any. By participant-mean centring, we have ensured that any observed improvement in model fit can only be due to improved modelling of *within-participants* variance, which is the portion of the variance we are interested in modelling in this exercise. (Similarly, since the predictor 'c_esteem' was centred around a mean of zero, the 'fixed estimate' for the intercept should be more or less unchanged from that in the null model.)

Testing identity process theory (model 2)

You should now run the *identity process theory* model to test H2 and H3:

1 Close the output window and open the 'configuration' window (by clicking on the tab). In the 'title 2' box, type in a new name: 'Identity process theory (model 2)'. Rename the definition and output files, 'model2.def' and 'model2.out'.
2 Now click on the 'variables' tab and change the 'number of fixed effects' from 1 to 4. Add the 'fields' (14, 15, 16) and the 'variable labels' for 'c_distin', 'c_contin' and 'c_effica', and run the analysis.

There are now two model comparisons you can make. First, you can check the significance of the model as a whole by comparison with the null model: calculate the likelihood ratio statistic for identity process theory, as you did for the self-esteem model; note that this time you have 4 degrees of freedom, since you have included four predictors which were not in the null model. Is the overall model fit significant?

Second, equivalent to *change statistics* in multiple regression, you can test whether this more complex model fits the data *significantly better* than the simpler self-esteem model: perform another likelihood ratio test comparing log likelihood statistics for the *self-esteem model* and *identity process theory*; here you have 3 degrees of freedom, since you have three predictors in the latter model which were not included in the former. If the test is significant, then you have evidence supporting H2: theorizing these four motives rather than just a self-esteem motive does significantly improve predictions of the perceived centrality of identity elements.

If so, you will probably also want to know – as you did for the self-esteem model – how well identity process theory predicts the perceived centrality of identity elements: how much variance in perceived centrality have you modelled using identity process theory? You can calculate R^2_w by comparing the 'residual variance' of this model with that of the null model, exactly as you did for the self-esteem model. What percentage of the variance have you modelled, and how much better are predictions using this more complex model rather than the self-esteem model?

Now examine the 'fixed parameter estimates' and associated 'p-values' for 'c_esteem', 'c_distin', 'c_contin' and 'c_effica'. According to identity process theory, the more an identity element is associated with feelings of self-esteem, distinctiveness, continuity and efficacy, the more it will be perceived as central within identity: are all of the fixed parameter estimates *positive*, as you would expect? Furthermore, are *all four* motives necessary for your predictions, as we have hypothesized (H3): does *each* predictor contribute significantly to your model *after accounting for effects of the other three*? As with the *B* weights in traditional multiple regression, the 'p-values' attached to the fixed parameter estimates allow you to test this hypothesis.

Testing for gender differences (models 3 and 4)

Finally, you should test whether there are significant gender differences in the strengths of any of the effects in the identity process theory model. This involves testing the significance of the cross-product terms, 's_esteem', 's_distin', 's_contin' and 's_effica', which you created to test for interaction effects of each rating with sex. Note that to test the significance of a two-way interaction effect you must have both main effects also included in your model (Agresti & Finlay, 1999): to see whether including the cross-product terms in the model significantly improves predictions of perceived centrality, you must first add 'sex' into the identity process theory model (model 3) and only then test the effect of adding the cross-product terms (model 4).

Run model 3 by changing the 'title', renaming the 'definition' and 'output' files, and adding a fifth 'fixed effect' for 'sex' (field 9 in your data). Note down the 'log likelihood' for this model. Now run model 4, adding 'fixed effects' for the four cross-product terms, 's_esteem', 's_distin', 's_contin' and 's_effica' (fields 17–20). You can test for gender differences (H4) by comparing the 'log likelihood' values of models 3 and 4 using a *likelihood ratio test* with 4 degrees of freedom (since you have added four predictors). If there are gender differences in the strengths of each motive in identity process theory, you can expect to see a significant improvement in fit from model 3 to model 4, which includes the four predictors modelling these gender differences.

If you do find a significant improvement from model 3 to model 4, you will want to describe the differences which exist between male and female participants in your sample. Look at the 'fixed parameter estimates' and associated 'p-values' for the four interaction effects, 's_esteem', 's_distin', 's_contin' and 's_effica': is the direction of the estimates negative or positive, and which of them are significant? As with the zero-order correlations, for any given motive, a negative estimate means that the motive is stronger among males, whereas a positive estimate means that the motive is stronger among females. You may also want to know how much additional variance you have modelled with these interaction effects: does allowing for gender differences dramatically improve your prediction of perceived centrality, or is the improvement only quite slight? You can calculate R^2_w by comparing the 'residual variance' with that of the null model, as you did previously. How much more variance have you modelled than you were able to account for without the interaction terms?

Notes for the Course Leader

TEACHING VALUE OF THE EXERCISE

This research exercise provides students with experience of collecting survey data and introduces multilevel regression analysis. Multilevel modelling – of which multilevel regression is the most common form – is increasingly used in social psychology as software becomes more available and user-friendly, and this has begun to be reflected in undergraduate and postgraduate research methods classes. Students should already have a fairly secure background in multiple regression: if so, this exercise will help to consolidate and expand their learning, dealing with issues such as modelled variance, model comparison approaches, and interaction effects.

The exercise also encourages students to engage with the rapidly developing body of research literature on identity motives. Currently there is little theoretical consensus over the core motives involved in identity processes, and so students will have the opportunity to engage with a body of literature in which the 'right answers' are not already given and to consider how their findings relate to this literature.

NECESSARY RESOURCES

For data collection, each group of students will need to produce about 100 copies of an eight-page questionnaire. The questionnaire requires a fairly large volume of printing/photocopying, and some students may also need help with the questionnaire layout, which is especially important in this exercise, as mentioned above.

Of key importance is the availability of multilevel modelling software. The exercise has been written for analysis using the MIXREG software program (Hedeker & Gibbons, 1996), which is available free from Don Hedeker's web site (http://tigger.uic.edu/~hedeker/mix.html). The analyses could equally be performed using HLM, MLwiN or any other multilevel modelling package. I have chosen MIXREG because the interface and output are comparatively user-friendly for students coming to the exercise with experience of SPSS multiple regression.

POSSIBLE MODIFICATIONS OF THE EXERCISE

As already noted, a simple modification to the exercise would be to adapt the hypothesis about gender differences to make a different group comparison: subject to the availability of participants, students might compare occupational groups, age groups or – perhaps for a dissertation topic – participants of different nationalities. Note that if more than two groups are to be compared, the calculation of interaction effects will be rather more complicated, as the sex variable will have to be replaced by a set of contrasts rather than a single dummy variable, and cross-product terms will have to be calculated with each contrast. Unless there are especially strong reasons to compare more than two groups, it is strongly advised to stick to the design used here, simply substituting another two groups for males and females in the analysis.

Another possibility would be to compare a different set of theoretical models, involving a different set of hypothesized motives. Several theorists have proposed identity motives or needs which are not included in identity process theory, such as a need for belonging (Brewer, 1991; Leary & Baumeister, 2000) and a need for meaning (Baumeister, 1991; Hogg, 2000). Ambitious students might think of suitably worded questions to rate identity elements with respect to these or other motives and modify the questionnaire and analysis accordingly. When conducting likelihood ratio tests, note the constraint that it is only valid to compare 'nested' models, in which the more complex model includes all parameters of the simpler model.

For advanced groups, a further modification would be to model individual differences in the strengths of each motive using models with *random slopes*. In this exercise, I have included models with *fixed slopes* only, in which the regression weights of each predictor of perceived centrality cannot vary between participants. The only *random effect* is that of the intercept, which is used to estimate the level 2 residual variance in each model. More complex are models with *random slopes*, which could be used here to estimate the extent to which participants vary in the regression weights of each predictor (see Vignoles et al., 2002a). Note that R^2_W is no longer meaningful in models with random slopes (Kreft & de Leeuw, 1998).

FURTHER READING

Although this exercise does not require any previous experience in multilevel modelling, it would be an advantage to run the exercise in conjunction with a statistics lecture on this topic. An accessible introductory text is by Kreft & de Leeuw (1998). Alternative texts include more detailed coverage of some advanced topics (Bryk & Raudenbush, 1992; Snijders & Bosker, 1999). Applications of multilevel modelling to social psychological questions are discussed by Pollack (1998), Nezlek (2001) and Wright (1998). See Hofmann & Gavin (1998) for a useful discussion of various centring options in multilevel modelling; see Snijders & Bosker (1994) for an advanced discussion of the nature and the calculation of modelled variance.

Students basing a report on this exercise should read Vignoles et al. (2002a), which describes a very similar study. For further multi-level studies, see also Almeida & Kessler (1998), Jex & Bliese (1999), Reis et al. (2000), Rice, Carr-Hill, Dixon & Sutton (1998) and Vignoles, Chryssochoou & Breakwell (2002b). For recent studies into identity motives and their implications for various outcomes, see Ethier & Deaux (1994), Fein & Spencer (1997), Hornsey & Hogg (1999), Mullin & Hogg (1999), Pickett et al. (2002), Sedikides (1993), Sheldon & Bettencourt (2002), Sherman, Nelson & Steele (2000), Speller, Lyons & Twigger-Ross (2002), Taylor et al. (1995), and Timotijevic & Breakwell (2000).

REFERENCES

Abrams, D. & Hogg, M. A. (1988). Comments on the motivational status of self-esteem in social identity and intergroup discrimination. *European Journal of Social Psychology, 18,* 317–34.

Agresti, A. & Finlay, B. (1999). *Statistical methods for the social sciences* (3rd edn.). Upper Saddle River, NJ: Prentice Hall.

Alicke, M. D., Klotz, M. L., Breitenbecher, D. L., Yurak, T. J. & Vredenburg, D. S. (1995). Personal contact, individuation, and the better-than-average effect. *Journal of Personality and Social Psychology, 68,* 804–25.

Almeida, D. M. & Kessler, R. C. (1998). Everyday stressors and gender differences in daily distress. *Journal of Personality and Social Psychology, 75,* 670–80.

Baumeister, R. F. (1991). *Meanings of life.* New York: Guilford.

Baumeister, R. F. (1998). The self. In D. T. Gilbert, S. T. Fiske & G. Lindzey (eds.), *Handbook of social psychology* (4th edn., pp. 680–740). New York: McGraw-Hill.

Baumeister, R. F., Smart, L. & Boden, J. M. (1996). Relation of threatened egotism to violence and aggression: The dark side of high self-esteem. *Psychological Review, 103,* 5–33.

Breakwell, G. M. (1987). Identity. In H. Beloff & A. Coleman (eds.), *Psychology Survey No. 6.* (pp. 94–114). Leicester, UK: British Psychological Society.

Breakwell, G. M. (1988). Strategies adopted when identity is threatened. *Revue internationale de psychologie sociale, 1,* 189–203.

Breakwell, G. M. (2001). Social representational constraints upon identity processes. In K. Deaux & G. Philogene (eds.), *Representations of the social: Bridging theoretical traditions* (pp. 271–84). Oxford: Blackwell.

Brewer, M. B. (1991). The social self: On being the same and different at the same time. *Personality and Social Psychology Bulletin, 17,* 475–82.

Brewer, M. B. (1999). Multiple identities and identity transition: Implications for Hong Kong. *International Journal of Intercultural Relations, 23,* 187–97.

Brewer, M. B. & Gardner, W. (1996). Who is this 'we'? Levels of collective identity and self representations. *Journal of Personality and Social Psychology, 71,* 83–93.

Bryk, A. S. & Raudenbush, S. W. (1992). Hierarchical linear models: Applications and data analysis methods. Newbury Park, CA: Sage.

Campbell, K. W. & Sedikides, C. (1999). Self-threat magnifies the self-serving bias: A meta-analytic integration. *Review of General Psychology, 3*, 23–43.

Deaux, K. (1992). Personalizing identity and socializing self. In G. M. Breakwell (ed.), *Social psychology of identity and the self concept* (pp. 9–33). London: Surrey University Press.

Deaux, K. (2000). Models, meanings and motivations. In D. Capozza & R. Brown (eds.), *Social identity processes: Trends in theory and research* (pp. 1–14). London: Sage.

Ethier, K. A. & Deaux, K. (1994). Negotiating social identity when contexts change: Maintaining identification and responding to threat. *Journal of Personality and Social Psychology, 67*, 243–51.

Fein, S. & Spencer, S. J. (1997). Prejudice as self-image maintenance: Affirming the self through derogating others. *Journal of Personality and Social Psychology, 73*, 31–44.

Gecas, V. (1982). The self-concept. *Annual review of sociology, 8*, 1–33.

Green, R. J. & Werner, P. D. (1996). Intrusiveness and closeness-caregiving: Rethinking the concept of family enmeshment. *Family Process, 35*, 115–36.

Greenwald, A. G. (1980). The totalitarian ego: Fabrication and revision of personal history. *American Psychologist, 35*, 603–18.

Hedeker, D. & Gibbons, R. D. (1996). MIXREG: A computer program for mixed-effects regression analysis with autocorrelated errors. *Computer Methods and Programs in Biomedicine, 49*, 229–52.

Hofmann, D. A. & Gavin, M. B. (1998). Centering decisions in hierarchical linear models: Implications for research in organizations. *Journal of Management, 24*, 623–41.

Hogg, M. A. (2000). Subjective uncertainty reduction through self-categorization: A motivational theory of social identity processes. *European Review of Social Psychology, 11*, 223–55.

Hornsey, M. J. & Hogg, M. A. (1999). Subgroup differentiation as a response to an overly-inclusive group: A test of optimal distinctiveness theory. *European Journal of Social Psychology, 29*, 543–50.

Hox, J. J. (1995). *Applied multilevel analysis.* Amsterdam: TT-Publikaties.

Jex, S. M. & Bliese, P. D. (1999). Efficacy beliefs as a moderator of the impact of work-related stressors: A multilevel study. *Journal of Applied Psychology, 84*, 349–61.

Kreft, I. & de Leeuw, J. (1998). *Introducing multilevel modeling.* London: Sage.

Kruglanski, A. W. (1996). Motivated social cognition: Principles of the interface. In E. T. Higgins & A. W. Kruglanski (eds.), *Social psychology: Handbook of basic principles* (pp. 493–520). New York: Guilford.

Kuhn, M. H. & McPartland, T. S. (1954). An empirical investigation of self-attitudes. *American Sociological Review, 19*, 68–76.

Leary, M. R. & Baumeister, R. F. (2000). The nature and function of self-esteem: Sociometer theory. *Advances in Experimental Social Psychology, 32*, 1–62.

Miller, D. T. & Ross, M. (1975). Self-serving biases in the attribution of causality: Fact or fiction? *Psychological Bulletin, 82*, 213–25.

Mullin, B. A. & Hogg, M. A. (1999). Motivations for group membership: The role of subjective importance and uncertainty reduction. *Basic and Applied Social Psychology, 21*, 91–102.

Nezlek, J. B. (2001). Multilevel random coefficient analyses of event- and interval-contingent data in social and personality psychology research. *Personality and Social Psychology Bulletin, 27*, 771–85.

Pickett, C. L., Bonner B. L. & Coleman J. M. (2002). Motivated self-stereotyping: Heightened assimilation and differentiation needs result in increased levels of positive and negative self-stereotyping. *Journal of Personality and Social Psychology, 82*, 543–62.

Pollack, B. N. (1998). Hierarchical linear modeling and the 'unit of analysis' problem: A solution for analyzing responses of intact group members. *Group Dynamics: Theory, Research, and Practice, 2*, 299–312.

Reis, H. T., Sheldon, K. M., Gable, S. L., Roscoe, J. & Ryan, R. M. (2000). Daily well-being: The role of autonomy, competence, and relatedness. *Personality and Social Psychology Bulletin, 26*, 419–35.

Rice, N., Carr-Hill, R., Dixon, P. & Sutton, M. (1998). The influence of households on drinking behaviour: A multilevel analysis. *Social Science and Medicine, 46*, 971–79.

Robins, R. W., Hendin, H. W. & Trzesniewski, K. H. (2001). Measuring global self-esteem: Construct validation of a single-item measure and the Rosenberg self-esteem scale. *Personality and Social Psychology Bulletin, 27*, 151–61.

Rosenberg, M. (1986). *Conceiving the self.* Malabar, FL: Krieger.

Sedikides, C. (1993). Assessment, enhancement, and verification determinants of the self-evaluation process. *Journal of Personality and Social Psychology, 65*, 317–38.

Sedikides, C. & Strube, M. J. (eds.) (1995). Motivational determinants of self-evaluation: Working toward synthesis (Special issue). *Personality and Social Psychology Bulletin, 21*(12).

Sedikides, C. & Strube, M. J. (1997). Self-evaluation: To thine own self be good, to thine own self be sure, to thine own self be true, and to thine own self be better. *Advances in Experimental Social Psychology, 29*, 209–69.

Sheldon, K. M. & Bettencourt, B. A. (2002). Psychological need-satisfaction and subjective well-being within social groups. *British Journal of Social Psychology, 41*, 25–38.

Sherman, D. A. K., Nelson, A. D. & Steele, C. M. (2000). Do messages about health risks threaten the self? Increasing the acceptance of threatening health messages via self-affirmation. *Personality and Social Psychology Bulletin, 26*, 9, 1046–58.

Snijders, T. A. B. & Bosker, R. J. (1994). Modeled variance in two-level models. *Sociological Methods & Research, 22*, 342–63.

Snijders, T. A. B. & Bosker, R. J. (1999). *Multilevel analysis: An introduction to basic and advanced multilevel modeling.* London: Sage.

Snyder, C. R. & Fromkin, H. L. (1980). *Uniqueness: The human pursuit of difference.* New York: Plenum Press.

Speller, G., Lyons, E. & Twigger-Ross, C. (2002). A community in transition: The relationship between spatial change and identity processes. *Social Psychological Review, 4,* 39–58.

Steele, C. M. (1988). The psychology of self-affirmation: sustaining the integrity of the self. In L. Berkowitz (ed.), *Advances in Experimental Social Psychology* (vol. 21, pp. 261–302). San Diego, CA: Academic Press.

Swann, W. B., Jr., Griffin, J. J., Predmore, S. & Gaines, B. (1987). The cognitive-affective crossfire: When self-consistency confronts self-enhancement. *Journal of Personality and Social Psychology, 52,* 881–9.

Taylor, S. E. & Brown, J. D. (1988). Illusion and well-being: A social psychological perspective on mental health. *Psychological Bulletin, 103,* 193–210.

Taylor, S. E., Neter, E. & Wayment, H. A. (1995). Self-evaluation processes. *Personality and Social Psychology Bulletin, 21,* 1278–87.

Tesser, A. (2000). On the confluence of self-esteem maintenance mechanisms. *Personality and Social Psychology Review, 4,* 290–9.

Timotijevic, L. & Breakwell, G. M. (2000). Migration and threat to identity. *Journal of Community and Applied Social Psychology, 10,* 355–72.

Vignoles, V. L. (2000). Identity, culture and the distinctiveness principle. Unpublished doctoral thesis, University of Surrey, Guildford, UK.

Vignoles, V. L., Chryssochoou, X. & Breakwell, G. M. (2000). The distinctiveness principle: Identity, meaning and the bounds of cultural relativity. *Personality and Social Psychology Review, 4,* 337–54.

Vignoles, V. L., Chryssochoou, X. & Breakwell, G. M. (2002a). Evaluating models of identity motivation: Self-esteem is not the whole story. *Self and Identity, 1,* 201–18.

Vignoles, V. L., Chryssochoou, X. & Breakwell, G. M. (2002b). Sources of distinctiveness Position, difference and separateness in the identities of Anglican parish priests. *European Journal of Social Psychology, 32,* 761–80.

Wright, D. B. (1998). Modelling clustered data in autobiographical memory research: The multilevel approach. *Applied Cognitive Psychology, 12,* 339–57.

Zuckerman, M. (1979). Attribution of success and failure revisited: or The motivational bias is alive and well in attribution theory. *Journal of Personality, 47,* 245–87.

CHAPTER NINE

The Analysis of Equivocation in Political Interviews[1]

Peter Bull

The prime focus of this chapter concerns the analysis of data elicited from archival sources (i.e. recordings of media interviews of politicians). It shows how one particular type of discourse analysis can be used to record and interpret such data. Discourse analysis and the traditional techniques of experimental social psychology are typically seen as mutually exclusive alternatives. The design of the exercise described here makes it possible for students to perform some analysis of naturally occurring language, and to incorporate those results into a more traditional experimental research design using sophisticated techniques of statistical analysis. The specific aspect of natural language under investigation will be equivocation. This has been defined as 'nonstraightforward communication; it appears ambiguous, contradictory, tangential, obscure or even evasive' (Bavelas, Black, Chovil & Mullet, 1990, p. 28). The purpose of the practical exercise is to examine equivocation both as it occurs in the context of a political interview and as it is perceived by others. The hypothesis to be tested is whether voters perceive responses from a politician of a different political persuasion as themselves as more equivocal than responses from a politician of the same persuasion as themselves.

The Analysis of Political Interviews

In the age of television, televised interviews have become one of the most important means of political communication. In the United

Kingdom, the first such interview appears to have taken place in 1951 when Anthony Eden, a senior member of Winston Churchill's government, was interviewed by a BBC announcer called Leslie Mitchell; however, it was all so stage managed that Cockerell (1988), in his history of television in British politics, refers to it as a 'cod interview'. The early 1950s was still the time when the BBC had a monopoly in broadcasting, and during this period a highly deferential style of interviewing was employed (Day, 1989). But with the introduction of the commercial channel ITV in 1955, the political interview was transformed from what has been referred to as the 'pat-ball' interview to a more aggressive and challenging kind of encounter (Bull, 1998a).

The most prominent exponent of this new style was Sir Robin Day, who had originally trained as a barrister. He wrote in his autobiography, 'The sixties was the period when the television interview became established as a new branch of journalism, as part of the political process, and increasingly as a political event in its own right' (Day, 1989, p. 142). Day claimed that by the 1980s interviewing had become harder, as politicians had become progressively more at ease in set-piece interviews. Politicians had become much more professional in the way they handled television, paying greater attention to impression management, to interview technique, to the rules of engagement under which interviews were conducted, even to the interview set itself (Jones, 1992). Indeed, it began to appear to some commentators (including Sir Robin Day) as if the political interview had been effectively neutralized (Jones, 1992). Nevertheless, televised political interviews in Britain show no sign whatsoever of decreasing in frequency. In the 2001 British General Election they played as prominent a role as ever, and as such must continue to be considered one of the most important and characteristic means of political communication in contemporary British politics.

The televised political interview has also become the theme of a substantive research literature. This can be seen in the wider context of research on what are termed 'news interviews', radio and television interviews not only with well-known public figures (such as politicians), but also with ordinary members of the public who may be experiencing such an interview for the first (and possibly only) time (Greatbatch, 1988). A principal theme of this research is the nature of the interaction that takes place. To some extent, this interaction is a kind of illusion: what appears to be a conversation is in fact a performance, transmitted to an overhearing audience potentially of millions (Heritage, 1985). It is also a performance governed by its own special set of rules, in which the type of conversation which takes place is quite distinctive. Characteristic features include the pattern of turn-taking, the frequent occurrence of both interruptions and equivocation, and the central role of self-presentation and face management (Bull, 1998a). A brief introduction is given below to these distinctive features of interaction in political interviews, before moving on to a detailed consideration of the analysis of equivocation.

TURN-TAKING

A number of observers have commented on the distinctive nature of turn-taking in political interviews. Typically, the interviewer both begins and ends the interview; he or she is also expected to ask questions and the interviewee is expected to provide replies (e.g. Clayman, 1989; Greatbatch, 1988; Heritage, Clayman & Zimmerman, 1988). Even when the interviewer departs from the question and answer format, for example by making a statement, the statement will typically be followed with a question or concluded with a tag in the form of 'isn't it?' or 'wasn't it?' The question/answer format is considered to be the principal means used by the participants to create and sustain talk (Schegloff, 1989), although interviewers may engage in non-questioning actions in order to open and close interviews (Heritage & Greatbatch, 1991).

The way in which news interviews are terminated is significantly affected by the pattern of turn-taking, according to Clayman (1989). Given that interviewees are not expected to speak unless the interviewer has asked them to do so, termination can be accomplished in a unilateral fashion by the interviewer; this is in contrast to ordinary conversation, where it is jointly managed by the participants. The opening sequence of a news interview also differs from ordinary conversation in a number of important respects, Clayman (1991) maintains: in particular, the primary task of the opening is to project the agenda for the interview, whereas topics in ordinary conversation are not predetermined but negotiated during the course of the interaction.

Turn-taking in political interviews may break down if interruptions are excessive, and one of the most well-known studies was concerned with this theme (Beattie, 1982). A detailed analysis was made of two political interviews in the 1979 British General Election: one between Margaret Thatcher (at that time leader of the Conservative opposition) and Denis Tuohy; the other between Jim Callaghan (Labour prime minister, 1976–9) and Llew Gardner. It was found that whereas the interviewer interrupted Margaret Thatcher almost twice as often as she interrupted him, the pattern for Jim Callaghan was the reverse:

he interrupted the interviewer more than he was interrupted. Beattie claimed that Margaret Thatcher was often interrupted following the display of turn-yielding cues, in particular at the end of clauses associated with drawl on the stressed syllable and a falling intonation pattern. According to Beattie, Margaret Thatcher was excessively interrupted because these turn-yielding cues were misleading, giving the interviewer the impression that she had completed her utterance. The interviewer then attempted to take over the turn, whereupon Margaret Thatcher continued speaking.

Another study of interruptions in political interviews was conducted by Bull and Mayer (1988), this time based on the 1987 British General Election. They compared Margaret Thatcher (Conservative prime minister, 1979–90) and Neil Kinnock (leader of the Labour opposition, 1983–92). They found no significant difference in the extent to which the party leaders made or received interruptions; indeed, the pattern of interruptions between the two leaders was markedly similar and correlated at a highly significant level. These results were quite contrary to Beattie's (1982) belief that Margaret Thatcher's interview style invited excessive interruptions. Where the politicians did differ was in the frequency with which Margaret Thatcher explicitly protested at being interrupted, with comments such as 'please let me go on' or 'may I now and then say a word in my own defence'. On at least two occasions, she objected to being interrupted where there was no sign of an interruption, the interviewer (Jonathan Dimbleby) even openly protesting on one occasion that he was not about to interrupt! The frequent use of such comments may have given the misleading impression that she was being excessively interrupted, although the objective evidence showed that this was not the case.

EQUIVOCATION

In the study reported above, a content analysis was also conducted of the reasons for interrupting in political interviews; this showed that the most frequent reason was to reformulate questions (Bull & Mayer, 1988). Thus interruptions may be closely linked to equivocation: if a politician talks at length while failing to answer a question, the interviewer must be able to interrupt effectively in order to pursue an appropriate reply. Hence, a further study was conducted in order to provide some basic information on equivocation in political interviews (Bull & Mayer, 1993).

Results showed that Margaret Thatcher replied to only 37 per cent of the questions put to her, and Neil Kinnock to only 39 per cent.

This is directly comparable to an independent study by Harris (1991), who found in an analysis of a different set of political interviews (principally with Thatcher and Kinnock) that the politicians gave direct answers to just over 39 per cent of the questions asked. By way of comparison, it is interesting to consider reply rates in televised interviews for other leading public figures who are not politicians. The late Diana, Princess of Wales, in her celebrated interview with Martin Bashir (20 November 1995), replied to 78 per cent of the questions put to her (Bull, 1997). Louise Woodward, the British au pair who was convicted for the manslaughter of eight-month-old Matthew Eappen, in an interview with Martin Bashir (22 June 1998) replied to 70 per cent of the questions (Bull, 2000). Monica Lewinsky replied to 89 per cent of questions posed by Jon Snow (4 March 1999) in an interview concerning her affair with President Clinton (Bull, 2000). The mean reply rate of 79 per cent across all three interviews is effectively double that reported by Bull and Mayer (1993) for the eight interviews with Margaret Thatcher and Neil Kinnock, and this difference is statistically significant (Bull, 2000). Thus, overall, the evidence is consistent with the popular view that politicians do not reply to a large proportion of questions in political interviews, hence that equivocation is a characteristic feature of discourse in this social situation.

BAVELAS ET AL.'S THEORY OF EQUIVOCATION

A theory of equivocation has been proposed by Bavelas et al. (1990), according to whom equivocation can be understood in terms of four dimensions. This is based on the proposal that 'Communication always involves a sender, some content, a receiver and a context' (Bavelas et al., 1990, p. 33). In Bavelas et al.'s theory of equivocation, *sender* refers to whether the response can be understood as the speaker's own opinion. *Clarity* (content) refers to whether the response is clear or unclear, and can be distinguished from *context*, the extent to which the response is a direct answer to the question. *Receiver* refers to the extent to which the message is addressed to the other person in the situation (an equivocal message would make the recipient unclear).

The importance of these distinctions is that a message can be equivocal on any one of these four dimensions. For example, when asked for his or her own personal opinion on a particular issue, a politician may do no more than reiterate party policy. This would be equivocation in terms of *sender*, because it is still unclear what is the politician's own personal opinion. Again, if the response is contradictory, vague or obscure, it may be seen as equivocal in terms of *clarity*. However, even if a response is clear, it may still be equivocal, for example, if a politician gives a clear response to a different question from that posed by the interviewer (*context*). Finally, a message may be equivocal if it is not clear to whom it is addressed (*receiver*). For example, if a politician uses the interviewer's name in responding to the interviewer's question, it is perfectly clear who is the addressee; in other instances, it may not be clear to whom the politician's response is addressed. Bavelas et al. have devised rating scales to measure each of these four dimensions, which will be used in the exercise to assess whether the politician's responses to questions are perceived as equivocal.

Bavelas et al. (1990) further propose that people typically equivocate when posed a question to which all of the possible replies have potentially negative consequences, but where nevertheless a reply is still expected. This situation they refer to as a communicative or *avoidance–avoidance* conflict. Their underlying argument is that equivocation does not occur without a situational precedent; thus, although it is individuals who equivocate, this has to be understood within the context of the individual's communicative situation.

Bavelas et al.'s theory is not restricted to any particular social setting, but they do argue that communicative conflicts are especially prevalent in interviews with politicians. For example, Bavelas et al. point out that there are many controversial issues on which there is a divided electorate. Politicians often seek to avoid direct replies supporting or criticizing either position, which would offend a substantial number of voters. Another set of conflicts, they argue, is created by the pressure of time limits. If the politician is under pressure to respond briefly to a complex question, he or she has to make a choice between two unattractive alternatives: reducing the issue to a simple and incomplete answer, or appearing long-winded, circuitous and evasive. In addition, Bavelas et al. propose that a further set of conflicts may occur if the candidate lacks sufficient knowledge of the political issue being addressed. In this circumstance, he or she has to make the unfortunate choice between acknowledging ignorance, or improvising – even fabricating – an answer.

THE ROLE OF FACE MANAGEMENT IN
POLITICAL INTERVIEWS

In their analysis, Bavelas et al. do not present any unifying theoretical explanation for what it is that politicians are seeking to avoid. The author and his colleagues (Bull, Elliott, Palmer, & Walker, 1996) have argued that in the context of political interviews it is the danger of losing face which is an important source of communicative conflicts. That is to say, politicians seek to avoid making certain kinds of responses which may put them in a bad light. This emphasis on losing face is not presented as an alternative to the concept of the communicative conflict, rather as an explanation as to why politicians find particular responses aversive (Bull, 1998b). Nor is it being proposed that communicative conflicts in political interviews will *only* be created by threats to face. For example, when President Clinton was questioned over the Monica Lewinsky affair, he was not only at risk of looking incompetent, treacherous and downright deceitful, he was also in real danger of criminal prosecution and impeachment (Bull, 2000).

On the basis of this analysis in terms of face, a study was carried out of the 1992 British General Election, based on 18 televised interviews with the leaders of the three main political parties at that time (John Major, Conservative prime minister 1990–97; Neil Kinnock, leader of the Labour Party, 1983–92; Paddy Ashdown, leader of the Liberal Democrats, 1987–99). A new typology of questions in political interviews was developed, based on their face-threatening properties. Nineteen different types of face-threat were distinguished, divided into the three superordinate categories of face which politicians must defend – their own personal face, the face of the party which they represent and the face of significant others. All the interviews were analysed using the new question typology, and the results showed that almost every question (99%) possessed at least some face-threatening properties. A distinction was also made between two types of question: those where each of the principal modes of response were considered to present some kind of threat to face, and those where it was considered possible to make a response which was not damaging to face.

Thus, there were some questions (40.8% of all questions) which were so tough that each of the principal modes of response open to the politician was considered to present some form of face-threat (hence, they created a communicative conflict). For example, Sir Robin Day posed this kind of problem to Neil Kinnock, when he asked him whether under a Labour Government the trade unions would recover much of their pre-Thatcher power. If Kinnock answered yes to this question, he would run the risk of offending that proportion of the electorate who are opposed to trade unions and fearful of their excessive influence. If he replied no, he would risk offending that proportion of the electorate who favour trade unions, as well as offending the trade unions themselves and their supporters within his own party. If he failed to reply, he might simply be seen as evasive. Thus each of the principal response options presents some kind of threat to face; in the event, Kinnock made the best of a bad job by simply stating Labour Party trade union policy, without indicating whether or not this meant they would recover much of their pre-Thatcher power under a Labour Government. Most of the communicative conflict questions in the Bull et al. data (87%) were couched in a 'yes–no' format (Quirk, Greenbaum, Leech & Svartvik, 1985). Given that there are three principal modes of responding to such questions (confirm, deny, equivocate), the probability of an equivocal response occurring by chance is 33 per cent; in fact, the total proportion of equivocal responses to the yes–no questions was 66 per cent. The finding that equivocation occurred at twice the rate expected by chance alone supported Bavelas et al's proposition that equivocation does occur in response to questions that create communicative conflicts.

But not all questions pose the politicians with this kind of dilemma. It was considered that there were some questions to which the politician could respond without necessarily threatening face, in the sense that it was possible to produce a response that did not incur any of the 19 face-threats specified in the coding system. Where it was considered that such a response could be made, that response option was coded as *no necessary threat*. So, for example, some questions are so favourable that they give the politician an open invitation to make positive statements about him or herself and the party the politician represents. Thus, Day asked John Major: 'Why do you deserve . . . why does the Conservative Party deserve under your leadership what the British people have never given any political party in modern times – a fourth successive term of office?'

In replying to this question, Major was given the opportunity to present both himself and the Conservative Party in a favourable light. Failure to reply would be extremely face-threatening, since it would imply that neither he nor the Conservative Party deserved a fourth term of office. Questions where a *no necessary threat* response was judged possible comprised 59.2 per cent of the questions in all 18 political interviews. Given the postulated importance of face management in political interviews, it was hypothesized that where a *no necessary threat* response was possible, this would be the response the politician would produce. Such questions most typically were couched in a 'yes–no' format (66% of *no necessary threat* questions); the total proportion of *no necessary threat* responses to these questions was 87 per cent (proportion expected by chance 33%, as argued above).

Subsequently, a second study on face management was conducted, which took advantage of a novel development in political

broadcasting in the 2001 General Election (Bull, 2003). In the traditional interview, one politician is typically questioned by just one professional interviewer. Growing dissatisfaction with this arrangement
has led broadcasters to experiment with different formats that allow for
some form of audience participation. The 2001 General Election was
the first in which both major television channels gave members of the
general public the opportunity alongside professional interviewers to
put questions directly to the leaders of the three main political parties.

What makes this situation so interesting is that members of the
general public may differ from political interviewers in the kinds of
questions that they ask. In particular, given the more complex structure of communicative conflict questions, members of the public might
be expected to ask them less frequently. Whereas interviewers might
seek through such questions to highlight inconsistencies in policy,
voters may be more concerned simply to establish where a party
stands on a particular issue. Consequently, if members of the public
pose fewer communicative conflicts, then politicians might be expected
to give them significantly more replies. To test these hypotheses, an
analysis was conducted of six sessions in which the party political
leaders were questioned by both professional interviewers and members of the general public (Bull, 2003).

Results showed that politicians replied to 73 per cent of questions
from members of the public, and to 47 per cent of questions from
political interviewers ($p < .025$). In addition, it was found that political
interviewers used a significantly higher proportion of communicative
conflict questions than members of public (58% cf. 19%, $p < .025$).
Finally, a significant Phi correlation of 0.76 ($p < .05$) between questions and responses showed that equivocation by the politicians was
associated with communicative conflict questions from the political
interviewers. The comparable correlation for questions and responses
from members of the audience just missed significance (Phi = 0.70,
$p > .05$). Thus professional interviewers received significantly fewer
replies from the politicians, and asked significantly more communicative conflict questions than members of the public.

A good example of threats to face in questions that either do or do
not pose communicative conflicts can be seen in the following extract.
It was taken from the BBC1 Question Time programme in the 2001
General Election with Tony Blair and David Dimbleby (Bull, 2003):

Audience member:	Why is it that er after four years of office the railways are in a worse state than we've ever seen in this country given that the policy is to encourage us not to use our cars?

Blair: Because the railways have been er because the railways have been under-invested for a very long period
of time, and if we don't get the money into the railways, then we will carry on with a second or third
class service.

Dimbleby: Are you ashamed of British railways?

Blair: I'm not proud of the state of British railways no I
mean I think you'd be pretty odd if you said that . . .

The question from the audience member, although face-threatening, did not present Blair with a communicative conflict. This is because he could reply by drawing attention to the chronic long-term under-investment in the railways that preceded his own government. However, the question from Dimbleby did place Blair in a commun-icative conflict. If Blair said yes, he was ashamed of British railways, it would be damaging both to his own personal face and that of his party, given that New Labour had already been in power for four years. To say no, he was not ashamed of British railways would simply stretch credibility, given the problems of major train accidents, cancellations and frequent delays in the years immediately preceding the 2001 General Election. Blair resolved this problem by equivocat-ing, saying that he was not 'proud of the state of British railways'. This did not directly answer Dimbleby's question, but enabled Blair to provide a credible response that was less face-damaging than either of the two possible replies. In this way, it can be seen how Blair equivocated in response to the communicative conflict created by David Dimbleby, but could give a reply to a similar question from the member of the public without incurring serious face damage.

STRATEGIC ADVANTAGES OF EQUIVOCATION

Bavelas et al. (1990), in their analysis of equivocation, focus speci-fically on the causes of equivocation, namely, the occurrence of communicative conflicts. However, whereas in existing theory, equi-vocation is presented as an essentially negative phenomenon (a means of not giving replies to awkward questions), equivocation also needs to be understood in terms of its *consequences* as well as its *causes* (Bull, 1998b).

There are many different ways of equivocating: at least 35 different forms of non-reply have been distinguished (Bull, 2003; Bull & Mayer, 1993). Not all of these are by any means equivalent; consideration needs to be given to potential strategic advantages of different forms of equivocation. For example, in an analysis of the celebrated interview between Princess Diana and Martin Bashir (20 November 1995), Bull (1997) focused on Diana's use of implicit criticisms. Her use of implicit responses, it was argued, could be readily understood as reflecting the kind of communicative conflict analysed by Bavelas et al. Thus if Diana had been too outspokenly critical in this interview, she might have alienated public opinion and exacerbated and embittered an already difficult situation with her husband and with the Royal Family; she might even have been frightened of some form of retaliation. Conversely, if she avoided comment on her husband and the Royal Family, or even denied there were any problems between them, she would not be able to give her side of the story, and would look foolish for having agreed to give the interview in the first place. But her use of answers by implication could also be seen to have distinct strategic advantages. In effect, it enabled her to put over her side of the story concerning the breakdown of her marriage to Charles without having to be too outspoken in her criticisms of him or of other members of the Royal Family.

Highly skilled use of equivocation was also observed in televised interviews given by Tony Blair during the 1997 British General Election campaign (Bull, 2000). The analysis was set in the context of the so-called 'modernization' of the British Labour Party, the dramatic policy changes which took place in the years following Labour's disastrous electoral defeat in 1983 and which culminated in its landslide victory in 1997. The 1983 Manifesto was memorably dubbed by Gerald Kaufman (a leading member of Labour's Front bench at the time) as 'the longest suicide note in history'. It called for unilateral nuclear disarmament, withdrawal from the Common Market, massive nationalization and renationalization with much greater planning of the economy, exchange controls and trade barriers. But by 1997, the Manifesto had an explicit commitment to *retaining* the Trident nuclear deterrent, to the rapid *completion* of the European Union single market, to the *retention* of the Conservative trade union legislation of the 1980s, and a five-year pledge to no increases in income tax: in short, a complete reversal of what the Labour Party stood for in 1983.

Such dramatic changes typically pose political parties with a major problem of presentation. A complete about-turn inevitably reflects badly on what has gone before: there is a clear implication that the previous policies were ill-judged and inappropriate. Presenting the new policies also creates a problem; they may be depicted as cynical, opportunist and unprincipled, simply a means of currying support with the electorate. Nowhere is this problem of presentation more pronounced than in the context of a political interview, where interviewers can ask repeated questions, challenge equivocal responses and draw attention to contradictions in policy.

In an analysis of five televised political interviews from the 1997 General Election campaign (Bull, 2000), it was hypothesized that questions about these policy changes would pose Blair with a classic communicative conflict, and that his responses would be characterized by equivocation. It was in fact in the General Election of 1983 that Blair was first elected to Parliament, as a Member of Parliament for what has come to be known as 'old Labour'. Thus, if he condemned the old Labour Party, he would at the very least be open to the charge of inconsistency; if he were to admit to any lack of belief in the manifesto of 1983, then he would be open to the further charge of hypocrisy. In addition, if he was too critical of old Labour, it might also make his party look bad, and he might well alienate support within his own party. Conversely, as the man pre-eminently associated with the 'modernization' of the Labour Party, if he failed to acknowledge criticisms of old Labour, then it would naturally invite the question as to why all the changes to what has become known as New Labour had taken place.

Just as predicted, it was found that Blair equivocated to questions about policy changes judged as creating a communicative conflict, and replied to those questions judged as not creating such a conflict. However, Blair's use of the term 'modernization' enabled him to do much more than just avoid replying to awkward questions. In particular, it had the advantage of enabling him to emphasize both continuity and change. For example, with regard to old Labour, he stated 'I believed in the values of the Labour Party', whereas the process of modernization has been '. . . to keep [the Labour Party] true to its principles but put those principles properly in a modern setting . . .' This allowed Blair not only to explicitly acknowledge the changes that had taken place, but also to present them as principled – as representing an adaptation of the traditional values of the Labour Party to the contemporary political situation. In this way, he could claim a positive face for his party, as both principled but also moving with the times. At the same time, change could be acknowledged without condemning or criticizing the old Labour Party, in order to minimize the risk of alienating traditional Labour support. Although Blair was invited to criticize or condemn old Labour in almost half the questions about policy changes, it is notable that he never did so.

Equivocation has recently been defined as the 'intentional use of imprecise language' (Hamilton & Mineo, 1998). In these terms, Blair's strategic use of the imprecise language of 'modernization' could certainly be regarded as a highly skilled form of political communication.

Not only did it provide him with a means of avoiding the risks of making face-damaging remarks, it also enabled him to present the best possible face for himself and the party which he represents, by striving to create a highly inclusive identity for New Labour. In fact, the very name 'New Labour' could be seen to project this inclusive identity, emphasizing change while still preserving the link with the Labour Party of old. Blair's use of this 'rhetoric of modernization' can thus be seen as representing a high level of communicative skill, which arguably played a crucial role in the Labour Party's stunning landslide victory in the British General Election of 1997.

Blair's mastery of the arts of equivocation is arguably an important element of his political skill, a point not lost on his political opponents. It was discussed in some detail by William Hague, the former leader of the Conservative opposition (1997–2001), writing in the *Guardian* (26 April 2002), five years on from Blair's landslide victory in the 1997 General Election. He singled out what he called Blair's 'skill for ambiguity' as one of his key political strengths, as one of the features which both helped him into power and helped keep him there. In contrast, Blair's stance over the Iraq war in 2003 was untypically unambiguous. It is interesting that the first serious doubts to be publicly expressed about Blair's continued premiership were voiced in response to a pro-war stance that was so uncharacteristically unequivocal.

THE SPECIFIC HYPOTHESIS UNDER TEST

The above analyses suggest that equivocation is an important form of discourse in political interviews. It can be seen both as a response to the kinds of communicative problems posed by questions in political interviews, as well as a distinctive form of communication which has significant strategic advantages in its own right. But the studies reported above are all based on the detailed analysis of natural language in political interviews; as yet we know very little about how political equivocation is perceived. Furthermore, although Bavelas et al. have worked extensively on ratings of equivocation, they have never investigated whether ratings of equivocation differ between groups. There is in fact ample evidence to show that attitudes exert selective effects on information processing through selective perception, selective evaluation and selective memory biases (e.g. Eagly & Chaiken, 1993). But this has yet to be investigated with regard to judgements of equivocation. Thus the specific hypothesis to be tested is whether voters rate responses from a politician of a different political persuasion to themselves as more equivocal than a politician of the same political persuasion.

A Specific Exercise

PARTICIPANTS

An interview between a politician and an interviewer will form the basis of this study.

Participants to complete the questionnaire will be selected according to voting preference, by asking them either 'Which way did you vote at the last General Election?' or alternatively 'If there was a General Election tomorrow, which way would you vote?' Two possible designs are proposed:

1 Design A. There might be 10 Labour, 10 Conservative and 10 Liberal Democrat voters, with five men and five women in each group. Although this design does not allow sufficient data to enter gender as a separate factor in analysis of variance (only five participants in each cell), it does control for its effects.
2 Design B. Alternatively, a more ambitious design might have 20 participants of each political persuasion, with 10 men and 10 women in each group. This allows sufficient data for gender to be entered as a separate factor in analysis of variance.

APPARATUS

1 Students are provided with an audiocassette recording and a transcript of a political interview.
2 The author (Bull, 1994) has devised a set of criteria for the purpose of identifying question-response sequences in interviews, and a summary of these criteria is provided in Appendix 9.1.
3 In addition, a copy is provided of the Bavelas et al. (1990) scales for rating *sender, receiver, context* and *clarity* (Appendix 9.2).

Each of the four Bavelas et al. dimensions is measured in terms of a single continuous line. So, for example, the question 'How clear is this message in terms of just what is being said?' is answered by placing a mark somewhere on a line that is only denoted as *completely clear* at one end and *completely unclear* at the other. The experimenter can then subsequently measure exactly where the mark was placed (in centimetres) and standardize these numbers. Bavelas et al. (1990, p. 36) considered that this procedure is more natural and less obtrusive than having a Likert-type scale of, say, just five or seven points. However, it is also much more time-consuming, because each response to each dimension has to be measured. Thus the student may wish to convert the Bavelas et al. dimensions into seven-point Likert-type scales to speed up the whole procedure. This also has the advantage that conventionally it is not regarded as necessary to ipsatize the scores from Likert scales, in contrast to the data obtained from Bavelas et al.'s continuous lines (for a full discussion of ipsatizing, see Results subsection below).

It should be noted that one of the Bavelas et al. scales – the *receiver* dimension – has had to be modified to take account of the particular problems posed by the analysis of equivocation in broadcast news interviews. In the original *receiver* scale, the rater is asked to assess 'To what extent is the message addressed to the other person in the situation?' Because the original scales were developed to rate question–response sequences in conversation, it is typically clear who the receiver might be. However, this is not the case in broadcast news interviews. When the politician is posed a question, it is not clear whether the receiver is the interviewer, the viewing audience, some particular section of the viewing audience or another politician or group of politicians. To cope with the special problems posed by the *receiver* dimension in broadcast interviews, the scale has been revised in the following way to take account of multiple recipients of the message:

How clear is it to whom the message is addressed?

_____

Completely Clear   Completely Unclear

Obvious to whom the message   Completely unclear to whom
is addressed, could only be   the message is addressed.
addressing that person.

In addition, the rater is asked to state to whom he or she thinks the message is addressed.

PROCEDURE

Students are asked to go through the interview, identifying question–response sequences, according to Bull's (1994) procedures. From this analysis, students then select out 12 question–response sequences, according to the following criteria. Four responses should be explicit replies to questions, another four should be outright non-replies. The remaining four should be what are termed answers by implication. In an answer by implication, the politician makes his or her views clear, but without explicitly stating them (Bull, 1994, p. 127).

So, for example, in the 1987 General Election, Sir Robin Day asked Margaret Thatcher whether, if the Labour Party won the election and decommissioned Polaris, she thought it would be the duty of the Chiefs of Staff to resign. In an extended answer, Thatcher stated:

> I know what I would do I just could not be responsible for the men under me under those circumstances it wouldn't be fair to put them in the field if other people had nuclear weapons . . . but they are free to make their decision that's a fundamental part of the way of life in which I believe.

In giving this reply, Margaret Thatcher made her own views quite clear without ever explicitly stating that she believed it would be the duty of the Chiefs of Staff to resign.

The 12 responses selected should be such that students can reach unequivocal agreement in coding them according to whether they are explicit replies, implicit replies or non-replies. They should also be such that they can 'stand alone' in a questionnaire, that is to say, they are not heavily dependent on contextual information for comprehension. For example, the following sequence from an interview between David Dimbleby and Tony Blair (7 April 1997) is still comprehensible when taken out of the context of the interview:

David Dimbleby: But did you believe in old Labour
Tony Blair: I believed in the values of the Labour Party yes.

Conversely, the second sequence reproduced below (from the same interview) is not fully comprehensible out of context, since it is not clear to what 'all that' refers. Hence, these kinds of sequences should not be selected for the questionnaire.

David Dimbleby: So all that was wrong
Tony Blair: No I don't say all that was wrong.

The 12 question–response sequences are then reproduced in the form of a questionnaire. Participants are asked to rate each of the 12 responses in terms of Bavelas et al.'s four dimensions *sender, clarity, context* and *receiver*.

RESULTS

One problem in analysing the Bavelas et al. rating scales is that people may use them in different ways. So, for example, some judges use the entire length of the line, while others avoid the extremes and place most of their messages within the centre third of the line; still others mostly use the lower (or upper) half of the line. These differences are systematic in the sense that any given judge is consistent in how he or she divides and uses the line (Bavelas et al., 1990, p. 44). However, this can become problematic if one wishes to combine the ratings of different judges.

The solution recommended by Bavelas et al. (1990, pp. 45–6) is to standardize the ratings statistically, by calculating what are called z scores. The procedure involves taking a judge's raw scores for a particular set of messages on one of the dimensions, and calculating the mean and standard deviation. This mean is then subtracted from the raw score for each message, and the difference is divided by the standard deviation. Because the judge's raw scores are being transformed by the use of his or her own mean and standard deviation (rather than a group mean and standard deviation), the resulting values are referred to as *ipsatized* (self-standardized) scores. Following this procedure, each set of new scores will have a mean of zero and a standard deviation of 1, as do all standard scores. With the effects of idiosyncratic means and standard deviations removed, it then becomes possible to combine the ratings of different judges for the same messages.

However, it should be noted that Bavelas et al.'s interest was in *combining* ratings from judges for the same material, not in performing group comparisons. If comparisons are to be made *between* groups, then a further modification of their ipsatizing technique is required. This is because the effect of standardizing the raw data to z scores on a particular dimension is to create a mean score of zero. Hence, if the raw data for two groups are both standardized, the mean score for each group will be zero, and no meaningful comparison is possible. The solution recommended here is to standardize the scores by taking the mean and the standard deviation not for each rating scale, but for all the rating scales combined. The raw scores can then be converted to z scores as before. Assuming that each participant will use the four rating scales in much the same way, their scores can still be standardized, but without the problem of creating a group mean of zero. In this way, group comparisons can be made using z scores.

The rating scale data can then be subjected to analysis of variance. It is, of course, possible to combine the ratings from all four scales into one overall measure of equivocation, but only at the loss of sensitivity to different aspects of equivocation. It would also be possible to include dimension of equivocation as one of the factors in one overall analysis of variance (with four levels), but this might make the analysis unnecessarily complex and difficult to interpret. Hence, it is recommended that four separate analyses of variance should be performed, one each for *sender, clarity, context* and *receiver*.

If Design A is adopted, gender is controlled for but not entered as a separate factor in the analyses of variance. Using this design, four separate two-way split-plot 3 × 3 analyses of variance would be conducted on the ratings for *sender, clarity, context* and *receiver*. The between-participants factor would be *political persuasion*, at three levels (Labour, Conservative, Liberal Democrat). The within-participants factor would be *response*, again at three levels (*explicit reply, implicit reply, non-reply*). If Design B is adopted, gender is introduced as a separate factor in what would now be four three-way 3 × 2 × 3 split-plot analyses of variance. The between subjects factors would be *political persuasion* (three levels, as for Design A) and *gender* (two levels); the within-participants factor would be *response* (again at three levels, as for Design A).

In evaluating the results, one feature of interest is the status of implicit replies. Bavelas et al. (1990) in their theory of equivocation make no particular distinction between replying to a question indirectly (what they call hinting at an answer) and not replying to it at all. They regard equivocation as a continuum, arguing that such an approach is far more useful than a dichotomy of equivocal/unequivocal, since it is more likely to detect subtle differences between messages (Bavelas et al., 1990, p. 31). However, in the analysis of the interview between Diana, Princess of Wales, and Martin Bashir, Bull (1997) argued that Diana's use of answers by implication had distinct interactional advantages over non-replies, and that this strategic advantage is not adequately represented in Bavelas et al.'s existing theory of equivocation. Hence, in the context of this debate, it is of interest to see how implicit replies are perceived in relation to explicit replies and non-replies: whether these three types of response are perceived as a continuum, or whether implicit replies are seen as more similar to explicit replies or to non-replies.

Notes for the Course Leader

RECORDING THE INTERVIEW

The course leader would need to record a political interview from radio or television, and have a transcript made of the interview. It is advisable that the interview should be at least 30 minutes in length, to ensure that there is sufficient material to obtain a good sample of question–response sequences. Multiple copies of the recording can then be made onto audio cassette. Most universities in the United Kingdom have an Educational Recording Agency licence which entitles them to make copies of off-air material for educational purposes. Check with your Audio-Visual Department if unsure about this. The course leader will also need audio cassette recorders for the practical class. Students can work in groups of two or three, using one machine per group. But each student should have their own transcript.

TRANSCRIPTS

Transcripts are essential for this kind of work. There are many different ways of making a transcript, and how this is done rather depends on what is the purpose of the transcript (see, e.g. Roger and Bull, 1989, pp. 141–212). Some notes of guidance are given below. These are not intended to be in any way prescriptive, they are simply points that the author has found useful in preparing his own transcripts:

1 The transcript should give the name of interviewer and interviewee, the date, time and television/radio channel on which it was broadcast, and the total duration of the interview.
2 The transcript should be as *accurate* as possible. This may seem blindingly obvious, but an inaccurate transcript is not only very irritating, it is also time-consuming to correct, and can lead to faulty analysis. The transcript should attempt to reproduce everything the participants say, including filled pauses ('um', 'er' etc.) and laughter. Faulty grammar or slips of the tongue should not be corrected, but reproduced as faithfully as possible.
3 *Punctuation* should be used as little as possible, only when it is necessary to ensure comprehensibility. For example, question marks in particular should be avoided. It is not always obvious whether an utterance should be understood as a question, and one of the purposes of this exercise is for students to gain some basic experience in the problems of identifying questions in naturally occurring discourse.
4 If *interruptions and simultaneous speech* are ignored in producing a transcript, this can produce a very misleading impression of the nature of the interaction. To indicate interruptions and simultaneous speech, vertical bars can be used, as well as careful alignment of text to show that overlap is occurring. To demonstrate this, an

example of text, transcribed from an interview between Tony Blair (TB) and David Dimbleby (DD) in the General Election campaign of 1997 (7 April 1997) is reproduced below

DD: no did you believe in what they stood for did you believe in CND did you believe in union power not being curtailed did you believe in nationalization no privatization

TB: there were a whole series of policy positions that I adopted with along with the rest of the labour party but the very process of modernization has been the very process that I have undertaken in the labour party for example yes
                                                                                          |
DD: I know that
but did you have you abandoned have you did you believe what you said you believed in the eighties

TB: look of course we always believed in the idea of a more just a more fair society and the labour party believed for a long period of time that the way to do that was for example greater nationalization er was for example simply more in-creased state spending the whole process of modernization David has been to take the labour party away from that to keep true to its principles but put those principles properly in a modern setting now |
DD: so all that was wrong
TB: no I don't say all that was wrong I simply say . . .
                                                  |
DD: most of it was wrong
TB: er I simply say what is important is to apply those principles to the modern world

PROCEDURE

1 I normally have people analyse the interview in class, working in small groups, for say about an hour. After a break, I then have a second session with the group as a whole, going through the tape, and discussing how people have analysed particular responses. This in itself can be quite instructive.

2 Students then complete the questionnaire part of the practical in their own time. If they work in small groups, this reduces the overall workload considerably by sharing the task of questionnaire administration. But if they do this, they should each write up their own report independently.

Appendix 9.1: Identifying questions, replies and non-replies to questions (from Bull, 1994. Reprinted by permission of Sage Publications, Inc.)

1 Questions typically – but not always – take interrogative syntax (subject–verb inversion and/or interrogative word).
2 One way of deciding whether an utterance constitutes a question is to consider its function – whether it constitutes a request for information.

Responses to questions can be coded along three main dimensions:

1 *Replies* – in which the information requested is given. (Delayed replies sometimes occur in which the answer to a question is given later on in the interview.)
2 *Non-replies* – in which none of the information requested is given. A typology of 35 different ways of not replying to a question is given in Bull (2003).
3 *Intermediate replies*. There are certain utterances that cannot be regarded as either replies or non-replies:
   • *Answers by implication*. The politician makes his or her views clear without explicitly stating them.
   • *Incomplete replies*. The politican gives some but not all of the requested information.
   • *Interrupted reply* – not possible to say whether the politician was going to answer the question because of an interruption by the interviewer

Note that in Bavelas et al.'s theory, incomplete replies, answers by implication and non-replies are all regarded as different forms of equivocation.

There are three principal types of question in English. Identifying these different types of question can help in deciding whether or not the politician has given a reply:

1 *Yes-no questions* invite the response yes or no, and if this response is given, it can be seen as constituting a reply. Note that the words 'yes' or 'no' do not have to be used, and occasionally if used may be misleading! What you have to decide for a reply is whether the respondent has affirmed or denied the proposition in the question.
2 *Interrogative-word questions* (sometimes confusingly called wh-questions). Interrogative-word questions (what, when, why, who, how, which and where) ask for a missing variable, and if the respondent supplies that missing variable, he or she can be seen

as having answered the question; for example, 'what' asks for a selection from an indefinite number of possibilities, or for the specification of amount, number or kind.

3 *Disjunctive questions* pose a choice between two or more alternatives. If the respondent chooses one of the alternatives, then this can be seen as constituting a reply. However, it is often also possible to offer a third alternative, which might also be regarded as a reply.

Appendix 9.2:   Rating scales for equivocation (based on the rating scales devised by Bavelas et al., 1990; reproduced with permission).

---

1 How clear is this message, in terms of just *what is being said*?

Completely Clear	Completely Unclear
Straightforward, easy to understand, there is only one possible meaning.	Totally vague, impossible to understand; no meaning at all.

2 To what extent is this message the *speaker's own opinion*?

Definitely	Not at all
It is very evident that the message is the speaker's opinion; it is obviously the speaker's personal opinion, not someone else's.	Someone else's opinion is being expressed, and you have no idea what the speaker's opinion is

3 To what extent is the message *addressed to the other person in the situation*?

Definitely	Not at all
Obviously addressing the other person; could only be addressing that person.	The message is not addressed to the other person in the situation.

4 To what extent is this a *direct answer to the question*?

Definitely	Not at all
This is a direct answer to the question asked.	The response is 'way off' the question; seems totally unrelated to the question.

NOTE

1 The author would like to acknowledge many useful and instructive comments from undergraduates who have taken part in practicals on equivocation in the Department of Psychology at the University of York.

REFERENCES

Bavelas, J. B., Black, A., Chovil, N. & Mullett, J. (1990). *Equivocal communication*. Newbury Park, CA: Sage.

Beattie, G. W. (1982). Turn-taking and interruptions in political interviews – Margaret Thatcher and Jim Callaghan compared and contrasted. *Semiotica*, *39*, 93–114.

Bull. P. E. (1994). On identifying questions, replies and non-replies in political interviews. *Journal of Language and Social Psychology*, *13*, 115–31.

Bull, P. E. (1997). Queen of Hearts or queen of the arts of implication? Implicit criticisms and their implications for equivocation theory in the interview between Martin Bashir and Diana, Princess of Wales. *Social Psychological Review*, *1*, 27–36.

Bull, P. E. (1998a). Political interviews: Television interviews in Great Britain. In O. Feldman & C. De Landtsheer (eds.), *Politically speaking: A worldwide examination of language used in the public sphere* (pp. 149–60). Westport, CT: Greenwood Publishing Group.

Bull, P. E. (1998b). Equivocation theory and news interviews. *Journal of Language and Social Psychology*, *17*, 36–51.

Bull, P. E. (2000). Equivocation and the rhetoric of modernisation: An analysis of televised interviews with Tony Blair in the 1997 British General Election. *Journal of Language and Social Psychology*, *19*, 222–47.

Bull, P. E. (2003). *The microanalysis of political communication: Claptrap and ambiguity*. London: Routledge.

Bull, P. E., Elliott, J., Palmer, D. & Walker, L. (1996). Why politicians are three-faced: The face model of political interviews. *British Journal of Social Psychology*, *35*, 267–84.

Bull, P. E. & Mayer, K. (1988). Interruptions in political interviews: A study of Margaret Thatcher and Neil Kinnock. *Journal of Language and Social Psychology*, *7*, 35–45.

Bull, P. E. & Mayer, K. (1993). How not to answer questions in political interviews. *Political Psychology*, *14*, 651–66.

Clayman, S. E. (1989). The production of punctuality: Social interaction, temporal organization and social structure. *American Journal of Sociology*, *95*, 659–91.

Clayman, S. E. (1991). News interview openings: Aspects of sequential organization. In P. Scannell (ed.), *Broadcast talk* (pp. 48–75). London: Sage.

Cockerell, M. (1988). *Live from number ten: The inside story of prime ministers and television*. London: Faber & Faber.

Day, R. (1989). *Grand inquisitor: Memoirs*. London: Weidenfeld & Nicolson.

Eagly, A. H. & Chaiken, S. (1993). *The psychology of attitudes*. Orlando, FL: Harcourt Brace Jovanovich, Inc.

Greatbatch, D. (1988). A turn-taking system for British news interviews. *Language in Society, 17*, 401–30.

Hague, W. (2002). What I learned about Tony – the hard way. *Guardian G2*, 26 April, pp. 2–5.

Hamilton, M. A. & Mineo, P. J. (1998). A framework for understanding equivocation. *Journal of Language and Social Psychology, 17*, 3–35.

Harris, S. (1991). Evasive action: how politicians respond to questions in political interviews. In P. Scannell (ed.), *Broadcast talk* (pp. 76–99). London: Sage.

Heritage, J. C. (1985). Analyzing news interviews: aspects of the production of talk for an overhearing audience. In T. van Dijk (ed.), *Handbook of discourse analysis* (vol. 3, pp. 95–117). New York: Academic Press.

Heritage, J. C., Clayman, S. E. & Zimmerman, D. (1988). Discourse and message analysis: The micro-structure of mass media messages. In R. Hawkins, S. Pingree & J. Weimann (eds.), *Advancing communication science: Merging mass and interpersonal processes* (pp. 77–109). Newbury Park: Sage.

Heritage, J. C. & Greatbatch, D. L. (1991). On the institutional character of institutional talk: The case of news interviews. In D. Boden & D. Zimmerman (eds.), *Talk and social structure* (pp. 93–137). Cambridge, UK: Polity Press.

Jones, W. (1992). Broadcasters, politicians and the political interview. In W. Jones & L. Robins (eds.), *Two decades in British politics* (pp. 53–77). Manchester, UK: Manchester University Press.

Quirk, R., Greenbaum, S., Leech, G. & Svartvik, J. (1985). *A comprehensive grammar of the English language*. London: Longman.

Roger, D. B. & Bull, P. E. (eds.) (1989). *Conversation: An interdisciplinary approach*. Clevedon, UK: Multilingual Matters.

Schegloff, E. A. (1989). From interview to confrontation: Observations on the Bush/Rather encounter. *Research on Language and Social Interaction, 22*, 215–40.

CHAPTER TEN

Interpretative Phenomenological Analysis

Jonathan A. Smith & Mike Osborn

This chapter describes interpretative phenomenological analysis (IPA), which involves self-report data elicitation through interview associated with a sophisticated thematic analysis. The approach is idiographic and invariably linked to non-experimental research designs. The IPA training exercise presented provides details of how to construct an appropriate interview schedule and the steps in recording and then reporting data. The chapter is appropriate for intermediate level courses.

What is Interpretative Phenomenological Analysis?

Interpretative phenomenological analysis is a relatively recent qualitative methodology developed specifically for psychology. Interpretative phenomenological analysis (IPA) recognizes that different people perceive the world in very different ways, dependent on their personalities, prior life experiences and motivations. It attempts to explore/understand/make sense of the subjective meanings of events/experiences/states of the individual participants themselves. This is in contrast to most psychology which is concerned with: (1) trying to test pre-existing hypotheses on the part of the researcher, (2) finding average results for a group of participants as a whole or (3) attempting to produce a quantitative measure of an objective reality. IPA is strongly influenced by phenomenology, a term used for a range of psychological approaches concerned with subjective experience and which in turn developed out of Husserl's philosophical phenomenology.

While IPA is committed to the value of attempting to understand the world from the perspective of one's participants, it also recognizes that this cannot be done without interpretative work by the researcher who is trying to make sense of what the participant is saying. This explains the interpretative part in the name of the methodology.

IPA is an idiographic approach. It begins with the detailed analysis of case studies and only cautiously moves to more general statements about groups of individuals. IPA studies are usually conducted with small numbers of participants (e.g. six to fifteen) because the aim is to present an intimate portrayal of individual experience. Such detailed examination of individuals is rare in psychology. However, IPA believes that studies concerned with documenting the existence of actual patterns of life have an important contribution to make to the discipline.

There are now a number of qualitative approaches to psychology. One which has established a high profile in social psychology, particularly in the UK, is discourse analysis. IPA has very different theoretical commitments from discourse analysis. Discourse analysis is interested in how verbal accounts given in conversations, interviews and written documents are linguistically constructed, and the social tasks people are trying to perform when they use particular verbal expressions. Discourse analysis as understood by most current social psychologists is sceptical about looking beyond what people are saying in order to inquire into how they are thinking or feeling about a particular topic.

IPA by contrast is very interested in cognitive and emotional entities and, when an IPA researcher is looking at what a person is saying or writing, the researcher is concerned with trying to find out what that person thinks and feels about what they are talking about.

To give an example, two different researchers might look at the transcript of an interview with a hospital patient. One of the researchers uses IPA and wants to find out how the patient is responding to the particular condition they are suffering from. What are the particular ways this condition is affecting this person? What influences in the person's biography affect their response? How does the condition affect the person's sense of identity? How does the person interpret the diagnostic label they have been given for their condition? In contrast, the discourse analysis researcher would be interested in questions such as: what language does the participant use to construct her/himself as a patient with a particular condition? What existing models or discourses of illness and health that are available in our society are they drawing on in order to present themselves in this way? What effect do the interview context and the presence of the interviewer have on how the patients talk about themselves? How might they talk differently to a different interviewer? See Smith (1996) or Smith and Osborn (2003) for more on the theoretical underpinnings of IPA.

How Do You Do Interpretative Phenomenological Analysis?

This section will give a brief overview of the stages involved in conducting a research study using IPA. In a subsequent section, a worked example will be provided which can form the basis for a practical exercise with students.

IPA is suitable for a very wide range of research questions in psychology where one is interested in finding out more about the meaning of experiences to participants. It is particularly suitable where the topic under investigation is novel or under-researched, where the issues are complex or ambiguous and where one is concerned to understand something about process and change. Examples of projects which have used IPA: how does a woman's sense of identity change during the transition to motherhood? How do health professionals think about patients who are suffering from anorexia nervosa? How do religious converts describe the conversion process? How do people react to being told they have been adopted?

SAMPLING

IPA uses a form of purposive sampling. Given that the numbers involved in an IPA study are inevitably small, IPA makes no pretence of attempting to obtain a random sample or one representative of a large diverse population. Rather, IPA operates from the logic of attempting to understand this specific phenomenon from the perspective of this particular group, in the same way that an anthropologist wants to understand one particular culture in detail rather than being able to talk about all cultures.

Consonant with that, IPA researchers usually try to find a fairly homogenous sample. Thus having determined which group would be suitable for one's research question, one attempts to make the group similar on obvious socio-economic variables: gender, age and

so on. Having established which particular group would be important, interesting and practical to approach for one's study, one then
draws a boundary around the claims to generalizability one can make.
Thus if the study is on attitudes to political activism in Britain today
and is based on data collected from six African-Caribbean women
in their twenties, one would hope to say: (1) a lot about the particular participants in the study, (2) something about the broad group
they represent, but (3) one would not be able to say anything
about people outside that group. What would be the problem with
having a more heterogeneous group? If the group was made up of
people of different ages, genders, ethnic group and so forth, then
it would be difficult to decide whether patterns of similarity and
difference that were found in the data were more to do with individual characteristics of the particular individuals or the social variable they represented. And of course, this is not to say that what
people from other groups would have to say about the topic would
not be interesting. On the contrary, it could form the basis for a later
study.

COLLECTING DATA

For IPA, one is seeking a data collection technique which provides
the flexibility to allow the participant to provide a detailed account
in their own words. Thus it is argued, for the purposes of IPA, that
existing questionnaires would constrain the participant too much –
only allowing short responses to pre-specified questions which are
testing the researcher's pre-defined hypotheses. Instead IPA researchers
usually engage in semi-structured interviews with participants where
the researcher has a set of questions to ask but these are used very
flexibly in the interview.

It is useful to contrast this approach to interviewing with the
more commonly used structured interview. The structured interview
shares much of the rationale of the psychological experiment. Generally the investigator decides in advance exactly what constitutes
the required data and constructs the questions in such a way as to
elicit answers corresponding to, and easily contained within, predetermined categories which can then be numerically analysed. In
order to enhance reliability the interviewer should stick very closely
to the interview schedule and behave with as little variation as
possible between interviews. Thus the interviewer will aim to read
the question exactly as on the schedule and ask the questions in the
identical order specified by the schedule. In many ways, the structured

interview is like the questionnaire; and indeed the two overlap to the extent that often the interview is simply the investigator going through a questionnaire in the presence of a respondent, the interviewer filling in the answers on the questionnaire sheet based on what the respondent says.

With semi-structured interviews the investigator will have a set of questions on an interview schedule but the interview will be guided by the schedule rather than be dictated by it. Here then, the ordering of questions is less important, the interviewer is freer to probe interesting areas that arise and the interview can follow the respondent's interests or concerns. Thus the interviewer may decide that it would be appropriate to ask a question earlier than it appears on the schedule because it follows from what the respondent has just said. Similarly how a question is phrased, and how explicit it is, will now partly depend on how the interviewer feels the participant is responding.

It is quite possible that the interview may enter an area that had not been predicted by the investigator but which is extremely pertinent to, and enlightening of, the project's overall question. Indeed these novel avenues are often the most valuable, precisely because they have come unprompted from the respondent and, therefore, are likely to be of especial importance for him or her.

These differences between structured and semi-structured interviewing follow from the theoretical premise underlying IPA. The investigator has an idea of the area of interest and some questions to pursue. At the same time, there is a wish to try to enter, as far as is possible, the psychological and social world of the respondent. Therefore the respondent shares more closely in the direction the interview takes and the respondent can introduce an issue the investigator had not thought of.

Given this, why is it still important when working in this way to produce an interview schedule in advance? Producing a schedule beforehand forces you to think explicitly about what you think/hope the interview might cover. More specifically it enables you to think of difficulties that might be encountered, for example, in terms of question wording or sensitive areas and to give some thought to how these difficulties might be handled. Having thought in advance about the different ways the interview may proceed allows you, when it comes to the interview itself, to concentrate more thoroughly and more confidently on what the respondent is saying.

Other forms of data collection are possible for IPA, for example asking the participant to write autobiographical accounts or keep diaries, but most IPA researchers have found the semi-structured

interview the best way to collect material. Interviews with participants are tape-recorded and transcribed verbatim, as there is no way
the interviewer can document everything that is being said in the
interview in sufficient detail to allow a thorough analysis afterwards.

ANALYSIS AND WRITING UP

One begins with the first transcript and engages in a systematic search
for themes that arise in it. One then attempts to forge connections
between these themes and establish superordinate themes for the
case. Having done this for the first case, one moves to the second and
slowly works one's way through the participants. One then looks for
patterns between cases with the aim of establishing the master themes
for the group as a whole. This set of master themes is presented in a
table, with examples of each theme to support it. This part of the
process of IPA will be described in detail in the worked example
provided below. This is taken from the authors' study of the personal
experience of chronic back pain.

Having established what the main themes are for one's group of
participants, one then translates the master table of themes into a
narrative account, introducing the topic and then each superordinate
theme in turn. The themes are described in detail and supported with
verbatim extracts taken from the interviews with the participants.
This way the participants can be said to have a presence or voice in
the final write-up produced.

The analysis will form the results section of a project write-up,
dissertation, book chapter or paper for publication. It will be preceded
by an introduction, outlining the rationale for the study, and a method
section describing what was done in the project. After the results
section, the discussion relates the analysis to some relevant literature
and discusses the implications of the study.

What Type of Studies
Have Been Done Using IPA?

IPA is a relatively recent qualitative approach to emerge in psychology. Here are two examples of studies which have been conducted.
The first author has been involved in IPA studies looking at the
psychological impact of the rapid advances in human genetics. In
one study, individuals who are considering taking the genetic test for

a seriously debilitating condition – Huntington's disease – were interviewed on their decision-making processes. One of the findings from that study was that individuals conceptualize what may seem a similar factor in very different ways. Thus while all the interviewees wanted to do what was right for their own children, different individuals interpreted 'doing the right thing' in very different ways. Thus two women both wanted to take the genetic test for the sake of their children, but while one mother believed that a positive test result should force her children to behave in a particular way, the other mother believed it was important not to influence her children to her own way of thinking. Thus the first woman declared that if she had a positive test result, her children should also take the test and if they too had a positive test result then they should not have children, because of the possibility of passing on the faulty gene. The second woman, on the other hand, recognized the danger of interfering in her children's decision making and stated that it would be important for them to retain the freedom to make their own decision about what to do. It is this very possibility of putting moral pressure on his children which leads a third interviewee towards the decision that he will not take the genetic test – that way he will not find out information which could be too loaded for his children. IPA enables us to explore in detail the particular ways the individuals are thinking through the process (Smith, Stephenson, & Quarrell in an unpublished manuscript 'Factors influencing the decision-making process with the genetic test for Huntington's Disease', 2003; see also Michie, Smith, Heaversedge & Read, 1999).

The first author also used IPA to explore how women's sense of identity changed during the transition to motherhood. A small number of women were followed through their first pregnancy, being interviewed when three, six and nine months pregnant and then five months after the birth of the child. They were asked to describe themselves and how the pregnancy was affecting them. This was written up in terms of the relational self. The women talked a great deal about significant relationships and it appeared that during the pregnancy the women saw themselves as becoming psychologically more like these significant others in their lives. It was suggested that the women are able to use their relationships with these important others who are already parents to help prepare themselves psychologically for becoming mothers (see Smith, 1999).

Examples of other published studies using IPA are: gay men's perceptions of sex and sexual behaviour (Flowers, Hart & Marriott, 1999); how individuals deal with the death of their partner (Golsworthy and Coyle, 1999); the experience of delusions (Rhodes and Jakes, 2000);

theoretical models used by mental health nurses (Carradice, Shankland & Beail, 2002).

A Training Exercise in IPA

This section outlines in sequence the stages involved in conducting a training exercise in IPA. The full exercise is run over two sessions of about two and a half hours each and is made up of a combination of didactic input from the teacher and hands-on practical work from the class working in small groups. While students are doing the practical work, the tutor and teaching assistants wander between groups, checking the process, offering assistance and stimulating the group work. The exercise takes the students through the stages in conducting an IPA project: thinking of a research topic, constructing the interview schedule, interviewing, transcription, analysis and writing up, so that by the end of it they are better placed to embark on research projects using the approach. The full sequence involves: session A: decide on a topic, construct interview schedule, practise interviewing; between sessions: conduct interview and transcribe it; session B: analysis.

INTRODUCTION TO IPA AND FORMING SMALL GROUPS

1 A short lecture is given to the class, outlining the key principles and methodological features of IPA and explaining how the practical exercise will work. The tutor can draw on material from this chapter, along with more details in reading mentioned in the list at the end of the chapter.
2 The class should be divided into groups of between four and six students. The students will work in the same group throughout the class, generating and analysing their own data.

CHOOSING A TOPIC

The group needs to choose a topic to investigate. The topic should be one which is consonant with the principles of IPA and for which it is a suitable approach. It should be of sufficient interest to them and relevant to the respondent who will be a peer, that is, a fellow student. It should also be of psychological relevance. However, given that the students are new to this way of working, it is best to avoid topics which are potentially highly sensitive. It is best for students to choose their own topic with approval from the class tutor. They are then likely to be more engaged in the exercise. However, if necessary, the tutor can suggest possible topics.

CONSTRUCTING THE INTERVIEW SCHEDULE

The group constructs a short interview schedule which will be used for a 15-minute interview. The exercise begins with a short presentation by the tutor. Students then work as a group to produce the schedule. During this, they can review the guidance provided in this chapter and should look at the sample schedule provided in Box 10.1. This is taken from a project conducted by the first author on kidney disease patients' response to their illness and dialysis treatment. The students are not expected to produce a schedule as long as this but it gives them an idea of what a real one looks like.

Box 10.1: Sample interview schedule – patient's experience of renal dialysis

A.   Dialysis
 1 Can you tell me the brief history of your kidney problem from when it started to you beginning dialysis?
 2 Could you describe what happens in dialysis, in your own words?
 3 What do you do when you are having dialysis?
 4 How do you feel when you are dialysing?
    prompt: physically, emotionally, mentally
 5 What do you think about?
 6 How do you feel about having dialysis?
    prompt: some people – relief from previous illness, a bind
 7 How does dialysis/kidney disease effect your everyday life?
    prompt: work, interests, relationships
 8 If you had to describe what the dialysis machine means to you, what would you say?
    prompt: what words come to mind, what images, do you have a nickname for it?

B.   Identity
9 How would you describe yourself as a person?
   prompt: what sort of person are you, most important char-
          acteristics, happy, moody, nervy?
10 Has having kidney disease and starting dialysis made a dif-
    ference to how you see yourself?
   prompt: if so, how do you see yourself now as different to
          before you started dialysis? how would you say
          you have changed?
11 What about compared to before you had kidney disease?
12 What about the way other people see you?
   prompt: members of your family, friends? changed?

C.   Coping
13 What does the term illness mean to you? How do you
    define it?
14 How much do you think about your own physical health?
15 Do you see yourself as being ill?
   prompt: always, sometimes? would you say you were an
          ill person?
16 On a day-to-day basis how do you deal with having kidney
    disease (the illness)?
   prompt: do you have particular strategies for helping you?
          ways of coping – practical, mental?
17 Do you think about the future much?

1 The lecturer gives a short presentation on constructing an interview
   schedule.
2 The group decides the broad range of question areas to be covered
   in the interview. Three areas is about the right number for this
   exercise. The three areas in the kidney dialysis project are: personal
   description of dialysis, effect on self, coping strategies.
3 The question areas are put in the most appropriate sequence. Two
   questions may help here. What is the most logical order to address
   these areas in? Which is the most sensitive area? In general it is a
   good idea to leave sensitive topics till later in the interview to allow
   the respondent to become relaxed and comfortable with speaking.
   Thus an interview on political affiliations might begin with questions
   on what the different political parties represent, then move on to

the question of societal attitudes to politics before, in the final section, asking about the person's own political views and voting behaviour – thus leaving the most personal and potentially most sensitive area till last.

4 The group thinks of three or four good questions for the first section. Questions should be neutral rather than value-laden or leading: 'What do you think of the prime minister's record in office so far?' is better than 'Do you agree that the prime minister is doing a bad job?' Jargon should be avoided. This can be done by thinking of the language of the respondent and framing questions in a way they will feel familiar and comfortable with. Questions can be seen as merely cues to try to get the person to speak. Constructing questions like this can be difficult for psychologists trained in experimental and quantitative methodology. Thus, in the course of constructing a schedule, the first draft questions may be too explicit and linked to specific hypotheses and assumptions. With redrafting, these become gentler and less loaded but sufficient to let the respondent know what the area of interest is and recognize that they have something to say about it. One member of the group can suggest a possible question and the group can then discuss it and suggest possible reformatting.

5 Prompts should be constructed to follow some of the questions where this is felt necessary or useful. Sometimes a question will be insufficient to elicit a satisfactory response. This may be because the issue is a complex one or the question is too general or vague for this particular participant. To prepare for this, prompts can be constructed, which are framed more explicitly. Some of the group's first draft questions may be able to act as these prompts. Prompts do not need to be prepared for every question and are not expected to be used with every respondent – just where he or she is having difficulty with the initial question. See the examples of prompts in Box 10.1.

PRACTICE INTERVIEWING

During this exercise, students practise interview skills by engaging in practice interviews in their small groups, different members of the group taking different roles. The exercise begins with the tutor giving a short presentation on interviewing and on ethics in relation to research interviews, and during it students can look at the notes on interviewing in this chapter and in Box 10.2.

Box 10.2:   Interviewing tips

1 Try not to rush in too quickly. Give the respondent time to finish a question before moving on. Often the most interesting questions need some time to respond to and richer fuller answers may be missed if the interviewer jumps in too quickly.

2 If the respondent is entering an interesting area, minimal probes are often all that is required to help them to continue, for example 'can you tell me more about that?' Or more specific probes may be appropriate in certain circumstances, for example, to tap affect – 'how did you feel about that?' or to focus on awareness – 'what do you think about that?'

3 Ask one question at a time. Multiple questions can be difficult for the respondent to unpick and even more difficult for you subsequently, when you are trying to work out from a transcript which question the respondent is replying to.

4 Monitor the effect of the interview on the respondent. It may be that the respondent feels uncomfortable with a particular line of questioning and this may be expressed in their non-verbal behaviour or in how they reply. You need to be ready to respond to this by, for example, backing off and trying again more gently or deciding it would be inappropriate to pursue this area with this respondent. As an interviewer you have certain ethical responsibilites towards your respondent.

1 The tutor gives a short lecture on interviewing and on the ethics of research interviews.

2 Students should review the material on interviewing in the earlier section of the chapter and read the guidance in Box 10.2.

3 The group engages in a practice interview. Individuals should volunteer for or be elected to roles: interviewer, interviewee, timekeeper. The remaining members of the group are observers. The interviewer takes five minutes to familiarize her/himself with the schedule. The interviewer and interviewee engage in a five-minute interview using the prepared schedule as a starting point. Obviously in five minutes the interview will only cover a small part of the schedule. The aim of the exercize is to give practice at interviewing skills and offer material which will then allow a review of some of the questions on the schedule. The interviewee takes the role of someone who has agreed to take part in the project and be

interviewed on this particular topic. The timekeeper begins the interview and stops it after five minutes.

4 Once the interview is finished, the group discusses how it went. It can be useful for one or two observers to begin this discussion by commenting on their reactions: what sense of the process did they have overall? Was the interviewee put at ease? Did the interviewer follow up interesting things that arose or was there a tendency to stick too closely to the schedule? This discussion should last for five minutes.

5 Members of the group then swap roles so new individuals take up the role of interviewer, interviewee and timekeeper, and the exercise is repeated with five minutes of interview and five minutes of discussion. Hopefully much will have been learned from the first trial and the second exercise should be showing signs of good practice.

6 The schedule is reviewed in the light of the practice exercize. It may be that certain questions need to be reworded, or the sequence of the interview adjusted or it may be considered that there are too few or too many questions for a full interview.

7 The tutor/teaching assistant asks each group to elect one member to conduct the interview proper with an interviewee between the two classes.

8 The whole class comes together for a brief discussion of their experience in the practice interviews. The lecturer asks a small number of questions to elicit discussion, for example: how did people find the exercise? what have you learned? how was the second interview different from the first?

9 The tutor conducts a brief summary on where the class has got too, and on what remains – conducting the proper interview and transcribing it before the next session when the group will analyse it.

THE INTERVIEW

Outside the first class, one student uses the interview schedule to interview one participant for 15 minutes. The interview is tape-recorded and transcribed verbatim.

1 Before conducting the interview, the interviewer should learn the schedule by heart, so that they will not be tempted to constantly refer to it in the interview.

2 The interviewer should review the notes on interviewing in this chapter and tips in Box 10.2 and acquaint him/herself with the ethical guidelines in Box 10.3.

Box 10.3:   Ethical guidelines

Potential interviewees need to be informed of what the project is about – that it is being conducted as part of a degree exercise – and what is expected of them – that they will be taking part in a short interview which will be tape-recorded and transcribed.

Rights. The participant is free to stop the interview at any point and free to state that they no longer wish to take part in the project at any point. This should be explained to them.

Confidentiality. The participant needs to have confidentiality explained – that any identifying information will be removed from the transcript, and that only a small number of people will hear the tape itself. It may be a good idea to give the tape of the interview to the interviewee once the whole exercise is completely finished.

Possible distress. The interview should be planned not to cause distress – through avoiding overly sensitive topics, thinking carefully about question wording and selection of interviewee. However, it is possible that the interviewee may become distressed inadvertently during the interview. It is the responsibility of the interviewer to check the demeanour of the interviewee to check for any signs of distress. If they occur, it may be possible to change tack, or it may be necessary to stop the interview. If the participant is upset, it is important to ensure that they are comfortable before leaving them. It may be advisable to suggest that the interviewee talks to a friend. It is a good idea to have the phone number of the student counselling service to hand in case the interviewee is very upset, and the interviewer may suggest that the interviewee considers contacting a counsellor.

3 The nominated interviewer will need to find a volunteer to take part in the interview which will form the basis for the group's analysis. Fellow students for whom the interview topic is considered relevant can be approached. The purpose of the task, what will be required of them and their rights to stop the interview at any time should be explained. Tutors may choose to require participants to complete an informed consent sheet. One possibility is for arrangements to be made between different groups in the

class, whereby individuals from two groups join up to form interviewer–interviewee pairs.

4 The interviewer should arrange to conduct the interview in a suitable venue at a time which is convenient to the interviewee. The interview should be conducted without anyone else present.[1] This should be a room which is quiet and where they will be undisturbed for the duration of the interview. It could be the place of residence of the interviewer, interviewee or another place convenient to both parties – perhaps a small room in the psychology department.

5 The interview will need to be tape-recorded and the interviewee will have to agreed to this. A tape recording allows a much fuller record than notes taken during the interview. It also means that the interviewer can concentrate on how the interview is proceeding and where to go next, rather than laboriously writing down what the respondent is saying. It is easiest if the interviewer uses a tape recorder they own and are already familiar with. Otherwise the interviewer will need to borrow one.

6 At the appointed time the interview is conducted. The interviewer should briefly recap the purpose of the interview and the rights of the interviewee to stop the interview at any time if they so wish. The interviewer should turn the tape recorder on and for the first few minutes the aim is to chat with the respondent to put them at ease. The aim is to make the interviewee feel comfortable talking to the interviewer before any of the substantive areas of the schedule are introduced. Hopefully then this positive and responsive 'mental set' will continue throughout the interview.

7 The interviewer can then ask the first question on the schedule. The interviewer's role in a semi-structured interview is to facilitate and guide, rather than dictate exactly what will happen during the encounter. If the interviewer has learnt the schedule in advance then he or she can concentrate during the interview on what the respondent is saying, and occasionally monitor the coverage of the scheduled topics. Thus the interviewer uses the schedule to indicate the general area of interest and to provide cues when the participant has difficulties, but the idea is to follow up interesting areas that arise and probe the interviewee for more details. In this way the respondent is allowed a strong role in determining how the interview proceeds. The aim should be for the interview to last approximately 15 minutes.

8 At the end of the interview, the interviewee is thanked and the interviewer should check that the respondent is comfortable with the interview being used for analysis and that the interviewee has not been distressed by the interview. In the unlikely event that

the interviewee is distressed, the interviewer will need to follow the procedure outlined in Box 10.3.

9 The tape recording is transcribed. A verbatim written record of everything said by interviewer and interviewee needs to be produced. This can either be handwritten, if the transcriber has good handwriting, or it can be typed. Gaps should be left to indicate change of speakers and there should be wide margins on both sides of the page. See Box 10.4 for a small piece of interview data

---

Box 10.4:   Extract from beginning of transcript of interview on dialysis treatment

I: Okay could could we start by erm you just just describing in your own words what you think is happening during dialysis what what you think the process involved is medically.

R: Mm well the way I understand is er there are two main functions and that is (a) to er take out you know toxins in the blood and er secondly er to take off er fluid obviously when they er when the kidneys pack well in my case and in I believe most cases that er you know kidney patients stop passing water as such now I myself pass a little bit but not much and the second process of dialysis is er to take off the fluid that stays on board.

I: Right.

R: Which I think is probably the most important part of dialysis.

I: Yeah.

R: So if you've got er if I've was to carry on drinking the way I used to drink well I was a big drinker up to now they say you need about 8 to 10 pints of fluids passing through the body a day as a normal person which if I did that today it have it have er you know a serious affect on my heart I believe.

I: So what what limit do you have now?

R: At the moment I'm er on about er a litre a litre and a half which is about 3 pints a day.

I: Right.

R: Which is not a lot.

to illustrate what a transcription looks like. During the transcription, any identifying information (names mentioned, occupation or degree subject, home town) about the interviewee needs to be removed or amended – it is appropriate to provide fictional identifying data for the interviewee. It is easiest if the interviewer does the transcription, as they will be familiar with the voices. However, this is putting a considerable burden on one person. It may be possible for someone else in the group to do the transcription. For a 15-minute interview, transcription will take an hour or maybe even longer.

10 Copies of the transcript should be made so that each member of the group has their own and one is also provided for the tutor/teaching assistant working with that group. These copies should be made available at the beginning of the second session.

ANALYSIS

After a short presentation on analysis from the lecturer the group goes through the stages of analysis on the transcript of their interview.

Step 1   The lecturer gives a brief presentation on IPA analysis.
Step 2   The students should review the earlier part of this chapter on analysis and read through the stages below before beginning. In addition, a worked example of the stages applied to an extract from an interview on the personal experience of pain is provided in Box 10.5; it is keyed to the steps in this sequence. This example should be referred to as the analysis is being conducted. Some notes on different types of analysis can be seen in Box 10.6. It is also useful to look at these.

WRITING UP

It can be a useful way to end the exercise to ask the students to write up a short project report. This may also be used to provide an assessment for the exercise. If this is the case the write-up can be done by each student individually or the group can allocate different sections in the write-up among themselves and the group be awarded one mark. A short extract from the results section of an IPA paper is provided in Box 10.7 to illustrate what the finished analysis can look like.

Box 10.5:   Worked example of stages of analysis – the experience of pain

Initial individual comments (Step 3)[2]

I: What's it like being in pain?

shoulds, ideals
expectations

frustration
other people
mobility restriction
trapped

L: I'm only 50, and I should be doing this and that and the other cos they say life begins at 40 but I can't and I suppose it does bother me. It's frustrating that people of my own age are, you can see them flying their kite and you feel as if you can't, well you can't.

I: You can't.

compared to sisters

compared to past when
fit/strong
ideal past/doubt,
'I thought' not 'I was'
adjustment, shock/loss/change

L: No which is so stupid, I just think I'm the fittest because there are 3 girls [she and her sisters] and I'm the middle one and I thought well I'm the fittest and I used to work like a horse and I thought I was the strongest and then all of a sudden it's just been cut down and I can't do half of what I used to do.

Deciding the themes (Step 4)
I: What's it like being in pain?

L: I'm only 50, and I should be doing this and that and the other cos they say life begins at 40 but I can't and I suppose it does bother

comparison with ought self

loss

me. it's frustrating that people of
my own age are, you can see them   social comparison – others
flying their kite and you feel as if
you can't, well you can't.

I: You can't.

L: No which is so stupid, I just   social comparison – family
think I'm the fittest because there
are 3 girls [she and her sisters] and
I'm the middle one and I thought   nostalgia – selective recall
well I'm the fittest and I used to
work like a horse and I thought I
was the strongest and then all of a   sense of self / loss of self
sudden it's just been cut down and
I can't do half of what I used to do.

Listing the themes (Step 5)
– Trying to make sense
– Searching for an explanation
– Uncertainty
– Lack of understanding
– Frustration
– Confusion and anger
– Implications for the self-concept
– Sense of self
– Self-critical
– Self-doubt
– Social comparisons with others
– Social comparison within family
– Social comparison with self
  before the pain
– Bereavement and shock
– Mobility/physical restrictions
– Adjustment
– Nostalgia/selective recall of the
  past
– Planning activity
– Social problems
– Social withdrawal

Clustering into superordinate themes (Steps 6 and 7)

1 Searching for an explanation
   a Lack of understanding   'no idea'
   b Frustration   'can't do it'
   c Anger and self-criticism/   'mad at myself'
      doubt
2 Self-evaluation and social
   comparison
   a With others   'other people'
   b Within family   'fittest of all'
   c Nostalgic recall of self   'like a horse'
      before pain
   d Index of loss/bereavement/ 'used to be'
      shock
3 Social problem
   a Withdrawal   'stay in'

Box 10.6:   Types or levels of analysis

While analysing, think about what sort of level or type of explanation is emerging. In general, the level and type of explanation should emerge in tandem with the analysis, rather than be imposed on it. What sort of argument would one want to make about this person's responses? Possibilities might be:

1 *Classification/typology.* You may find that you are able to present the range of views a participant has about a particular subject or a typology of the different explanatory styles the respondent uses.
2 *Development of theory.* You may be able to use the themes that have emerged to begin to produce your own theory about, or explanation for, the respondent's position, drawing on examples from the respondent's answers as evidence.
3 *Complexity/ambiguity.* At a more detailed level, you may decide that the most important finding that emerges from your analysis is the complexity of a particular theme, and wish to explicate that complexity. It may be that the person's views

on this topic are more detailed and complicated than envisaged. It may be that they appear contradictory or ambiguous and you may decide that is the most important aspect to capture in your write-up.

4 *Life history*. It may be that the participant's own life story is the most significant or interesting aspect of the data and therefore you may wish to write this up as a narrative life history.

Step 3   Students read the transcript for their group individually. This should be done quietly, carefully and slowly, using one margin to annotate points of interest and importance as they arise. Some of these comments may be attempts at summarizing, some may be associations/connnections that come to mind, others may be initial interpretations.

Step 4   Once all members of the group have finished the individual reading and annotation, they engage in a group discussion, going through the transcript chronologically and comparing the notes they have made. This discussion provides the basis for deciding the themes which are in the transcript, and the right-hand margin should be used to record these as they are agreed, using key words to capture the essential quality of what you are finding in the text. Some of the themes will be governed by, and follow closely, questions on the schedule, but others may well be completely new. Some of these may be because the respondent has tackled the subject in a different way from that anticipated. Other themes may be at a higher level, acting as pointers to the respondent's more general beliefs or style of thinking and talking. For example, the topic under discussion may be attitudes towards public transport but what emerges from the transcript is a sense of the respondent's generally left-wing political leanings and a self-deprecatory style of presentation. These therefore may inform what becomes a theme. These emergent themes may force the group to think about the focus of the project and take it in a slightly different direction.

Step 5   Once the group has gone through the whole transcript, one member lists all the themes, in chronological order, as a column on one sheet of paper. Please note

the list in box 5 shows the themes for the whole interview, not just the extract illustrated.

Step 6   The group discusses the list and puts the items into
related groupings. This form of analysis involves a close
interaction between researcher and the text, the analyst
attempting to understand what the person is saying
but, as part of the process, drawing on his or her own
interpretative resources. The analyst is now attempting
to create some order from the array of concepts and
ideas extracted from the participant's responses. Analysis is a cyclical process – students should be prepared
to go through the stages a number of times, dropping a
master theme if a more useful one emerges. During the
process it is worth asking: do some of the themes act
as a magnet, seeming to draw others towards them and
helping to explain these others? Also, this is a selective
process – some of the themes may drop out as not
being of sufficient importance to the overall analysis.
A name should be given to each cluster and the group
of related themes is described as a superordinate theme.

Step 7   A master table is produced, presenting the superordinate themes for the interviewee, and the themes within
each superordinate category. For each theme, a few
verbatim words from the interviewee should be used to
signal an example of the theme in the transcript. The
code for the theme (e.g. 1a, 2b) should be used to annotate the transcript where the examples can be found.

1 The tutor gives a brief presentation on writing up IPA and tells the
class what is required for their write-up.
2 Outside the class, students prepare a short write-up:
   i   *Introduction* (half side) stating what the project is about, what
   approach was used;
   ii *Method* (1 side + table) This should briefly outline the stages in
   the project – constructing the interview schedule, how the participant was selected, how the interview was conducted, how
   analysis was done. The interview schedule should be included
   as a table.
   iii *Results* (2–3 sides + table) The table of superordinate themes
   should be presented. Then the first superordinate theme is taken

Box 10.7: Extract from write up of IPA

As participants described their pain, they compared themselves with other people and with themselves both in the past and projected into the future. This creative process of comparison captured the pernicious impact of their pain. One participant, Linda, appeared to reach out to what she saw, by comparing her present situation with selected events she had witnessed, and used those comparisons as benchmarks:

> I'm only 50 and I should be doing this that and the other cos they say life begins at 40 but I can't and I suppose it does bother me, it's frustrating that people of my age are you can see them flying their kite and you feel as if you can't.

Linda could not do the things she felt she should be able to do like other women her age who were active and enjoying life. Her comparison was not just of reduced mobility but of the denial of pleasure in activity. Others her age could enjoy their life and celebrate it free from pain, 'you can see them flying their kite', and this emphasized her feelings of loss. In one passage, Linda recalls a description of her pain-free self set amidst her immediate family:

> I just think I'm the fittest because there were 3 girls and I'm the middle one I thought well I'm the fittest and I used to work like a horse and I thought I was the strongest and then all of a sudden it's just been cut down and I can't do half of what I used to do.

Linda's description of her loss was exacerbated by the recall of an idealized past where she was not only fit but the fittest and worked not just hard but 'like a horse'.

and introduced. The report should then describe each of the themes in the first superordinate theme in turn, explaining why they are important and providing short verbatim extracts from the transcript to illustrate the point being made. Again this process is iterative. It is important to keep thinking while doing the

write-up, because the interpretation is likely to become richer as
one goes through this process. It is only necessary for students
to write up the first master theme.

iv *Conclusion* (half a side) what has the group learned from the
exercise – about the topic, about qualitative methodology, about
themselves as researchers.

Notes for the Course Leader

ASSUMPTIONS MADE

Level of student

This exercise has been used successfully with second level undergraduates. It is likely that by this point they have had some training
in quantitative methodology which will enable them to contextualize
the issues involved in doing qualitative research. It is not necessary for
students to have had any previous experience of qualitative methodology. The exercise has also been run on postgraduate masters' courses.

Class size

The exercise has been conducted in classes of between 20 and 42
students. With the latter size, students can work in seven groups with
six students in each. Where a large class is being taught, there needs
to be sufficient space for students to work in small groups without
being too distracted by other groups. The ideal would be a large room
with small rooms leading off it so that the class could move easily
between settings. Other configurations can be adapted.

Time available

The complete exercise can be run over two classes of two and a half
hours duration, although this can be quite rushed and three hours is
a better time slot for each class. Between classes, one student from
each group needs to conduct a 15-minute interview with a fellow
student and this interview needs to be transcribed, which may take
up to two hours.

Materials needed

The interviews conducted by students between the two classes need
to be tape-recorded. It is useful to ask at the beginning of the class for

students who own a tape recorder which can be used to tape-record an interview to identify themselves. Then groups can be built around these individuals. This reduces the need for a large number of tape recorders to be loaned from the department. Groups who do not have access to their own tape recorder may be able to borrow one from the department.

Teaching assistance involved

Students need support at each stage of the exercise. For a class of 42, two teaching assistants would be optimal. Then each of the assistants can be responsible for two groups of students and the tutor helps three groups, moving between them during the practical exercises.

ADDITIONAL READING

Smith (1996) describes the theoretical positioning of IPA. Fuller descriptions of the stages of conducting a project using IPA are available in Smith and Osborn (2003) and Smith, Osborn and Jarman (1999): the former details all the stages from interview schedule construction to write up, while the latter provides more detail on analysis. A chapter providing a short introduction to IPA and giving illustrations from three studies using it is found in Smith, Flowers and Osborn (1997). Empirical examples of studies employing IPA can be found in Carradice et al. (2002), Flowers et al. (1999), Golsworthy and Coyle (1999), Michie et al. (1999), Osborn and Smith (1998), Rhodes and Jakes (2000) and Smith (1999).

NOTES

1 In certain research projects, there are exceptions where this would neither be practical nor sensible. For example it may not be advisable with young children where it would be appropriate for an adult known to the child to be present. However, it is expected that all the interviews conducted for this exercise will be with fellow students.
2 (Step 3) indicates the step in the Analysis subsection which is being illustrated.

REFERENCES

Carradice, A., Shankland, M. & Beail, N. (2002). A qualitative study of the theoretical models used by UK mental health nurses to guide their assessments with family caregivers of people with dementia. *International Journal of Nursing Studies, 39,* 17–26.

Flowers, P., Hart, G. & Marriott, C. (1999). Constructing sexual health: Gay men and 'risk' in the context of a public sex environment. *Journal of Health Psychology, 4,* 483–95.

Golsworthy, R. & Coyle, A. (1999). Spiritual beliefs and the search for meaning among older adults following partner loss. *Mortality, 4,* 21–40.

Michie, S., Smith, J. A., Heaversedge, J. & Read, S. (1999). Genetic counseling: Clinical geneticists' views. *Journal of Genetic Counseling, 8,* 275–87.

Osborn, M. & Smith, J. A. (1998). The personal experience of chronic benign lower back pain: An interpretative phenomenological analysis. *British Journal of Health Psychology, 3,* 65–83.

Rhodes, J. & Jakes, S. (2000). Correspondence between delusions and goals: A qualitative analysis. *British Journal of Medical Psychology, 73,* 211–25.

Smith, J. A. (1996). Beyond the divide between cognition and discourse: Using interpretative phenomenological analysis in health psychology. *Psychology & Health, 11,* 261–71.

Smith, J. A. (1999). Towards a relational self: Social engagement during pregnancy and psychological preparation for motherhood. *British Journal of Social Psychology, 38,* 409–26.

Smith, J. A., Flowers, P. & Osborn, M. (1997). Interpretative phenomenological analysis and health psychology. In L. Yardley (ed.), *Material discourses and health* (pp. 68–91). London: Routledge.

Smith, J. A. & Osborn, M. (2003). Interpretative phenomenological analysis. In J. A. Smith (ed.), *Qualitative psychology: A practical guide to methods* (pp. 51–80). London: Sage.

Smith, J. A., Osborn, M. & Jarman, M. (1999). Doing interpretative phenomenological analysis. In M. Murray & K. Chamberlain (eds.), *Qualitative Health Psychology: Theories and Methods* (pp. 218–40). London: Sage.

CHAPTER ELEVEN

Cognitive Mapping: Generating Theories of Psychological Phenomena from Verbal Accounts and Presenting them Diagrammatically

Tom Farsides

This chapter presents a technique that typically uses semi-structured in-depth interviews to elicit self-report data (often referred to as 'accounts') from individuals. These accounts are subjected to analysis in order to identify and then depict graphically the relationships between the concepts used in them. The way such 'cognitive mapping' can be used to erect psychological theories is described. The exercise is suitable for introductory or intermediate level courses.

A Hypothetical Research Project

A RESEARCH AIM

How would you find out what your best friend *really* thinks about your other friends? Maybe you believe you don't need to find out, as you already know. Perhaps you've talked to your best friend about your other friends, you've seen your best friend spend time with your other friends, and you've heard tales of your best friend's exploits with your other friends when you haven't been there. So what's to know? But let's suppose someone has accused you of not really knowing your best friend very well at all. Perhaps this person has claimed your best friend has only been pretending to like your other friends as a kindness to you. As this seems at least plausible, you decide that you do need to check – or perhaps find out – what your best friend really does think of your other friends. Such a goal is very similar to the sort of research aim you will be set in the assignment contained in this chapter. But how are you going to achieve such an aim?

DATA COLLECTION

The chances are that your first step will be to ask your best friend if it would be possible to have a 'serious chat'. You will also probably try to subtly manage this chat in whatever ways seem most likely to get your best friend to reveal what they 'really' think. You will probably start by trying to put your best friend at ease, perhaps indulging in some idle small talk while you get them a drink and a snack. You might then inform them that you genuinely want to know what they think about something and that it is really important to you that they tell the truth, no matter how they think you might react. Perhaps you will then ask directly what they think about your friends 'generally', before going on to ask for more specific information about what they think of particular friends. Whatever your friend says, you might be suspicious. Perhaps they are still trying to say whatever they think is in your best interest, whatever the truth of the matter. Perhaps they do not want to admit that they have been fooling you all these years. Perhaps they have never really thought about how they feel towards the rest of your friends. So you will try to tease apart when your friend is telling things as they 'really are', when they are trying to hide the way things 'really are', and when they are discovering (or making up?) the way things 'really are' as they talk.

Sometimes you might have trouble accepting what your friend says. Perhaps they will claim something that does not quite square with things you have observed in the past. Perhaps they will say things that directly conflict with things they or other people have told you on previous occasions. Perhaps they will say one thing in one breath and then something entirely incompatible with it in the next. What are you going to do if this occurs? Most likely, you will challenge your friend's account. Doing your best not to antagonize them or make them defensive, you will point out the difficulties you are having and ask them to help you resolve those difficulties. Eventually, you will decide you have found out all you can by chatting and so you will thank your friend and find some way of showing your appreciation for them talking to you in such an intimate way. At this point you will have just completed a semi-structured in-depth interview, very similar to the one in the assignment set in this chapter.

THEORY GENERATION AND VALIDATION

Later that night, you might think over (and over) what your best friend has said. Suddenly you achieve a flash of insight. You realize that your friend believes something that they are not even fully conscious of but which nevertheless leads them to talk, think and act the way they do. Excited, but nevertheless making the effort to be tactful and sensitive, you reach for the phone and try out this revelation on your best friend. 'Could it be the case that you really think such and such and that this is why . . . ?' Your friend is doubtful at first, saying they have always avoided 'thinking too much' about such things. But the excitement you feel at obtaining clarity makes you persist. You point out how your conception makes everything so much easier to understand. You argue that a great deal of what your best friend has said and done makes so much more sense than it did previously if what you have realized about them is true. As you speak, recognition and conviction becomes evident in your friend's voice. They chuckle and observe, once again, that no one understands them like you do, not even them. Were this to occur, you would have just successfully used 'respondent validation' to provide support for a 'theory' you 'inductively generated' from – and defended partially with reference to – your friend's 'account' of their own views. In doing so, you would have done all that is required, and more, in the assignment set below.

Cognitive Mapping

Tolman (1932) proposed that humans and other animals have mental representations of their physical environments. He called these representations 'cognitive maps'. While such specifically geographical mental representations continue to be researched to this day (e.g. O' Laughlin & Brubaker, 1998; Reid & Staddon, 1998), this chapter is concerned with how people conceptualize their environments more generally. Swan (1995, p. 1257) draws a distinction between the theoretical and the practical concerns of the sort of cognitive mapping we are interested in here. At a theoretical level, our concern is with the mental 'concepts and relations among concepts' implied by people's verbal accounts of any aspect of their experience or their understanding of the world and of their place in it (e.g. Cacioppo, von Hippel & Ernst, 1997). At a practical level we are concerned with how best to identify and represent such concepts and relations. It may help your understanding at this early stage if you immediately look at the example cognitive map included in Figure 11.1. The 'shapes' represent concepts the participant is considered to employ and the 'lines' represent postulated connections between such concepts.

Axelrod is generally credited with initiating cognitive mapping research (e.g. Axelrod, 1976), largely in an attempt to synthesize and extend five earlier bodies of work (Young, 1996). Since then, cognitive mapping has been developed in a bewildering number of ways in a variety of disciplines. Huff (1990) lists five 'generic families' of purposes to which cognitive mapping has been put. Of these, the one most pertinent here is sometimes called 'causal mapping', as this particular form of cognitive mapping attempts to represent *causal* relationships between concepts. However, as we are also interested in mapping some non-causal relationships between concepts (e.g. correlational, logical), we shall continue to use the more generic term of cognitive mapping.

Although a number of techniques exist for generating cognitive maps, only one method will be described in this chapter. This method employs both qualitative data collection and qualitative data analysis, with 'qualitative' in this context meaning little more than 'non-numerical', concerned with identifying the nature (i.e. the qualities) of things rather than with identifying how many things there are. Specifically, the method described in this chapter uses semi-structured interviews to obtain respondents' views of a topic of the researcher's choosing (here, attitudes towards organ donation). Next, a form of qualitative content analysis is used to identify the concepts and connections between them used and implied by respondents during their interviews. Finally, selected concepts and connections are represented diagrammatically, that is, 'mapped'.

The goal of this method of cognitive mapping is to represent people's cognitive structures and processes to try to understand what they think about a given topic and why. It is a 'theory *building*' approach, as the representation we will produce will be primarily inferred from things respondents tell us, that is, the data. This approach may be contrasted with ones in which theories are *tested*, for example by seeing how well respondent-produced data 'fits' existing psychological models. The current approach may also be contrasted with other less empirically derived forms of theory generation, such

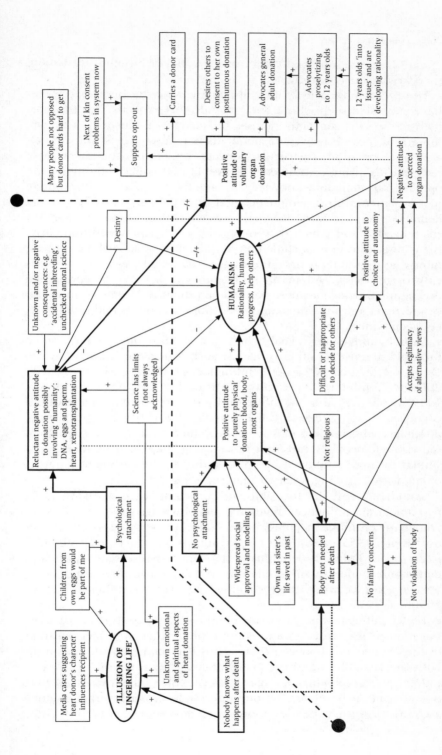

Figure 11.1 A cognitive map of one interviewee's views on organ donation

as via generalization, bold conjecture, researcher 'insight', revelation, speculation, or whatever.

The theories we will build will employ concepts that respondents have suggested themselves. They may do this explicitly, for example by using specific conceptual terms, such as 'heart', 'justice', 'attitude', 'upset', or 'gift'. However, respondents may also suggest the import- ance and operation of particular concepts only implicitly, for example by explicitly using a number of concepts that collectively imply the operation of some unacknowledged 'underlying' concept. An example of this latter process would occur if a respondent's explicit verbal behaviour implied racist views the respondent did not make explicit reference to (and which they might deny if 'challenged'). Similarly, the connections to be included on our cognitive maps will be connec- tions that respondents have themselves suggested, again either expli- citly or implicitly. All manner of connections may be represented on cognitive maps, but here we will be primarily interested in causal connections and in connections reflecting similarities and differences between concepts.

Causal connections reveal beliefs that certain concepts have some form of influence on other concepts. Such beliefs are indicated by the use of words such as 'caused', 'influenced', 'encouraged', 'provoked', 'hindered', 'inhibited', 'prevented'. Attribution theory (see Hewstone, 1989) is often cited as an influence by researchers employing causal cognitive mapping (e.g. Huff & Schwenk, 1990). This is unsurprising, as Kelley, who made a massive contribution to attribution research, represented people's causal schema using graphic techniques very similar to those employed by Axelrod during the early development of cognitive mapping research (e.g. see Kelley, 1972).

'Another' Kelly, but this time with only one 'e', is a second social psychological influence regularly acknowledged by researchers employing cognitive mapping. Based on Kelly's personal construct the- ory (Kelly, 1955), and often employing his repertory grid technique to do so (see Fransella & Bannister, 1977), these researchers primarily endeavour to identify the similarities and differences that respondents believe exist between their cognitive concepts (e.g. Reger, 1990a, 1990b).

The cognitive mapping described in this chapter concerns both iden- tification of the structure and content of concepts and identification of the connections between them. Thus it resonates with work from both the attribution and the personal construct traditions. However, rather than employing or investigating existing theories of attribu- tion, cognition or whatever, our interest lies in using respondents' accounts to *generate* theories of how they represent their worlds. Thus, conceptually, the methods employed in this chapter have more in common with practices such as exploratory factor analysis (and certain other multivariate statistical techniques) and some forms of 'analytic induction' (e.g. Bloor, 1978), which take raw data and try to identify the building blocks of theory from it (see also Lofland, 1995).

There are many advantages to deriving theory from data. To the extent that the theories we develop are genuinely and demonstrably derived from participants' accounts, these theories may be said to be 'grounded' in those accounts. Further, to the extent that those accounts may be said to derive from the participants' mental processes, it is possible to argue that the concepts and connections represented in our cognitive maps are to some degree 'grounded' in the psychological structure and processes that 'actually exist' within our participants' minds. Thus cognitive mapping is a way of empirically 'grounding' theories of mind by inferring those theories from data assumed to be products of the minds theorized about (cf. Smith, 1996).

Conceived in this way, cognitive mapping is an appropriate tool for researchers adopting or accepting a realist philosophy of science (Sayer, 2000). Realism claims that certain things have an existence independent of being perceived. Further, when these things are perceived, the perceptions will be determined by an interaction of the qualities possessed by the things perceived, the qualities possessed by perceivers, and the qualities of anything mediating the perceptual process. To give an example, realists will argue that the book in your hands has a real existence, even when thrown under your bed and perceived by no one. Further, realists will claim that the book has certain qualities when in such a state, although such qualities can of course only be inferred, never directly perceived (as we are talking about qualities that exist *independent* of perception). Finally, realists will assert that your direct perceptions of the book will be affected by the sort of thing you are (e.g. in terms of your sensory and cognitive faculties) and the qualities of the medium through which your perception of the book occurs (e.g. how light it is if you are looking at the book, how impregnated with aromas the air is if you happen to try to smell the book), as well as by the qualities of the book itself. For realists, then, the job of science is to investigate what things exist 'in the world', what qualities those things have, and what influences those things have on other things by virtue of the qualities possessed by all involved.

As presented here, cognitive mapping accords with mainstream social psychology in adopting a realist conception of psychological processes. A realist social psychology claims that people and other objects of psychological study have an existence independent of being perceived by a particular researcher. Further, it is claimed that such objects have structures and processes (i.e. qualities) that also exist independent of being researched. Realism therefore assumes that the job of social psychology-as-a-science is to describe the qualities of the objects it studies and to explain why these objects and qualities are perceived as they are, for example by people in particular situations, with both the nature of the people and the nature of the situations interacting with the nature of the things perceived to determine the exact form of the perception that occurs. Similarly, cognitive mapping as presented in this chapter attempts to describe the structure and processes that really exist in other people's heads, even though (1) no one, not even the participants themselves, may have direct perceptual access to the objects of study, and therefore (2) the qualities of the things studied can only be inferred from the products of particular interactions between those and other things.

To consider the more concrete implications of these rather abstract reflections, cognitive mapping, in common with mainstream social psychology, attempts to identify (and represent for the purposes of communication) enduring and causally efficacious beliefs, values and attitudes that research participants have. Because researchers cannot have direct access to such things, their nature has to be inferred from certain of their products, in this case the accounts produced during semi-structured interviews. Such inference is made both tricky and possible because of all the other things that influence the direct objects of study – that is, respondents' accounts – such as temporal, geographic, and social factors at work during their production (Ericsson & Simon, 1980, 1984). Such factors make inference tricky, because the complexity of the situations in which the things are studied mean that it is rather easy to make erroneous causal attributions, for example claiming that someone has a shy disposition when in fact one's (mis)perceptions of shyness are due to factors other than dispositional shyness (e.g. actor–observer differences, Jones & Nisbett, 1972). Nevertheless, this same complexity makes inference possible. The realist researcher's job is to come up with the most coherent and persuasive theory they can to account for all the phenomena of which they are aware (Collier, 1994). Sometimes, this will be best achieved by attributing particular cognitive structures and processes (e.g. personality traits) to their respondents.

Having provisionally generated a theory that tentatively explains the relevant phenomena (e.g. the participants' accounts), both in terms of identifying 'latent' determinants (e.g. beliefs) and situational 'triggers' (e.g. interview questions), the nature of realist science dictates that researchers must test the adequacy of those theories. This is done by formulating theory-consistent hypotheses that may be supported or undermined by subsequently examined evidence, particularly empirical evidence.

Note that none of the above means that the content of people's accounts of their own cognitive processes must be taken at face value – quite the opposite. Although psychological processes are thought to (partially) cause participants' verbal accounts, this is not to say that they will do so in any 'direct' or 'obvious' way. Psychologists are well aware that all manner of things may lead to a discrepancy between attitudes and behaviour, including verbal behaviour (Nisbett & Wilson, 1977; Wilson, 1985). Nevertheless, practitioners of cognitive mapping assume that obtaining people's verbal accounts of what they think is often a fruitful means by which to obtain valuable information about what they do, in fact, think. First, people sometimes *do* have valuable – and often unique – access to their own cognitive processes. Secondly, whether or not that is the case in any given instance, sensitive researchers may infer a lot about cognitive contents and processes from an important product of these things, namely, people's (credible or otherwise) accounts of what and how they are thinking.

Cognitive mapping is therefore a method of generating theories about people's cognitive content and processes by inferring what people think from what they say about what they think (and from what they say about other things assumed to be affected by what they think, e.g. their feelings and their behaviour). Data collection is therefore relatively straightforward: one obtains accounts from people about whatever it is one is researching. Typically, this will be done, at least in major part, using semi-structured in-depth interviewing. Some structure is necessary during such interviewing, as researchers wish to keep their interviewees focused on aspects of the topic of interest that the researchers think are likely to be especially revealing about the interviewees' underlying cognitive processes. But interviews cannot be fully structured, as participants' accounts must be unconstrained enough for inferences to be made from them about the cognitive processes assumed to be partially determining those accounts. In addition, it must be repeated that inferences about people's cognitive content and processes may be assisted by information about *other* products of such cognitive processes, that is, beyond the interview-produced verbal account. Thus there are good reasons to supplement interview-based methods of data collection during theory-generation as well as using such 'alternative' methods during theory testing.

The purpose of data analysis has already been mentioned: it is to infer the concepts and relationships between those concepts that are implied by participants' own accounts obtained during interview, possibly with the aid of data also collected by other means. Such analysis may be attempted in many ways, employing any number of quantitative or qualitative techniques. In this chapter we will be using a qualitative method of analysis. There are various rules of thumb available to the qualitative analyst, but for those with a realist bent the overall guiding principle is a search for coherence. Thus analysts ask themselves the 'transcendental' question (Collier, 1994): 'What psychological structures and processes might be at work that would provide the best explanation for what the interviewees say about how they think, feel and act?' In attempting to answer this question, researchers will want to know: (1) how interviewees achieve a subjective sense of coherence between the things they seem to believe; (2) how to provide a coherent account of their own (i.e. the researchers) perceptions of the things the interviewees say and do; and (3) how best to understand the relationship between their (i.e. the researchers) emerging theories and those they are already familiar with (i.e. from their own lives and from their knowledge of the relevant research literature).

Cognitive mapping as presented in this chapter is closely aligned to several existing content-analytic qualitative methodologies, particular those falling under the grounded theory umbrella (Glaser & Strauss, 1967). Cognitive mapping's primary distinctiveness, however, lies in its *essential* production of a relatively detailed graphic representation of the '*inter-relationships* between', as well as the more commonly identified (other) 'qualities of', the principal components of participants' cognitive structures and processes. (Something similar is advocated – but rarely practised – in certain forms of grounded theory.) When there is a single interviewee, this 'map' attempts to show the main aspects (including causes and consequences) of 'how that person thinks', in terms of the concepts they employ *and* the inter-relation between those concepts. When there is more than one person, the principal 'map' will attempt to show the main concepts and connections that a collection of people or some other social entity employ when evaluating or expressing their 'approach' to the subject in question (cf. Ford & Hegarty, 1984; Weick & Bougon, 1986).

As with other forms of qualitative analysis, research reports resulting from cognitive mapping of the form discussed here attempt as far as possible to allow readers to judge for themselves the adequacy of the analyses reported. Thus one or more main cognitive maps will form the centrepiece of the report, along with extensive accompanying text providing researchers' rationales for representing the map(s) as they have. The more 'raw data' that can be included, the better.

The worked example shown below will provide more details about the practice and rationale of cognitive mapping, often repeating and extending the general information provided here.

Strengths and Limitations of Cognitive Mapping

Cognitive mapping is a form of qualitative data collection and analysis and, as such, has some predictable strengths and limitations. On the plus side:

- it forces the researcher to get very 'close' to both the research participants and the data they provide, facilitating an understanding of the data (not necessarily the only one) that genuinely accords with that of the research participants;
- it provides very 'rich' data, allowing revelation and appreciation of complexity, structure and meaning;
- it attempts research relatively unaffected by preconceptions, as theory is flexibly and sensitively built from emerging data rather than data being forced into Procrustean beds of existing categories of interest within the research community;
- similarly, it allows research participants to identify, use and define concepts and relationships that they consider important for an adequate description of the phenomena of interest, rather than forcing them to either rate the usefulness of researchers' own concepts or indeed to use such concepts irrespective of their subjective worth;
- it captures the uniqueness of individuals' own points of view, as well as allowing identification of points of commonality across a (limited) number of individuals;
- it allows investigation and representation of an enormous number of variables and of the relationships between them, far more than would be practical within most forms of quantitative research, as well as potentially including and noting the importance of many variables that might be very difficult to identify and evaluate via other methods;
- it presents theory in such a way as to make part–whole relationships easily comprehensible, also enabling researchers to move 'back and forth' between holistic and detailed considerations;
- it allows representation of various ways in which particular concepts are relatively important, for example in terms of being 'central' or 'well-connected';
- it allows readers to evaluate the adequacy of the method by which the theory has been generated.

As a form of qualitative research that is nevertheless compatible with a realist philosophy of science, cognitive mapping is potentially susceptible to criticism from two 'opposite' sides. Realists (and similar) with a penchant for quantitative methods might complain that cognitive mapping faces limitations because it practically allows investigation of only relatively small numbers of research participants, leading to questionable generality and external validity for any theory generated. They might also point out that methods similar to cognitive mapping are typically used to generate theories that are, in fact, seldom tested or practically employed. Similarly, they would point to the relative infrequency with which supplementary methods are used to bolster the findings obtained by analysis of participants' (unsubstantiated) accounts. Finally, such critics might make the incontestable observation that there are as yet no commonly agreed procedures for demonstrating or evaluating the quality of any form of qualitative research, that is, in terms of reliability, validity and similar.

On the other hand, researchers who reject realist (and similar) philosophies of science might complain that cognitive mapping, especially as presented in this chapter, shares far too many of the 'fallacious' assumptions of mainstream social science. Most of these criticisms in truth stem from a rejection of realism, that is, of the philosophy of science underlying the method, rather than a rejection of the method of cognitive mapping *per se*. That is, many limitations of the method are considered to be entailed by its 'faulty' underlying rationale. This is not the place to debate such things. Thus I will content myself with asserting that (1) cognitive mapping may be employed in much the same way as presented here by researchers with philosophies of science other than realism (who will simply *interpret* the maps differently), and (2) the adequacy of any 'realistic' research is ultimately an empirical matter. If a theory can be used to effectively predict or control events, that theory has a degree of 'practical adequacy' within a realist conception of science. Thus if cognitive mapping produces theories that allow prediction or control, those theories are worthwhile products of science, no matter how much the process of science itself is debated.

My own view is that the criticisms from the 'realist quantitative' camp are not much more compelling than those from the 'anti-realist qualitative' camp. Some of those criticisms concern poor current practice within qualitative research, for example a lack of use of supplementary methods, and an inclination to consider initial theory generation as a legitimate ultimate goal. Such limitations may easily be remedied, at least in principle. Other criticisms are simply inappropriate, essentially attacking the method for not being something other than it is, that is, a method particularly suited to theory generation (and theory refinement). Still other criticisms are true but – to adopt a wonderfully irritating phrase beloved of philosophers – only 'trivially' so. Thus cognitive mapping does of necessity involve small samples and techniques that do not yet have *universally* agreed criteria for assessing their adequacy.

In response, I would argue that generating theory from participants' extensive accounts is often preferable to the alternative more often used by 'realist quantitative' researchers, namely identifying a few variables (for subsequent arrangement into a 'theory' that is then tested) on the basis of researchers' introspection; a shallow trawl of research literature that is, of necessity, inadequate for the purpose of theory *generation*; or some poorly specified and wholly unevaluated 'pilot study'. Further, it must be recognized that a small sample size is often a problem more for *demonstrating* external validity than it is for being susceptible to not *having* such validity. As far as having external validity is concerned, the extent of the problems associated with small sample sizes is inversely related to the 'universality' of the phenomena studied. If the phenomena of interest are widespread, small sample sizes become increasingly likely to 'capture' such phenomena. Finally, and most importantly, the theories generated by cognitive maps – although they have many admirable qualities as a result of being generated from and therefore grounded in empirical research – are just that, theories. And, within the realist tradition, theories must continually be tested by whatever means seem appropriate.

As far as conceptual concerns go, then, I would argue that on balance cognitive mapping has considerable strengths and no limitations strong enough to cancel out or otherwise invalidate such strengths. However, it must be noted that cognitive mapping has a number of practical limitations that anyone considering adopting the approach would be wise to bear in mind. I shall simply list them and let prospective users of the method evaluate their legitimacy and strength for themselves. First, cognitive mapping of the form advocated here has never to my knowledge been explicitly used within social psychology or within psychological science more generally. Thus there is little specific guidance or existing practice available for consultation. Second, and following on from points made above, cognitive mapping is a relatively unknown form of qualitative research and qualitative research has yet to establish itself within the psychological mainstream. Thus research employing cognitive mapping may not receive a sympathetic welcome from 'traditional' social psychologists. Third, cognitive mapping, at least as presented here, is a form of qualitative analysis that does not endear itself to those who champion qualitative methods as an alternative or even an antidote to 'mainstream' social psychology (and to science more generally). Thus research employing cognitive mapping may not receive a sympathetic welcome from psychologists prominent for challenging the mainstream. It can be noted that the last two points in combination may contribute to the first point being a matter of concern for some time to come. Finally, cognitive mapping is 'expensive' to do, in that data takes a long time to collect and analyse 'per research participant'. Researchers therefore need to convince themselves of the method's worth before making the investment necessary to use this method, especially if the research is destined to be evaluated by psychologists wedded (explicitly or 'by default') to philosophies of science suggesting antagonism (justified or otherwise) toward the method.

Further Reading

For guidance on conducting qualitative interviewing, see Kvale (1996) and Robson (2002).

For guidance on how to how to manually produce cognitive maps from semi-structured interview data, see Jones (1985), Huff, Narapareddy & Fletcher (1990) and especially Miles & Huberman (1994). Personally, I have found chapters 2, 6 and 10 of the latter reference invaluable, with section 6D (pp. 151–65) being particularly pertinent here.

For further information and references on theories and techniques of cognitive mapping in fields allied to psychology, see Daniels, Chernatony & Johnson (1995), Huff (1990), Swan (1995), Sergeev, Akimov, Lukov & Parshin (1990), and Young (1996).

For further information about techniques for qualitatively analysing textual data, see Miles & Huberman (1994) and also consider sources describing grounded theory, for example Glaser (1992) and Strauss & Corbin (1998). Although I have presented the form of cognitive mapping described here in terms of its 'alignment with' grounded theory, this has been mainly to sidestep some very complex debates. In truth, I consider this form of cognitive mapping to be a development of one *aspect* of grounded theory (to be used in conjunction with the 'constant comparative method', 'theoretical sampling', 'theoretical saturation', etc.). For an excellent account of the content of various forms of 'grounded theories' and their relation to one another and to other approaches, see Willig (2001).

For an extremely useful and accessible comparison between five types of qualitative research, see Cresswell (1998).

For a consideration of issues associated with producing and evaluating qualitative research, see (among many others) Elliot, Fischer & Rennie et al. (1999), Henwood & Pidgeon (1992), LeCompte & Goetz (1982), Murphy, Dingwall, Greatbatch, Parker & Watson (1998), Pidgeon & Henwood (1997), Sadler (1981) and Searle (1999).

For an admirably balanced evaluation of qualitative and quantitative research and of their relationship with one another, see Bryman (1988).

To discover more about issues surrounding realist approaches to social science, see Madill, Jordan & Shirley (2000) and Sayer (2000). To read defences of realism in human and social science similar to the one presented here, see Hammersley (1992) and Miles & Huberman (1994).

A Specific Example

INTRODUCTION

This section describes a workshop assignment set for students on a second year course at the University of Sussex, entitled Research Methods in Social Psychology. The first sub-section below describes the assignment set. The second sub-section uses interview data collected by Hannah Mitchell (who was a student on the course) to demonstrate how a cognitive map may be developed and used.

THE ASSIGNMENT

The general task is to *use semi-structured interviewing and cognitive mapping to investigate one person's views of organ donation*. Students are encouraged to seek the tutor's permission should they wish to investigate alternative research questions.

Students are asked to collaborate with one or two other students from their class to develop a single semi-structured interview guide common to each of them. Each member of these groups then uses their group's interview guide to conduct a single tape-recorded, semi-structured, in-depth interview with one interviewee. Interviews are expected to last a minimum of 30 minutes. Additional data gathering methods and techniques are permitted but not required. Students are strongly encouraged but not required to transcribe at least part of their interview data.

Students then produce a cognitive map of their own interview, using techniques described in class and described (in fuller form) by Huff et al. (1990), Jones (1985) and Miles & Huberman (1994). Additional data analytic methods and techniques are permitted but not required.

Students then write a research report of their interviewee's views on organ donation, presented as an exercise in theory generation.

Precise guidelines are then provided and discussed in relation to every aspect of the assignment. Some of these will not be mentioned in this chapter, as they are dealt with elsewhere in this volume. Thus nothing will be said here about such things as how best to go about producing interview guides, general interviewing techniques, ethical concerns associated with interview research, or transcription conventions. Other precise guidelines provided during the setting of this exercise concern possibilities for supplementary data collection and analysis. The sub-section 'Ringing the changes' at the end of this chapter contains some information about what these techniques are and where to find advice on how to employ them. Finally, some precise guidelines concern techniques and practices that may be fruitfully employed when (1) conducting interviews to collect data from which cognitive maps are to be produced, and (2) actually producing such a map. In this chapter, such procedures are described in general terms above and are illustrated in more detail in the worked example immediately below.

A STEP-BY-STEP EXAMPLE AND EXPLANATION

The set assignment does much to constrain the research question (i.e. 'What views on organ donation does an individual of your choosing have?'), the data-gathering technique to be employed (i.e. a semi-structured, in-depth interview), and the data analytic method to be use (i.e. cognitive mapping). Nevertheless, there are still many decisions to be made.

Producing the interview guide

Cognitive mapping relies in this assignment on data collected from a semi-structured interview. Thus one of the first decisions you must make is what to include in your interview schedule. Organ donation is a big topic with lots of facets and you will need to decide which of these you definitely want discussed by all the people who will be interviewed by students in your working group. You will also need to decide which supplementary topics it might be nice or necessary to cover if discussion of the essential topics is over too soon. When you have chosen your central and additional topics, you will need to decide whether or not you want them covered in any particular order. Finally, you will need to decide whether or not to have very specific questions and probes to initiate discussion on certain topics, or whether you think it more appropriate to ask more general open-ended questions throughout.

Possible topics for inclusion may be obtained by brainstorming within your working group (e.g. 'What are our views on organ donation?') and by reviewing the relevant literature (e.g. Farsides, 2000). Your tutor may also want everyone in the class to cover one topic of the tutor's choosing. Hannah's interview schedule included the following topics: 'general views on organ donation', 'personal experience with organ donation and organ donors', 'consistency of views towards donation of different organs and other bodily products', 'regulation of organ donation', and 'xeno- (i.e. cross-species) transplantation'.

As well as providing guidance on the topics to be discussed, interview schedules may be used as more general prompts for interviewers. Thus you will need to decide whether or not you want to include such things as scripted introductions and terminations, general prompts that may be used to elicit further information, reminders to collect supplementary data, sources of further information that inter-viewees may request or benefit from and any number of other things that might enable interviewers to collect their data with maximum effectiveness.

Choosing whom to interview

When you have the choice, there are several characteristics you would be wise to seek in your interviewee. First, you should choose some-one who is unlikely to get too distressed by the subject matter or suffer any aversive longer term consequences as a result of talking about it (e.g. 'falling out' with you). Secondly, although it does not matter how much they know about the subject, you should choose someone who is likely to be willing (and ideally eager) to explore and share their views on it with you. Thirdly, you should choose someone who is likely to talk clearly, freely, deeply and at length on relevant (and ideally only relevant) topics. Finally, you should choose some-one whose views are likely to be potentially significant for theory development. Thus you may decide that the various members of your working group should interview people whom you suspect will have interestingly divergent views. Whatever you decide, remember to bear these constraints in mind when both analysing your data and evaluating the strengths and weakness of the emergent theory.

Conducting the interview

General guidance on how to conduct semi-structured interviews is plentifully available and will not be repeated here (e.g. Kvale, 1996). However, the fact that cognitive maps are to be produced suggests that interviewers for this assignment should be especially attentive to three things: (1) similarities and differences among the interviewee's concepts, (2) causal and other connections between those concepts, and (3) apparent contradictions within participants' accounts.

Primarily because of its partial origins in personal construct theory (Kelly, 1955), but nonetheless in common with many other forms of qualitative (and indeed quantitative) analysis, cognitive mapping pays special attention to perceptions of similarity and difference. Thus you should be particularly alert to comparisons and contrasts that interviewees make spontaneously, as well as in response to questions deliberately seeking such information. Hannah specifically asked her interviewee about the similarities and differences between her views towards donation of various organs, but she also made special note of when the interviewee spontaneously likened organ donation to blood donation.

Cognitive mapping goes beyond content analysis (Holsti, 1969; Krippendorff, 1980) in trying to 'map' relations between concepts in ways that go beyond similarities and differences in their form or content. Thus you should make special efforts to encourage your interviewee to make perceived connections between concepts as explicit and precise as possible. The more you do this, the more confident you will be that your cognitive map and its associated narrative reflect the interviewee's own views, rather than your expectations, inferences and guesswork about their views. In particular, where interviewees identify or imply causal relations between concepts, you are likely to find cognitive mapping easier if you try to establish during the interview whether postulated causes and reasons (see Buss, 1978) are perceived to be necessary ('required') or sufficient ('enough') to bring about suggested consequences. The person interviewed by Hannah thought an absence of religious beliefs was contributory to their positive attitude towards organ donation but they appeared to consider secular views as neither necessary nor sufficient to result in such positive attitudes.

Cognitive mapping may be done at various 'depths'. The shallowest analyses 'merely' graphically represent more or less everything of seeming importance the interviewee has said, with concepts being identified by little more than parsing (splitting up) the interviewee's sentences. Deeper levels of analysis attempt to identify relatively few 'central' and 'underlying' concepts that 'explain' the relatively unstructured and chaotic 'manifest' patterns revealed by shallower levels of analysis. It is extremely satisfying when analysis suggests the existence of a very few concepts that seem so central and organizing that they might be termed 'core categories' or similar (Glaser & Strauss, 1967). In my experience, the key to identifying such core categories is spotting and trying to comprehend apparent contradictions and inconsistencies within an interviewee's expressed views. Often, it seems, people have two or more 'perspectives' that they use to provide guiding principles in life but which are not wholly compatible with each other. Thus, they tend to 'flip' between one ideology or identity and another to provide self-guides that, as a consequence, lead to seemingly contradictory or inconsistent views and behaviours. In everyday conversation people reveal the commonness of such phenomena when they say things like, 'my head tells me one thing and my heart another'. The views of Hannah's interviewee form an understandable and revealing 'whole' when cognitive mapping reveals core categories that echo this everyday experience. Most of the time, and by choice, the interviewee is guided primarily by her head, that is, by principles akin to humanism (roughly, using rationality to promote human progress). However, some of the time, and in part 'against her will', the interviewee's use of rationality is kept in check by her heart, that is, by intuitions and superstitions (as her humanism would see them) akin to what Sanner (1994) describes as 'the illusion of lingering life' (i.e. believing that aspects of 'the self' may be retained and transported within body parts and products that become divorced from one's own central nervous system).

Cognitive mapping

Cognitive mapping relies on identifying a person's (manifest and deep) concepts (e.g. constructs, categories) and the perceived relationships between them. There are no hard and fast rules about how this is to be done. What follows is one possibility. Huff (1990), Jones (1985), and Miles & Huberman (1994) describe more comprehensive schemes (see also Lofland 1995).

Comprehension of this sub-section is likely to be enhanced if it is read in conjunction with the cognitive map presented in Figure 11.1.

Transcription. As soon as possible after the interview, transcribe the tape recording you have made. Do this on a word processor and save at least two copies of the transcript, for example one on a hard disc and one on a floppy. Make sure you keep one 'untainted' copy of the transcript safe, that is, do not edit the only copy of your transcript during analysis and then decide you would like to start again from scratch. Unless you are already familiar with transcribing conventions, transcribe more or less as you would normally write, using standard punctuation to reflect pauses, new topics and so on. Much information about the content of the interview that cannot be represented in this way may be done by adding contextualizing material in square brackets, for example: [Seemed confused and stopped talking at this point. After a short, reflective break started talking again, fairly rapidly and with some excitement]. How much of the interview you transcribe and in how much detail will depend on how long and focused the original interview was. My preference is to transcribe everything that is not *very* clearly irrelevant and to capture as much as I can of hesitations, repetitions and so on. This is frequently of great benefit when one wishes to engage in relatively 'deep' levels of analysis.

Surface level analysis. Begin by producing a 'surface' analysis of your material. This is a little like producing a 'flow-diagram' of everything the interviewee expressed. Thus you identify 'manifest' concepts and provisionally represent connections between concepts as explicitly suggested by the interviewee. Unless you are confident to do otherwise, start by considering complete phrases or sentences as concepts. Hannah's interviewee opened her contribution to the interview by saying, 'Yes, an organ donation is a good thing. I carry a donor card'. As a first step, this suggests two connected concepts, one indicating a positive attitude towards organ donation and another showing that the interviewee carries a donor card.

It would be a serious mistake to assume that surface level analysis avoids interpretation by the researcher. In my cognitive map of Hannah's interview I have represented the interviewee's positive attitude towards (voluntary – see below) organ donation as *leading to* or in some sense *accounting for* the fact that she carries a donor card. You may note that this is not what the interviewee said. Cognitive dissonance (Festinger, 1957) and self-perception theories (Bem, 1972) might suggest the opposite causal relationship, namely that Hannah's interviewee has a positive attitude towards (voluntary) donation *because* she carries an organ donor card (and has done since she was 12 years old). Alternatively and additionally, Hannah's interviewee may both carry a donor card and express positive attitudes to organ donation because of some third factor, for example a desire to express her self-image as a 'humanist'. The necessity of interpretation is one of the main reasons why qualitative analysts like to provide readers with the 'raw data' they have used in their analysis. However, as well as being clear about the interpretative aspect of cognitive mapping, you might like to reflect on how likely it is that readers would check or even spot interpretations as 'intuitively' appealing as the one I have just been discussing.

Diagrammatic representation conventions. Relatively 'manifest' concepts may be represented by oblongs, with text inside either giving a label for the concept in terms of its content (e.g. 'positive view of organ donation') or showing the text that led to identification of that concept (e.g. 'organ donation is a good thing').

Assuming you are new to cognitive mapping, I would recommend using three forms of connection between concepts. Use arrows to indicate causal 'therefore' relationships between concepts, with the arrow head pointing towards the ('target') concept influenced by the ('source') concept the arrow stems from, for example 'organ donation is a good thing' → 'I carry a donor card'. Arrows may be annotated with plus or minus signs, to indicate whether the source concept 'encourages' or 'discourages' the target concept. Concepts that influence each other may be joined with arrowheads at each end.

Use straight lines between concepts to indicate relationships not identified to be causal or identified to be definitely non-causal. I use such connections most commonly to represent 'nevertheless' relationships. Thus, 'I'm not religious, but organ donation shouldn't be compulsory if people do hold religious beliefs' might become 'Not religious' – 'Accepts legitimacy of alternative views'.

Dotted lines may be used to indicate potentially contrasting or qualifying ('but') relationships. Sometimes these will highlight a genuine contradiction in views expressed by interviewee's, for example 'once I'm dead, I'm dead' . . . 'nobody knows what will happen after death'. At other times dotted lines may draw the analyst's or reader's attention to concepts that need to be considered together if misrepresentation is to be avoided, for example 'positive attitude to *voluntary* donation' . . . 'negative attitude to *coerced* donation'.

Both concept outlines and the connections between them may be highlighted to show relative importance compared to other attributes shown within the map.

Following depth analysis (see below), I think it makes sense to highlight core categories by representing them with ellipses instead of oblongs. Such categories deserve highlighting for several reasons. First, such highlighting distinguishes the core categories as distinct from more 'peripheral' or 'surface-level' categories. Second, it acknowledges the fact that these categories are primarily *inferred* by the analyst from a *number* of aspects of the interviewee's data, rather than being relatively directly *derived* from perhaps more *occasional* instances of that data. Third, it allows the reader to quickly get an overall 'sense' of what is 'driving' the interviewee's views. Fourth, and bearing the former points in mind, highlighting core categories provides the reader with clues about where it is most important for them to interrogate the adequacy of the analysis they are being presented with.

When identification of core categories reveals two relatively contrasting or competing 'cognitive systems' (e.g. ideologies, identities, belief or value systems), I like to try and delineate the boundaries of those systems by using a heavy dashed line with shaded circles at each end. The core categories then provide quick 'explanations' of those systems for the readers, thus providing a fifth reason for highlighting them.

Depth analysis. As you analyse the 'manifest' level of your interview data, you will begin to develop expectations about what sorts of views your interviewee will express on topics that you think are related to those already explored. Sometimes, your expectations either do not materialize or are explicitly denied by your interviewee. They may make (or fail to make) distinctions that surprise you. They may express uncertainty or ambivalence where you expected confidence and clarity. They may express adherence to identities you did not anticipate or distance themselves from ones you might have taken for granted. They may fail to acknowledge causal connections you expect, or claim ones seemingly inconsistent with others they have already drawn upon. In short, something the interviewee says will seem odd in relation to the broader picture you are developing on the basis of what they have said so far. In large part, depth analysis occurs by trying to come up with hypotheses – grounded in the interview data – that, if true, would explain how it is possible for your interviewee to hold a set of views which, considered as a whole, seem surprising, for example contradictory or incoherent (Collier, 1994).

In terms of the physical process of drawing the map, the need and appropriateness of depth analysis is suggested whenever you find yourself redrawing or rearranging particular areas or you find it especially difficult to decide how to connect concept boxes together. Depth analysis is also suggested whenever your map contains the dotted lines between boxes that signify 'contrasting' or qualifying concepts. Whenever such things occur, ask yourself: is there any possible 'latent' concept or process that might explain these difficulties or complications?

Hannah's interviewee expressed a view early in the interview that organ donation is almost unreservedly both a good thing and without costs. She listed a whole raft of consistent reasons for her views and mentioned a plethora of personal actions and attitudes that were compatible with the self-portrait she was painting. It was clear that she thought posthumous organ donation equivalent to blood donation, and had no more attachment to the material stuff of organs than she had to blood (or probably any other non-essential bodily products). But then she surprised me. She talked with empathy about a child who wished to refuse a heart transplant for fear that it would change her identity. She was also impressed by a heart transplant recipient who went to a medium to confirm that her perceived post-operation personality change was due to having received the heart of a teenage male biker. Finally, Hannah's interviewee took a very tough line against egg donation, with her concern to help others and improve the lot of humankind trumped by a desire to avoid having 'children walking around that were *part of me* that I didn't know about'.

As well as surprising me, Hannah's interviewee clearly recognized for herself a tension associated with the views she was expressing. Where her views were clear, or at least set, she expressed them succinctly and with confidence. When expressing views that (ultimately) surprised me, however, she spontaneously felt some pressure to either qualify views she had expressed earlier or at least critically examine the relationship between the various views that seemed to have a rather uncomfortable 'fit' with each other.

As a result of all these 'clues', the need for some 'depth analysis' seemed clear. And, as a result of Hannah's interviewee being so intelligently self-reflective, identifying 'latent' constructs and processes was relatively straightforward (which is not to say it was quick or undemanding). As already mentioned, I surmised that a 'humanist' ideology was the dominant attitude and action-guide Hannah's interviewee lived by, but that in certain circumstances (which I would claim are now relatively predictable) a 'non-humanist' ideology 'took over'. These 'ideologies' co-existed with some tension, but they are not incomprehensible. The form of 'humanism' Hannah's interviewee subscribes to considers rationality to be subservient to and appropriately used in service of the needs of humans. That is, humans are 'special'. Further, rationality, appropriately applied, suggests humility and a willingness to admit only partial and tentative knowledge. In combination, the privileged status of humankind and the acknowledged imperfections of rationality led Hannah's interviewee to become increasingly cautious and challenging of her 'usual' ideology whenever it threatened to over-reach itself and prioritize 'rationality' over the (unknown and possibly unknowable) 'essence' of humanity.

Theory validation

Cognitive mapping is an exercise in theory generation. Social psychology is a science and scientific theories need testing, however well 'grounded' they are in empirical data. One form of theory testing is to investigate the validity of the process by which the theory was generated. Within quantitative methods, this is usually indicated by reliability. If two or more people using the same method can get similar results, or if one person can get similar results using the same method on different occasions, the method is said to be reliable and the validity of that method is inferred. Cognitive mapping lends itself to a limited form of reliability testing. Different people can independently produce cognitive maps from the same data and then compare the results. These are unlikely to be identical, but it should be possible to ascertain the extent to which they are telling 'the same story', or parts thereof. Similarly, different people can interview the same interviewee on the same topic and see to what extent cognitive maps developed from each interview are similar.

Cognitive mapping also lends itself to a further form of testing the validity of the method of theory generation. Analysts can explain, to each other or to third parties, *how* and *why* they developed the cognitive maps they did. It is common for researchers publishing the results of qualitative analysis to try to provide enough 'raw material' to allow readers to evaluate theories the analyst has generated. It is also common, in a process known as 'respondent validation', for researchers using qualitative analytic methods to explain to interviewees (or whomever provided the raw data) how and why they developed the theories they did. Thus people other than the person generating the theory have an opportunity to critique the method by which the theory was generated. They and the theory generator may then enter into a debate about what can and cannot be validly inferred on the basis of the available data (cf. Rorty, 1987).

The discussion above primarily concerns testing the validity of the method by which theories are developed. We should also be concerned with the validity of the theories themselves. Qualitative analysts are fond of relying on respondent validation for this purpose (as well as for testing the validity of the method of theory generation), but a respondent's views on the adequacy of theories seem rather weak for this purpose. Interviewees may have privileged information about what they meant by what they said (i.e. the data from which theories were developed), but in psychology there is plenty of reason to suspect that they will not always have privileged access to their own thoughts, feelings, views and reasons for action (Bem & McConnell,

1970; Loewenstein & Schkade, 1999; Markus, 1986; Nisbett & Wilson, 1977; Wilson, 1985).

It is increasingly common for qualitative analysts to recommend 'methodological triangulation' as a method for validating their theories (but see Searle, 1999). This simply means using a variety of methods to investigate the same phenomenon and investigating the extent of any consistency between the accounts of that phenomenon generated by each of the methods. I can do nothing but (1) wholly endorse such a prescription, and (2) note how infrequently it is put into practice.

Within traditional realist conceptions of psychology (as opposed, particularly, to 'critical realist' conceptions), the best test of the validity of theories is the extent to which those theories may be used to obtain accurate prediction and control. If a cognitive map of a single person's views is correct, it should be possible to infer all sorts of things about how the person thinks and acts. On the basis of my cognitive map, for example, I might predict all manner of attitudes I think Hannah's interviewee is likely to hold but which were not explicitly discussed by her in her interview with Hannah, for example liberal attitudes towards homosexuality and recreational 'soft' drug use, negative attitudes towards racism and sexism, and ambivalent attitudes towards genetic testing and population control. I might also predict certain of her behaviours, for example a tendency to form close and intense relationships, be highly motivated in work and leisure pursuits of her choosing, prefer 'argumentative' to 'fact-gathering' academic topics. Finally, I could try to use my cognitive map to 'control' Hannah's interviewee, for example by inferring how to balance 'rational' and 'non-rational' attempts at persuasion and influence (cf. Petty & Cacioppo, 1986).

Cognitive mapping of the form described here, in common with other qualitative techniques, relies on small sample sizes and consequently provides little to ground claims of generality. It is, however, perfectly possible to test the validity of theories generalized from cognitive mapping. First, one may critically examine the theory in the light of existing literature. Despite being based on a sample of one, and seeming to result from a sophisticated but presumably relatively idiosyncratic mix of belief and value systems, it is striking how consistent the cognitive map discussed in this chapter is with the known psychological determinants of organ donation (Farsides, 2000). Secondly, one may test the generality of theories developed by cognitive mapping (or parts of those theories) by testing hypotheses derived from those theories on a wider sample. This may be done 'qualitatively' (as in 'theoretical sampling' within grounded analysis, Glaser &

Strauss, 1967), where people are selected for interview (which is subsequently qualitatively analysed) on the basis of being most likely to present a challenge to the theory developed so far. Or it may be done 'quantitatively', for example by developing questionnaire measures on the basis of concepts identified in the map, or by designing experiments to test contingencies suggested by the map.

The assignment described in this chapter does not insist on any form of validation of method or of the theory developed from it. A lack of requirement does not entail prohibition, however. You will almost certainly improve the quality of your project (and the quantity of the mark it receives) if you incorporate methods that will allow validation as described above (see the final sub-section of this chapter, 'Ringing the changes', for some specific ideas).

Report writing

I recommend that you write the project outlined here using the 'standard' format of the dominant psychology journals. Many of the sections and sub-sections will differ little in style or content from those that would appear in a 'quantitative' study. Thus, you will have an *Abstract*, summarizing your research aims, method, sample, main results, main conclusion and implications. You will have an *Introduction*, outlining what the project is, why it is needed, what it hopes to achieve, a rationale for the methods employed and an explicit statement of the research aims. There will be a *Methods* section, in which you provide the reader with details of who took part in the study and how they were selected for inclusion (in the 'Participants' sub-section), how the data was gathered (in the 'Procedure' sub-section), and what analytic method was used and how it was put into practice (in an 'Analysis' sub-section), along with details of any other data-gathering techniques (e.g. for validation purposes). You will have a *Results* section, discussed in the remaining paragraphs of this sub-section. There will be a *Discussion* section, in which your main results are summarized, the implications of them for the issues raised in the Introduction are discussed (e.g. for existing theory, for future research, for policy making), and strengths and weaknesses of the study are evaluated (with guidance for future researchers). You will have the standard *References* section. And you will have appropriate *Appendices*. These may include one or more cognitive maps, full or partial transcripts of the interview, copies of the interview schedule used, a copy of the recorded interview, and so forth.

The major difference between a report written for this assignment and ones written for more 'quantitative' ones will occur in the Results section. The 'good news' for many students is that there will be no statistical analyses (unless required for analysis of supplementary data you have collected). Instead, there will be an account of how your cognitive map was developed and what its major characteristics are. As an example of qualitative analysis, it is essential that it gives readers of your report as much chance as possible to evaluate the quality of your theory development, for example in terms of validity, depth, sophistication and insight. It is therefore imperative that you include a diagram of at least the 'final' map (ideally in such a way that it may be easily referred to while simultaneously reading about the development of it). Some people also find it helpful to provide earlier 'drafts' of the map to explain how their thinking developed during analysis. Additionally or alternatively, some people like to include 'summary' maps as well as 'full' ones, so that major themes may be discussed before and in more detail than supplementary or minor themes.

Apart from the maps, which may be included within the Results section or within Appendices, the main body of the Results section will be a textual discussion of the development and character of the final map. The former essentially comprises an argument that your analysis is appropriate, in the sense of being 'adequately grounded' in the data. Thus you want to do all you can to convince your reader that such grounding is 'secure'. It is usually a good idea to quote extensively from your interview to justify interpretations you have made about the appropriate representation of mapped concepts and connections between them. Prior transcription will obviously facilitate this, as well as allowing the reader to evaluate the context in which your quotes occurred (as long as you have included your transcript in an Appendix or otherwise made it available for inspection, e.g. by posting it on a web-page – having obtained your interviewee's permission to do so). Particular justification is required if you have identified 'latent' level (e.g. 'core') categories. There is no way to provide detailed guidance on how best to do this, but here is a tip. Once you have completed your map, think about how you would describe your interviewee's attitudes towards organ donation (or whatever) to someone unfamiliar with your project. The chances are you will say something like, 'Well, overall they expressed [whatever] view, but some things they said seemed not to fit too well with that, for example . . . When I tried to make sense of everything they said, I found that I could best do so if I assumed that 'underneath it all' they thought [account of the core categories]. Once I did this, it was clear that they thought both [whatever] and [seemingly inconsistent whatever else] because [explanation of how core category resolves or makes possible the apparent inconsistency]'. If you then 'formalize' that summary and supplement it with a justification of the postulated core categories (e.g. by referring to things the interview said), you will be well on your way to identifying a very effective structure for your Results section.

Notes for the Course Leader

STUDENT EXPERIENCE

The exercise I have described above is one (using different topics) that I have set at two universities over the space of about a decade. My overall evaluation is that students feel very insecure about their abilities both to conduct an interview and develop a cognitive map from the data obtained. Nevertheless, they invariably do a very good job, with many students excelling and none who put the effort in doing atrociously. As important, most overcome their anxieties and end up thoroughly enjoying the assignment. Despite this, it must be noted that until very recently few students have gone on to use similar methods in their final year projects. Common reasons offered for this include suspicions that markers will be less 'tolerant' of qualitative projects than of quantitative ones and that examiners will assume that only 'weak' students use such methods. To the extent that such fears exist, validly or otherwise, it might be particularly worth stressing the advantages of employing 'mixed-methods'.

TEACHING FORMAT

The assignment described above is a 'bare-bones' one. It is typically set for students early in their second undergraduate year when they have almost no experience with or knowledge of qualitative methods. It is an infinitely flexible exercise, although I typically teach it using two lectures and two associated workshops.

The first (one hour) lecture covers interviewing skills and methods in general and guidance on conducting interviews for the purpose of generating cognitive maps in particular. The accompanying (two-hour) workshop is used to demonstrate some interview techniques (by me interviewing one or more student), to give students practice of the same (by interviewing each other), and to split students into groups for the purpose of developing their common interview schedule (completed outside of workshop time if necessary). Students are also instructed to conduct their interview before the next workshop (although they are explicitly given the option of waiting until after the second lecture should they wish to do so).

The second (one hour) lecture covers 'qualitative methods' generally, including the 'qualitative versus quantitative' and 'realists versus the rest' debates. It does this fairly swiftly in broad terms and then moves on to talking specifically about cognitive mapping as an illustrative example. I then explicitly put my view across about the consistency of 'qualitative' and 'quantitative' methods within the framework of a realist conception of social psychology as a science. I also, of course, highlight the existence of alternatives views and the reasons for and consequences of holding them. The accompanying (two-hour) workshop begins with me describing the details of producing a cognitive map and demonstrating how it may be done by use of a worked example, very much as described above. After a general discussion and a question and answer session, students are free to begin cognitive mapping of their own data or, if they have already started doing so, to ask me or the demonstrator for advice on problems and difficulties they may be facing. After the second workshop is over, students complete their analysis and write up a report to be handed in for marking.

Lectures are usually intended for the whole year-group (about 65 students) and, because the tasks involve small group work, workshops work well with groups of up to 30 or more, especially if you have a demonstrator or similar support.

No specialist equipment is needed. I encourage students to use their own recording equipment, which most are happy and able to do. If any students do not have recording equipment and are not willing or able to borrow some, we have a small stock from which students may sign out the equipment they require.

RINGING THE CHANGES

The exercise above was designed to introduce students to qualitative data collection and analysis methods with the minimum of effort and pain on all sides. Students of all abilities and most motivation levels can complete the assignment and, I believe, enjoy learning a lot about qualitative methods as they do so. However, there is clearly much that can be done to extend (or shrink) and improve the assignment, given the inclination and resources.

Most obviously, some of the 'optional' aspects of the assignment above can be made 'obligatory'. Thus you might require students to supplement their interviewing with other methods of data collection, either within or without the interviewing situation, for example having them administer small questionnaires, employ projective techniques or engage in participant or other observation. Additionally or alternatively, you might require group members to produce cognitive maps from each other's interview data as well as their own, allowing comparison of different maps produced from the same data and comparison of maps across cases. Again, you might insist that students attempt respondent validation.

If it is not possible or not desirable for students to collect data, even from each other, they can be asked to map one or more transcripts provided for them.

Throughout the mapping literature there is an emphasis on the cognitive, although clearly there has been some 'underground' interest in potentially distinct psychological phenomena, such as emotions, evaluations and motivations. You could invite your students to imagine what an 'emotional map' of any given subject might be like and to consider to what use it might be put. If they are able to do this, you might even get them to produce one.

You might also encourage students to think about how the theories they have generated might then be tested. Thus you might have them conduct further interviews, perhaps according to guidelines suggested by grounded theory. Alternatively, you might have them develop (and perhaps administer) a questionnaire based on their own cognitive maps.

Further, you might encourage students to think more seriously about the comparisons and contrasts between methods, both within the qualitative tradition and across the qualitative versus quantitative divide. Thus you might get students to analyse the same interview data using guidelines developed within different traditions (Cresswell, 1998 and Huff, 1990 would each be very useful here). Alternatively, you might attempt genuine methodological triangulation by having students use a variety of methods to examine (ostensibly) 'the same' phenomenon (but see Searle, 1999, chapter 5).

Another possibility is to get students to use cognitive mapping to 'test' existing social psychological theories. For example, you could get students to use their knowledge of social identity theory (Tajfel & Turner, 1979) to design a semi-structured interview schedule on the topic of 'How I feel about the groups I belong to'. Respondents' accounts could then be analysed in ways similar to those suggested in this chapter and then the resulting cognitive map could be considered for compatibility with the theory being 'tested'.

Finally, you could invite students to consider the conceptual similarities, differences and compatibilities of cognitive mapping (as presented in this chapter) as it might be used to investigate specific social psy-chological theories. For example, you could ask whether cognitive mapping is more suitable for use within the social cognition attitude paradigm (e.g. Ajzen & Madden, 1986; Fishbein & Ajzen, 1975), the social representation theory tradition (e.g. Moscovici, 1973, 1988) or both (see Augoustinos & Innes, 1990).

REFERENCES

Ajzen, I. & Madden, T. J. (1986). Prediction of goal-directed behaviour: Atti-tudes, intentions, and perceived behavioural control. *Journal of Experimental Social Psychology, 22*, 453–74.

Augoustinos, M. & Innes, J. M. (1990). Towards an integration of social representations and social schema theory. *British Journal of Social Psychology, 29*, 213–31.

Axelrod, R. (ed.) (1976). *The structure of decision: The cognitive maps of political elites*. Princeton, NJ: Princeton University Press.

Bem, D. J. (1972). Self-perception theory. In L. Berkowitz (ed.), *Advances in Experimental Social Psychology* (vol. 6, pp. 1–62). New York: Academic Press.

Bem, D. J. & McConnell, H. K. (1970). Testing the self-perception explanation of dissonance phenomena: On the salience of pre-manipulation attitudes. *Journal of Personality and Social Psychology, 14*, 23–31.

Bloor, M. (1978). On the analysis of observational data: a discussion of the worth and uses of inductive techniques and respondent validation. *Sociology, 12*, 545–52.

Breakwell, G. & Canter, D. (eds.) (1993). *Empirical approaches to social represen-tations*. Oxford: Oxford University Press.

Bryman, A. (1988). *Quantity and quality in social research*. London: Sage.

Buss, A. R. (1978). Causes and reasons in attribution theory: A conceptual critique. *Journal of Personality and Social Psychology, 36*, 1311–21.

Cacioppo, J. T., von Hippel, W. & Ernst, J. M. (1997). Mapping cognitive structures and processes through verbal content: The thought-listing tech-nique. *Journal of Consulting and Clinical Psychology, 65*, 928–40.

Collier, A. (1994). *Critical realism*. London: Verso.

Creswell, J. W. (1998). *Qualitative inquiry and research design: Choosing among five traditions*. London: Sage.

Daniels, K., de Chernatony, L. & Johnson, G. (1995). Validating a method for mapping managers' mental models of competitive industry structures. *Human Relations, 48*, 975–91.

Elliot, R., Fischer, C. T. & Rennie, D. L. (1999). Evolving guidelines for publication of qualitative research studies in psychology and related fields. *British Journal of Clinical Psychology, 38*, 215–29.

Ericsson, K. A. & Simon, H. A. (1980). Verbal reports as data. *Psychological Review, 87*, 215–51.

286 Tom Farsides

Ericsson, K. A. & Simon, H. A. (1984). *Protocol analysis: Verbal reports as data.* Cambridge, MA: MIT Press.

Farsides, T. L. (2000). Winning hearts and minds: Using psychology to promote voluntary organ donation. *Health Care Analysis, 8,* 101–21.

Festinger, L. (1957). *A theory of cognitive dissonance.* Stanford, CA: Stanford University Press.

Fishbein, M. & Ajzen, I. (1975). *Belief, attitude, intention, and behaviour: An introduction to theory and research.* Reading, MA: Addison-Wesley.

Ford, J. & Hegarty, H. (1984). Decision makers' beliefs about the causes and effects of structure: An exploratory study. *Academy of Management Journal, 27,* 271–91.

Fransella, F. & Bannister, D. (1977). *a manual for repertory grid technique.* New York: Academic Press.

Glaser, B. G. (1992). *Emerging vs. forcing: Basics of grounded theory analysis.* Mill Valley, CA: Sociology Press.

Glaser, B. G. & Strauss, A. L. (1967). *The discovery of grounded theory: Strategies for qualitative research.* Chicago: Aldine.

Hammersley, M. (1992). *What's wrong with ethnography?* London: Routledge.

Henwood, K. L. & Pidgeon, N. F. (1992). Qualitative research and psychological theorising. *British Journal of Psychology, 83,* 97–111.

Hewstone, M. (1989). *Causal attribution: From cognitive processes to collective beliefs.* Oxford: Blackwell.

Holsti, O. R. (1969). *Content analysis for the social sciences and humanities.* Reading, MA: Addison-Wesley.

Huberman, A. M. & Miles, M. B. (2002). *The qualitative researcher's companion.* London: Sage.

Huff, A. S. (1990). Mapping strategic thought. In A. S. Huff (ed.), *Mapping strategic thought* (pp. 11–49). Chichester, UK: John Wiley & Sons.

Huff, A. S., Narapareddy, V. & Fletcher, K. E. (1990). Coding the causal association of concepts. In A. S. Huff (ed.), *Mapping strategic thought* (pp. 311–25). Chichester, UK: John Wiley & Sons.

Huff, A. S. & Schwenk, C. R. 1990. Bias and sensemaking in good times and bad. In A. S. Huff (ed.), *Mapping strategic thought* (pp. 89–108). Chichester, UK: John Wiley and Sons.

Jones, E. E. & Nisbett, R. E. (1972). The actor and the observer: Divergent perceptions of the causes of behaviour. In E. E. Jones, D. E. Kanouse, H. H. Kelley, R. E. Nisbett, S. Valins & B. Weiner (eds.), *Attribution: Perceiving the causes of behaviour* (pp. 37–52). Morristown, NJ: General Learning Press.

Jones, S. (1985). The analysis of depth interviews. In R. Walker (ed.), *Applied qualitative analysis* (pp. 80–5). Aldershot, UK: Gower.

Kelley, H. H. (1972). Causal schemata and the attribution process. In E. E. Jones, D. E. Kanouse, H. H. Kelley, R. E. Nisbett, S. Valins & B. Weiner (eds.), *Attribution: Perceiving the causes of behaviour* (pp. 151–74). Morristown, NJ: General Learning Press.

Kelly, G. A. (1955). *The psychology of personal constructs* (vols 1 and 2). New York: Norton.

Krippendorff, K. (1980). *Content analysis: An introduction to its methodology*. Beverly Hills, CA: Sage.

Kvale, S. (1996). *Interviews: An introduction to qualitative research interviewing*. London: Sage.

LeCompte, M. D. & Goetz, J. P. (1982). Problems of reliability and validity in ethnographic research. *Review of Educational Research, 51*, 31–60.

Loewenstein, G. & Schkade, D. (1999). Wouldn't it be nice? Predicting future feelings. In D. Kahneman, E. Diener & N. Schwartz (eds.), *Understanding well-being: The foundations of hedonic psychology* (pp. 85–105). New York: Russell Sage Foundation.

Lofland, J. (1995). Analytic ethnography: Features, failings, and futures. *Journal of Contemporary Ethnography, 24*, 30–67. Reprinted in A. M. Huberman & M. B. Miles, *The qualitative researcher's companion* (pp. 143–4). London: Sage.

Madill, A., Jordan, A. & Shirley, C. (2000). Objectivity and reliability in qualitative analysis: Realist, contextualist and radical constructionist epistemologies. *British Journal of Psychology, 91*, 1–20.

Markus, G. B. (1986). Stability and change in political attitudes: Observe, recall, and 'explain'. *Political Behaviour, 8*, 21–44.

Miles, M. B. & Huberman, A. M. (1994). *Qualitative data analysis: An expanded source book* (2nd edn.). London: Sage.

Moscovici, S. (1973). Foreword. In C. Herzlich, *Health and illness: A social psychological analysis*. London: Academic Press.

Moscovici, S. (1988). Notes towards a description of social representations. *European Journal of Social Psychology, 18*, 211–50.

Murphy, E., Dingwall, R., Greatbatch, D., Parker, S. & Watson, P. (1998). Qualitative research methods in health technology assessment: A review of the literature. *Health Technology Assessment, 2*, 1–292. Available on-line from links found at <http://www.soton.ac.uk/~hta> Currently (June, 2003) located at <http://www.hta.nhsweb.nhs.uk/fullmono/mon216.pdf>

Nisbett, R. E. & Wilson, T. D. (1977). Telling more than we can know: Verbal reports on mental processes. *Psychological Review, 84*, 231–59.

O' Laughlin, E. M. & Brubaker, B. S. (1998). Use of landmarks in cognitive mapping: Gender differences in self-report versus performance. *Personality and Individual Differences, 24*, 595–601.

Petty, R. E. & Cacioppo, J. T. (1986). The Elaboration Likelihood model of persuasion. In L. Berkowitz (ed.), *Advances in experimental social psychology* (vol. 19, pp 123–205). San Diego, CA: Academic Press.

Pidgeon, N. & Henwood, K. (1997). Using grounded theory in psychological research. In N. Hayes (ed.), *Doing qualitative analysis in psychology* (pp. 245–73). Hove, UK: Psychology Press.

Reid, A. K. & Staddon, J. E. R. (1998). A dynamic route finder for the cognitive map. *Psychological Review, 105*, 585–601.

Reger, R. K. (1990a). Managerial thought structures and competitive positioning. In A. S. Huff (ed.), *Mapping strategic thought* (pp. 71–88). Chichester, UK: John Wiley & Sons.

Reger, R. K. (1990b). The repertory grid technique for eliciting the content and structure of cognitive constructive systems. In A. S. Huff (ed.), *Mapping strategic thought* (pp. 301–9). Chichester, UK: John Wiley & Sons.

Robson, C. (2002). *Real world research: A resource for social scientists and practitioner researchers* (2nd edn.). Oxford: Blackwell.

Rorty, R. (1987). Science as solidarity. In J. S. Nelson, A. Megill & D. McCloskey (eds.), *The rhetoric of the human sciences: Language and argument in scholarship and public affairs* (pp. 38–52). Madison, WI: University of Wisconsin Press.

Sadler, D. R. (1981). Intuitive data processing as a potential source of bias in naturalistic evaluations. *Educational Evaluation and Policy Analysis, 3*, 25–31. Reprinted in A. M. Huberman & M. B. Miles, *The qualitative researcher's companion* (pp. 123–35). London: Sage.

Sanner, M. (1994). Attitudes towards organ donation and transplantation. *Social Science and Medicine, 38*, 1141–52.

Sayer, A. (2000). *Realism and social science*. London: Sage.

Searle, C. (1999). *The quality of qualitative research*. London: Sage.

Sergeev, V. M., Akimov, V. P., Lukov, V. B. & Parshin, P. B. (1990). Interdependence in a crisis situation: A cognitive approach to modelling the Caribbean crisis. *Journal of Conflict Resolution, 34*, 179–207.

Smith, J. A. (1996). Beyond the divide between cognition and discourse: Using interpretive phenomenological analysis in health psychology, *Psychology and Health, 11*, 261–71.

Strauss, A. & Corbin, J. (1998). *Basics of qualitative research: Techniques and procedures for developing grounded theory* (2nd edn.). London: Sage.

Swan, J. A. (1995). Exploring knowledge and cognitions in decisions about technological innovation: Mapping managerial cognitions. *Human Relations, 48*, 1241–70.

Tajfel, H. & Turner, J. C. (1979). An integrative theory of group conflict. In W. G. Austin & S. Worchel (eds.), *The social psychology of intergroup relations* (pp. 33–47). Monterey, CA.: Brooks.

Tolman, E. C. (1932). *Purposive behaviour in animals and men*. New York: Appleton-Century-Crofts.

Weick, K. E. & Bougon, M. G. (1986). Organisations as cognitive maps: Charting ways to success and failure. In H. P. Sims & D. A. Gioia (eds.), *The thinking organisation: Dynamics of organisational social cognition* (pp. 102–35). San Francisco: Jossey-Bass.

Willig, C. (2001). *Introducing qualitative research in psychology: Adventure in theory and method*. Buckingham, UK: Open University Press.

Wilson, T. D. (1985). Strangers to ourselves: The origins and accuracy of beliefs about one's own mental states. In J. H. Harvey & G. Weary (eds.), *Attribution: Basic issues and applications* (pp. 9–36). New York: Academic Press.

Young, M. D. (1996). Cognitive mapping meets semantic networks. *Journal of Conflict Resolution, 40*, 395–414.

CHAPTER TWELVE

The Multiple Sorting Procedure (MSP)

Julie Barnett

This chapter describes the multiple sorting procedure (MSP). MSP is a way of eliciting structured self-report data from individuals or groups. It can be used in any type of research design (from the completely experimental to the totally non-experimental). It is essentially a technique for examining how participants place constructs (that can be defined in any way the researcher chooses) into categories and how they then label the distinctions between the categories. The procedure is used in collaboration with advanced statistical techniques that generate graphical representations of the relationships between constructs and between categories. The exercise given in the chapter allows the research question to be chosen by the students but takes them step by step through the collection and analysis of their data. This chapter is suitable for introductory level courses.

The Multiple Sorting Procedure

The multiple sorting procedure (MSP) is a technique that is used most frequently in the context of an interview with an individual but it can be used with a group as part of a joint interactive data elicitation process. It is a simple procedure for eliciting structured self-report data yet it allows subsequently for sophisticated treatment of those data. Like virtually all data-elicitation techniques, it can be used to address a wide variety of research questions.

This chapter will address three aspects of the MSP. It will:

- outline the principles upon which it is based,
- explain the procedure itself,
- illustrate the process of analysis.

Following this, the steps that students should take to use this methodology are outlined and an illustrative exercise summarized. Finally there are some notes for class leaders that will be of value to further refine research skills in this area.

PRINCIPLES

The MSP is based on:

- established psychological theory regarding the importance of categorization processes,
- the importance of personal meaning.

The importance of categorization processes has long been recognized in psychology (Bruner, Goodnow & Austin, 1956; Rosch, 1977; Deschamps & Doise, 1978). To avoid every situation and object being classed as unique, they are considered as belonging to particular categories (Smith & Medin, 1981). So to understand the way in which the individual relates to and responds to the world, it is necessary that the conceptual system of constructs and categories that are used is understood. The uniqueness of the way that people see the world and the importance of personal meaning constitutes an equally pervasive theme within psychology (Kelly, 1955; Shepherd & Watson, 1982). Much attention over the years has been given to developing methods that reflect these two themes. Indeed, an examination of the history of sorting tasks might suggest such influences. For some the emphasis has been on the cognitive processes of concept formation, and sorting tasks were designed to reflect this (Vygotsky, 1934; Bruner et al., 1956; Rosenberg & Kim, 1975). Latterly this focus on the cognitive dimension has seen the use of sorting tasks to explore cognitive structure in relation to illness representations (Hampson & Glasgow, 1996). The emphasis of this use of sorting tasks focuses on elements of cognitive structure such as cognitive complexity rather than looking at the content of a substantive area that inhabits these structures.

The precursor of the sorting task that focuses upon the importance of personal meanings is undoubtedly best exemplified in the work of Kelly and the subsequent development of the repertory grid by Fransella and Bannister (Fransella & Bannister, 1977). Although sorting tasks can be put to different uses, they have the common requirement that respondents 'make discrete categorizations of a set of elements based on judgements of relative similarities among those elements' (Groat, 1982, p. 6). This task is referred to as a 'sort'. However, within this, and depending on the specific purpose of the research, there is a good deal of variation in the degree of constraint that the task places on the respondent – that is, in the extent to which the researcher specifies the basis of the sort, the categories that these elements should be sorted into and the constraints upon the number of elements within each category. Of all the types of sorting tasks, the MSP places the fewest constraints upon respondents insofar as participants can be free to specify the basis of the sort, to decide how many categories this can be divided into and how the elements should be distributed within these. Recent developments in non-metric multidimensional scaling procedures enable the resulting data to be systematically analysed and yet retain and portray the essentially personal meanings that each sort conveys.

The MSP can be used to explore a variety of research questions using an exploratory or a confirmatory (or restricted, see Hammond 2000) approach. For example, it can set out to understand the way in which people think about a particular area where the researcher has no preconceived ideas about the constructs and categories that people are likely to use. In contrast, it can also be used to test hypotheses that particular relationships exist between the variables. Although touching upon a much wider research literature,the reader should be aware that the MSP in both exploratory or confirmatory mode has often been situated within facet theory (Brown, 1985). Whatever the approach of the research, the MSP can focus on the relationship between constructs, elements or people. It can be used as a 'within-individual' approach, taking an in-depth look at the way in which an individual conceptualizes a particular area, maybe using it to look at changes that occur over time. It can also be used as a 'within-group' approach. Here the focus might be on the way in which different members of a group conceptualize particular elements and the differences between individuals. Or it can be used to look at research questions focusing on the differences between groups. The focus here might be whether belonging to a particular group was associated with the use of particular constructs or particular groupings of elements. It is this 'between-group' approach that is most commonly represented in the published literature of research that uses the MSP.

As far as the content of research in this area is concerned, the MSP has probably been most widely used in environmental psychology, for example in relation to the evaluation of places (Kramer, 1995) architecture (Groat, 1982; Wilson & Canter, 1990) and landscapes (Scott & Canter, 1997). Conceptualizations of work in a clinical setting (Morrison & Bauer, 1993) and the way in which different groups classify sexual offences have also been explored (McGuickin & Brown, 2001). Many of these studies illustrate the way in which the MSP can be used to explore the conceptual systems of groups, with the differences in the perceptions of lay people and professionals being a strong theme. For examples of research focusing upon single individuals see Canter, Brown, & Groat (1985) and Sixsmith & Sixsmith (1987).

In summary then, using the MSP enables an understanding of how people conceptualize a particular area and the constructs and categories that they use. Individuals are free to express and articulate what they consider to be the important issues, and yet these personal meanings can be explored in a systematic and structured manner. This contrasts with using a questionnaire where participants are asked to use set response categories to respond to particular elements of the research question. This can often minimize the differences between groups and mask the possibility of discovering subtle differences in evaluations (Hubbard, 1997). The MSP is a highly flexible tool that can accommodate wide variations in the nature of the sorting task and can thus be adapted to address a wide variety of research questions.

PROCEDURE

The MSP requires that participants sort a set of elements into different categories. What are the elements? The answer to this question is a function of the nature of the research question and the ingenuity of the researcher. They are generally cards with words (e.g. labels, descriptions), drawings or photographs that represent the domain of interest. However they could be anything – objects, for example, or video clips. In the rest of this chapter, however, we will call these elements 'cards'. To assist the researcher in the process of recording the details of each sort each card should be numbered; 15 to 25 is the ideal number of cards to sort (Canter et al., 1985).

Participants are asked to sort the elements into groups such that all the elements in one group are similar to each other in some important way and different from the other groups. There is no restriction on either the number of groups or on the number of elements in each group. This is called a *free sort* – participants can choose the basis of the sort and within that are free to allocate the elements to categories in any way they choose.

When they have finished a free sort participants are asked about *why* they have sorted in the way that they have and what it is that the elements in each group have in common. The researcher records the sort information (see below) and the interviewee is asked to sort again. This is repeated until the participant is no longer able to devise alternative themes. Sometimes participants feel they can only do one or two sorts. However, when the elements are concrete and familiar to them many more sorts can result.

It may be that the researcher would also like the participants to sort the cards in a particular way, using predefined response categories. This is a *structured sort*. The reader will understand that in effect this provides similar information to completing a rating scale on a questionnaire. It is different in that the allocation of each card to a category involves some consideration of the positioning of the other cards that it is or is not being grouped with. It is also likely that the reasons participants give provide valuable additional information that would remain untapped by a questionnaire. Structured sorts can also be useful insofar as they can also be related to the information gained from free sorts (see below).

When doing a sorting task, participants can be encouraged to verbalize anything that occurs to them and even to think aloud as they are devising categories and assigning the elements to these. This material is valuable in its own right but is also useful in refining the interpretation of the analysis.

People generally find that completing an MSP is a stimulating, engaging, enjoyable and yet simple task. Another strength of the methodology is that it can be completed by people who do not have strong verbal skills and who may not be able to articulate the reasoning behind their card groupings.

The use of the multiple sorting procedure can be illustrated in relation to an area where an understanding of people's conceptual systems is of growing importance. In the light of the completion of the Human Genome Project (Evans, 1999) future genetic research is increasingly likely to depend on the voluntary donation of human biological samples and associated personal medical information. It is therefore important to understand the ways in which attitudes in this area might lead to the legitimacy of work in human genetics being questioned (Martin & Kaye, 1999). In order to facilitate effective communication, awareness and engagement (Merz, 1997), those responsible for developing a practical and legislative framework need to be aware of the way in which it is represented both by the general public and by particular interest groups.

How do people think and feel about these issues? What categories and constructs are used to order them? One way of exploring this would be to use the MSP. This could be done by asking people to sort various scenarios that are concerned with the collection and storage of human biological material for research purposes. Group differences between experts and lay publics, ethnic or religious groups or those who have or have not had personal experience of disabilities or illnesses with a genetic component might be explored.

A number of scenarios could be generated within this domain. Scenarios might include the following examples:

- A man waiting to undergo surgery gives his permission for small samples of skin to be donated to a research programme in a private clinic. The sample would be held in a 'biobank' until it was used.
- A multinational biotechnology company advertised on the Internet for volunteers to donate saliva samples to a new research programme. Personal health information would be also be needed. Samples would be held for a number of years and used in a variety of research programmes.
- Before an operation for breast cancer a woman is asked to sign a form giving permission for tissues that were removed to be stored in case they were necessary for research purposes in the future. Although she was assured of anonymity, the samples would be kept in conjunction with her hospital notes.

As well as doing 'free sorts', it may be that there is a question that the researcher would like all of the participants to answer. In this case it would be useful to include a 'structured sort'. For example, participants might be asked to sort the cards into two categories:

1 Situations in which you feel sure that your personal details would remain confidential,
2 Situations in which you are unsure whether your personal details would remain confidential.

It is useful to record details of each sort in the following way (see Figure 12.1). A *description of the category* scheme is noted along with the *groupings of the sort* and *labels for each of the groups* within the sort. All of this information is brought to bear upon the analysis and interpretation of the data.

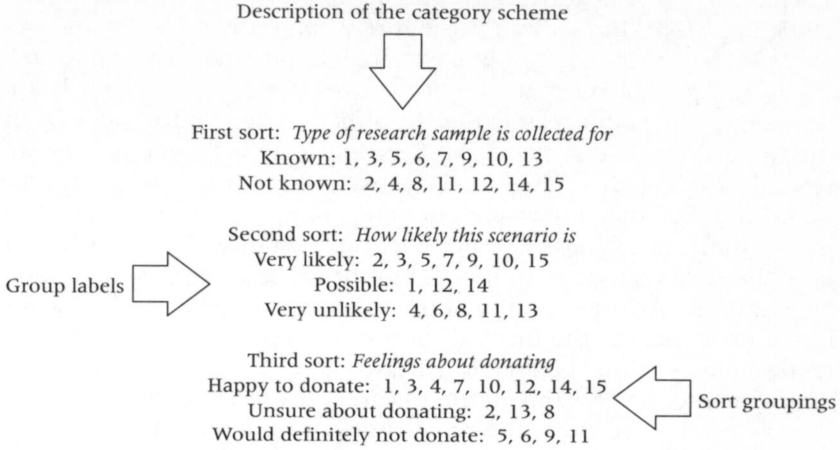

Description of the category scheme

First sort: *Type of research sample is collected for*
Known: 1, 3, 5, 6, 7, 9, 10, 13
Not known: 2, 4, 8, 11, 12, 14, 15

Second sort: *How likely this scenario is*
Very likely: 2, 3, 5, 7, 9, 10, 15
Group labels   Possible: 1, 12, 14
Very unlikely: 4, 6, 8, 11, 13

Third sort: *Feelings about donating*
Happy to donate: 1, 3, 4, 7, 10, 12, 14, 15
Unsure about donating: 2, 13, 8   Sort groupings
Would definitely not donate: 5, 6, 9, 11

Figure 12.1   Card sort recording scheme

PROCESS OF ANALYSIS: DESCRIBING CARD SORT DATA

The initial task for the researcher is to describe the data from the free sorts. The descriptors of the sort themes can be content analysed (and subjected to appropriate assessments of reliability). A table can be compiled depicting the themes/category schemes of the sorts and show-ing, if appropriate, the ways in which they were used by different groups. It may be that some themes are predominantly used by par-ticular groups (Hubbard, 1997) or that themes vary in the way that they are used by the same group at different points in time (Wilson & Canter, 1990). More cognitive information can also be noted. For example, the number of categories within a designated sort could be used as a measure of the dimensional complexity within a particular area (Hampson & Glasgow, 1996).

However, it is generally more informative to consider how the various sorts relate to each other and what the relationships between the cards are. This can be done using multidimensional scaling tech-niques such as the multiple scalogram analysis (MSA) which forms part of the Guttman–Lingoes package of statistical procedures (Lingoes, 1968) Relatively simple accounts of this procedure can be found in Zvulun (1978) and Wilson & Hammond (2000). The strength of this procedure is that 'it only deals with each response as a categorical one comparing the categories with each other. No order is assumed between the various categories, nor is any similarity of meaning assigned to the categories for each of the variables' (Canter et al., 1985, pp. 97–8). In this way it is entirely appropriate for the analysis for MSP data as it does not impose any inappropriate assumptions.

The key part of the MSA output is a scatter plot where cards are represented as points. Cards that have been often conceptualized in the same way, that is, that have been put into the same group, are plotted close together. Thus spatial proximity is equated with conceptual similarity, and conversely difference (i.e. when cards have been put in different groups) is represented by distance. The question of how the space can be partitioned into meaningful regions must then be addressed. As the meaning of the space is derived from the meaning of the variables, the first task of the researcher is to decide where partition lines should be drawn. These partition lines should be drawn on the plot to indicate the groups of cards that were generally seen in the same way. Secondly, the researcher has to determine the nature of these similarities and differences and label the partitioned regions accordingly. Both of these tasks are addressed by projecting the variable categories, that is, the information about the individual sorts, into the same space. How the researcher moves from the information that has been gathered about individual sorts to an interpretation of the MSA plot can be outlined as follows.

First, the information about each sort has to be converted to numbers. A data matrix is constructed such that each card is represented by a row and each sort by a column. Each cell of the matrix contains a number representing the group that an item has been assigned to. The data matrix in Table 12.1 represents the data in Figure 12.1. So for example, in the second sort ('How likely this scenario is'), the cards were sorted into three categories (very likely, possible, very unlikely). Seven cards (2, 3, 5, 7, 9, 10 and 15) were put in the category designated by the researcher as being group 1 ('very likely'), and are thus represented by the number 1 in the intersections of the second sort column and the rows representing Cards 2, 3, 5, 7, 9, 10 and 15.

By varying the arrangement of the data matrix, it is also possible that the points on the plot can represent people rather than cards. However, for now, bearing in mind that the main point of the MSP is to understand the way in which people conceptualize a particular area, let us assume that the points on the plot represent cards. This data matrix forms the core part of the input for analysis.

When the analysis has been run, it is generally helpful to open it in a word processing application in order that the text and page layout can be formatted appropriately. Font size can be adjusted; however, the font style must be retained in order to maintain the relative positions of the points on the plot.

Table 12.1 Card sort data matrix

Cards	Sort 1	Sort 2	Sort 3
Card 1	1	2	1
Card 2	2	1	2
Card 3	1	1	1
Card 4	2	3	1
Card 5	1	1	3
Card 6	1	3	3
Card 7	1	1	1
Card 8	2	3	2
Card 9	1	1	3
Card 10	1	1	1
Card 11	2	3	3
Card 12	2	2	1
Card 13	1	3	2
Card 14	2	2	1
Card 15	2	1	1

As noted above, the main focus of the analysis is a visual representation of the similarities and differences between the cards. However,
depending which program is used, there are other parts of the output
that can be instructive when faced with the task of making sense of
the overall plot. For example:

- A list of elements/cards with similar profiles (i.e. when two (or
  more) cards have been categorized in exactly the same way for all
  sorts in the analysis). One number is thus used in the output to
  represent those cards.
- The coordinates for the items in the space. These may be useful for
  tracking down points you can't find, for example if they are located
  on the border of the plot. They can also be used if a graphing
  program is chosen to reproduce the plot.

Following this information is the 'overall' or 'top plot' followed by a
number of 'item' or 'variable plots' – one for each sort in the analysis.

Figure 12.2 gives a hypothetical example of what this 'overall plot'
might look like in relation to the example given in Table 12.1. Each
number represents one of the 15 cards/scenarios that were sorted. An
immediate impression can be gained from this plot of the cards that
were seen as being similar and different, that is, which ones are close

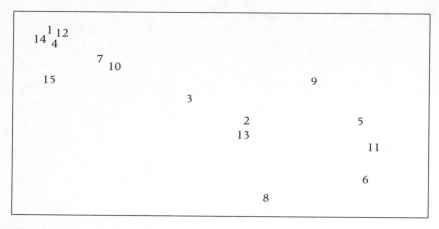

Figure 12.2   An example top plot

together and which are more distant from each other. However, the crucial part of the interpretive process involves bringing the information associated with the item plots to bear upon the overall plot. It is the reasons given for grouping the cards together in each of the individual sorts that enable the researcher to partition the overall plot and to label the resulting regions.

The first step involved in interpreting the plot is to label the points on the overall plot to indicate which card or cards each point represents. Remember that one point may represent more than one card.

Following the overall plot in the output are the item plots, one for each sort that was included in the analysis and in the order in which they appeared in the matrix. On each of these plots the configuration of points (i.e. cards) is exactly the same as on the overall plot; however, here the points are represented by a number that refers to the category that the card was placed in for that particular sort. Figure 12.3 provides an example of this in relation to the third sort in Table 12.1.

The researcher should attempt to partition each item plot so that each category of the sort can be contained within a different region; that is, to draw lines that maximally separate the ones from the twos and so on. Each region should be labelled with the reason that the participant gave for putting those cards together. The regions that are partitioned and labelled in Figure 12.3 are very clear-cut; this is not always the case. Don't worry about this too much although it is true that the clearer the partitions are on the item plots, the more straightforward the partitioning and labelling of the overall plot is.

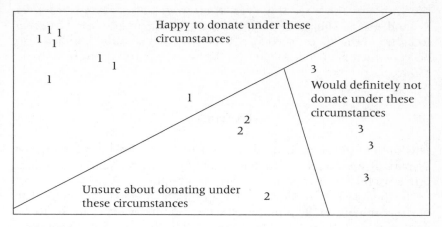

Figure 12.3   An example item plot

The crucial part of the exercise is then to overlay the partitions from each item plot onto the overall plot in order to start developing an understanding of the reasons for the proximity and distance of the points. This informs the way in which the overall plot might in turn be partitioned and of the labels that can best be used to identify each of the regions in the space. In this way the meaningful partitions from the item plots are used to establish the multivariate nature of the region. Because of the researcher's reliance upon the item plots to direct the partitioning and define the regions it can happen that two points that are close together fall into different regions of the space. Scott & Canter (1997) say that this 'indicates a construct on which these items are similar, but which is not as strong as the constructs which have created the divisions' (p. 267). For a fuller explanation of how to interpret the output of an MSA see Wilson & Hammond (2000).

The reader will be aware of the way in which the output of this analysis differs from more conventional statistical analyses, namely that in making sense of the data, there is no significance level towards which to gravitate. The MSA analysis does provide a *coefficient of contiguity* to indicate that the degree of distortion between the data and its representation is not unacceptable. Researchers in this area would generally accept a coefficient of contiguity of 0.9. It may seem to the reader that the method of analysis and interpretation outlined above appear to be more subjective than the apparent objectivity afforded by levels of significance. There is no 'right' way of locating the best partition of the space and 'wiggly' lines can sometimes be the order of the day. However, there are safeguards against over dependence on subjective judgement. First, straight lines can be drawn to partition the space. Secondly, selectivity and sensitivity indices can be constructed to indicate how effective the partitioning is (Shalit, 1977).

Exercise

This outline of the procedure and process of analysis can be distilled as part of an exercise into the following practical steps that might prove useful for anyone new to the technique.

The first task is to devise an appropriate research question. The most positive and helpful introduction to the MSP is likely to be derived where this can be operationalized in a set of 15 to 25 concrete elements that are familiar to the intended participants (e.g. drugs, crimes, places, hazards, people). It might be an interesting and valuable exercise to explore differences in the conceptualizations of different groups in the chosen area, for example first and final year students, males and females, experts and lay publics. Other groups may be specific to particular research questions. If the research question was 'What dimensions do undergraduates use to conceptualize different types of holiday resort?', the elements chosen would be 15 to 25 holiday resorts and obviously the sample would be undergraduates.

The question then arises as to how the specific elements are to be derived and the range of elements to be used. Some guidance is given by Canter et al. (1985) and Sixsmith & Sixsmith (1987) on these issues. For present purposes the researcher should aim to generate elements to be broadly representative of the research domain, so a variety of types of holiday destinations would be chosen.

Each element should be transferred to a card and the cards should be numbered. Instructions to participants should be finalized and made specific to the research question being addressed (Canter et al., 1985). Sheets for recording the details of each sort should also be prepared. The details of any structured sorts that are required should also be finalized.

The fact that the MSP is used in tandem with a form of analysis that permits smaller sample sizes means that it is quite realistic to partition a plot resulting from the sorts of about six people. Obviously if two or more groups are being compared there should be a corresponding increase in the sample size.

Once willing participants have been identified the task is carried out as follows. First, the purpose of the task is explained. The interviewee is then given the cards and asked to familiarize him or herself with them. The instructions for the sorting task are read to them and they would carry out as many free sorts as they were able. Following these, or possibly interspersed with these, they are asked to complete any structured sorts as appropriate. During this process participants are encouraged to verbalize what they are doing (this can be recorded with the informed consent of participants and appropriate assurances of anonymity or confidentiality). Participants are thanked for their time and given the opportunity to receive details of the results if they are interested.

The researcher should record all the sort information as outlined above and proceed with the process of describing, analysing and interpreting the data. When the focus of the research question is on the way in which different groups might conceptualize a particular domain, the researcher should present the overall plot for each group that has the elements labelled and that is partitioned on the basis of the item plots. It is also possible, and can be useful, to present altern- ative partitionings. The coefficient of contiguity for each overall plot should also be reported. If this task is completed for an assignment it is helpful to include the item plots as an appendix in order that the plausibility of the interpretation can be assessed. Wilson & Hammond (2000) suggests that a more cautious approach to partitioning may be advisable at the early stages. Here the overall plot would be presented simply with the points labelled. Provisional assessments of the rela- tionships between the elements would be discussed in the light of the partitioned item plots.

Notes for the Course Leader

Use of the recommended non-metric multidimensional scaling pro- cedures is tolerant of small sample sizes. Thus for a class exercise, students could work in groups of three or four and not need ask more than two people each to participate in the sorting task in order to generate an appropriate data matrix. Of course if the focus of the exercise were located in a research question that required exploration of the differences between groups, a corresponding increase in the number of participants would be required.

It can be useful to initially input the data into a program such as Excel. This allows for more convenient manipulation of the data file. For example, the student may have a rationale for only including particular sorts in the analysis. The necessary deletion of columns is easier and less likely to lead to error outside of a DOS environment.

The MSP and its associated analyses allow a flexible exploration of conceptual systems for both individuals and groups. It has a number of possible applications and can help answer a number of different research questions.

Further ways in which the exercise might be refined would include the following.

- As noted, the MSP can be very effective in exploring differences between the groups. One group may see several cards as being very similar, another group may see them as quite different. It may be that that the cards are profiled in a similar way by different groups but that there are quite different reasons for this. The analysis and interpretation of the MSP can depict both of these possibilities.

- Other information, from either the sorting task or from other interview material, can be superimposed on to the plot, for example if, as a structured sort, participants were asked to sort the elements in relation to how much they knew about them, a mean knowledge score could be derived for each element and these can be mapped on to the points in the overall plot. This allows some assessment of the extent to which a particular parameter (e.g. knowledge) may or may not underlie the representations of a particular group.

- It is also possible to assess the difference that the introduction of a new piece of information makes to the way in which people sort the cards. An example of this can be seen in the work of Scott & Canter (1997). Initially photographs of places were sorted. In a second sort participants were asked to look at the photos but to sort them on the basis of what their imaginations told them that the place looked and felt like and how it would be experienced. In this way the focus was moved from the photograph to the place itself.

- It can be informative to limit the sorts that are included in the analysis. For example, first sorts only could be used, or only sorts that refer to a particular theme. This would give a clearer picture of how the elements were conceptualized with respect to one issue only. In some versions of available programs there are restrictions on the numbers of columns and rows that can be included.

All of these possible uses of the MSP and the associated analyses have the potential to systematically capture complex, perhaps ambivalent and apparently contradictory attitudes and represent these visually.

REFERENCES

Brown, J. (1985). *An introduction to the uses of facet theory*. New York: Springer Verlag.

Brown, J. & Barnett, J. (2000). Facet theory: an approach to research. In G. Breakwell, S. Hammond & C. Fife-Schaw (eds.), *Research methods in psychology* (pp. 105–18). London: Sage.

Bruner, J., Goodnow, J. & Austin, G. (1956). *A study of thinking*. New York: Wiley.

Canter, D. V., Brown, J. & Groat, L. (1985). A multiple sorting procedure for studying conceptual systems. In M. Brenner, J. Brown & D. V. Canter (eds.), *The research interview: Uses and approaches* (pp. 79–104). London: Academic Press.

Deschamps, J.-C. & Doise, W. (1978). Crossed category memberships in intergroup relations. In H. Tajfel (ed.), *Differentiation between social groups: Studies in the social psychology of intergroup relations* (pp. 141–58). London: Academic Press.

Evans, G. A. (1999). The Human Genome Project and public policy. *Public Understanding Of Science, 8*, 161–8.

Fransella, F. & Bannister, D. (1977). *A manual for repertory grid technique*. London: Academic Press.

Groat, L. (1982). Meaning in post-modern architecture: An examination using the multiple sorting task. *Journal of Environmental Psychology, 2*(3), 3–22.

Hammond, S. (2000) Introduction to multivariate data analysis. In G. Breakwell, S. Hammond & C. Fife-Schaw (eds.), *Research Methods in Psychology* (pp. 372–96). London: Sage.

Hampson, S. E. & Glasgow, R. E. (1996). Dimensional complexity of older patients' illness representations of arthritis and diabetes. *Basic and Applied Social Psychology, 18*, 45–59.

Hubbard, P. (1997). Diverging attitudes of planners and the public: An examination of architectural interpretation. *Journal of Architectural and Planning Research, 14*, 317–28.

Kelly, G. (1955). *The psychology of personal constructs*. Norton: New York.

Kramer, B. (1995). Classification of generic places – explorations with implications for evaluation. *Journal of Environmental Psychology, 15*, 3–22.

Lingoes, J. (1968). The multivariate analysis of qualitative data. *Multivariate Behavioral Research, 3*, 61–94.

Martin, P. & Kaye, J. (1999). *The use of biological sample collections and personal medical information in human genetics research*. The Wellcome Trust, November 1999. Avalable at <http://www.wellcome.ac.uk/en/images/DNAsamplecollection_background_2261.pdf>.

McGuickin, G. K. & Brown, J. (2001). Managing risk from sex offenders living in communities: Comparing police, press and the public. *Risk Management: An International Journal, 3* (1).

Merz, J. F. (1997). Psychosocial risks of storing and using human tissues in research. *Risk: Health, Safety and Environment, 8*, 237.

Morrison, P. & Bauer, I. (1993). A clinical-application of the multiple sorting technique. *International Journal of Nursing Studies, 30,* 511–18.

Rosch, E. (1977). Human categorization. In N. Warren (ed.), *Studies in cross cultural psychology* (vol.1, pp. 1–49). London: Academic Press.

Rosenberg, S. & Kim, M. P. (1975). The method of sorting: A data gathering procedure in multivariate research. *Multivariate Behavioral Research,* October, 489–502.

Scott, M. J. & Canter, D. V. (1997). Picture or place? A multiple sorting study of landscape. *Journal of Environmental Psychology, 17,* 263–81.

Shalit, B. (1977). Structural ambiguity and limits to coping. *Journal of Human Stress, 3,* 32–46.

Shepherd, E. & Watson, J. P. (1982). *Personal meanings.* Chichester, UK: Wiley.

Sixsmith, J. A. & Sixsmith, A. J. (1987). Empirical phenomenology: principles and method. *Quality and Quantity, 21*(3), 313–33.

Smith, E. E. & Medin, D. L. (1981). *Categories and concepts.* London: Harvard University Press.

Vygotsky, L. (1934). *Thought and language.* Hillside, NJ: Erlbaum.

Wilson, M. & Canter, D. V. (1990). The development of central concepts during professional education: an example of a multivariate model of the concept of architectural style. *Applied Psychology: An International Review, 39*(4), 431–55.

Wilson, M. & Hammond, S. (2000). Structuring qualitative data: Multidimensional scalogram analysis. In G. Breakwell, S. Hammond & C. Fife-Schaw (eds.), *Research Methods in Psychology* (pp. 281–93). London: Sage.

Zvulun, E. (1978). Multi-dimensional scalogram analysis: The method and its application. In S. Shye (ed.), *Theory construction and data analysis in the behavioural sciences* (pp. 237–64). San Francisco: Jossey Bass.

CHAPTER THIRTEEN

The Laddering Technique

Susan Miles & Gene Rowe

This chapter introduces the laddering technique. This is an approach to self-report data elicitation and data recording that can be used in interviewing to impose a systematic framework upon questioning, and in analysis to allow complex themes across answers to be represented. The technique incorporates the sorting procedures described in chapter 12. However, instead of relying solely on statistical procedures to reveal patterns in the data, laddering can also require participants to expose and explain such patterns. Laddering is concerned with linkages between concepts elicited from the participant, for instance between behaviour, beliefs, attitudes and values associated with a specific object. This chapter is suitable for advanced level courses.

Introduction: What is the Laddering Technique?

Combining data from separate interviews can be difficult, even if this is a desirable objective (i.e. if one wishes to draw trends from several interviews rather than treating each as, effectively, a unique case study). The extent to which this is practical and theoretically possible varies according to the amount and similarity of structure that exists across and within the different interviews. Essentially, the greater the similarity of any set of interviews (in terms of location, interviewer, questions asked, and so on), the more valid it becomes to merge the obtained data and perform quantitative, as opposed to qualitative, analyses. Over recent years, a specific form of interviewing called 'laddering' has emerged, that seeks to take a structured approach to the data-gathering process. Although it initially had its roots in the domain of personality psychology, it has been primarily used as a knowledge-elicitation technique in the field of advertising and marketing (e.g. Gutman, 1982; Reynolds & Gutman, 1984). Its precise aim is to get from attributes of a product to the underlying personal values thought to influence purchase decisions. It does, however, have wider potential applicability, and it has recently been applied in the social psychology domain to investigate consumer attitudes (Bredahl, 1999; Miles & Frewer, 2001).

Although the term 'laddering' refers specifically to the interview process, the technique comes with associated procedures for dealing with the pre- and post-interview context that might also be considered to belong to the technique as a whole. In this chapter, we consider laddering using this wider, more inclusive, definition. We take the reader through the entire 'laddering' process, from the elicitation of the attributes that form the focus of the laddering interview, through the conduct of such interviews, to the various means for representing the interview results and for analysing the obtained data. A questionnaire-based alternative to the laddering interview, namely, the 'paper-and-pencil' method, will also be detailed.

ORIGINS IN PSYCHOLOGY: PERSONAL CONSTRUCT THEORY

The origin of laddering is attributed to Hinkle (see Butt, 1965). It was developed as a method for use with the repertory grid technique in order to elicit and organize 'personal constructs' as theorized in Kelly's personal construct theory (1955). The importance of this theory to the development and present practice of the laddering approach is tenuous, but it is worth briefly noting the key aspects of the theory and describing the repertory grid, which may be included as part of the wider laddering approach.

Kelly's theory posits that humans are, in essence, natural scientists. We hold theories about the world through which we predict events. Depending upon actual outcomes, and importantly, how we interpret these outcomes, our theories may be perceived to be validated or falsified, with implications for our subsequent behaviour. These personal theories are based upon our 'personal constructs', which in traditional personal construct theory are dichotomous distinctions (good–evil, happy–sad and so on) that are organized in a hierarchical way. Constructs that are higher up the construct system are in a sense more fundamental to us, to our personality, and how we perceive the world. Understanding these constructs, and how they are arranged, therefore has significance for human personality and implications for psychopathology.

The repertory grid method was developed to elicit such personal constructs. It was designed to help the participant discover the fundamental constructs they use for perceiving and relating to others. As traditionally used in clinical settings, the participant is required to name the most important figures (people) in their life, which are known as 'elements'. These elements are written on separate cards. Next, the participant is presented with three of the elements and asked to say in what way two are alike, and different from the third. The participant's responses constitute their personal constructs, and are expressed in a bipolar way. For example, the difference between two alike people and the different third may be that the two are friendly and the third is unfriendly, hence a friendly–unfriendly dichotomous construct. The participant then assigns each of the remaining elements to one pole of the construct, in this example classifying each named person (element) as friendly or unfriendly. The participant is then presented with further combinations of three elements, and generates other constructs distinguishing between these. This process is repeated until the participant has produced all the constructs they can or until the investigator judges a sufficient number has been produced (Gross, 1996).

Although the repertory grid procedure identifies constructs, it says little about the hierarchical relationship between these. Laddering was developed with the aim of clarifying the relations between constructs that have been elicited using the repertory grid method, and ordering them into hierarchical relations. In particular, laddering was used to elicit superordinate constructs from subordinate ones (Hinkle, 1965, cited in Butt, 1995). We will describe in detail how it tries to do so later.

DEVELOPMENT IN ADVERTISING: MEANS–END THEORY

Although the origin of laddering is attributed to a domain of psychology, its growth and development has subsequently come about in an entirely different field with a different theoretical underpinning. That is, the laddering technique (modelled after Hinkle's technique) has become a tool used in the advertising and marketing domain, based on means–end theory.

Means–end theory is concerned with the meanings consumers obtain from products they purchase and use/consume. It suggests that the physical attributes of products have personal relevance or meaning for consumers on which they base, for example, purchasing decisions (e.g. Gengler, Mulvey & Oglethorpe, 1999). In particular, it posits that consumers select products with attributes that lead to desired consequences, which are determined by personal values associated with those consequences (Mulvey, Olson, Celsi & Walker, 1994; Gengler et al., 1999). It is useful to distinguish between three levels of abstraction. *Attributes* are the concrete, physical or observable characteristics of the product. *Consequences* are more abstract and refer to what the product does for, or provides to, the consumer (at the functional or psychosocial level) in terms of benefits or costs. *Values* are highly abstract; they are the higher-order outcomes or ends, representing the consumers' needs, goals and beliefs. They are the end states the consumer is trying to achieve through purchase behaviour. As an example, consider the following attribute-consequence-value chain for chocolate: attribute = creamy texture, consequence = enjoy taste, value = happiness. The pattern of associations from product attributes, through the consequences produced by these attributes to the end values, represents a knowledge structure called a means–end chain, and also referred to as an attribute-consequence-value (ACV) chain.

Means–end theory posits that there is a hierarchical structure linking attributes of a product to consequences attained by that product and then to personal values held by consumers (Gengler et al., 1999; ter Hofstede, Audernaert, Steenkamp & Wedel, 1998). The laddering technique can be used to assess such hierarchical structures. The technique is known as 'laddering' because it forces the participant up a 'ladder of abstraction' by linking concrete product attributes with more abstract consequences and values (Gengler et al., 1999). Specifically, it aims to elicit the associations between the attributes of a product (the means), the consequences for the participant provided by the attributes, and the participant's personal values (the ends). Initially, the participant is asked to generate important attributes that they associate with a product. They are then asked why these attributes are important, using simple probes like 'Why is that important to you?' The elicited reason is probed until the ACV chain is exhausted, with responses moving from tangible product attributes to personally relevant and desired end values. In the next section, we discuss the method more fully.

The Laddering Technique

The laddering technique can be considered to comprise three parts. In the first part, concrete attributes are elicited. In the second, the attributes are laddered to produce attribute-consequence-value chains.

This can be done using a laddering interview (a one-to-one in-depth interview providing qualitative information) or the 'paper-and-pencil' technique (a questionnaire-based version of the interview). In the third part, results from the laddering are represented and analysed. In this section we consider, in turn, the methods and issues related to the three parts of the technique.

ELICITING ATTRIBUTES

Attributes can range from physical characteristics of products (as in the advertising domain) to personality characteristics of people (as in clinical settings). In other words, they are lower order characteristics that are in some sense associated with, or have implications for, higher order cognitive processes (beliefs, attitudes, etc.). Various methods exist (often borrowed from elsewhere in psychology) for eliciting these attributes (Reynolds & Gutman, 1988). In this section we describe these methods and discuss their relative merits.

Methods of elicitation

Bech-Larsen, Nielsen, Grunert & Sorensen (1997) identify five main methods, which we describe below.

1 *Triadic sorting*. This is the elicitation procedure used in the repertory grid method developed by Kelly (1955). In this, participants are asked to consider three items and come up with ways in which two are similar and yet different from the third. The responses are taken as the attributes that will be used in the laddering interview. Responses are likely to be bipolar. For example, in considering three brands of chocolate (in an advertising context), the distinction might be that 'two are sweet and one is not', in which case 'sweetness' would be taken as the attribute.
2 *Ranking*. This is also known as 'preference-consumption differences' when investigating products. In this, participants generate a preference order for items and then say why they prefer the most preferred item to the second, and so on. These preference reasons are the attributes that will be used in the laddering interview.
3 *Attribute list*. In this, the participants are provided with a list of previously generated attributes and have to pick their preferred attributes according to some criteria, such as perceived importance. For example, clothing might be described as 'comfortable', 'warm', 'colourful', 'stylish' and so on, and participants might be asked to

choose which are most important to them when deciding upon whether to buy clothes. The preferred attributes are used in the laddering interview. The list is generated prior to the laddering interview, and can be produced by the investigator or by the same participants (on a different occasion), or by other participants, for example during a focus group. When the attribute list is generated by the investigator, the exercise may generally be considered to have less ecological validity than when participants themselves are responsible for the list, but this may be justified for practical or theoretical reasons (e.g. when testing a specific hypothesis).

4 *Free sorting.* Here, participants group a large number of products or items (usually presented on cards) in terms of similarities between products in a group, and differences compared to products in another group. The participant states the ways in which the products in each group are similar to each other and different from products in other groups. This method is similar to the triadic sorting method, although in free sorting there can be as many groups, and products in each group, as the participant wishes.

5 *Free/direct elicitation.* In this method, participants generate the attributes most important to them when they are thinking about, or choosing between the products or items. The *context distinction* technique can be used prior to elicitation using any of these methods. Here, the participant is presented with a meaningful context in which they can make distinctions (Reynolds & Gutman, 1988). For example, a participant might be asked to imagine the last time they had bought a similar product, or asked to envisage going into a shop under certain defined circumstances.

Which elicitation technique is best?

The types of attributes elicited will depend upon the elicitation method used (Grunert, Grunert & Sorensen, 1995). However, there is little evidence to suggest which technique is most appropriate in any given situation. One study has compared the five elicitation techniques described above on a number of criteria for low-involvement products (Bech-Larsen et al., 1997). The authors concluded that the elicitation technique selected should be determined by the purpose of the study, suggesting that one should use the *attribute list* elicitation technique when the goal is to *predict choice*, use *free sorting* when the aim is to *identify participant cognitive structure* with respect to the product or topic, and use *free/direct elicitation* for *exploratory studies of new areas of behaviour* (the reader should be aware, though, that this report is not peer reviewed and more research is required in this area).

Bech-Larsen et al. (1997) further suggest that elicitation techniques that only constrain and guide the answers of participants to a limited degree (e.g. free/direct elicitation), can result in attributes that are viewed as more important by participants than attributes generated by techniques such as triadic sorting and free sorting. Grunert et al. (1995) pointed out that elicitation techniques such as triadic and free sorting emphasize the visible differences between the products being sorted, and as such may lead to the generation of irrelevant attributes such as size or colour of packaging, which in turn may lead to short, inconsequential ladders.

Another practical aspect that needs to be considered in the choice of elicitation method is the time constraints in conducting interviews, with the time required generally increasing with the number of attributes being laddered. Generally, the number of attributes elicited will be a consequence of (1) the complexity of the issue, and (2) the constraints posed by the investigator through the choice and enact-ment of elicitation method. Indeed, an elicitation exercise might eas-ily generate too many attributes to ladder, necessitating the selection of a reduced sub-set. But how should one determine which attributes to ladder? The number of elicited attributes may be constrained by the investigator so that the numbers problem never becomes evident; this is true for each of the five elicitation techniques (e.g. one could determine to elicit only five attributes per participant, and conduct only enough triadic comparisons to achieve this). However, in a com-plex task, such constraints may inadequately sample participants' understanding of the issue. Regardless of the attribute elicitation method chosen, there are two ways of selecting the attributes to be laddered: attributes may be selected by the investigator on the basis of their own prior knowledge of the product category or topic, or the participants may be allowed to choose themselves, through rating the elicited attributes on some scale (such as 'importance'), with those attributes receiving the highest rating being subsequently laddered (Reynolds & Gutman, 1988). There is no evidence as to which of these two approaches is best, but clearly the latter has greater ecological validity (although at the expense of less control).

THE LADDERING INTERVIEW

Having elicited the attributes and selected those that will be laddered, the laddering interview begins. Essentially, this involves the particip-ant being asked why each attribute (in turn) is important, using a simple probe like 'Why is that important to you?' The reason given in response to this probe is similarly questioned. This process continues until the participant can respond no further. The procedure is then repeated for the rest of the attributes.

Hard and soft laddering

Before conducting the laddering interview, it is necessary to select the type of laddering that will be used. There are two types of laddering: hard and soft (Grunert et al., 1995). The hard laddering technique forces the participant to produce attribute-consequence-value chains one by one. Responses become increasingly more abstract as they move from attributes through consequences to values. In contrast, the soft laddering technique involves the participants' natural flow of speech being constrained as little as possible; it resembles a dialogue, with the ladders being constructed afterwards.

Jonas & Beckmann (1998) compared the responses of participants interviewed using both the hard and soft laddering techniques in the context of consumer perception of functional foods. Their results indicated that the hierarchical value maps (described in a later section) developed from interviews using hard laddering were more comprehensive and detailed than those developed from soft laddering interviews. The authors suggested that this could be due to hard laddering forcing participants to make more extensive use of their cognitive structures. However, in this study the participants had little natural knowledge about the topic. In other contexts, in which participants have a greater familiarity with the issue, it is possible that a soft laddering approach might result in a much richer and more comprehensive conceptualization of the issue. In any case, one might anticipate that the output from a soft laddering interview will be less clearly structured in terms of ACV chains than the output from hard laddering, requiring a greater amount of interpretation by the investigator.

Jonas & Beckmann also found that participants interviewed using hard laddering had a tendency to perceive the topic (functional foods) as positive (or at least, not negative), whilst participants interviewed using soft laddering were more sceptical about it. They suggested that this might be due to the participants interviewed using hard laddering only being required to say if an attribute is important or not, without being allowed to say *why* it is important. In contrast, participants interviewed using soft laddering are encouraged to say *everything* they want to about the product, which can include both positive and negative aspects. It is likely that this particular result was dependent upon the precise context of the interviews, and we should not generalize this finding of more positive perceptions from hard laddering to all situations without further research.

The interview environment

It is important to consider the interview environment to gain the most from the interview. Essentially, the interview environment should be non-threatening. It is important to gain and maintain rapport. The participants should view their responses as being recorded rather than judged. It has to be made clear before the interview that there are no right or wrong answers, and that the whole purpose of the interview is to understand the ways in which the participants see this particular set of products or topic. The participants are positioned as the experts, as the goal of the questioning is to understand the way in which they see the world. The interviewer is merely a trained facilitator of the discovery process and should be perceived as an interested, but neutral, recorder of information. The participants need to be willing to be introspective and look inside themselves for the underlying motivations behind their perceptions of a given product class or topic (Reynolds & Gutman, 1988).

Techniques used in the laddering interview

Often, during the course of an interview, participants may find it difficult to answer the question 'Why is that important to you?' Reynolds & Gutman (1988) describe a number of techniques that can be used in the interview process to overcome this.

1 The investigator provides a context for the participant to imagine whilst responding, for example: 'Imagine a situation where you are choosing a box of chocolates for a friend's birthday.'
2 The investigator can change the conversation to the third person by asking the participant how other people they know might act or feel in similar circumstances, for example: 'Why do you think your friends buy this brand of chocolate?' This technique can be useful if the issue becomes too sensitive (e.g. nearer the top of the ladder).
3 When the technique becomes too sensitive, another approach is for the investigator to leave that particular line of questioning and come back to the area later in the interview.
4 The investigator can ask the participant why they *do not* do certain things, or *do not* want to feel certain ways, for example: 'Why *wouldn't* you buy that particular brand of chocolate?' This technique is known as *negative laddering*.

5 Along similar lines, the investigator can ask the participant to imagine what it would be like if the product, attribute or consequence *was not present*, for example: 'What would you purchase if this brand of chocolate was not available to you?'
6 The investigator can ask the participant to imagine their behaviour some time in the past, and say how this compares to now, for example: 'Is there a difference in your purchase behaviour compared to a couple of years ago?'
7 The investigator can wait silently for the participant to continue.
8 The investigator can repeat back what the participant has just said and ask for clarification, for example: 'Now, let me see if I understand what you're saying. By 'quality' you mean . . . Is that right? So, why is that important to you?'
9 The investigator can rephrase the question or prompt to make it more concrete.

Methods of recording laddering interview data

The participants' responses in the laddering interview can be recorded in a number of different ways. They can be recorded using a Dictaphone, or recorded graphically or textually by the interviewer during the course of the interview. Such records will illustrate how each response leads to others. Graphical or textual recording during the interview enables the investigator to keep track of the participants' responses, to obtain clarification, or to check if the participants have anything more to add to a response. Dictaphone recording can be used in conjunction with graphical or textual recording. Below are examples of how you might record data. The topic under investigation here is chocolate.

In *textual* recording the starting item is followed by a line to separate it from subsequent responses. For example:

---

creamy texture
    enjoy taste
    good quality

enjoy taste
    happiness

In *graphical* recording the starting item is drawn in a bubble, and this is linked to other items by arcs. For example:

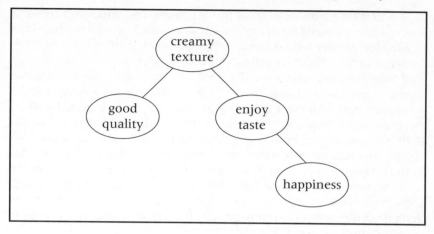

There is no evidence to suggest which recording method is best, but we would generally recommend graphical for hard laddering where typical ACV chains will be elicited, and textual for soft laddering where the participants' responses are likely to be less structured. Dictaphone recording is likely to be more useful when the soft laddering technique has been used, as the ladders have to be created from the participants' responses *after* the interview.

REPRESENTING AND ANALYSING THE RESULTS

Representing and analysing the results from laddering interviews can be a time-consuming affair. In order to aid in the process there is a software package known as 'LadderMap'. This program can be used to assist in content analysis, to create the implication matrix and to draw the hierarchical value map (see Gengler and Reynolds, 1995, for a description of its use). We describe all of the aspects involved in representation and analysis of data in the following section, taking the reader through the process in a step-by-step manner.

Content analysis

If soft laddering has been used, the raw interview data needs to be broken down into 'chunks' of responses before content analysis can be carried out. In contrast, if the hard laddering technique or 'paper-and-pencil' laddering have been used (see later section) the data will likely already be in chunks of responses that can be content analysed.

The first step is to classify all the interview responses as attributes, consequences or values. In the second stage, the investigator examines the laddering data with the goal of developing a comprehensive list of 'content codes'. These content codes consist of single words or phrases that together summarize *all* the responses made by the participants (there is no 'other' category). The aim is to be able to group similar responses and represent them by the same content code (Nielsen, Bech-Larsen & Grunert, 1998). The content codes will be more abstract than the answers themselves. For example, if laddering interviews about chocolate have resulted in the responses 'I love the taste of that brand', 'It tastes nice' and 'It has a good flavour', then an appropriate content code might be 'enjoy taste'. There is no formal approach to specifying content codes in laddering; content codes are simply developed through the common sense determination by the investigator of similarities between elicited statements. It is important to have codes that are general enough to allow replication of meaning, that is, to ensure that the cell frequencies in the aggregate implication matrix (described below) are not so low that the hierarchical value map (see below) cannot be created, but not so general that too much meaning is lost or dissimilar concepts are coded into the same content code (Reynolds & Gutman, 1988; Grunert et al., 1995).

In the third stage, the investigator and another rater assign all of the verbatim interview responses to the content codes (Reynolds & Gutman, 1988). Disagreements should be discussed until all the responses are categorized. At this time, a measure of inter-rater reliability can be taken to assess agreement between the two raters (often this is merely a figure for percentage agreement, although more formal methods also exist). It should be noted that not all ladders will follow the attribute, consequence, value sequence: some ladders may start at the attribute level and end at the consequence level, while others may start with consequences and may or may not end with values (Reynolds & Gutman, 1984).

Summary matrix

It is useful at this point to draw up a summary matrix (Reynolds & Gutman, 1988). Each content code is given a code number. Next, all of the ladders for each participant are drawn out in rows from left to right, with each row representing one ladder from one participant. Each participant can have multiple rows because they can have multiple ladders. This is known as a summary matrix because it summarizes all of the data from all the laddering interviews. It can be seen in Figure 13.1 that the interview participant Sam generated two ladders.

Participant						
Sam 1	1	3	15	20	30	
Sam 2	1	5	10	14		
Jo 1	1	10	12	15	33	46

Figure 13.1 An example summary matrix

The first ladder contained five concepts, and was thus five content codes long, and the second was four content codes long. In Figure 13.1, content code '1' might refer to the attribute 'creamy texture', whilst '3' might refer to the consequence 'good quality'.

The summary matrix allows the investigator to see the dominant connections, and provides the means for the data to be summarized by sub-groups if desired, such as gender (Reynolds & Gutman, 1988). The summary matrix represents the 'ladders' that have been elicited from participants. In contrast, the aggregate implication matrix and the hierarchical value map represent chains of concepts associated with the product or topic under investigation.

Aggregate implication matrix

The next step is to construct what is known as the aggregate implication matrix. This represents the linkages between the concepts (attributes, consequences and values) identified in the laddering interviews. These linkages are often called implications (Mulvey et al., 1994). It is a square table in which both the rows and the columns represent the content codes. The entries in the cells of the table illustrate the number of time each content code leads to each other content code across *all* participants. Here the aim is not to represent individual ladders, as was seen in the summary matrix, but to produce an aggregate representation of all the interview data.

One important decision that needs to be made when constructing the aggregate implication matrix is whether to count each time a single participant makes a connections between two concepts, or just count once. Mulvey et al. (1994) argue for counting connections made on a number of occasions by a participant only once, as this avoids over-weighting connections mentioned by verbose subjects. We concur and suggest this approach.

It is usual to represent both direct and indirect relations on the aggregate implication matrix. Direct relations are those in which one

	1 creamy texture (A)	2 enjoy taste (C)	3 good quality (C)	4 happiness (V)
1 creamy texture (A)		10.5	10.8	2.11
2 enjoy taste (C)	1.0		2.1	8.6
3 good quality (C)	0.0	2.0		10.8
4 happiness (V)	0.0	0.2	1.1	

Figure 13.2   An example aggregate implication matrix

content code leads directly to another. Indirect relations are those in which one content code leads to another with one or more other content codes in between. In the following example, *creamy texture – enjoy taste – happiness*, the links of *creamy texture* to *enjoy taste*, and *enjoy taste* to *happiness*, are direct relations, and the link of *creamy texture* to *happiness* is an indirect relation. In the aggregate implication matrix, direct and indirect relationships are both represented in the matrix cells in the format *direct.indirect* (see Figure 13.2).

In the example aggregate implication matrix illustrated in Figure 13.2 we see that content code '1 creamy texture' *leads to* '2 enjoy taste' 10 times directly and five times indirectly, and to '3 good quality' 10 times directly and eight times indirectly, and to '4 happiness' twice directly and 11 times indirectly. In contrast, '1 creamy texture' *follows* '2 enjoy taste' once directly (or, to put it another way, '2 enjoy taste' leads to '1 creamy texture' directly once and not at all indirectly). Cell diagonals are always 0, as a meaning cannot lead to, or be followed by, itself.

It is from the aggregate implication matrix that the hierarchical value map (HVM) is constructed. The HVM represents the content and structure of consumer knowledge regarding the product/topic in a graphical way.

Abstractness and centrality

Measures of abstractness and centrality can be calculated for all of the concepts represented in the implication matrix if the researcher desires (Botschen and Hemetsberger, 1998; Pieters, Bottschen & Thelen, 1998).

Centrality is a measure of the extent to which a concept is connected to all other concepts in the implication matrix. It is a measure of the importance of a concept in the means–end structure. Its value ranges from 0 to 1, where 0 indicates that the concept is not connected to any other concepts, and 1 indicates that it is connected to all other concepts. It is defined as *the ratio of the row sum plus the column sum of a meaning over the sum of all cell entries in the matrix*. For example, in Figure 13.2 'creamy texture' has a row sum of 46 (i.e. there are 22 direct and 24 indirect links to other concepts in the matrix) and a column sum of 1 (i.e. 1 direct and no indirect links). The sum of all the cell entries is 88 (i.e. all the values in the matrix, both direct and indirect). Therefore, the centrality value is $(46 + 1)/88 = 0.534$.

Abstractness is a measure of the extent to which concepts are predominantly means (at the beginning of ladders) or ends (at the end of ladders) in the perceptions of the participants. It ranges from 0 (less abstract) to 1 (more abstract). Means are low in abstractness and ends are high. It is defined as *the ratio of the column-sum to the column-sum plus the row-sum of a particular concept in the implication matrix*. For example, in Figure 13.2 'creamy texture' has a row sum of 46 and a column sum of 1. Therefore, the abstractness value is $1/(1 + 46) = 0.021$.

Abstractness and centrality values may be used for a number of purposes. They may aid in constructing a form of the HVM called the *directed graph* (see below). They may also be used as values for analysis, for example in comparing the most central concepts across different experimental groups. Pieters, Baumgartner & Stad (1994) describe an additional measure that can be calculated from the implication matrix, which they term 'prestige', but as this is not widely used we will discuss it no further.

Hierarchical value map (HVM)

There are two important considerations before drawing the HVM. First, it is necessary to decide whether to include both direct and indirect relations, or just direct. The advantage of representing the indirect relations is that, for example, content code 1 may lead to content code 3 on many occasions, but not enough times directly to be included. In addition, it may be that content codes 1 and 3 are indirectly linked by many participants though separated by different intermediate content codes, such that the implied link between these two codes may be lost from the hierarchical value map if indirect relations are omitted. As such, we suggest that both indirect and direct relations are used in constructing the HVM.

Secondly, it is necessary to decide upon a cut-off level (i.e. the number of times two content codes must have been linked to be included on the HVM). Reynolds & Gutman (1988) recommend using a cut-off level of 3–5 for 50–60 participants. However, Gengler &

Reynolds (1995) note that at least 70 per cent of the implications derived from the raw interview data should be represented. It is common practice to produce HVMs for several cut-off points and then select which one best represents the data in terms of interpretability (e.g. Bredahl, 1999; Reynolds & Gutman, 1988).

Having made these decisions, it is now time to draw the HVM. The aim of the HVM is to represent the interview data by ensuring that the dominant connections are illustrated, whilst still maintaining interpretability. As it is important that the HVM is readable, crossed lines should be avoided. Redundant connections do not need to be represented on the HVM. For example, if the connection between 'creamy texture' and 'enjoy taste' and the connection between 'enjoy taste' and 'happiness' are represented on the HVM, it is not necessary to represent the connection between 'creamy texture' and 'happiness' as this is implied by the other two connections (Gengler et al., 1999).

First, mark all the cells in the aggregate implication matrix that contain a value above the cut-off point (direct and indirect relations should be added together at this stage if both are being represented in the HVM). If we use a cut-off of 3, examining the example aggregate implication matrix in Figure 13.2, it can be seen that the connections '1 creamy texture – 2 enjoy taste', '1 creamy texture – 3 good quality', '1 creamy texture – 4 happiness', '2 enjoy taste – 3 good quality', '2 enjoy taste – 4 happiness' and '3 good quality – 4 happiness' all exceed the cut-off point, and thus will be represented on the HVM.

The next step is to examine the first row of the aggregate implication matrix for cells that exceed the cut-off. It can be seen that 'creamy texture – enjoy taste' has a value of 10.5 (indicating 10 direct and 5 indirect relations). This attribute-consequence connection is represented on the HVM by writing 'creamy texture' (an attribute) at the bottom of the page, then a line is drawn up to connect it with 'enjoy taste' (a consequence). This chain is continued by examining row 2 for 'enjoy taste' for associations above the cut-off. It can be seen that 'enjoy taste – good quality' exceeds the cut-off, and so a line is drawn across from 'enjoy taste' to 'good quality' (these are both consequences). The chain is then continued by examining connections in row 3 for 'good quality'. This is connected with 'happiness' and so a line is drawn up from 'good quality' to 'happiness' (a value). It is customary to draw HVMs so that the attributes are at the bottom of the page, and these are connected to consequences positioned higher up the page, and then to values that are at the top of the page (see Figure 13.3). This chain is complete, as examination of row 4 for 'happiness' does not reveal any further connections exceeding the cut-off value. The process continues by returning to row 1 and drawing

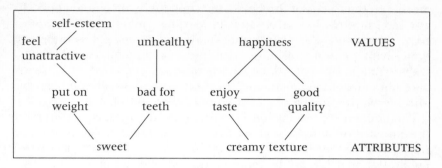

Figure 13.3 An example hierarchical value map (HVM)

out other connections between 'creamy texture' and other concepts that exceed the cut-off value. Thus connections between 'creamy texture', 'good quality' and 'happiness' need to be represented. However, the connection between 'creamy texture' and 'happiness' does not need to be represented, as it is a redundant connection: it is implied by the connections between 'creamy texture' and 'enjoy taste', and 'enjoy taste' and 'happiness'. This process continues until all the connections between the concepts above the specified cut-off value have been represented on the HVM, either in actuality or by implication (see the right side of the example HVM illustrated in Figure 13.3).

Generally this procedure will be fairly straightforward to implement for most data. Occasionally, however, the data represented in the implication matrix may prove more difficult to plot. This may occur, for example, when two consequences are found that both lead to each other and follow each other on enough occasions for both the cell entries to exceed the cut-off point, and hence, both relationships should in theory be plotted. Consider the consequences 'enjoy taste' and 'good quality' (see Figure 13.2). It is possible that a participant might say that 'enjoy taste' is important because it implies 'good quality', while another participant might say that 'good quality' is important to them in that it implies that they will 'enjoy the taste'. In Figure 13.2 we see that 'enjoy taste' leads to 'good quality' twice directly and once indirectly, and thus would be included on the HVM (because cut-off value has been set at 3). In contrast, 'good quality' leads to 'enjoy taste' twice directly, and in this case would not be included on the HVM. When both relationships occur often enough to exceed the cut-off, they should both be plotted, but how should one indicate hierarchical directionality here? There is no clear answer to this. One solution might be to indicate the relationship by including arrows on both ends of the line connecting the two content codes. In any case, it might be useful to reconsider the way in which the items have been content coded as they may in fact be representing the same theme, and might be recoded into one content code. Alternatively, it might be that a hierarchical relationship between the items does not in fact exist and one might want to consider alternative ways of representing the data (e.g. Miles & Frewer, 2001).

The strength of association between related concepts, in terms of the number of times a link between two content codes was made (as represented by the direct and indirect relations on the aggregate implication matrix), can be represented on the diagram in one of two ways. Numbers, representing the number of participants associating two content codes, can be placed beside the line connecting the two content codes (Miles & Frewer, 2001). Alternatively, the thickness of the line connecting two content codes can be used to represent the strength of association. Thicker lines can be used to link content codes that were associated together by more participants, and thinner lines can link content codes associated by fewer participants (Mulvey et al., 1994).

There are several alternatives to the HVM in terms of illustrating the interview data. One such alternative is the adaptation implication map (AIM). This is created in the same way as the HVM: its only difference is that instead of attributes, consequences and values, the concepts elicited and represented on the AIM are *customer perception cues, adaptive responses to those cues,* and the *consumer goals these adaptive responses are aimed at delivering* (Gengler, Howard & Zolner, 1995). Another variation is the consumer decision map (CDM), which is again created in the same way as the HVM, but with differently termed components (Gengler et al., 1999).

A third alternative is a directed graph (Pieters et al., 1998). This uses the concepts of abstractness and centrality. In essence, abstractness is plotted on the y axis and centrality on the x axis. Both values range from 0 to 1; however, centrality goes from 0 to 1 and then back to 0, in order that the most central concepts appear in the centre of the graph rather than at one extreme. A technique known as the additive tree (described below) is used to group related meanings either to the left or the right of the most central meanings. However, the values of abstractness and centrality used to create a directed graph are not the 'raw values' described above, but 'normalized' values that are transformed to ensure that the fullest range of values are graphed (i.e. that values range from 0 to 1, rather than from the narrower range that generally obtains). The formula is specified in Pieters et al. (1998).

Interpreting the data and further analysis

In most laddering studies the final stage of analysis is the interpretation of the HVM. The chains represented on the HVM are viewed as perceptual orientations regarding the product or topic under investigation (Reynolds & Gutman, 1988). Interpretation of the HVM generally consists of simply describing the connections between the concepts (attributes, consequences and values). However, some investigators have proposed use of supplementary analysis to add to the rigour of interpretation. Nielsen et al. (1998) used a correspondence analysis of the frequency with which a specific attribute was mentioned to supplement their HVMs. Grunert et al. (1995) note that techniques such as correspondence analysis result in a representation where cognitive categories are not linked in a network (as is the case with an HVM), but are placed in a multidimensional space, where distances are used to express association. Pieters et al. (1998) performed additive tree analysis on their implication matrix. This method illustrates groupings of related concepts, but does not indicate the direction of connections between concepts (the investigators used this method in combination with a directed graph, which does allow examination of which concepts *lead to* which other concepts). The precise ways to conduct these analyses are beyond the scope of this chapter, and the reader is directed to the noted references.

In the example provided in Figure 13.3, the HVM could be interpreted in the following way: *the brands of chocolate were associated with two attributes, 'creamy texture' and 'sweet'. Participants perceived the sweet taste of chocolate to be associated with the consequences of 'putting on weight' and 'being bad for teeth'. The negative effect of chocolate on teeth was associated with the value 'unhealthy'. The consequence 'put on weight' was associated with two values, 'feel unattractive' and 'self-esteem'. In contrast, the chocolate attribute 'creamy texture' was associated with the benefit 'enjoy the taste' and the perception of a creamy texture implying a 'good quality' chocolate. Both these consequences resulted in 'happiness'. Thus the perception of consumers with regard to these brands of chocolate are being directed by underlying values associated with happiness, health, feeling unattractive and self-esteem.*

VALIDATION AND PAPER-AND-PENCIL LADDERING

One of the difficulties with laddering interviews is the relatively small sample size obtained, and hence the issue arises as to the generalizability of results to the wider population. For this reason, it is preferable to validate the results of the interviews with a larger sample.

There are various ways of doing this. Grunert et al. (1995) described three ways of validating laddering data. In the first, participants are presented with a card-sorting task, in which the attributes, consequences and values derived from an earlier laddering study are written on three piles of cards. Participants are then required to pick the most important attribute for the product in question, and then the most important consequence and value following on from this. This procedure can be repeated for the second most important attribute, and so on. According to Grunert et al., this method has the advantage of producing ladders, as in a real laddering interview, so that similar analysis can be conducted as per the laddering interview. A second form of validation involves presenting participants with the actual ACV chains produced in the interviews and requiring them to rate how well the chain fits the product in question. For the best-fitting chains, the separate attributes, consequences and values can also be rated in terms of 'credibility' (i.e. how believable the chain is). A third method involves employing conjoint analysis (a complex analysis technique that we will not discuss here). All three methods assume that data collection has resulted in attribute-consequence-value chains (refer to Grunert et al., 1995 for further details of these studies).

A fourth validation method involves using data reduction techniques, such as principal components analysis (PCA). Statements may be created to represent the concepts (i.e. the attributes, consequences and values) identified in the laddering interviews. These statements may then be presented to a new (larger) sample of participants to be rated in terms of some criteria, such as participant agreement with the statement. Data reduction analysis may then be conducted to examine the relationships between statements, and to compare these relationships with the pattern of concepts identified in the laddering interviews (Miles & Frewer, 2001; Jansen-Verbeke and van Rekom, 1996). The item loadings on resulting components/factors can be compared to the associations of the concepts on the HVM. The two studies using this form of validation have each noted some success (see the next section, which describes the empirical laddering studies).

There is, however, a version of laddering that may not require validation because of its ability to be used with a larger sample of participants. This was developed by Walker & Olsen (1991) and is known as *paper-and-pencil laddering*. The technique may also be used as a method of validating the results from laddering interviews. Essentially it entails the use of a self-administered questionnaire. The process begins with the investigators deciding how many attributes they want the participant to generate (typically, participants are asked to generate four attributes) and how many subsequent responses they

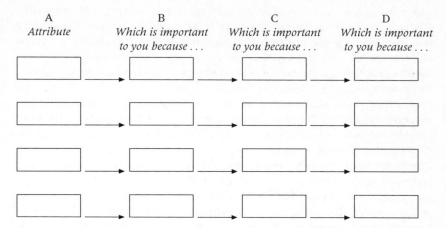

A	B	C	D
Attribute	*Which is important to you because . . .*	*Which is important to you because . . .*	*Which is important to you because . . .*

Figure 13.4   An example of the structure of a paper-and-pencil laddering questionnaire

require. The latter can be limited, for example, to three further responses, as illustrated in Figure 13.4, or the investigator can allow the participants to continue until they can go no further. In the questionnaire, this is operationalized through rows of boxes linked by arrows for each attribute.

First, the participants are required to state up to four important attributes concerning the product/topic under investigation. They write these in the boxes in column A (Figure 13.4). Next, the participants are required to state why the first attribute is important to them. This will usually produce a higher order response, for example a consequence. This response is placed in the box in column B, linked to the appropriate attribute by an arrow. The participants are then required to write why that response is important to them in the next box in column C. This pattern continues until the last box in the row is completed or until participants can respond no further. The procedure is repeated for the remaining attributes (Mulvey et al., 1994; Botschen & Hemetsberger, 1998).

There are several advantages to the paper-and-pencil version. First, data collection will be more driven by the participants' cognitive structures and thought processes than by the investigators'. Second, interviewer biases in both data collection and interpretation are reduced. Third, the participants are in more control of the procedure. Finally, data can be collected from a larger, more representative sample easily and cost-effectively (Botschen & Hemetsberger, 1998). The primary disadvantage of the paper-and-pencil version is that participants are often limited to a set number of attributes and subsequent responses for each attribute, although in reality their cognitive structure regarding the product or topic under investigation is likely to be more complex (Pieters et al., 1998). Furthermore, the absence of an interviewer means that there is no one to aid in the process should the participant have difficulty in completing the task.

Another method that may be used to validate data from laddering interviews is called the association pattern technique (APT). This may also be considered as an alternative method of measuring means–end chains. This is a quantitative method that can be used in mail questionnaires, allowing the investigators to collect from larger, more representative samples of consumers. Furthermore, it does not require any content analysis. The APT is inspired by Gutman (1982), who proposed that for measurement purposes the means–end chain can be conceived as a series of connected matrices. In APT there are two matrices, an AC-matrix (attribute-consequence) and a CV-matrix (consequence-value). The AC-matrix consists of *columns of attributes* and *rows of consequences*, resulting in a table of all combinations of attributes and consequence. The CV-matrix consists of *columns of consequences* and *rows of values* (ter Hofstede, Steenkamp & Wedel, 1999). The attributes, consequences and values to be used in the matrices can be obtained from a number of laddering interviews prior to implementation of the APT, or may be pre-specified by the investigator. The participants are presented with the AC-matrix and, taking each column (attribute) in turn, they are required to indicate (by a tick in the appropriate matrix cell) which consequences that attribute leads to. This procedure is repeated for the consequences and values in the CV-matrix.

The APT assumes that AC and CV linkages are independent (this is why the means–end chains can be separated into the two matrices), that is, that any links between a consequence and a value in the CV-matrix are independent of the links the participant makes between any attribute and that particular consequence in the AC-matrix.

One study examining the differences in the obtained data from laddering interviews and the APT found that the strengths of the linkages did not differ between laddering and APT (ter Hofstede et al., 1998). However, the two techniques differed in the content of the means–end chains network identified. Generally, the APT produced higher frequencies of occurrence of concepts than laddering did. The investigators suggested that this was to be expected, given that the APT involves *recognition* of concepts in the matrices while laddering involves *recall* of concepts associated with the product or topic under investigation. It is not possible to say which technique produces the most valid information, as in a recognition task participants may select more concepts than are actually relevant, and in a recall task participants may not remember concepts, or may mention unimportant concepts as a response to the interview situation. One disadvantage of the APT technique is that it provides a simplified representation of the means–end chain network in that it only considers links between concepts at adjoining levels, that is, A to C and C to V, not A to V.

Use of the Laddering Technique: Empirical Studies

In Table 13.1 we describe the published articles that have used the laddering technique empirically. The papers reported were found by searching the social science section of the Web of Science database of published research, using the search term 'laddering'. Additional studies (e.g. from edited books) were located by considering the references cited in the initially identified papers. It is unlikely that the included papers represent the entirety of published laddering studies, but they are likely to typify such research.

Table 13.1 details the various uses of the laddering techniques and the specific methods employed in the identified empirical papers. The first column provides references. The second column describes the tasks considered in the research, describing these as either 'exploratory' or 'hypothesis testing', and gives precise details of their aims. Columns three, four and five detail the elicitation method, laddering technique and representation/analysis of results, respectively. The final column comments upon additional issues of potential interest, such as methodological idiosyncrasies and results.

As can be seen from column two, most empirical studies have used laddering as an exploratory tool, often to consider the nature of cross-cultural differences, usually regarding beliefs about certain products. However, there are three examples of hypothesis testing. In each case, participants were effectively divided into two groups, and aspects of the results from the laddering process were compared using various types of inferential statistics. Gengler et al. (1995) tested whether automobile salesmen of low and high experience varied in terms of the numbers of concepts generated regarding consumers. Mulvey et al. (1994) considered whether degree of 'involvement' with a product (high or low) was related to number of concepts derived from laddering. And Pieters et al. (1994) tested whether software managers who varied on a personality scale had different numbers of concepts and links between these with regard to word processing

Table 13.1 Methodological details of the published empirical laddering studies

Reference	Task (exploratory or hypothesis testing)	Elicitation	Laddering details	Representation and analysis	Comments
Fotopoulos, Krystallis & Ness (2003)	Exploratory (perception of wine in organic and non-organic food buyers)	Attribute list (weight importance on 1–3 scale when purchasing wine; 'important' attributes laddered)	Interviews. No validation. 2 judges coded content.	HVMs. Used LadderMap software.	Authors stated that they used a 'soft laddering' approach.
Grunert, Lähteenmäki, Nielsen, Poulsen, Ueland & Åström (2001)	Exploratory (cross-cultural perception of genetically modified and non-genetically modified food products)	Ranking (ranking product descriptions according to buying intention)	Interviews. No validation. Individually coded in each country, then one researcher synchronized codes from the different countries.	HVMs. Used LadderMap software. Multiple Correspondence Analysis.	Found that 'non-genetically modified' was a value in itself; differences in perceptions found between the products, dependent on extent of genetic modification.
Jaeger & MacFie (2001)	Exploratory (perception of apples)	Free/direct elicitation (attributes considered when purchasing apples)	Interviews. No validation. 2 judges coded content.	HVMs. Used LadderMap software.	Laddering study included in appendix – used to provide data on means–end chains for use on study on expectations of advertising.
Klenosky, Templin & Troutman (2001)	Exploratory (collegiate student athletes school choice decisions)	Free/direct elicitation (attributes leading to choice of school)	Interviews. No validation. 2 judges coded content.	HVMs. Used LadderMap software.	Identified influences on students' selection of competing athletic programs.

Study	Purpose	Elicitation	Data collection	Analysis	Comments
Miles & Frewer (2001)	Exploratory (public perception of five food hazards)	Free/direct elicitation (what comes to mind about food hazard)	Interviews. Validation by principal components analysis (PCA) of questionnaire data from larger sample. 2 judges coded content.	HVMs (referred to as 'results diagrams').	Hazard characteristics and concerns elicited instead of attribute-consequence-value chains. PCA item loading matched pattern of associated characteristics and concerns on results diagrams for 3 of the 5 hazards.
Hunter & Beck (2000)	Exploratory (cross-cultural perceptions of systems analysts)	Triadic sorting (attributes of good systems analysts)	Interviews. No validation.	Repertory grid.	Only partial use of the technique: laddering used to help understand attitudes to the topic and aid repertory grid construction.
Roininen, Lähteenmäki & Tuorila (2000)	Exploratory (consumer perceptions of health/hedonic aspects of food)	Free sorting (sorting food into four groups re health/hedonic characteristics)	Interviews. No validation.	HVM. Multiple Correspondence Analysis.	Unclear number of content coders. Laddering not to value level (attribute and consequences only). After free sorting, attributes are generated for one 'representative' food in each of the four categories.
Bredahl (1999)	Exploratory (cross-cultural perceptions of genetic modification in food products)	Ranking (attributes of genetically modified products)	Interviews. No validation. One researcher synchronized codes from the different countries.	HVM. Multiple Correspondence Analysis.	More complex cognitive structures for some nationalities than others as seen in differences in HVMs.
Gengler, Mulvey & Oglethorpe (1999)	Exploratory (mothers' motivation to initiate/terminate breastfeeding)	Free/direct elicitation (attributes of initiating and terminating breastfeeding)	Interviews (by phone). No validation. 2 judges coded content.	Consumer Decision Map (like HVM). Thematic Analysis. Used LadderMap software.	Identified differences in initiating/terminating breastfeeding.

Table 13.1 (cont'd)

Reference	Task (exploratory or hypothesis testing)	Elicitation	Laddering details	Representation and analysis	Comments
Grunert & Beckmann (1999)	Exploratory (cross-cultural perceptions of food products)	Triadic sorting (attributes of food products)	Interviews. No validation.	HVMs. Used LadderMap software.	Differences in HVM structure between the groups, suggesting one had lower habitualisation in shopping behaviour than other (i.e. thought more about purchases).
Langerak, Peelen & Nijssen (1999)	Exploratory (experts establishing sequence for new product development – NPD–approaches)	Attribute list (selected which of nine NPD acceleration approaches they would use)	Interviews. No validation.	Abstractness, centrality and prestige indices calculated. Hierarchy of objectives guiding NPD approach selection developed using implication matrix.	Does not follow classic attempt to establish attributes, consequences and values. Experts selected which of nine generic NPD approaches they would use in future projects, then used laddering to identify objectives they seek to meet with each approach. Links between objectives generated, rather than typical ACV chains.
Ter Hofstede, Steenkamp & Wedel (1999)	Exploratory (cross-cultural perceptions of yoghurt)	Not clear: states 'the relevant attributes . . . were elicited' (p. 7)	Interviews. No validation per se, but data used to develop questionnaire for use on a larger sample.	A 'segmentation model' applied to questionnaire data revealing four segments charted in 'probabilistic means–end maps'.	Laddering interviews used to help define attribute–benefit and benefit–value matrices for inclusion in a questionnaire in which respondents indicated links between concepts. The procedure is referred to as the Association Pattern Technique (APT). Aim of paper to assess the segmentation model.

Reference	Purpose	Elicitation	Method	Analysis	Findings
Botschen & Hemetsberger (1998)	Exploratory (cross-cultural preferences for clothing brands)	Free/direct elicitation (four attributes of clothing)	Paper and pencil. 2 judges coded content.	Abstractness and centrality calculated and represented on HVMs.	Some differences in cognitive structures between nationalities, implying need for differential marketing for some aspects of product promotion.
Nielsen, Bech-Larsen & Grunert (1998)	Exploratory (cross-cultural perceptions of vegetable oils)	Free sorting into three groups, then ranking within the groups (attributes of vegetable oils)	Interviews. No validation.	HVMs. Correspondence analysis. Used LadderMap software.	Differences in structures found between the national groups in terms of knowledge and preference.
Pieters, Botschen & Thelen (1998)	Exploratory (consumer expectations of service employees when purchasing clothing)	Free/direct elicitation (four desired characteristics or behaviours of salespeople)	Paper and pencil. 2 judges coded content.	Abstractness and centrality calculated and used in developing HVMs. Additive Tree Analysis.	Additive tree analysis is described on p. 770. Results displayed in 'directed graphs'. Three orientations in consumer desire expectations identified.
Jansen-Verbeke & van Rekom (1996)	Exploratory (tourist motives for visiting museum)	Triadic sorting (attributes of why people visit a museum)	Interviews. Validation by factor analysis of questionnaire data from larger sample	HVMs. Additive Tree Analysis.	Identified five main motives, three of which seemed to correspond to factors in validation. Generally, this is a difficult to understand paper, with missing details on methodological aspects.
Gengler, Howard & Zolner (1995)	Hypothesis testing (is experience of automobile salesmen related to their behaviour adaptability with consumers?)	Triadic sorting (attributes of car-buying customers)	Interviews. No validation. 2 judges coded content.	Adaptation Implication Matrix (similar to HVM, but content different). T-tests.	Hypothesis testing: more experienced staff use more cues/concepts (etc.) than less experienced. HVM represents attributes, consequences and values; AIM represents customer perception cues, adaptive response to cues, and customer goals cues aimed at delivering.

Table 13.1 *(cont'd)*

Reference	Task (exploratory or hypothesis testing)	Elicitation	Laddering details	Representation and analysis	Comments
Mulvey, Olson, Celsi & Walker (1994)	Hypothesis testing (does higher 'involvement' activate more product-related knowledge re tennis rackets?)	Free/direct elicitation (four attributes considered when purchasing a tennis racket)	Paper and pencil. 2 judges coded content.	HVM. ANOVAs. Logistic regression analysis. Used LadderMap software.	Higher involvement activated more product-related knowledge during decision making. Sample was separated according to score on involvement measure into low, medium and high involvement, and differences between the groups analysed.
Pieters, Baumgartner & Stad (1994)	Hypothesis testing (are managers' perceptions of word processing software related to scores on an adaptive-innovative personality scale?)	Free/direct elicitation (five attributes of word processing software)	Paper and pencil. 2 judges coded content.	Abstractness, centrality and prestige calculated, and represented in HVM. Multiple correspondence analysis conducted but results not shown. Logistic regression analysis.	Respondents completed an adaptation-innovation scale, and were divided into two types, adaptive personality and innovative personality. Differences were found between these in terms of the number of meanings and nature of connections between meanings, according to predictions.

software. In each case, the issues considered had implications for advertising issues rather than fundamental research, although this does not mean that the technique may not be used for such purposes.

Of the five main types of elicitation procedure described earlier, each type is represented in the table, although two types (free/direct elicitation and triadic sorting) have been more commonly used in published empirical studies/research than the remaining three (column three of Table 13.1). It should be noted that the free/direct elicitation method is usually employed when the paper and pencil method is used. Gengler et al. (1999) conducted their laddering interviews over the phone, which may have practically limited their choice of elicitation method to the free/direct elicitation method.

Regarding the use of laddering *per se*, the table shows that there have been more uses of the interview than the paper and pencil approach. In the interview studies the use of validation is rare, only being described in two papers (Miles & Frewer, 2001; Jansen-Verbeke & van Rekom, 1996). In each case, questionnaires were produced on the basis of interview data, and data reduction analysis (e.g. factor analysis or principal components analysis) was conducted on the questionnaire results to see whether the factor structure bore any similarity to the means–ends chains initially produced (and indeed, both showed some similarity, partially validating the interviews). Validation is not generally necessary for paper and pencil laddering, as a larger, potentially more representative sample of the population of interest may be obtained. It is notable that two of the three studies which involved hypothesis-testing tasks used the paper and pencil method, which is perhaps apt, given the greater control of the process that exists with this method than with the interview (in which interviewer effects are potentially large), and given that it may be conducted with a large enough sample to enable inferential statistics to be used on results with the hope of obtaining significant findings. If one considers the 'representation and analysis' column in Table 13.1, it is clear that results from laddering interviews have tended to be displayed graphically, using the HVM, and then described from observation, rather than using inferential statistics.

In the 'laddering details' column we note whether the content coding of laddering data was conducted by multiple judges or not. Generally, there is an inconsistency in the reporting of laddering details, and hence the omission of a note about content analysis for any particular study should not be taken to mean that there were no reliability checks between coders, but that such details were unclear in the paper. In either case, however, this represents poor practice, either in terms of method reporting or enactment.

The Advantages and Disadvantages of the Laddering Technique

The question arises as to the utility of laddering and its value in comparison to other methods. Aside from the study of ter Hofstede et al. (1999), which investigated the association pattern technique as an alternative to laddering, there are no studies of which we are aware that compare the wider laddering technique (as a method for eliciting concepts and determining the links between these and their hierarchical structure) with other techniques that might fulfil similar functions. However, the laddering technique considered as a knowledge elicitation tool has been compared with a number of other knowledge elicitation techniques in several studies in the expert knowledge elicitation domain. In one such study, laddering interview data was compared with the data obtained from card sorting, interviewing and self-report (using role play) in the domain of expert medical diagnosis (Corbridge, Rugg, Major, Shadbolt & Burton, 1994). Results indicated that, whilst laddering took more time than card sorting, considerably more *concepts* were elicited. The traditional interviewing task and the self-report technique also resulted in fewer elicited concepts than the laddering task. Similar results have been reported by Burton and his colleagues in other expert knowledge domains (Burton, Shadbolt, Hedgecock & Rugg, 1987; Burton, Shadbolt, Rugg & Hedgecock, 1988). This suggests that the laddering interview is a fairly effective method for eliciting information. What is more, the information that laddering elicits is structured, and arguably easier to analyse than that obtained from less-structured approaches, such as the standard interview. Furthermore, the wider laddering technique provides a common framework for representing and analysing that data.

There are, however, several disadvantages to laddering interviews (Durgee, 1985/6). First, the interviews are both time-consuming and costly – although perhaps not more so than alternative procedures. Second, they require highly trained interviewers – though, again, the training should be no more difficult than for standard interviewing, and the laddering approach might easily be added to interviewer training courses. Both of these factors might militate against using this technique to collect data from large, representative samples (ter Hofstede et al., 1999), although this problem can be overcome by using laddering on a small sample and then validating the interview data with a larger sample. A third disadvantage is that the laddering interview process may lead to participant fatigue and boredom, particularly as the questioning method is very repetitive (this, however, is a hazard associated with other techniques). Relatedly, participants may not be able or willing to give honest answers. Furthermore, laddering might result in an artificial set of answers, as participants are forced to give justifications for things/feelings/behaviours that may mean very little in their everyday life. To some extent, these various concerns can be overcome by skilled interviewing, and by ensuring that the topic under consideration is of personal interest and meaning to the participants. A fourth difficulty is that both the interview and the analysis can be affected by interviewer bias. Once more, this is a problem that afflicts other procedures (e.g. traditional interviewing and interpreting answers to open-ended questions in questionnaires), and biases in analysis can be reduced by having several coders conduct the content analysis.

It has also been argued that the laddering interview, as traditionally used in advertising, tends not to produce anything new, but merely pulls out standard perceptions of the product (Durgee, 1985/6). This is unlikely to be such a concern when the laddering technique is used, for example, in an exploratory manner to investigate new topics, or to examine cross-cultural differences or when hypothesis testing.

One further potential problem that should be noted is that laddering leads to the aggregating of information over a number of people. To what extent it makes sense to merge the different links between concepts across people to produce an aggregate hierarchy is a matter of debate. This issue, however, is of more fundamental research interest, and one we cannot go into here.

The Exercise: What Makes a Good Lecturer?

This exercise is intended to provide the student with experience in the laddering technique. The formal procedure can be time-consuming, particularly with regard to the generation of content codes to describe interview data, and as such, the exercise is simplified to enable it to be conducted during a laboratory class. The exercise nevertheless requires the student to use many of the procedures that are typically used in the full laddering technique. Although you are free to choose any issue as a topic of research, we would suggest that the class investigate the question: 'What makes a good lecturer?' The following exercise (suitably adapted) might be used with any other question, although the alternative question/topic chosen should be one of personal relevance and importance to the class.

ORGANIZATION OF THE EXERCISE

For purposes of this exercise, the class should be split into pairs. One of each pair will act as the interviewer, and the other will act as the participant. Naturally, good practice in a real study dictates the use of only one or two interviewers in order to reduce variance from interviewer differences, but for the sake of the exercise this will be overlooked. The pairs should be spread throughout the room, or preferably dispersed to separate rooms if possible (again, it should be emphasized that in a 'real' exercise there should be a careful consideration of the interview environment).

Stage 1: introduction

First, the interviewer needs to explain the process to the participant. In their introductions, they should note the following things:

- The aim of the interview. Here, the topic is 'what do students believe makes a good lecturer?' The interviewer should explain that the interview aims to find out what the participant thinks are the characteristics of good lecturers, and to find out why.
- The interviewer needs to emphasize that there are no right or wrong answers and that the only goal of the interview is to find out what the participant thinks.
- The interviewer also needs to explain that the questioning may get a little repetitive, and needs to reassure the participant that this is just the questioning method.

Once the participant acknowledges that they understand the aims and process of the interview, then the exercise can begin.

Stage 2: attribute elicitation

The interviewer should contextualize the attribute elicitation by asking the participant to remember the last good lecture they attended, for example, saying: 'Remember the last good lecture you attended; think about why you felt it was good.' Give the participant a few moments to bring to mind the event.

The elicitation method we recommend here is the free/direct attribute elicitation method. This is the simplest approach. If more time is available, or the class is more advanced, then the triadic sorting or free sorting elicitation approaches might be tried, perhaps for comparison.

Using the direct elicitation method, interviewers need to ask the participants to name a certain number of attributes. In this case, we suggest that interviewers should ask participants to 'Name five attributes of a good lecturer'. This stage will result in five attributes that can be laddered.

Stage 3: the laddering interview

The hard laddering method will be used, as this provides data that requires less interpretation at the content analysis stage. The interviewer must also decide how he or she will record the interview data, either textual or graphical. In this case, we recommend using the graphical approach.

The interviewer begins by taking the first of the attributes, and asking the participant why that attribute is important to them. For example, try: 'When I asked you to name five attributes of a good lecturer, you responded *gives good handouts*. Please can you tell me why *gives good handouts* is important to you when you are thinking about good lecturers?'

Hopefully, this should result in the participant giving a 'higher order' (i.e. more abstract) response. For example: 'It means that I can check my lecture notes afterwards to be sure I understood what was said.'

The interviewer now needs to repeat the probe: 'Why is that important to you?' Here, for example, the participant might say: 'This improves my chance of getting good grades.' This process is repeated until the participant can respond no further. The aim is to elicit highly abstract values. In the case of this possible chain, the final item might be something like: 'Because it gives me a sense of self-importance.'

The interviewer should be careful to ensure that when the participant claims that they can go no further that they really cannot, by using some of the further prompting techniques as described in the subsection 'Techniques used in the laddering interview' above. We suggest that the interviewer has reference to this subsection and experiments with a variety of techniques throughout the interview.

Following the elicitation of the first ladder, the interviewer repeats the whole laddering process for the remaining four attributes in turn.

Stage 4: representation and analysis of results

Construction of the content code list cannot feasibly be done in a group situation. It is a time-consuming process that can take a couple of days. Usually it is done by one rater, and then the interview responses are allocated to the content codes by two raters (to ensure and check for reliability). We suggest that the course leader formulate a list of codes that he or she would expect to be appropriate given the research question. There is no simple rule for predicting the number of codes that may be needed. We would suggest generating about 30 codes, assuming approximately 30 students (approximately 15 attribute codes, 10 consequence codes and 5 value codes). For example, attributes might be: 'gives good notes', 'approachable', 'talks slowly'. Consequences might include: 'I have time to write notes', 'I understand the lecture'. And values might include 'personal self-esteem', 'desire to better self'. The reader must be aware that this is a simplification, and that, in practice, codes are generated from the data, not *a priori*.

Each student should allocate the concepts generated from their own ladders to the content codes, after which a group summary matrix can be created. During this process, the students will find that not all concepts can be allocated to the pre-generated codes. For example, in a particular ladder three of the four concepts might have appropriate codes and one might not. Clearly, one could not produce summary or aggregate implication matrices with such missing data. At this point, in the class, the group should consider all those concepts that the students have been unable to code, and additional codes should now be created. Once concepts from all students have been coded, redundant codes from the pre-generated set should be dropped.

Next, a summary matrix containing the interview data from each pair of students needs to be created. One person from each pair should write down the ladders generated from their interviews, in terms of the content codes, onto a blackboard/whiteboard in front of the class. Students should copy the entire summary matrix down.

There are now two options for this exercise depending on the time available in the class, or whether the course leader wants to dedicate another lesson to this exercise. If time is running short, the students can be instructed to complete the rest of the exercise at home individually or in the interviewer–interviewee pairs, to be handed in as an assignment or reported at a subsequent lesson. If time is not a problem then the following procedures can be carried out in class as a group exercise.

The first objective is to turn the summary matrix into the aggregate implication matrix. Summarize the ladders in the format of direct. indirect relations between the different concepts. Now decide upon a suitable cut-off value. Normally this would be determined by the complexity of the interview data, but we would suggest using a level of three, or two if the sample size is very small (of course this exercise is for demonstrative purposes, and students should be made aware of the importance of appropriate sample sizes and cut-off values). If a low cut-off means that too much data will be included on the HVM, a higher cut-off should be used. If a high cut-off means that the HVM is very 'bare', a lower cut-off should be used. Remember the aim of the HVM is to represent the interview data in an *interpretable* form.

The second objective is to calculate measures of centrality and abstractness from the aggregate implication matrix. Refer to the instructions in the subsection 'Abstractness and centrality' above to do this. Now, draw out the hierarchical value map using the aggregate implication matrix, as described in the subsection above on the HVM. The more 'abstract' concepts should occur at the top of the HVM, and the least 'abstract' at the bottom. The concepts with the highest 'centrality' scores should be connected to more of the other concepts than those with lower scores.

Finally, it is up to the students to interpret the HVM. Usually this is simply done by describing the pattern of relationships between the concepts. The students need to answer the question 'What do students believe makes a good lecturer?' The advanced students might wish to consider alternative questions, such as, how do male and female students differ in their perceptions (this would require dividing the data set into that from male and female students, and developing two aggregate implication matrices and two HVMs). Further analysis, using inferential statistics (t-tests, ANOVAs) might also be conducted, for example comparing the number of concepts generated by males and females during the exercise. Finally, the class should discuss the advantages and disadvantages of using the laddering technique.

Notes for the Course Leader

Although we suggest the question of what makes a good lecturer, the course leader is of course free to choose an alternative topic. The essence is that it must be a topic that the students have some interest and involvement in, that is, which is pertinent to them.

There may be a number of practical constraints that lead the course leader to prefer to use the 'paper-and-pencil' laddering technique for this exercise. For example, the 'paper-and-pencil' technique is quicker to complete, and can result in data that requires less interpretation at the content analysis stage.

Level of student. This exercise is suitable for any level of student.

Class size. Ideally one should have at least 30 students, but more is better. This would allow for 15 interviewers, with 15 interviewees providing data. If using the 'paper-and-pencil' technique, then each student would be providing data (there are no interviewers) and so a lower number would be acceptable.

Time available. This exercise should take around three hours, and would be suitable for a half-day experimental session. However, the time will clearly depend on the number of students, and a variety of other factors (e.g. how experienced the course leader is at using the technique). If time does prove to be a problem, the exercise can be split into two. The interviewing could take place on the first occasion and the analysis on the second. Alternatively, the analysis could be completed by the students out of course time and discussed in a later session.

Materials needed. Paper and pens are needed for recording the interview data and conducting the analysis. Ideally tape recorders/ Dicatophones should be used, but they are not necessary for this demonstration exercise.

The teaching assistants involved. No additional teaching assistants are necessary, although it would be useful to have one or more assistants circulating the room to ensure that the interviews are being conducted effectively.

The preparatory reading required. Reynolds & Gutman (1988), and Pieters et al. (1998) (if centrality and abstractness are to be calculated).

The statistical competence of the students. Generally, only low-level statistical competence is needed. In this exercise, basic mathematical skills are required to construct the implication matrix. Interpreting the HVM requires no additional skills. However, should some form of hypothesis testing take place, for example on differences between the perceptions of males and females, then competence in simple inferential statistics (t-tests and ANOVAs) is required.

REFERENCES

Bech-Larsen, T., Nielsen, N. A., Grunert, K. G. & Sorensen, E. (1997). Attributes of low involvement products – A comparison of five elicitation techniques and a test of their nomological validity. MAPP Report, No. 43. Aarrhus, Denmark: Centre for Market Surveillance, Research and Strategy for the Food Sector <http://www.mapp.hha.dk/default.html>.

Botschen, G. & Hemetsberger, A. (1998). Diagnosing means–end structures to determine the degree of potential marketing program standardization. *Journal of Business Research, 42,* 151–9.

Bredahl, L. (1999). Consumers' cognitions with regard to genetically modified foods. Results of a qualitative study in four countries. *Appetite, 33,* 343–60.

Burton, A. M., Shadbolt, N. R., Hedgecock, A. P. & Rugg, G. (1987). A formal evaluation of knowledge elicitation techniques for expert systems: Domain 1. In D. S. Moralee (ed.), *Research and development in expert systems IV* (pp. 136–45). Cambridge, UK: Cambridge University Press.

Burton, A. M., Shadbolt, N. R., Rugg, G. & Hedgecock, A. P. (1988). Knowledge elicitation techniques in classification domains. In Y. Kodratoff (ed.), *ECAI-88: Proceedings of the 8th European conference in artificial intelligence* (pp. 85–90). London: Pitman.

Butt, T. (1995). Ordinal relationships between constructs. *Journal of Constructivist Psychology, 8,* 227–36.

Corbridge, C., Rugg, G., Major, N. P., Shadbolt, N. R. & Burton, A. M. (1994). Laddering: Technique and tool use in knowledge acquisition. *Knowledge Acquisition, 6,* 315–41.

Durgee, J. F. (1985/86). Depth-interview techniques for creative advertising. *Journal of Advertising Research, 25*(6), 29–37.

Fotopoulos, C., Krystallis, A. & Ness, M. (2003). Wine produced by organic grapes in Greece: Using means–end chains analysis to reveal organic buyers' purchasing motives in comparison to the non-buyers. *Food Quality and Preference, 14,* 549–66.

Gengler, C. E., Howard, D. & Zolner, K. (1995). A personal construct analysis of adaptive selling and sales experience. *Psychology & Marketing, 12*(4), 287–304.

Gengler, C. E., Mulvey, M. S. & Oglethorpe, J. E. (1999). A means–ends analysis of mothers' infant feeding choices. *Journal of Public Policy & Marketing, 18*(2), 172–88.

Gengler, C. E. & Reynolds, T. J. (1995). Consumer understanding and advertising strategy: Analysis and strategic translation of laddering data. *Journal of Advertising Research*, July/August, 19–33.

Gross, R. (1996). *Psychology: The Science of Mind and Behaviour* (3rd edn.). London: Hodder & Stoughton.

Grunert, K. G. & Beckmann, S. C. (1999). A comparative analysis of the influence of economic culture on East and West German consumers' subjective product meanings. *Applied Psychology: An International Review, 48*(3), 367–90.

Grunert, K. G., Grunert, S. C. & Sorensen, E. (1995). Means–end chains and laddering: An inventory of problems and an agenda for research. MAPP Working Paper, No. 34. Aarrhus, Denmark: Centre for Market Surveillance, Research and Strategy for the Food Sector <http://www.mapp.hha.dk/default.html>.

Grunert, K. G., Lähteenmäki, L., Nielsen, N. A., Poulsen, J. B., Ueland, O. & Åström, A. (2001). Consumer perceptions of food products involving genetic modification – results from a qualitative study in four Nordic countries. *Food Quality and Preference, 12,* 527–42.

Gutman, J. (1982). A means–end chain model based on consumer categorization processes. *Journal of Marketing, 46,* 60–72.

Hunter, M. G. & Beck, J. E. (2000). Using repertory grids to conduct cross-cultural information systems research. *Information Systems Research, 11*(1), 93–101.

Jaeger, S. R. & MacFie, H. J. H. (2001). The effect of advertising format and means–end information on consumer expectations for apples. *Food Quality and Preference, 12,* 189–205.

Jansen-Verbeke, M. & van Rekom, J. (1996). Scanning museum visitors: Urban tourism marketing. *Annals of Tourism Research, 23*(2), 364–75.

Jonas, M. S. & Beckmann, S. C. (1998). Functional foods: Consumer perceptions in Denmark and England. MAPP Working Paper, No. 55. Aarrhus, Denmark: Centre for Market Surveillance, Research and Strategy for the Food Sector <http://www.mapp.hha.dk/default.html>.

Kelly, G. (1955). *The psychology of personal constructs.* Norton: New York.

Klenosky, D. B., Templin, T. J. & Troutman, J. A. (2001). Recruiting student athletes: A means–end investigation of school-choice decision making. *Journal of Sport Management, 15,* 95–106.

Langerak, F., Peelen, E. & Nijssen, E. (1999). A laddering approach to the use of methods and techniques to reduce the cycle time of new-to-the-firm products. *Journal of Product Innovation Management, 16,* 173–82.

Miles, S. & Frewer, L. J. (2001). Investigating specific concerns about different food hazards. *Food Quality and Preference, 12*(1), 47–61.

Mulvey, M. S., Olson, J. C., Celsi, R. L. & Walker, B. A. (1994). Exploring the relationships between means–end knowledge and involvement. *Advances in Consumer Research, 21,* 51–7.

Nielsen, N. A., Bech-Larsen, T. & Grunert, K. G. (1998). Consumer purchase motives and product perceptions: A laddering study on vegetable oil in three countries. *Food Quality and Preference, 9*(6), 455–66.

Pieters, R., Baumgartner, H. & Stad, H. (1994). Diagnosing means–end structures: The perception of wordprocessing software and the adaptive-innovative personality of managers. In J. Bloemer, J. Lemmink & H. Kaspar (eds.), *Proceedings of the 23rd EMAC Conference, 17–20 May* (pp. 749–62). Maastricht: EXAC.

Pieters, R., Botschen, G. & Thelen, E. (1998). Customer desire expectations about service employees: An analysis of hierarchical relations. *Psychology and Marketing, 15*(8), 755–73.

Reynolds, T. J. & Gutman, J. (1984). Laddering: Extending the repertory grid methodology to construct attribute-consequence-value hierarchies. In R. E. Pitts and A. G. Woodside (eds.), *Personal values and consumer psychology* (pp. 155–67). Lexington, MA: Lexington Books.

Reynolds, T. T. & Gutman, J. (1988). Laddering theory, method, analysis, and interpretation. *Journal of Advertising Research, 28*(1), 11–31.

Roininen, K., Lähteenmäki, L. & Tuorila, H. (2000). An application of means–end chain approach to consumers' orientation to health and hedonic characteristics of foods. *Ecology of Food and Nutrition, 39,* 61–81.

ter Hofstede, F., Audernaert, A., Steenkamp, J-B. E. M. & Wedel, M. (1998). An investigation into the association pattern technique as a quantitative approach to measuring means–end chains. *International Journal of Research in Marketing, 15,* 37–50.

Ter Hofstede, F., Steenkamp, J-B. E. M. & Wedel, M. (1999). International market segmentation based on consumer-product relations. *Journal of Marketing Research, 36,* 1–17.

Walker, B. A. & Olsen, J. C. (1991). Means–end chains: Connecting products with self. *Journal of Business Research, 22*(2), 111–18.

CHAPTER FOURTEEN

Focus Groups

Sue Wilkinson

This chapter introduces the principles and practicalities of running and analysing focus groups. A focus group is essentially an observational data elicitation method. It is a forum that allows the researcher to observe and record in a structured or semi-structured fashion the interactions (verbal and non-verbal) between a small group of individuals, around topics chosen by the researcher and most often in a direction stimulated by the researcher. It is thus an observational approach that normally involves substantial participation from the researcher. This chapter describes the use of thematic and content analysis for the recording and treatment of data elicited. It also provides a valuable appendix on handling the problems that sometimes emerge in running a focus group. The exercise involves a non-experimental design and is suitable for introductory level courses.

Introducing Focus Group Research

Most people these days have heard of focus groups. This is likely to be either in the context of market research, or in the contemporary political arena as a popular – if controversial – gauge of 'public opinion' (Wilkinson & Kitzinger, 2000). Focus groups are also a widely used research method across the social sciences – although, despite their popularity elsewhere, they were little used in social psychology until the 1990s.

The history of focus groups in social science research dates back to the 1920s, when psychologists Emory Bogardus and Walter Thurstone used them to develop survey instruments (although their 'invention' is more often credited to sociologist Robert Merton and his colleagues in the 1940s). Prior to the late 1970s, the main use of focus groups was as a market research tool, and most published studies were in the field of business and marketing – this is still an active area of focus group research today (Greenbaum, 1998). In the 1980s health researchers pioneered the use of focus groups in social action research, particularly in the fields of family planning and preventive health education; the method was then widely used to study sexual attitudes and behaviours, particularly in relation to HIV/AIDS; and it continues to be used extensively today in the areas of health education and health promotion (Basch, 1987), as well as in health research more generally (Carey, 1995; Wilkinson, 1998a). In the 1990s the burgeoning popularity of focus group research created a substantial literature on the method across a much wider range of disciplines, including education, communication and media studies, feminist research, sociology and social psychology (see Morgan 1996; Wilkinson, 1998b for reviews).

Focus group methodology is, at first sight, deceptively simple. It is a way of collecting data which essentially involves engaging a small number of people in an informal group discussion (or discussions), 'focused' around a particular topic or set of issues. This could be, for example, young women sharing experiences of dieting, single parents evaluating childcare facilities or sports enthusiasts comparing and contrasting training regimes. The discussion is usually based on a series of questions (the focus group 'schedule'), and the researcher generally acts as a 'moderator' (or facilitator) for the group: posing the questions, keeping the discussion flowing and encouraging people to participate fully. The moderator does *not* ask questions of each focus group participant in turn – but facilitates group discussion, actively encouraging group members to interact *with each other*. This interaction between research participants is a key feature of focus group research – and the one which most clearly distinguishes it from one-to-one interviews (Morgan, 1997). Compared with interviews, focus groups are much more 'naturalistic' (i.e. closer to everyday conversation), in that they typically include a range of communicative processes – such as storytelling, joking, arguing, boasting, teasing, persuasion, challenge and disagreement. The dynamic quality of group interaction, as participants discuss, debate and (sometimes) disagree about key issues, is generally a striking feature of focus groups – which, sometimes, may even have 'the feel of rap sessions with friends' (Jarrett, 1993, p. 194). Typically, the focus group discussion is audiotaped, and the data transcribed and then analysed using conventional techniques – most commonly content or thematic analysis.

However, as we shall see, focus group methodology involves much more than is initially apparent in terms of planning and preparation, and also requires a range of skills in data elicitation and analysis.

One likely reason for the contemporary popularity of focus group research is the flexibility of the method. Focus groups can be used as a stand-alone qualitative method, or combined with quantitative techniques as part of a multimethod project. They can be used within the social psychology laboratory or out in the field, to study the social world or to attempt to change it, for example in action research projects (see Wilkinson, 1999 for a review). At almost every stage of a focus group project, there are methodological choices to be made. A good way to get a sense of this variety is to flip through one of the recent edited collections of focus group research such as Barbour & Kitzinger (1999) or Morgan (1993). A focus group project can involve a single group of participants meeting on a single occasion, or it can involve many groups, with single or repeated meetings. It can involve as few as two, or as many as a dozen or so participants (the norm is between four and eight). These participants may be pre-existing groups of people (e.g. members of families, clubs or work teams), or they may be brought together specifically for the research, as representative of a particular population, or simply on the basis of shared characteristics or experiences (e.g. middle-aged men, sales assistants, sufferers of PMT). In addition to (or instead of) a set of questions, the moderator may present group members with particular stimulus materials (e.g. video clips, advertisements); and in addition to (or instead of) discussing particular questions, they may be asked to engage in a specified activity (e.g. a card-sorting task, a rating exercise). Kitzinger (1990) provides examples of a range of such activities in the context of researching AIDS media messages. The moderator may be relatively directive, or relatively non-directive. Proceedings may be audiotaped or videotaped (the former is more common in social science research). Data transcription may be more or less detailed – ranging from simple orthographic transcription (which preserves just the words spoken) to the complex form of transcription favoured by conversation analysts (which also preserves a range of linguistic and paralinguistic features, such as false starts, self-corrections, overlapping speech, pauses, volume and intonation). Data analysis may be by hand or computer-assisted (using programs such as NUD.IST or THE ETHNOGRAPH); and a variety of different types of data analysis may be undertaken – including content analysis, thematic analysis, narrative/biographical analysis and discursive/conversation analysis (see Wilkinson, 2000 for a comparison of three methods of analysis of a focus group on breast cancer).

Focus group research is not tied to a specific theoretical framework: the method can be used either within an 'essentialist' or within a 'social constructionist' framework. Focus group research conducted within an essentialist framework, like most psychological research, rests on the assumption that individuals have their own personal ideas, opinions and understandings, and that the task of the researcher is to access or elicit these 'cognitions'. Within this framework, the particular advantage of focus groups is the more comprehensive elicitation of individuals' ideas, opinions and understandings. Focus group research conducted within a social constructionist framework does *not* assume pre-existing cognitions located inside people's heads, but rather presupposes that sense-making is produced collaboratively, in the course of social interactions between people. Within this framework, the particular advantage of focus groups is the opportunity they offer for the researcher to observe how people engage in the process of collaborative sense-making: how views are constructed, expressed, defended and (sometimes) modified within the context of discussion and debate with others. The theoretical framework of the research will influence the kind of data analysis undertaken – essentialist research is likely to utilize content or thematic analysis, while social constructionist research is more likely to use narrative/biographical or discursive/conversation analysis.

Given this breadth and flexibility of use, focus groups are obviously a multipurpose method. However, they are not, as is sometimes assumed, 'a method for all seasons' – like any other method, they have particular advantages and disadvantages, and are demonstrably more suited to some kinds of research questions than others. Focus groups are a good choice of method when the purpose of the research is to elicit people's own understandings, opinions or views (this is an essentialist research question); or when it seeks to explore how these are advanced, elaborated and negotiated in a social context (this is often regarded as a social constructionist research question). They are less appropriate if the purpose of the research is to categorize or compare types of individuals and the views they hold, or to measure attitudes, opinions or beliefs (although they are sometimes used in this way). Focus group data are voluminous, relatively unstructured, and do not readily admit to summary analysis. While such data can be subjected to some limited quantification (as in content analysis), they are best reported in ways which preserve (at least some of) the participants' own words – that is, using illustrative quotations. Ideally, too, there should also be some analysis of group interactions (although, sadly, this is all too rare in the published literature). Focus groups are unlikely to be the method of choice when statistical data and generalizable findings are required: samples are usually small and unrepresentative, and it is difficult to make a good theoretical case for aggregating data across a number of diverse groups, or for making direct comparisons between groups (although, again, this is sometimes done).

There are also practical advantages and disadvantages to the use of focus groups. They have been seen as a way of collecting a large volume of data relatively quickly and cheaply. On the other hand, it can be difficult to recruit and bring together appropriate participants; moderating a group effectively is a skilled technique, which (ideally) requires training and practice; and data transcription and analysis (of whatever kind) is an extremely painstaking and time-consuming process, which requires a range of data-handling and interpretative skills. The following section offers a more detailed practical guide to what is involved in doing focus group research.

Doing Focus Group Research

The focus group literature includes a substantial number of 'handbooks', which offer a wealth of general information and advice about the process of doing focus group research, as well as a consideration of issues specific to particular types of focus group. The most useful of these guides for the social psychologist are: Krueger (1994), Morgan (1997), Stewart & Shamdasani (1990) and Vaughn, Schumm & Sinagub (1996); the most comprehensive is Morgan & Krueger (1998). Here, I draw both on the advice offered by these handbooks, and on my own experience of focus group research, to review the key stages of a focus project and to suggest the key practical considerations at each stage.

For any focus group to provide the best possible data (and to be a rewarding experience for the participants, which will also lead to the better data), two things – at least – are necessary: an effective moderator and a well-prepared session. Ideally, the moderator should have some basic interviewing skills, some knowledge of group dynamics and some experience of running group discussions. Although some of the skills involved in moderating a focus group are similar to those involved in one-to-one interviews (e.g. establishing rapport, effective use of prompts and probes, sensitivity to non-verbal cues), the number of research participants involved in a focus group requires more in terms of active 'people management'. The shy participant must be encouraged to speak, the talkative one discouraged at times, and instances of discomfiture and/or disagreement must be handled with care. The handbooks provide substantial detail on the principles of people management but are no substitute for the experience of moderating a focus group in practice. The most common mistakes of novice (and/or nervous) moderators are: failure to listen – and so follow-up appropriately, inability to tolerate silence, talking too much and sequential questioning. You should not embark on a focus group project without some kind of practice run – or, preferably, a full-scale pilot study. Proper preparation for, and efficient planning of, the focus group session itself is just as essential as moderator skills for obtaining high-quality data. A well-run focus group session might *look* effortless, but it almost certainly is not: a surprising amount of preparatory work is needed – before, during and after the session itself. Having determined that focus groups are an appropriate way to address your research question, here are some of the main practical considerations in setting up an effective focus group project.

DESIGN ISSUES

First, you will need to decide on the broad parameters of your project – that is, the overall timescale; how many focus groups you will run; what kind of focus groups they will be; the number and type of participants you will have (and how you will recruit them); and how you will record, transcribe and analyse your data. These parameters need to be set before you can address the more 'nitty gritty' practical issues below. In almost all cases the design of the research is likely to be a compromise between what would be ideal, and what is actually feasible, given the practical constraints of time, resources and your own expertise and energy.

ETHICAL ISSUES

Focus group research (like any other research in social psychology) must be conducted in accordance with ethical guidelines. Broadly speaking, you must obtain your participants' informed consent to take part, you are responsible for protecting their confidentiality and you should take all reasonable steps to ensure that they will not be subjected to any stress or anxiety over and above what they might reasonably experience in their everyday lives. Confidentiality is a particular issue within focus groups, because of the number of participants, and 'ground rules' must be set to ensure that personal details and potentially sensitive material are not discussed outside the context of the group. There are also some ethical issues specific to the interactional nature of focus group research. For example – very occasionally – a participant may be visibly worried or distressed by the experiences or opinions being aired, an argument may 'turn nasty' or several focus group members may collude to silence or intimidate a particular individual. It is important to handle such a situation immediately, within the group (this may include, in the last resort, terminating the session); it may also be necessary to address it further with the individual(s) involved once the group has finished. In practice, though, focus group research is usually an interesting, and often enjoyable, experience for all concerned, and such 'difficult situations' rarely occur. Finally, as with any research, it is a good idea to have contact details available for relevant counselling services, help lines, self-help groups and other sources of information, in case they are needed.

PREPARING MATERIALS

You will need (at least) a focus group schedule, perhaps also written or pictorial materials. In devising a schedule, make sure that it is likely to engage the participants, that it uses appropriate vocabulary, that the questions flow logically, that it provides the opportunity for a variety of viewpoints to be expressed and that it allows participants to raise points which may not have occurred to the researcher. Try out all the materials you intend to use – to ensure they are intelligible, legible, visible and the right length. If you are intending to use slides or video clips, make sure that the appropriate projectors are readily available, and that you know how to operate them. Write out your introduction to the session, including 'ground rules' for running it, and your closing comments (see also 'The session itself' below).

RECRUITING PARTICIPANTS

This is much harder than the novice researcher ever imagines. Make sure that potential participants know what's involved in the focus group procedure – this is part of giving informed consent. Consider whether you will pay them (or offer other incentives) and/or reimburse travel expenses. Always over-recruit by about 50 per cent (i.e. recruit nine participants for a six-person group) – however much enthusiasm/commitment participants express, some of them *always* fail to turn up on the day, for one reason or another. Make sure they have clear directions for finding the venue, and (particularly if you recruit some time in advance of the session) issue several reminders, including – most crucially – a phone call the day before the focus group itself.

CHOOSING THE VENUE

Sometimes – particularly in action research projects – there is no choice of venue: you have to conduct the focus group on the group's own 'territory' (e.g. wherever the participants usually meet, or wherever they are prepared to meet you), which may not be an ideal research environment. Where there is a choice, however, the main consideration is balancing participant comfort and a good recording environment. A few universities now have purpose-built 'focus group suites' (more often in the business school than the psychology department), and most psychology departments have a lab with a one-way mirror – this might be worth considering, particularly if observation/ videorecording is part of the project. Most important is a relatively comfortable quiet room where you won't be disturbed or under time pressure to finish. Participants should be seated in a circle – either in easy chairs, or around a table (note the different 'feel' of these two options). Easy access to lavatories and to a phone are essential.

PREPARING FOR THE SESSION

There are two aspects to this: thinking through the logistics of the day itself and preparing supplementary materials. It is ideal to have an assistant, especially for larger focus groups. Whether or not this is possible, think through how you will handle arrivals and departures (including late arrivals and early departures), refreshments, dealing with unforeseen queries or problems and taking notes and/or operating the recording equipment while moderating the group. Note that Murphy's law ('if anything can go wrong, it will') holds as much for focus groups as other types of research – but seems to apply particularly to recording equipment! This should be checked and double-checked before every group. In terms of supplementary materials, you will need some or all of the following:

- refreshments: water at least, preferably tea/coffee and biscuits (*not* alcohol) or depending on time of day and length of session, possibly simple food (e.g. sandwiches, pizza);
- writing materials (paper and pens) – for yourself and participants;

- informed consent forms and expenses claim forms;
- a box of paper tissues;
- name badges or cards (and marker pens to complete them);
- recording equipment, including spare tapes and batteries.

Set up the room well in advance, if possible, and check the recording equipment (again) just before using it.

THE SESSION ITSELF

The beginning and end of the focus group session entail specific practical considerations. The following activities are needed at the *beginning* of the session (not necessarily in this exact order):

- offering thanks, a welcome and introductions;
- attending to participants' comfort (refreshments, toilets, any special needs);
- signing consent forms (if not done at recruitment), including permission to record;
- reiterating issues of anonymity/confidentiality;
- completing name badges;
- recapping purpose of study;
- outlining procedure (including confirming finishing time);
- setting ground rules for running the group;
- providing an opportunity to ask questions.

Once it gets going, a good focus group discussion will appear almost to run itself. The discussion will 'flow' well – and it will seem to move seamlessly through the schedule – sometimes even without the moderator needing to ask the questions. Such apparent 'effortlessness' rests substantially upon good preparation and effective moderating skills (as well as a measure of good luck). A good focus group often over-runs, but always allow participants to leave at the agreed time, even if you haven't finished.

The following activities are needed at the *end* of the focus group (again not necessarily in this exact order):

- reiterating thanks;
- reiterating confidentiality;
- giving a further opportunity for questions;
- providing further information or possible sources of information (as appropriate);

- debriefing (as appropriate) – including on an individual basis as necessary;
- checking that participants have had a good experience (possibly formal evaluation);
- completing expenses claim forms (and making payment arrangements);
- offering appropriate farewells and/or information about any follow-ups.

TRANSCRIPTION AND ANALYSIS

The next step is to make back-up copies of all notes and tapes (which should be clearly labelled with the date, time and nature of the session). Keep them in a separate place from the originals. If you are transcribing your own data (as is usually the case), try to do this as soon as possible after the session, while it is still fresh in your mind. Transcription is really the first stage of data analysis, and a careful detailed transcription will facilitate the next steps (although the level of detail preserved in the transcription will depend on your research question and type of data analysis you plan to use – see earlier and example below). You should have decided long before this stage how you will analyse your data, in relation to your research question (again, see earlier, and examples of analysis given below). Both transcription and analysis are likely to take much longer than you might expect.

A Specific Exercise

So far, I have sketched out the process of doing focus group research in general terms. I move now to a specific exercise which can be conducted in social psychology practical classes.

A practical exercise using focus groups can only be regarded as a 'taster' for the method – but it is likely to give students a good sense of whether they might want to use it in future work. This part of the chapter details a specific focus group exercise, designed to be conducted over the course of (a minimum of) two three-hour undergraduate practical classes, including some (essential) student work between the two classes. I will assume a class of about 20 students (variations for smaller and larger classes are addressed in the tutor notes which follow). The procedure is greatly facilitated by the assistance of two demonstrators (although it can be managed with one).

The minimum facilities required are: two medium-sized rooms (preferably a lab and a 'comfortable room'), plus an additional small room; one set of audio-recording equipment (preferably plus an additional back-up set); tape-copying facilities; photocopying facilities; sticky labels and marker pens; and a range of paper-and-pencil materials as detailed in the Appendices below. Four 'Walkman'-type cassette players may also be needed for transcription (if students do not have their own).

The aims of the exercise are: (1) to use focus group methodology to investigate a substantive topic – cosmetic surgery; (2) to provide 'hands-on' experience of conducting a focus group and transcribing and analysing the data; (3) to compare two different methods of analysing focus group data (content analysis and thematic analysis); and (4) to evaluate focus group methodology as a research tool. The division of activities between weeks is as follows: in Week One, students are introduced to focus group research and run a focus group; between classes they transcribe the data; and in Week Two they work on data analysis and evaluation of the method. Typically, the analysis is not completed by the end of Week Two, but the framework(s) for analysis are in place, and the procedures to be followed are clear – enabling evaluation of the method to be undertaken (and also providing the option of students completing the analysis individually and submitting it as a piece of coursework, if desired). A third week would allow for completion of data analysis in class.

WEEK ONE

The students are not required to do any specific preparation before the first class – although they could be given a reading list on focus groups, and encouraged to look at at least one of the 'handbooks' (e.g. Krueger, 1994; Morgan, 1997) and/or at least one of the review articles (e.g. Morgan, 1996; Wilkinson, 1998b).

Step 1 – general introduction (30 mins max.)

The exercise begins with the tutor giving an introductory 'mini-lecture' on focus group research. This can be based on the first section of this chapter, augmented by some further details of specific focus group research projects – see the reference list below, particularly the edited collections by Barbour & Kitzinger (1999) and Morgan (1993). In case the tutor wishes to give the students the 'feel' of focus group research by means of an extended illustration from a single project,

I have included (in Appendix 14.1) a sample focus group schedule, taken from my own research on breast cancer (Wilkinson, 1998a, 1998b, 2000). A data extract from the same project is given as a sample transcript in Appendix 14.6, and also forms the basis for the sample analyses in Appendices 14.7 and 8.

Step 2 – overview of the exercise and possible research questions (c. 15 mins)

The tutor then outlines the specific focus group exercise to be followed and, ideally, gets the class to engage with the topic of cosmetic surgery (this is usually not too difficult). The 'hands-on' nature of the exercise should be stressed, and the need for students to volunteer to undertake particular tasks. The tutor should note that Week One will be devoted to data collection and Week Two to data analysis (with students undertaking a small amount of transcription between classes). The tutor should also explain that the exercise involves using two *different* methods of data analysis on the *same* data – in order to see the different kind of 'answers' they provide to research questions (this may well be a novel concept). It is not necessary at this stage to explain what is entailed in either content analysis or thematic analysis. Finally, some possible research questions should be identified. The students' initial 'buzz of interest' can often be channelled to generate specific research questions; alternatively, to save time (although less pedagogically desirable) these can simply be provided by the tutor as 'the kind of thing we will be looking at'. For example, possible research questions might include:

- What do participants think about cosmetic surgery?
- What factors influence their views on cosmetic surgery?
- Are some types of cosmetic surgery seen as more acceptable than others?
- What are the main reasons given for considering/having cosmetic surgery?

All of these are based on the focus group schedule to be used in this exercise, and all are suited to both content and thematic data analysis. (All are broadly 'essentialist' questions.)

Step 3 – setting up the focus group (c. 20 mins)

This entails dividing up the students and briefing them appropriately.

1 One student is designated as focus group moderator (a volunteer is desirable); a second student as recording assistant (again a volunteer is desirable); a further six to eight students as 'participants'; and the remainder as 'observers'.

2 One demonstrator takes the moderator and recording assistant into a separate room, and shows them the focus group schedule (Appendix 14.2) and informed consent form (Appendix 14.3). (The informed consent form given for this exercise is a very simple one; a more elaborate version – suitable for more advanced research purposes – can be found in ten Have, 1999.) The demonstrator then talks the moderator through what will be expected, using the moderator briefing notes (Appendix 14.4). Some degree of reassurance may well be needed, as well as answers to specific questions. The recording assistant is simply required to practise using the tape recorder and microphone.

3 The other demonstrator takes the participants into a separate room, briefs them and answers any questions. They are simply told that the focus group will last around 35 minutes and that they are to behave as if it were a 'real' focus group – that is, to participate fully in discussing the questions posed. They are also told that the focus group will be observed but that the observers will be concentrating on the dynamics of the group overall (rather than on what is said by individual participants).

4 The tutor briefs the observers, by talking through the observer record form (Appendix 14.5) which they will be expected to complete during the course of the focus group, and by answering any questions.

Note that in the case of a single demonstrator, the tutor does 3 and 4 sequentially.

Step 4 – strategic break (c. 10 mins)

As the briefings typically take different lengths of time, it is convenient to give the students a tea/coffee break here (allow 10 minutes for the moderator, who will be last to finish), with a specified return time. While the students are away the demonstrators set up the room in which the focus group will be held – with an inner circle of chairs for the moderator and participants, a corner table and chair for the recording assistant and an outer circle of chairs for the observers. (Alternatively, if a one-way mirror facility is available, the observers can be out of sight in an adjacent room.)

Step 5 – *running the focus group (c. 45 mins)*

This works best if neither tutor nor demonstrators is present. The tutor simply ensures that the students are seated appropriately, ready to participate in/observe the focus group; reminds the moderator to get the participants to complete name badges and informed consent forms before starting the focus group; checks that the recording assistant is ready to go; and then leaves them to it. A time of 30–45 minutes is suggested (allowing the moderator to run the group on to what seems like a natural 'close'). When the group is over, the students return to the main room/lab.

Step 6 – *focus group debriefing (45 mins max.)*

While the debriefing is taking place, one of the demonstrators makes four copies of the tape (the original is retained by the tutor).

1 The class is encouraged to offer a vote of thanks to the moderator (and the recording assistant).
2 The moderator is asked to feed back to the class on how it felt to moderate the group.
3 The participants are asked to feed back to the class on how it felt to participate in the group.
4 The observers are asked to feed back to the class their observations on how they think the group went (using their record forms as a prompt).
5 The class as a whole is asked to reflect on what they see as the pros and cons of focus group research so far (i.e. having only experienced data *collection*).

Step 7 – *setting up transcription (c. 15 mins)*

The tutor provides a brief introduction to simple orthographic transcription, and, if desired, an example of a sample transcript (Appendix 14.6). Four of the observers are then asked to undertake orthographic transcription of consecutive 10-minute segments of the tape (volunteers desirable) and to bring them the following week. They are each given a copy of the tape, and – if needed – a 'Walkman'-type cassette player (many students will have their own). A 'reserve transcriber' should also be appointed from amongst the observers for each segment, in case of illness or other problems (make sure the students have each others' contact details). A simpler – but less pedagogically desirable – alternative is to have the demonstrators transcribe the tape (and photocopy the transcript) between classes. In either case, however, it is essential to have a complete transcript of the tape ready for the beginning of the next class.

WEEK TWO

One of the demonstrators collects in the four segments of transcript and photocopies them for each student while the tutor begins the class.

Step 1 – transcription debriefing; introduction to analysis (c. 20 mins)

The tutor asks the transcribers to feed back to the class their experiences of transcription, noting in particular any difficulties they had, and whether/how these could be resolved. Once the transcripts have been handed out, it is a good idea to give the students a few minutes to familiarize themselves with the data in printed form. An easy way of getting into the analysis is to ask the students what strikes them as particularly interesting or noteworthy about the data – this can usually be related back to the putative research question(s), which should then be confirmed/reiterated. It is recommended that the selected research question(s) focus on a very few – and possibly just one – aspects of the data – it will not be feasible for the class to attempt a comprehensive analysis of the focus group transcript. The tutor reminds the students that the purpose of this part of the exercise is to compare and contrast two different ways of analysing focus group data: content analysis and thematic analysis. It is recommended that the analyses are undertaken sequentially, and then compared (rather than as a compare-and-contrast exercise from the outset).

Step 2 – introduction to content analysis (c. 10 mins)

The principles of content analysis can be introduced either in the abstract, or in relation to a sample content analysis of a data extract (provided in Appendix 14.7). The main points to emphasize are that content analysis is probably the most commonly used approach to analysing qualitative data; and that it involves coding participants' open-ended talk into closed categories, which summarize and systematize the data. These categories may be derived either from the data (as in this exercise) or from the prior theoretical framework of the researcher (which would entail prior familiarity with the literature on views of cosmetic surgery). Content analysis also allows for the conversion of qualitative data into a quantitative form by counting the number of responses falling within each category (i.e. their frequency or 'popularity') and then summarizing the number – or percentage – of responses for each category in tabular form.

Step 3 – doing content analysis (c. 30 mins)

The students are then divided into four or five groups, and each group works independently on developing a provisional category system for their data, and coding the data into the provisional categories. (Each group could be allocated a different research question; in any case, of course, each group will come up with a slightly different analytic framework for any single research question.) The tutor and demonstrators circulate round the groups to discuss the emerging analyses and to sort out any problems. The goal is for students to grasp the principles involved in content analysis, and to come up with a workable provisional framework, rather than to complete a content analysis. An 'end time' should be set for this small group activity.

A simpler – but less pedagogically desirable – alternative is to suggest to the students the kinds of categories they might use: for example, types of cosmetic surgery; reasons for having cosmetic surgery.

Step 4 – discussion of content analysis (c. 15 mins)

The class reconvenes as a whole and the students are asked to identify any problems they experienced in attempting a content analysis, and to suggest pros and cons of the method. Pros are likely to include the value of summaries, the potential for quantification, easy comparison with other studies; cons might include losing detail, losing a sense of individual participants (and interactions between participants) and a range of coding problems. Note that the end of this discussion is a good point at which to give the students a short break (c. 15 mins).

Step 5 – introduction to thematic analysis (c. 10 mins)

The principles of thematic analysis can be introduced either in the abstract, or in relation to a sample thematic analysis of a data extract (provided in Appendix 14.8). The main points to emphasize are that thematic analysis involves identifying major (and minor) 'themes' which run through the data, and selecting representative quotations which exemplify these themes. (Ideally, themes should cross-cut the questions in the focus group schedule.) There should be a specified basis for identifying key themes (e.g. frequency of mention, time taken up with discussing, expressed importance by the participants, perceived importance by the researcher) and the quotations used to illustrate them should be relevant, vivid, succinct and typical.

Step 6 – doing thematic analysis (c. 30 mins)

The students are then divided into four or five groups, and each group works independently on identifying a provisional set of 'themes' in the data, and selecting quotations from the data which best exemplify the themes. (Note that groups use the same research question(s) as they did for the content analysis; again, of course, each group will come up with a slightly different analytic framework for any single research question.) The tutor and demonstrators circulate round the groups to discuss the emerging analyses and to sort out any problems. Again, the goal is to grasp the principles involved in thematic analysis, and to come up with a workable provisional framework, rather than to complete a thematic analysis. An 'end time' should be set for this small group activity.

A simpler – but less pedagogically desirable – alternative is to suggest to the students the kinds of themes they might look for, for example dissatisfaction with appearance, 'socially desirable' norms of appearance, concern about the effects of ageing.

Step 7 – discussion of thematic analysis; comparison of content and thematic analyses (c. 20 mins)

The class reconvenes as a whole and the students are asked first to identify any problems they experienced in attempting a thematic analysis, and to suggest pros and cons of the method. Pros are likely to include compelling data extracts, preservation of detail, preservation of a sense of individual participants (and – at least potentially – interactions between them); cons might include the difficulty of identifying themes, difficulty of selecting quotations ('naturalistic' talk doesn't come in soundbites), ddifficulty of writing up.

They are they asked to compare and contrast content and thematic analyses in terms of the different kinds of 'answers' they provide to the same research question. The differences in form and content of the analyses are bound to be substantial, but if students have not got far enough in their own analyses to have a sense of an 'end product', it might be helpful to draw their attention to the sample content and thematic analyses in Appendices 14.7 and 8.

Step 8 – evaluation of focus group research (30 mins max.)

The last activity is to pull together students' experiences of the whole process of focus group research (i.e. data collection, transcription and different types of analysis) and to evaluate the method as a whole. In this discussion, focus groups may be considered as a 'stand-alone' qualitative method; they may be compared with other qualitative methods (such as interviews); or they may be taken as an exemplar of qualitative methods and compared with quantitative methods to which the students have been exposed (although note that content analysis is included here to demonstrate that it is possible to quantify focus group data, and content/thematic analyses by no means exhaust the range of possibilities for analysing focus group data). Students are likely to have developed a clear sense of the specific advantages of focus group research: many will have enjoyed the data collection phase but been dismayed by the time and effort required for transcription and analysis. There are also likely to be advocates for each of the types of data analysis sampled. This would be a good point to mention other forms of qualitative analysis – such as narrative/ biographical analysis (e.g. Reissman, 1993; Smith, 1994) and discursive/conversation analysis (e.g. Potter & Wetherell, 1987; ten Have, 1999). Finally, if desired, a piece of coursework could be set based on this exercise. This could be either (1) a semi-traditional 'lab report', for which students complete and write up their content and/or thematic analyses (in which case they may need to be given a 'template' for writing up qualitative research); or (2) an evaluation of focus group methodology, based on experiences in this exercise and on the focus group literature (in which case specific further reading should be suggested – see the references list).

Notes for the Course Leader

This final section of the chapter provides some more details for the tutor about what is needed to run this exercise successfully, and – in particular – outlines a number of variations than can be made with larger classes, and with more or less time available.

LEVEL OF STUDENT

This exercise is suitable for any level of undergraduate student (although the analysis may need to be simplified, or even omitted, for first years – see below), and I have also run it with postgraduate students, as part of their research methods training. No prior knowledge or expertise is required – although some familiarity with research methods in social psychology (including qualitative methods) is helpful, and maximizes the potential benefits to be gained from the exercise.

CLASS SIZE

It is relatively easy to run this exercise with a larger class of about 40 students, by dividing the class into two, and running two focus groups simultaneously (although this should not be attempted without the assistance of two demonstrators). For between 20 and 40 students, a strategic decision will need to be taken as to whether to run one or two focus groups (a single group becomes rather unwieldy with more than about 15 'observers').

EQUIPMENT

While highly specialized recording equipment is unnecessary, it is essential to use an omnidirectional flat microphone, in order to produce a recording clear enough for transcription. These can be purchased relatively inexpensively at large high street electrical retailers. In order to minimize the risk of recording failure, it is also desirable to use *two* sets of recording equipment, if possible (this also reduces the number of tape copies needed). A competent recording assistant can operate both sets, or two recording assistants can be appointed. Specialized transcribing equipment is also unnecessary for this exercise – but is strongly recommended for more advanced/extensive transcription work (the job of transcription is considerably facilitated by the use of a dedicated transcribing machine, and a much better quality transcript usually results).

VARIATIONS

It is relatively easy to modify and adapt this exercise for different groups of students, different purposes and according to the time available. For example:

1 The availability of a third three-hour session permits a more
   extended exercise, in a number of ways. Most obviously, a more

thorough job can be made of data analysis if Week Two is devoted to content analysis and Week Three to thematic analysis. Alternatively, for more advanced students, a comparison can be made between different *theoretical* frameworks (i.e. esssentialism and social constructionism), as well as between methods of analysis. In this case, students could be asked to derive 'essentialist' and 'social constructionist' research questions and to compare methods of analysis compatible with each (e.g. content/thematic analysis with discursive/conversation analysis). Finally, for less advanced students, more attention can be given to data collection than data analysis – by running a 'fun' focus group – see (3) below – in Week One; running a data-gathering focus group in Week Two; and discussing the principles of data analysis (and/or undertaking some very limited data analysis) in Week Three.

2   The exercise can also be reduced in complexity in a number of ways. Most obviously, this can be done by setting only one type of data analysis (i.e. either content analysis or thematic analysis), rather than asking students to undertake a comparison. Alternatively, the data collection and data analysis components can be uncoupled, obviating the need for audio-taping and transcription. In this variant, Week One is run (more or less) as above, but in Week Two the tutor provides some (previously collected and transcribed) focus group data for the analytic exercises. Finally, the exercise can be run in a single session by choosing to focus only on data collection (i.e. excluding data transcription and analysis, and also obviating the need to record the session). Again, in this case, Week One is run (more or less) as above – and students are simply asked to evaluate the data collection phase of focus group research.

3   Another possibility, if greater emphasis is to be placed on data collection than on data analysis is to run a 'fun' focus group – albeit with a serious pedagogic purpose. In this variant, potential 'problem participants' in focus groups, and the consequent need for 'people management' skills are highlighted; it works particularly well as the first of two focus groups, run in sequential weeks. It involves a similar procedure to setting up the focus group in Week One, but with the following amendments:

   • When the participants are briefed, they are assigned particular 'roles' to play in the group – for example 'the dominant talker', 'the shy or quiet participant', the 'rambler'. A list of six possible roles, plus role descriptions, is provided in Appendix 14.9. It works well to reproduce role titles/descriptions on slips of paper and to get students to 'pull them out of a hat'; if there are more

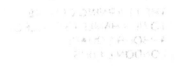

than six participants, additional slips reading 'ordinary participant – be yourself' can be added. They will need time to 'practise' the roles, and should be allowed to swap if difficulties arise. They should also be instructed *not* to reveal their roles to the moderator or observers in advance of the focus group.

- A reasonably outgoing and confident moderator should be appointed for this variant. The moderator briefing includes the information that participants are being briefed to be 'difficult' (but *not* that they are being given specific roles). The demonstrator should talk through with the moderator, in general terms, how he or she might handle talkative participants, quiet participants, and so on (some 'possible tactics' are given in Appendix 14.9 – which I usually give as a summary handout to the students at the end). Any necessary reassurance should also be provided.
- The observers' briefing includes the information that the participants will be 'playing roles' – and they are asked both to 'spot the roles' and to assess how the moderator deals with them. They can be given a supplementary observer record form for this purpose (Appendix 14.10).
- The tutor may prefer to be present for the running of the focus group. There is usually some initial hilarity, which quickly settles down as the students get into the exercise.
- The class debriefing should allow the moderator to give his or her reactions first (the moderator is likely to have spotted some of the roles); then the observers are asked to 'add roles'; and finally the participants are cued in to reveal any that might have been missed or misrepresented. The class discussion should then focus around how the moderator dealt with the 'problem participants', and elicit students' suggestions as to what else he or she might have done (see Appendix 14.9). The tutor should be alert to the moderator's sensibilities and set up an ethos of 'constructive feedback'.

FINAL CONSIDERATIONS

Focus group practical classes are not easy to run – they demand a lot of planning and organization in advance, and a lot of energy on the day. However, in my experience, they are immensely rewarding (for staff and students), and they undoubtedly provide the opportunity to learn a wide range of research skills, particularly in the handling of qualitative data.

THE LEARNING CENTRE
TOWER HAMLETS COLLEGE
ARBOUR SQUARE
LONDON E1 0PS

Appendix 14.1: Sample focus group schedule – breast cancer

This is drawn from the author's own focus group research (Wilkinson, 1998a, 1998b, 2000), in which women with breast cancer talk about their experience. The women were recruited through a symptomatic breast clinic at a general hospital in the north of England. Most were working-class, middle-aged or older, and within five years of diagnosis. A total of 77 women took part in 13 focus groups, each lasting one to three hours. The focus groups were held in a university setting, and each woman attended only one group on a single occasion. Data were audiotaped and transcribed orthographically.

(Note that a sample transcript of a data extract is given in Appendix 14.6, and sample analyses in Appendices 14.7 and 8.)

Introduction

Questions (These were used with every group)

1 How did you feel when you first became aware of a breast problem?
2 How did you feel when you were first told it was breast cancer?
3 How did people around you react to knowing you had breast cancer? – Partner/family/friends/others
4 What kind of support did you need? – When you were first aware of a problem? – When you knew for sure it was cancer?
5 What kinds of support did your partner/family/others close to you need? – When you were first aware of a problem? – When you knew for sure it was cancer?
6 What do you think caused your breast cancer?
7 What kinds of effects has having breast cancer had on your life? (including your general outlook on life) – On you personally? – On those around you?

Supplementary questions (There was rarely time for these)

8 What is the worst thing about having breast cancer?
9 Has anything good come out of having breast cancer? – What?
10 Have you been concerned about your appearance? – In what way? – Those around you? – In what way?
11 Is there anything else you'd like to say about your experience of breast cancer? – Or about this research project?

Conclusion

Appendix 14.2: Focus group schedule – cosmetic surgery

(Each participant should have completed an informed consent form, and be wearing a name badge, before starting the focus group.)

Introduction

- Welcome (thank participants, introduce self and topic);
- Overview of procedure (length and format of session);
- Ground rules (confidentiality, value range of opinions, OK to disagree but don't all speak at once!).

Questions

1 How do you feel about your appearance? – Are you happy with it, or not? Why/why not? – Are there aspects which you particularly like, or dislike?
2 Do you ever try to alter your appearance in any way? – If so, how? (e.g. ask about makeup, clothes, diets, etc.) – Why? – If not, why not?
3 How do you feel about the appearance of supermodels and media personalities? (e.g. Pamela Anderson, Naomi Campbell, etc.)? – Do you find them attractive, or not? – Would you like to look like they do? – Why/why not?
4 Do you think that media images of supermodels, etc. affect 'ordinary' women? – If so, how? – If not, why not?
5 What do you think about supermodels, etc. having cosmetic surgery (e.g. breast implants, liposuction, tummy tuck, nose job, facelift, jaw tightened, bags under eyes removed)? – Do you approve of these practices, or not? – If so, why? – If not, why not?
6 What do you think about 'ordinary' women having cosmetic surgery? – Is this any different from supermodels etc. having it? – If so, why? – If not, why not?
7 Would you ever consider having cosmetic surgery? – If so, what kind(s)? – Why would you do this? – If not, why not? – Can you think of anything which might make you change your mind? (e.g. getting older, weight gain, new job)
8 Is there anything else you would like to add to this discussion?

Conclusion

- Round off/sum up (say what you got from session, how valuable all views were, reiterate confidentiality);
- Give participants opportunity to ask you any questions;
- Thank everyone again and close session.

Appendix 14.3:   Informed consent form

(To be read out by the researcher/moderator before the beginning of the session. One copy of the form to be left with each participant; one copy to be signed by each participant and kept by the researcher/moderator.)

My name is _____ .
I am doing research on a project entitled Cosmetic Surgery.

My tutor/supervisor _____ is directing the
project and can be contacted at _____
_____ should you have any questions.

Thank you for agreeing to take part in this project. Before we start, I would
like to emphasize that:

- Your participation is entirely voluntary,
- You are free to refuse to answer any question,
- You are free to withdraw at any time.

The focus group will be tape-recorded, but the data will be kept strictly
confidential and will be available only to members of the research team.

Excerpts from the results may be made part of the final research report, but
under no circumstances will your name or any identifying characteristics be
included in the report.

Please sign this form to show that I have read the contents to you.

_____ (signed)

_____ (printed)

_____ (date)

(Researcher/moderator to keep signed copy and leave unsigned copy with
each participant.)

Appendix 14.4:   Moderator briefing notes

(Materials to be given to moderator(s) at briefing: Copies of focus group
schedule and informed consent forms, sticky labels and marker pens for
name badges.)

1 Show moderator(s) the focus group schedule, and answer any questions
   they may have about it. Remind them that the group members won't have
   seen it in advance (as in a 'real' focus group).
2 Go briefly through the role of the moderator, to ensure they know exactly
   what to do, and answer any questions. Suggest you cover: pre-group
   activities (name badges, informed consent forms), Introduction, lead-in
   question, getting people talking, using the questions as a guide only, prompts
   and probes, facilitating the flow of discussion, winding up and Conclusion.
   (Take it gently – and don't make it sound more difficult or daunting than
   necessary).
3 Emphasize that they may well need to exercise some 'people management
   skills', for example encouraging the quiet participant, discouraging the

talkative one, bringing the group back to the point if they seem to have wandered off it. (You could point out that these only develop through practice – and that the best way to learn them is to try them out.)

4 Get them to write out what they will say as Introduction and Conclusion (just a few sentences for each).

5 Give them time to familiarize themselves with the schedule.

6 Tell them they will have 35–40 mins to run the group as a 'real' focus group, including appropriate Introduction and Conclusion – and they should let it run (or steer it gently) into a 'natural' close, not just cut off discussion (so it's fine to run for less than 35 mins if the group 'dries up', or more than 40 mins if it's really 'taken off').

7 Keep the briefing fairly low key – and try to leave them feeling confident that they will be able to handle the task.

8 Let them have a short break before the agreed start-time for the focus group.

Appendix 14.5:   Observer record form

1 What were the main functions of the Introduction? (To what extent were these fulfilled?)

2 In general, did the schedule of questions enable the discussion to develop well? (Could it be improved?)

3 In general, did the way the questions were asked/followed up enable the discussion to develop well? (Could the moderator's technique be improved? Please be constructive in your suggestions!)

4 What were the overall group dynamics like? (Did conversation 'flow' – or was it stilted? Did this change over time?)

5 Any other comments about the group dynamics and flow of discussion?

6 Any other comments about the moderator's role?

7 What were the main functions of the Conclusion? (To what extent were these fulfilled?)

8 Any other impressions or comments you would like to make?

Appendix 14.6:   Sample transcript – breast cancer data

This data extract is taken from the transcript of a single focus group with three women who have breast cancer (Wilkinson, 2000). Here, the moderator has just asked the women if they have any idea what caused their breast cancer.

Gertie:	[cuts in] There's a lot of <u>stories</u> going about. I was once told that if you use them aluminium pans that cause cancer. I was also told that if you, if you eat tomatoes and plums at the same meal that-
Doreen:	[Laughs]
Gertie:	[To Doreen] Have you heard all these, those things?
Doreen:	[Laughs] No

[17 lines omitted here, in which there is laughter and disengagement from 'folklore']

Gertie: Now <u>I've</u> no views on this, [To Doreen] have you?

Doreen: No – The only thing is, I mean from my point of view, I don't know, they say that, they say that breast feeding is supposed to, erm [tch], give you some <u>protection</u>, well I breast fed and I mean [laughs], it obviously didn't work with me, did it? Erm, what's the other thing? Then they say that taking the pill, it's not proved to be [pause] have I got this right?, it's not proved that it's only, it's not caused an increase in breast cancer, so that, I mean I did t-, you know, obviously I took the pill at a younger age, I mean, I don't know whether the age at which you have children makes a difference as well because I had my [pause] eight year old relatively <u>late</u>, I was an old mum

[43 lines omitted here, in which Doreen details her sisters' gynaecological problems and Gertie talks about her sister, who was a nurse]

Freda: [cuts in] Sometimes I've heard that <u>knocks</u> can bring one on but I've never (had any knocks) [indistinct]

Gertie: No

Freda: [cuts in] (I don't think that) [indistinct]

Doreen: [cuts in] Well, I'd heard that from somebody else and so when I, when obviously this was sus-, my lump was suspicious, I then, I then remembered I'd <u>banged</u> my breast with this, erm [tch] you know these shopping bags with a wooden rod thing, those big trolley bags?

[Approx. 5 mins of tape omitted here – in which Doreen elaborates on her 'knock'; and they discuss breast feeding problems, including inverted nipples, and nipple discharge]

Freda: It's difficult to know what causes anything, isn't it really? I mean, looking years and years ago, I mean, everybody used to [laughs] sit about sunning themselves on the beach and now all of a sudden you get cancer from sunshine. Well, I mean, who told you years ago [indistinct], I don't think we were ever told it was a risky behaviour, or anything else, well, I don't know (about) all the chemicals in what you're eating and things these days as well, and

Doreen: Mm

Freda: how cultivated and everything

Doreen: Mm

Freda: I mean, I would feel, I, I should <u>hate</u> [pause], I think it's me surgery, 'cos I always sort of, I even treat <u>this</u> as just something you cut off the top, it's not about opening you up

Doreen: Mm

Freda: and he was saying, 'Oh they have'. I said, 'They haven't opened
          me up, they've only cut a bit of extra off the top' [laughs] sort of
          thing, but, but I always think that people go into hospital, even
          for an exploratory
Doreen: Mm
Freda: it may be all wrong, but I do think, well the air gets to it, it
          seems to me that it's not long afterwards before they [pause]
          simply find there's more to it than they thought, you know, and
          I often wonder if the air getting to your inside is- [pause] brings,
          brings on [pause] cancer in any form, not a breast cancer now,
          but any, you know, any cancers

(Abridged 'causes' extract from SW: BCP 12, 30–33)

Transcription key for this extract:

- underlining – emphasis;
- hyphen at end of word – word cut off;
- round brackets – used when transcriber is uncertain what was said, but is
  able to make a reasonable guess;
- square brackets – enclose comments made by transcriber; n.b. such comments include inability to make out what was said [indistinct], and sounds
  that are difficult to transcribe [tch], as well as interactional features of note
  – e.g. [cuts in], [laughs], [pause], etc.

Appendix 14.7:   Sample content analysis – breast cancer data

This analysis is based on the transcript of a single focus group with three
women who have breast cancer (Wilkinson, 2000). All talk in this focus
group about the 'causes' of breast cancer has been categorized systematically.
The categories are derived from Mildred Blaxter's (1983) classic study on
women talking about the causes of disease, and the analysis notes the frequency with which 'causes' falling into each category are mentioned.

1 *Infection* 0 instances
2 *Heredity or familial tendencies* 2 instances
        family history (×2)
3 *Agents in the environment: 'poisons', working condition, climate* 3 instances
        aluminium pans; exposure to sun; chemicals in food
   Drugs or the contraceptive pill 1 instance
        taking the contraceptive pill
4 *Secondary to other diseases* 0 instances
5 *Stress, strain and worry* 0 instances
6 *Caused by childbearing, menopause* 22 instances

not breast feeding; late childbearing (×3); having only one child; being single/
not having children; hormonal; trouble with breast feeding – unspecified
(×4); flattened nipples (×2); inverted nipples (×7); nipple discharge (×2)

7 *Secondary to trauma or to surgery* 9 instances
   knocks (×4); unspecified injury; air getting inside body (×4)
8 *Neglect, the constraints of poverty* 0 instances
9 *Inherent susceptibility, individual and not hereditary* 0 instances
10 *Behaviour, own responsibility* 1 instance
   mixing specific foods
11 *Ageing, natural degeneration* 0 instances

----

12 *Other* 5 instances
'several things'; 'a lot'; 'multi-factorial'; everybody has a 'dormant' cancer; 'anything' could wake a dormant cancer

Appendix 14.8: Sample thematic analysis – breast cancer data

This analysis is based on the transcript of a single focus group with three women who have breast cancer (Wilkinson, 2000). All talk in this focus group about the 'causes' of breast cancer has been reviewed, and two main themes identified, on the basis of time devoted to taking about them. Within each main theme, further sub-themes have been differentiated by topic. Illustrative quotations are provided for each sub-theme.

Main theme 1: Childbearing

Sub-theme 1(a): Breast feeding

I did have trouble breast feeding (Doreen)

. . . if you've an inverted nipple [. . .] be wary, and report it (Gertie)

. . . until I came to the point of actually trying to breast feed I didn't realize I had flattened nipples and one of them was nearly inverted or whatever, so I had a lot of trouble breast feeding, and it, and I was several weeks with a breast pump trying to um get it right, so that the he could suckle on my nipple, so I did have that problem (Doreen)

. . . inverted nipples, they say that that is one thing that you could be wary of (Gertie)

I fed the children, I thought, I began to notice it [. . .] then another time I went in and I brought it to the attention because by then . . . although you know it was more or less inverted, periodically it used to leak, only on a very small amount, but it was just a little bit of yellow [. . .] but over the years, every, I couldn't say it happened monthly or anything like that, it would just start throbbing this . . . leakage, nothing to put a dressing on or anything like that, but there it was, it was coming from somewhere and it were just kind of gently crust over (Gertie)

Sub-theme 1(b): Other childbearing

I mean, I don't know whether the age at which you have children makes a difference as well because I had my [pause] eight year old relatively <u>late</u>, I was an old mum when I got, I mean, [pause] yeah, I was thirty two when I-, just nearly thirty two when I had John, so I was a relatively <u>old</u> <u>mum</u> (Doreen)

They say that if you've only had <u>one</u> that you're more likely to get it than if you had a <u>big</u> family (Freda)

Main Theme 2: Trauma

Sub-theme 2(a): knocks

Sometimes I've heard that <u>knocks</u> can bring one on (Freda)

... when obviously this was sus-, my lump was suspicious, I then, I then remembered I'd <u>banged</u> my breast with this, erm [tch] you know these shopping bags with a wooden rod thing, those big trolley bags? (Doreen)

Sub-theme 2(b): other trauma

I do think, well the <u>air</u> gets to it, it seems to me that it's not long afterwards before they [pause] simply find there's more to it than they thought, you know, and I often wonder if the <u>air</u> getting to your inside is- [pause] brings, brings on [pause] cancer in any form, not a breast cancer now, but any, you know, any cancers (Freda)

... there are so many times you hear now 'He's gone in just for a routine operation' and then when they open him up they find he'll be riddled with cancer or something, and to me, I think, well, this is, is it because the <u>air</u> got to it, and it's, it brought it out [pause] (Freda)

Appendix 14.9: 'Problem' participants in focus groups

One of the advantages of focus groups is that they bring together a variety of people with different backgrounds and characteristics. Sometimes, however, particular kinds of participants can present special problems for the moderator. Six potential types of 'problem' participant are described below – and some strategies for dealing with them are also suggested.

The 'Expert'

Some people consider themselves experts because they have had particular experience with the topic under discussion, because they consider themselves to be influential or because they have previously participated in this type of session. Self-appointed 'experts' can present special problems in the focus group. What they say and how they say it can have an inhibiting influence on others in the group. Participants often defer to others who are perceived to be more knowledgeable or informed, or of higher status in some way (e.g. education, social class).

Possible tactics

Emphasize that everyone is an expert and that all participants have important perceptions and opinions that are of interest to the researcher. Also the introductory questions should avoid responses that would identify differences in status or educational background.

The Dominant Talker

Dominant talkers – who 'hog' the conversation – sometimes consider themselves to be experts, but much of the time they are unaware of how they are perceived by others (usually very negatively).

Possible tactics

If you identify someone as a dominant talker before the session, try to seat him or her beside the moderator, which will permit some control via body language (i.e. the moderator can turn away slightly, which is discouraging). Other non-verbal techniques include avoiding eye contact with the talker and appearing bored with the comments. Also you can verbally shift attention by saying things like: 'Thank you, Christopher. Do others want to comment on this question?', 'Does anyone feel differently?', 'That's one point of view. Does anyone have another point of view?' Do be tactful and kind, because harsh and critical comments may inhibit others in the group from speaking.

The Shy or Quiet Participant

Shy participants tend to say little, and/or speak with soft voices, so it is hard for others to hear. Extra effort is needed to get them to express their views and to feel their comments are wanted and appreciated (especially if they look down so that eye contact is limited).

Possible tactics

If possible, shy participants should be seated facing the moderator, so that eye contact, nods and smiles (all of which are encouraging) can be maximized. Verbal reinforcement can also be used (e.g. addressing the participant by name; saying things like: 'That's really interesting – do tell us more' and – as a last resort – inviting the individual to speak).

The Bored or Restless Participant

This participant seems to want to be elsewhere: he or she may fidget, shuffle, yawn, cough – or just stare out of the window. He or she may fail to contribute to the group, or contribute rarely, and apparently randomly, with points of little relevance.

Possible tactics

Try to engage the participant's interest, address him or her by name and offer positive reinforcement for any relevant contributions (as with the shy participant).

The Rambler

Rambling respondents use a lot of words and usually never get to the point, if they have a point. These individuals are comfortable with talking and seem to feel the obligation to say something. Unfortunately, they ramble all over the place, bore other participants with irrelevant detail, and use up a lot of precious discussion time.

Possible tactics

As with the dominant talker, discontinue eye contact with the rambler, turn away if possible, shuffle your papers, look at your watch or tap your pen (to look bored and impatient) – and as soon as the rambler stops or pauses, be ready to prompt others to speak or to introduce the next question. Limit eye contact with the rambler for the rest of the session.

The Obsessive

The obsessive is someone who seems only to have one point or main interest, and who keeps returning to it obsessively.

Possible tactics

As with the dominant talker and the rambler, avoid eye contact, look bored or impatient, move the discussion on at the first opportunity.

(Adapted and expanded from material in Krueger 1988).

Appendix 14.10:   Supplementary observer record form

What roles were played by 'problem' participants in the focus group? For each one you have identified, note below:

* How the moderator dealt with the problem
* Other possible tactics you think the moderator could have tried

Role:	How dealt with:	Other possible tactics:
-------------	----------------------	------------------------------
-------------	----------------------	------------------------------
-------------	----------------------	------------------------------
-------------	----------------------	------------------------------
-------------	----------------------	------------------------------
-------------	----------------------	------------------------------
-------------	----------------------	------------------------------
-------------	----------------------	------------------------------

REFERENCES

Atkinson, J. M. & Heritage, J. (1984). *Structures of social action*. Cambridge, UK: Cambridge University Press.

Barbour, R. & Kitzinger, J. (eds.) (1999). *Developing focus group research: Politics, theory and practice*. London: Sage.

Basch, C. E. (1987). Focus group interviews: An underutilized research technique for improving theory and practice in health education. *Health Education Quarterly, 154*, 411–48.

Blaxter, M. (1983). The causes of disease: Women talking. *Social Science & Medicine, 17*, 59–69.

Carey, M. A. (ed.) (1995). Special issue: Issues and applications of focus groups. *Qualitative Health Research, 5*(4).

Greenbaum, T. L. (1998). *The handbook for focus group research* (2nd edn.). Thousand Oaks, CA: Sage.

Jarrett, R. L. (1993). Focus group interviewing with low-income minority populations: A research experience. In D. L. Morgan (ed.), *Successful focus groups: Advancing the state of the art* (pp. 184–201). Newbury Park, CA: Sage.

Kitzinger, J. (1990). Audience understanding of AIDS media messages: A discussion of methods. *Sociology of Health and Illness, 12*(3), 319–55.

Krueger, J. (1988). *Focus groups: A practical guide for applied research* (1st edn.). Newbury Park, CA: Sage.

Krueger, R. A. (1994). *Focus groups: A practical guide for applied research* (2nd edn.). Newbury Park, CA: Sage.

Morgan, D. L. (ed.) (1993). *Successful focus groups: Advancing the state of the art*. Newbury Park, CA: Sage.

Morgan, D. L. (1996). Focus groups. *Annual Review of Sociology, 22*, 129–52.

Morgan, D. L. (1997). *Focus groups as qualitative research* (2nd edn.). Newbury Park, CA: Sage.

Morgan, D. L. & Krueger, R. A. (1998). *The focus group kit* (6 vols.). Newbury Park, CA: Sage.

Potter, J. & Wetherell, M. (1987). *Discourse and social psychology*. London: Sage.

Reissman, C. K. (1993). *Narrative analysis*. Newbury Park, CA: Sage.

Smith, L. M. (1994). Biographical method. In N. K. Denzin & Y. S. Lincoln (eds.), *Handbook of qualitative research* (pp. 286–305). Thousand Oaks, CA: Sage.

Stewart, D. W. & Shamdasani, P. N. (1990). *Focus groups: Theory and practice*. London: Sage.

ten Have, P. (1999). *Doing conversation analysis: A practical guide*. London: Sage.

Vaughn, S., Schumm, J. S. & Sinagub, J. (1996). *Focus group interviews in education and psychology*. Thousand Oaks, CA: Sage.

Wilkinson, S. (1998a). Focus groups in health research: Exploring the meanings of health and illness. *Journal of Health Psychology, 3*(3), 329–348.

Wilkinson, S. (1998b). Focus group methodology: A review. *International Journal of Social Research Methodology, 1*(3), 181–203.

Wilkinson, S. (1999). Focus groups: A feminist method. *Psychology of Women Quarterly, 23*, 221–44.

Wilkinson, S. (2000). Women with breast cancer talking causes: Comparing content, biographical and discursive analyses. *Feminism & Psychology*, *10*(4), 431–60.

Wilkinson, S. & Kitzinger, C. (2000). 'Clinton faces nation': A case study in the construction of focus groups as public opinion. *The Sociological Review*, *48*(3), 409–24.

INDEX